HISTORY OF
United States Naval Operations
IN WORLD WAR II

★

VOLUME THIRTEEN

The Liberation of the Philippines
Luzon, Mindanao, the Visayas
1944-1945

D1120346

From the painting by Albert K. Murray 1945

Admiral Thomas C. Kinkaid USN

HISTORY OF UNITED STATES NAVAL
OPERATIONS IN WORLD WAR II
VOLUME 13

The
Liberation of the Philippines

Luzon, Mindanao, the Visayas

1944-1945

SAMUEL ELIOT MORISON

UNIVERSITY OF ILLINOIS PRESS
Urbana and Chicago

First Illinois paperback, 2002
© 1959 by Samuel Eliot Morison; © renewed 1987
by Lawrence Coolidge and W. Sidney Felton
Reprinted by arrangement with Little, Brown and Company, Inc.
All rights reserved
Manufactured in the United States of America

P 5 4 3 2 1

∞ This book is printed on acid-free paper.

Library of Congress Cataloging-in-Publication Data
Morison, Samuel Eliot, 1887–1976.
History of United States naval operations in World War II / Samuel Eliot Morison
p.   cm.
Originally published: Boston : Little, Brown, 1947–62.
Includes bibliographical references and index.
Contents: v. 1. The Battle of the Atlantic, September 1939–May 1943—v. 2. Opera-
tions in North African Waters, October 1942–June 1943—v. 3. The Rising Sun in
the Pacific, 1931–April 1942—v. 4. Coral Sea, Midway and Submarine Actions, May
1942–August 1942—v. 5. The Struggle for Guadalcanal, August 1942–February
1943—v. 6. Breaking the Bismarcks Barrier, 22 July 1942–1 May 1944—v. 7. Aleutians, Gilberts and Marshalls, June 1942–April 1944—v. 8. New Guinea and the
Marianas, March 1944–August 1944—v. 9. Sicily—Salerno—Anzio, January 1943–
June 1944—v. 10. The Atlantic Battle Won, May 1943–May 1945—v. 11. The Invasion of France and Germany, 1944–1945—v. 12. Leyte, June 1944–January 1945—
v. 13. The Liberation of the Philippines—Luzon, Mindanao, the Visayas, 1944–1945
  ISBN 0-252-06963-3 (v. 1); ISBN 0-252-06972-2 (v. 2); ISBN 0-252-06973-0 (v. 3);
  ISBN 0-252-06995-1 (v. 4); ISBN 0-252-06996-X (v. 5); ISBN 0-252-06997-8 (v. 6);
  ISBN 0-252-07037-2 (v. 7); ISBN 0-252-07038-0 (v. 8); ISBN 0-252-07039-9 (v. 9);
ISBN 0-252-07061-5 (v. 10); ISBN 0-252-07062-3 (v. 11); ISBN 0-252-07063-1 (v. 12);
                ISBN 0-252-07064-X (v. 13)
    1. World War, 1939–1945—Naval operations, American. I. Title.
             D773.M6   2002
         940.54′5973—dc21   00-064840

University of Illinois Press
1325 South Oak Street   Champaign, IL 61820-6903
www.press.uillinois.edu

To
The Memory of
THEODORE EDSON CHANDLER
1894–1945
Rear Admiral, United States Navy

I firmly believe that it is not wise and statesmanly for our leaders, in this their darkest hour, to teach our people to avoid sufferings and hardships at the sacrifice of fundamental principles of government and the democratic way of life. On the contrary, it is their bounden duty and responsibility to inspire our people to willingly undergo any kind of difficulties and sacrifices for the sake of noble principles that they nourish deep in their hearts. Instead of depressing their patriotic ardor, the people should be inspired to be brave and courageous under all kinds of hardships and difficulties in defense of what they consider righteous and just. We shall never win or deserve the esteem and respect of other nations if we lack principles and if we do not possess the courage and valor to defend those principles at any cost.

— Tomás Confesor, Governor of Iloilo: *Reply to the demand of President Laurel that he surrender, January 1943.*

Preface

THE BATTLE FOR LEYTE GULF and the securing of the island of Leyte, as described in Volume XII, were the necessary preliminaries to operations described in this volume for the liberation of the rest of the Philippine Archipelago.

We begin by taking Mindoro as a steppingstone to Luzon. Next come the major landings on the shores of Lingayen Gulf, where the Kamikaze Special Attack Corps first showed what it could really do. The covering operations by Admiral Halsey's Third Fleet, including its ordeal in the typhoon of 18 December 1944 and the South China Sea raid, are related, as well as all naval aspects of the drive on Manila. We then take up the liberation of Palawan, Panay, Negros, Cebu, Bohol and Mindanao. In Part IV we gather in the amphibious landings which wrested Borneo from the Japanese, the patrols of Seventh Fleet submarines in 1945, and the extraneous but picturesque operations of Rear Admiral Miles's United States Naval Group, China. Except for these last, and those of the fast carrier forces, all naval operations described in this volume were in the theater of General of the Army Douglas MacArthur, and under the direct command of Admiral Thomas C. Kinkaid, Commander Seventh Fleet.

Research for this volume has been going on since 1945. The late Lieutenant Commander Henry Salomon USNR participated in the Lingayen landings as member of Vice Admiral Wilkinson's staff, and brought back both personal impressions and documents which were woven into my preliminary narrative of Parts I and II. Material on the Japanese side was obtained by Commander Salomon at Tokyo immediately after the surrender, by Mr. Roger Pineau and myself in 1950, and from Captain Toshikazu Ohmae at intervals ever since. With the assistance of Rear Admiral Bern Anderson USN (Ret.), working at the Naval War College at Newport, and Dr. K. Jack Bauer, working at Washington, I resumed work on this volume before XII was completed. Mr. Donald R. Martin, now in his seventeenth year of service to me and to naval history, prepared the task organizations and did various pieces of research. Yeoman 2nd Class Edward Ledford and Chief Yeoman Henry W. Sutphin shared with him the typing. The charts were done by Yeoman 3rd Class Alexander D. Henderson and Specialist 1st Class Jane M. Donnelly, shortly after the war, and later, at the Naval War College, by James A. Clarkson, under the oversight of Mr. John Lawton.

Rear Admiral Ernest M. Eller, Director of Naval History, and his exec., Captain F. Kent Loomis, and Vice Admiral Stuart H. Ingersoll, President of the Naval War College, Newport, have given this volume both countenance and support. Thanks are also due to Mr. John F. di Napoli, Director of Libraries, Naval War College and to Mr. Dean C. Allard, head of the Historical Records Branch of the Division of Naval History, Washington. My beloved wife, Priscilla Barton Morison, has patiently listened to many of the chapters and helped, by her criticism, to make them more readable.

Printed or mimeographed works used so frequently in the preparation of this volume that they are seldom cited in footnotes, are: —

Robert R. Smith *Triumph in the Philippines*, a volume in the U. S. Army in World War II series, of which the Army kindly gave me a mimeographed copy in advance of publication.

A number of books and pamphlets issued by General MacArthur's headquarters at Tokyo; indispensable because they were drawn from Japanese sources by a corps of Japanese experts. Also produced by the same headquarters, a series of some 180 *Japanese Monographs* on all phases of the Pacific War, of which a dozen or more were useful for this volume.

Based on these and other sources, the General's *Historical Re-*

port Vol. II (1951), representing the Japanese side, and *The Imperial Japanese Navy in World War II* (1952), a reference book and check list. JANAC (Joint Army-Navy Assessment Committee) *Japanese Naval and Merchant Ship Losses During World War II* (1947), another good reference work, is not wholly superseded by the book just mentioned. Differences in my attributions of sinkings from these two sources result from recent rechecking by Dr. Bauer, particularly with the Navy's Submarine Operations Research Group report, "Submarine Attacks According to Command and Month of Attack" (1945), and a 1946 list of antisubmarine attacks prepared by the office of the Chief of Naval Operations.

United States Strategic Bombing Survey, Pacific, Naval Analysis Division, *Interrogations of Japanese Officials*, 2 vols (1946). A highly important source; and there are other mimeographed USSBS interrogations not included in this printed work.

Sixth Army Report, printed in Japan shortly after the surrender, in four volumes: I Operational, II Maps, III General and Special, IV Engineers.

Engineers of the Southwest Pacific 1941–45, Vol. I, *Engineers in Theatre Operations* (1947), a valuable publication by Office of Chief Engineers, GHQ, U. S. Army Forces, Pacific; supplemented by Colonel Robert Amory *Surf and Sand: The Saga of the 533rd Engineer Boat and Shore Regiment* (1947), a useful regimental history.

Wesley F. Craven & James L. Cate *The Pacific: Matterhorn to Nagasaki* (1953), Vol. V, in *Army Air Forces in World War II* series, is supplemented, for Marine Corps aviation, by Major Charles W. Boggs *Marine Aviation in the Philippines* (1951) and Robert Sherrod *History of Marine Corps Aviation in World War II* (1952).

Two important narratives by commanding generals: General Walter Krueger, *From Down Under to Nippon* (1953), and General Robert L. Eichelberger *Our Jungle Road to Tokyo* (1950).

It should also be understood that the war diaries and action reports of ships, divisions, squadrons, task forces and fleets have been used constantly, and are the principal body of sources for this, as of other volumes. Wherever motor torpedo boats are mentioned I have largely depended on Commander Robert J. Bulkley USNR "PT: A History of Motor Torpedo Boats in the United States Navy" (1946), a manuscript prepared in the Division of Naval History.

The dates used for the operations described in this volume are East Longitude, and the times are Zone Item (Greenwich minus 9 hours).

Rear Admiral Theodore E. Chandler, to whose memory this volume is dedicated, was born at Annapolis in 1894, the son of Rear Admiral Lloyd H. Chandler USN. His grandfather, William Eaton Chandler, was Secretary of the Navy under President Arthur and subsequently United States Senator from New Hampshire. "Ted" Chandler, as his friends called him, graduated from the Naval Academy well up in the Class of 1915, which included such distinguished officers as the future Rear Admirals Lynde D. McCormick, Arthur D. Struble, Richard W. Bates, Forrest B. Royal, John L. McCrea and Allan E. Smith, and Major General Ralph J. Mitchell USMC. Theodore Chandler specialized in gunnery, served in World War I and subsequently as gunnery officer on various staffs, and as C.O. of destroyers *Pope* and *Buchanan*. At the outbreak of World War II, as C.O. of light cruiser *Omaha*, he was instrumental in capturing a German blockade runner.[1] Promoted Rear Admiral 1942, he commanded Allied naval forces in the Aruba-Curaçao sector of the Caribbean for a year. In Operation DRAGOON, the invasion of Southern France, he had charge of the "Sitka-Romeo Force," a collection of tough but undisciplined French, American and Canadian commandos, who saw to it that his good humor and capacity to command were well

[1] For references in this History to his service in World War II see Volume I p. 84; also X 204, XI 242, 251, and XII 224-226.

tested. In the Battle of Surigao Strait he commanded Batdiv 2 (*Tennessee*, flag) and shortly after was given command of Crudiv 4. In the kamikaze attack of 6 January 1945, in Lingayen Gulf, on his flagship (*Louisvillle*), he was overwhelmed by the flaming gasoline, tried heroically to carry on, but collapsed, and died next day.

Admiral Chandler was a quiet and efficient officer, thoroughly competent for his successive commands, knowing what should be done and how to do it, beloved both by his seniors and his juniors.

SAMUEL E. MORISON

U. S. NAVAL WAR COLLEGE
NEWPORT, R. I.
1 June 1959

Contents

     1. The "Rice Paddy Navy"   289
     2. The Pony-back Navy   294
     3. The Yangtze Raiders   295
     4. The Coast Watchers   296
     5. The Final Naval Battle of World War II   300

     Appendix   I Task Organization for the Invasion
                    of Luzon, *January 1945*   303

     Appendix   II Task Organization for Third Fleet,
                    1 December 1944–23 January 1945   315

     Appendix III Task Organizations in Operations to
                    Liberate the Southern Philippines,
                    February–April 1945   321

     Appendix   IV Ships Hit or Near-missed, and Casual-
                    ties Inflicted, by Kamikaze Attacks
                    in Lingayen Operation, *January 1945*   325

     Index   327

List of Illustrations

List of Maps and Charts

Abbreviations

Officers' ranks and bluejackets' ratings are those contemporaneous with the event. Officers and men named will be presumed to be of the United States Navy unless it is otherwise stated; officers of the Naval Reserve are designated USNR. Other service abbreviations are USA, United States Army; USCG, United States Coast Guard; USCGR, Reserve of same; USMC, United States Marine Corps; USMCR, Reserve of same; RAN, Royal Australian Navy; RN, Royal Navy; RNN, Royal Netherlands Navy; IJN, Imperial Japanese Navy.

See Preface for abbreviations of books in footnotes.

A.A.F. — United States Army Air Forces
Abda — American-British-Dutch-Australian Command
AGC — Amphibious Group Command flagship; AGP — Motor Torpedo Boat tender
AP — Transport; APA — Attack transport; APD — destroyer transport
A/S — Antisubmarine
ATIS — Allied Translator and Interpreter Section of General Headquarters
avgas — Aviation gasoline
Batdiv — Battleship division
BB — Battleship
BLT — Battalion Landing Team
Bu — Bureau; Buord — Bureau of Ordnance; Bupers — Bureau of Naval Personnel; Buships — Bureau of Ships
CA — Heavy cruiser
CAG — Commander Air Group
C.A.P. — Combat Air Patrol
Cardiv — Carrier division
C.I.C. — Combat Information Center
Cincpac — Commander in Chief, Pacific Fleet (Admiral Nimitz)
CL — Light Cruiser
C.O. — Commanding Officer
C.N.O. — Chief of Naval Operations
Com — before cardiv, desdiv, etc., means Commander Carrier Division, Commander Destroyer Division, etc.

Cominch — Commander in Chief, United States Fleet (Admiral King)

CTF — Commander Task Force; CTG — Commander Task Group

CV — Aircraft Carrier; CVE — Escort Carrier; CVL — Light Carrier

DD — Destroyer; DE — Destroyer Escort

ESB — Engineer Special Brigades

H.M.A.S. — His Majesty's Australian Ship; H.M.S. — His Majesty's Ship

H.Q. — Headquarters

IFF — Identification, Friend or Foe

J.C.S. — Joint Chiefs of Staff

LC — Landing craft; LCI — Landing craft, infantry; LCM — Landing craft, mechanized; LCS — Landing craft, support; LCT — Landing craft, tank; LCVP — Landing craft, vehicles and personnel; LSD — Landing ship, dock; LSI — Landing ship, infantry; LSM — Landing ship, medium; LST — Landing ship, tank; LSV — Landing ship, vehicle; LVT — Landing vehicle tracked (or Amphtrac). (A), (G), (L), (M) and (R) added to above types mean armored, gunboat, large, mortar and rocket.

N.A.S. — Naval Air Station; N.O.B. — Naval Operating Base

Op — Operation; Opnav — Chief of Naval Operations; op plan — Operation Plan

O.N.I. — Office of Naval Intelligence

O.T.C. — Officer in Tactical Command

PC — Patrol craft; PCE — Patrol craft, escort

R.A.F. — Royal Air Force

RCT — Regimental Combat Team

S.A.P. — Semi-armor-piercing

SC — Submarine chaser

s.f.c.p. — Shore fire control party

S.O.P.A. — Senior Officer Present Afloat

SS — Submarine

TBS — Talk Between Ships (voice radio)

TF — Task Force; TG — Task Group; TU — Task Unit

UDT — Underwater Demolition Team

U.S.C.G.C. — United States Coast Guard Cutter

U.S.S. — United States Ship

USSBS — United States Strategic Bombing Survey

VB; VC; VF; VT — Bomber; Composite; Fighter; Torpedo plane

WDC — Washington Document Center

YMS — Motor minesweeper; YP — Patrol vessel

AIRCRAFT DESIGNATIONS

(Numerals in parentheses indicates number of engines)

United States

A–20 – Boston, Army (2) light bomber

B–17 – Flying Fortress, Army (4) heavy bomber; B–24 – Liberator, Army (4) heavy bomber; B–25 – Mitchell, Army (2) medium bomber; B–26 – Marauder, Army (2) medium bomber; B–29 – Superfortress, Army (4) heavy bomber

C–47 – Skytrain, Army (2) transport; C–54 – Skymaster, Army (4) transport

"Dumbo" – PBY equipped for rescue work

F4F – Wildcat; F6F – Hellcat; F4U – Corsair; Navy (1) fighters

OS2U – Kingfisher, Navy (1) scout-observation float plane

P–38 – Lightning, Army (2); P–39 – Airacobra, Army (1); P–40 – Warhawk, Army (1); P–47 – Thunderbolt, Army (1); P–51 – Mustang, Army (1); P–61 – Black Widow, Army (2) fighters

PBM–3 – Mariner, Navy (2) patrol bomber (flying boat)

PBY – Catalina, Navy (2) patrol bomber; PBY–5A, amphibian Catalina; PB4Y–1 – Navy Liberator bomber (4); PB4Y–2 – Navy Privateer bomber (4). *See also* "Dumbo"

PV–1 – Ventura, Navy (2) medium bomber

SB2C and SBW – Helldivers; SBD – Dauntless; Navy (1) dive-bombers

SOC – Seagull, Navy (1) scout-observation float plane

TBF, TBM – Avenger, Navy (1) torpedo-bombers

Japanese

Betty – Mitsubishi Zero–1, Navy (2) high-level or torpedo-bomber

Hamp – Mitsubishi Zero–2, Navy (1) fighter

Jake – Aichi or Watanabe, Navy (1) reconnaissance bomber (float plane)

Judy – Aichi, Navy (1) dive-bomber

Nick – Kawasaki or Nakajima Zero–2, Army (2) fighter

Oscar – Nakajima, Army (1) fighter

Rufe – Mitsubishi, Navy (1) fighter (float plane)

Tojo – Nakajima Zero–2, Army (1) fighter

Tony – Zero–3, Army or Navy (1) fighter

Val – Aichi 99, Navy (1) dive-bomber

Zeke – Mitsubishi Zero–3, Navy (1) fighter

PART I

Planning and Preliminaries

CHAPTER I

Planning for Luzon[1]

October–December 1944

1. *Luzon, Not Formosa*

"LEYTE and then Luzon," said General MacArthur in July 1944. President Roosevelt and Admiral Nimitz agreed. But the question whether a landing on Luzon or on Formosa or somewhere else should follow Leyte was not settled by the Joint Chiefs of Staff until 3 October, about two weeks before Leyte A-day.

The reason why the J.C.S. took so long to reach a decision was the adamantine devotion of Admiral King to the Formosa concept. A glance at a chart of the Western Pacific will suggest many arguments in favor of taking Formosa, together with a beachhead at Amoy on continental China. It would "put a cork in the bottleneck" of Japan's communications with her conquests of 1942; it would be a step nearer the enemy's heart than would Luzon.[2] To invade Formosa after Leyte would continue the successful "leap-frog" strategy, leaving the most powerful Japanese strong points (of which Luzon was one) to "wither on the vine." But there were both practical and political considerations against it. Formosa was in Admiral Nimitz's bailiwick, so he would have to find the troops. He did not have nearly enough, especially service troops; he could

---

[1] Grace P. Hayes "History of the J.C.S. in World War II" Vol. II; Robert R. Smith *Triumph in the Philippines;* MacArthur *Historical Report* Vol. II and *The Philippines Campaign 1944-45* (see Preface); General Walter Krueger *From Down Under to Nippon* (1953); Sixth Army Report of Luzon Campaign, Vols. I and III. See also Vol. XII, chap. i, for discussion of strategy.

[2] Also, the presence of an Allied Army on the Chinese mainland at the end of the war with Japan might have helped Chiang to retain control of China.

get none from Europe until after Germany surrendered, nor could he borrow from MacArthur, who already had XXIV Corps on loan from Pacific Ocean areas. And the General was determined not to let Formosa be substituted for Luzon. He urged not only the dishonor involved in bypassing seven million Filipinos, but the value of having a loyal and coöperative native population to help our armed forces, in comparison with hostile or indifferent Formosans.

On 21 September, after the Leyte operation had been stepped up to 20 October, General MacArthur demonstrated to the Joint Chiefs of Staff the feasibility of landing on Luzon exactly two months later, anticipating that the next step could be Kyushu, particularly if the Bonins were attacked previously.

Admiral Spruance and Rear Admiral Forrest Sherman [3] now joined the Army leaders in breaking the deadlock between "Formosans" and "Luzonites." At Pearl Harbor, in late August or early September 1944, Spruance [4] told Admiral Nimitz that he considered the Bonins and the Ryukyus a more practical approach to Japan than Formosa and Amoy; and he pointed out that General MacArthur offered to liberate Luzon in late December with the same troops that were about to be employed at Leyte. Admiral Nimitz, after frequent discussions with Spruance and with Forrest Sherman, his chief planning officer, agreed on the general concept. Sherman, one of the most acute strategists in the United States Navy, made

[3] Forrest Sherman, b. New Hampshire 1896, Annapolis '18 (second in his class), served in gunboat *Nashville* and destroyer *Murray* in World War I; C.O. of *Barry* 1921; naval aviator 1922, assigned to Fighting Squadron 2, instructor at Pensacola and Naval War College course. Served in carrier *Lexington* for a year from her commissioning in 1927, then C.O. Scoutron 2 in *Saratoga*. After a year instructing at Annapolis he rejoined "Sara" on staff of Adm. Yarnell. C.O. Fightron 1, 1932–33, then a three-year tour of duty in charge of aviation ordnance section, Buord, Washington; fleet aviation officer on staff of Commander Battle Force. Between 1940 and 1942 he was in war plans division office of C.N.O., and had a marked influence on some of the basic plans of the war; at Argentia he was the naval aviation adviser to Admiral King. C.O. *Wasp* 1942, of which he was the last to leave when she was torpedoed by *I-19* (see Vol. V 131–36). Deputy chief of staff to Adm. Nimitz, and head of his war plans division from Nov. 1943 to the end of the war. Comcardiv 1 Oct. 1945, deputy C.N.O. for operations, Dec. 1945, Com U.S. Naval Forces, Medit. (Sixth Fleet) 1948; C.N.O. Nov. 1949; died at Naples 22 July 1951 while on an important diplomatic mission.

[4] Spruance had just turned over Fifth Fleet to Admiral Halsey, under whose command it became Third Fleet.

a fresh study of the problem and produced a plan to drop Formosa altogether, invade Luzon in December, and the Bonins and Ryukyus early in 1945. Nimitz would have enough ground forces to take Iwo Jima in the one group and Okinawa in the other, without drawing on Eisenhower or MacArthur.

This plan, with which Spruance cordially agreed, was presented at an informal conference in San Francisco on 29–30 September and 1 October, called by Admiral King. Present were Admirals Nimitz and Sherman and Lieutenant Generals Simon Bolivar Buckner and Millard F. Harmon, the top Army and Air Force commanders in Nimitz's Pacific Ocean Areas. The two generals, whose staffs also had been studying this problem, convinced Admiral King that they could not get the troops required for a successful assault on Formosa before June 1945, if then; they were satisfied that MacArthur could invade Luzon in December 1944 with what he already had and take Manila early in the new year; and the admirals agreed that the Navy was capable of supporting and covering MacArthur in his coveted return to the big island.

Admiral King growled a little; said he wanted nothing to do with that "sinkhole" Iwo Jima (a prophetic description), but agreed. And on 3 October 1944, only one week before the Leyte operation got under way, the Joint Chiefs of Staff issued their last important strategic directive of the war.

Its main provisions were: —

1. General MacArthur to invade Luzon 20 December 1944; Admiral Nimitz to provide cover and support.
2. Admiral Nimitz to invade one or more islands (such as Iwo Jima) of the Bonins-Volcano group on 20 January 1945, and one or more islands (such as Okinawa) in the Ryukyus on 1 March.
3. In deference to Admiral King, the invasion of Formosa was not canceled, but directives as to "possible operations" against Formosa, the Pescadores and points on the China coast would be "issued later." They never were.

2. The Planning Process

A-day for Leyte was 20 October 1944, and on the 24th and 25th the great Battle for Leyte Gulf, which we have described in Volume XII, was fought. The smoke had hardly cleared before the admirals who were to participate in the Luzon landings departed Leyte Gulf in their flagships, to make preparations for Lingayen and Mindoro.[5] General MacArthur's planning staff at Hollandia had already been working with Rear Admiral Clifford E. Van Hook, deputy commander Seventh Fleet, and with Captain David S. Crawford, Admiral Kinkaid's plans officer, on outline plans for the Luzon landings; one called MUSKETEER III was ready on 26 September. On 12 and 13 October, General MacArthur issued operational instructions for the Mindoro landings on 5 December and for Lingayen Gulf on the 20th, assigning the troop tasks to General Krueger's Sixth Army with Vice Admiral Kinkaid's Seventh Fleet to embark, transport, land and support them.

The weeks since mid-September had been grueling for the fleet commanders and staff officers who were responsible for executing the landings on Morotai, Peleliu, Angaur and Leyte, defending the Leyte beachhead, and fighting the several actions which made up the Battle for Leyte Gulf. Although these operations had gone off successfully, they had been exhausting for command staffs because of the sudden changes of objective, which meant scrambling old op plans and devising new ones at short notice. Much work of that sort had been done on board flagships *Wasatch, Mount Olympus* and *Blue Ridge* in Leyte Gulf under frequent "red" alerts and amid pressing problems that required immediate evaluation and decision. And although the great naval battles were over, Leyte itself was far from secured, Japanese air forces were making kamikaze attacks on

[5] Admirals Wilkinson and Barbey left Leyte 26 Oct. and arrived Hollandia 30 and 31 Oct. Admiral Kinkaid left 29 Oct. and arrived Hollandia 2 Nov. Admiral Oldendorf left same day, spent about three weeks with Third Fleet on its sweeps and arrived Hollandia 19 Nov. A letter from Admiral Kinkaid to the writer, 1 Dec. 1958, has greatly clarified the planning process.

ships in the Gulf, and reinforcement and supply of Sixth Army on Leyte was a major responsibility in which the Navy shared. Nevertheless, in the first week of November, naval staffs had to concentrate on planning for Mindoro and Lingayen, with target dates, at that time, of 5 and 20 December.

Time was short, but several factors softened the pressure on the planners. There was no great procurement problem. Most of the combatant ships, auxiliaries and merchant vessels which had been involved in the Leyte operation, most of the naval commanders, and many of the troops were available for Mindoro and Lingayen. The amphibious problems and the logistic requirements were much the same for these new operations as for Leyte. And the staffs of Admirals Kinkaid and Wilkinson had an ideal spot for such work — the shores of Lake Sentani, Netherlands New Guinea.

This beautiful body of water, cupped in the Cyclops Mountains — which rise to an elevation of 7000 feet — lies some twenty-five miles inland from Hollandia. On the crest of a hill overlooking the lake, General MacArthur had established his headquarters in the summer of 1944. General Krueger's were at Hollekang, on Hollandia Bay. Admiral Kinkaid set up Seventh Fleet headquarters on a hill, adjacent to General MacArthur's, where he found quarters for Admirals Wilkinson and Oldendorf and had frequent visits from Admiral Barbey. Thus, the naval plan could be worked out in Quonset huts within twenty yards of one another.

Admiral Kinkaid, after spending a few days with his planners at Hollandia, flew back to Leyte to look over the situation. During the two days that he spent there with General MacArthur, he communicated his feelings about the air situation. The existing plans for Mindoro and Lingayen assumed that by 5 December, target date for Mindoro, the A.A.F. based on Leyte would have complete control of the air over Leyte and the Central Visayas. But, as we have seen in the previous volume, the Japanese successfully disputed this control of the air. To the Admiral, it seemed highly unlikely that they would be knocked down by 5 December — then only three weeks away. MacArthur was adamant about the date;

and Kinkaid learned that Lieutenant General Richard K. Sutherland — MacArthur's chief of staff — and General Kenney of Far Eastern Air Forces had presented the same argument to MacArthur yet failed to move him.

Returning to Hollandia, Admiral Kinkaid held a final conference on the Mindoro-Lingayen plans, at which Rear Admiral Forrest Sherman was present. Since it was clear that the A.A.F. could not furnish air cover, the only alternative would be to attach escort carriers to the invasion convoys. It looked like sudden death to send CVEs into the Sulu Sea, where they would be surrounded by enemy airfields, but it had to be done; and although the "baby flat-tops" took another bad beating, as in the Battle off Samar, they came through.

Admiral Kinkaid issued his plan for the Mindoro landings on 9 November. The task was given to Rear Admiral Arthur D. Struble,[6] then commanding the Ormoc resupply convoys; and as the assigned troops were then fighting on Leyte, all detailed planning had to be done on that island. On 18 November Kinkaid's plan for Lingayen was issued. Wilkinson's followed on the 27th and Barbey's on 3 December. The distance of the Lingayen beaches from Hollandia was 2150 miles, but some of the troops assigned were 800 miles to the rear of Hollandia. This meant that the slower ships, such as LSTs, would have to be loaded and sailed as much as twenty days in advance of S-day (as D-day for Lingayen was designated). Most of the shipping assigned had to make at least one resupply run to Leyte before loading.

General Krueger, although directing the Leyte campaign in the field, gave considerable attention to planning for Lingayen. He called a conference of troop commanders at his headquarters on 15 November to outline his ideas. In spite of their preoccupation with the Leyte campaign, they had plans for Lingayen ready by 25 November.[7]

---

[6] See Volume XII of this History, p. 119*n*, for his brief biography.
[7] Sixth Army Report.

In the meantime, the kamikazes were raising the devil with Allied shipping in Leyte Gulf. Thus, the more that Kinkaid knew about conditions in the islands to be liberated, the less he liked the target dates of 5 and 20 December. So, toward the end of November, he made another visit to MacArthur's headquarters at Tacloban, again to argue postponement. Generals Sutherland and Kenney joined him. They did not enter into the discussion, which the Admiral remembered to have been "on the warm side." But they agreed with him, as did Admirals Nimitz and Halsey. The result was that General MacArthur agreed to postpone the Mindoro operation to 15 December, and the Lingayen landings to 9 January 1945.

A great relief it was to everyone concerned. Barbey and Wilkinson welcomed the delay for logistics, upkeep and time to conduct rehearsals. Admiral Halsey had already sortied from Ulithi with three carrier groups of Task Force 38 on 30 November to cover the Mindoro landing when he received the word. He ordered the carriers back to Ulithi with orders to make best use of the ten days' delay for rest, recreation and repairs. It was the first time since August that the ships had had so long a respite. And, as we have seen, Kinkaid used the delay to land a division at Ormoc, which advanced the Leyte campaign.[8]

A few days before the new D-day for Mindoro, General MacArthur held a top-level conference at his Tacloban headquarters. Here it came out that, despite the postponement, the Army Air Force would not be ready to take responsibility for air cover of the Mindoro convoys. Not only the airfield and weather problems, said General Kenney, but the inexperience of his pilots would preclude their taking off before daylight or landing after dark. General MacArthur then turned to Admiral Kinkaid: what could he do to fill the gap? The Admiral — after a private conference on the porch with one of his staff and with a member of Admiral Halsey's staff who was present — decided that it was a "good fighting proposition" to use escort carriers, much as he disliked the idea; and he so

---

[8] Described in Vol. XII chap. xvi.

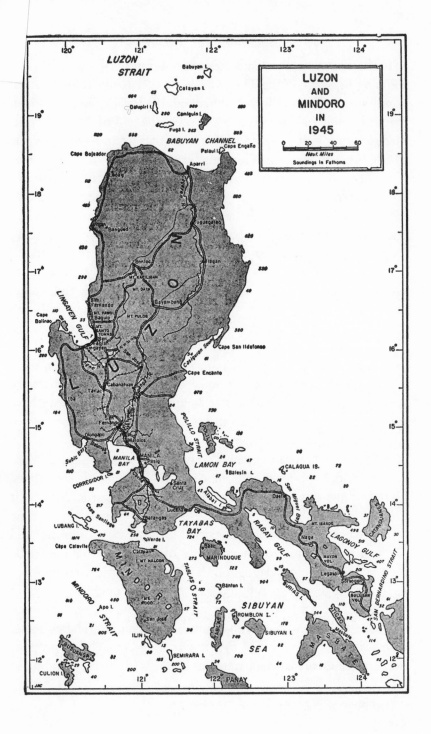

decided. General MacArthur remarked that it was the "best decision" that Commander Seventh Fleet had ever made.[9]

Admiral Kinkaid then organized a combat force of unusual composition — six escort carriers, three battleships, three heavy cruisers
and about 18 destroyers — to cover the transports from Leyte to
Mindoro, and back to Leyte.

3. *The Target and the Setup*

Luzon (population 7,384,798 before the war), although smaller
in area than New Guinea, Borneo, Sumatra or Java, by Western
standards is the most civilized of the greater islands. And it contains
Manila — then the largest and wealthiest city (population about
684,000) [10] in these Southwest Pacific islands. Luzon's irregular
shape has been compared to a dog's hindquarter, with Manila Bay,
one of the world's largest landlocked harbors, tucked in by the
hock. Guarding the entrance to the bay is Corregidor, off the Bataan Peninsula, twin symbols of dark days in recent history. Luzon
is mountainous and heavily forested, a notable exception being the
plain that lies between Manila Bay and Lingayen Gulf. That deep
indentation lies less than a hundred miles north of the capital.
Here is the natural landing point for a rapid advance to Manila;
it had been chosen by the Japanese in 1941 for their main invasion
of Luzon.[11] Another relatively level area is the Cagayan Valley,
formed by the river of that name which arises in the mountains
of Nueva Vizcaya Province and flows north into the Babuyan
Channel, some 250 miles from Manila, at the town of Aparri. A
landing at Aparri in addition to Lingayen was seriously considered
for a time, not with any idea of using the Cagayan Valley, but be-

[9] Adm. Kinkaid's letter to writer, 1 Dec. 1958.

[10] JANIS (Joint Army-Navy Intelligence Studies) No. 154, Study of the Philippines (1944); Cincpac-Cincpoa Information Bulletin 125–44, *Philippines and Hal-
mahera*. Total population of the Archipelago was 17,170,000 in 1941 (War Dept.
Survey of Philippines based on 1939 census).

[11] See Vol. III 174–81. There are also good beaches on the Bicol Peninsula, the
thin narrow part of the dog-leg southeast of Manila; but the exits from them are
easily defended defiles. The same is true of Batangas Bay.

cause General MacArthur planned originally to send the invasion convoy northwest, through Luzon Strait, and both Admirals King and Kinkaid thought that an air base near Cape Engaño would be necessary to protect that route. Kinkaid, however, pointed out that typhoons were to be expected in Luzon Strait around the target date and, supported by Nimitz, recommended the "back side" route through the Camotes and Sulu Seas to Lingayen. General Mac-Arthur accepted this in early November.

Lingayen Gulf offered so many advantages to an invader that it was decided to concentrate the landings there. The railroad north from Manila terminates at San Fernando (La Union) on the northern entrance, and the road network is the best in Luzon.

Both plan and command structure for Lingayen were similar to those which had been successful at Leyte. Vice Admiral Kinkaid in flagship *Wasatch,* with Lieutenant General Krueger embarked, would be in over-all command. Vice Admiral Barbey's VII 'Phib, with I Corps embarked, took the left flank; Vice Admiral Wilkinson's III 'Phib, with XIV Corps, the right flank, each amphibious force being divided into two attack groups, each under a flag officer. Vice Admiral Oldendorf and Rear Admiral Berkey commanded the bombardment and close covering groups, as before. Only the Spragues were missing; Rear Admiral Calvin T. Durgin, who had commanded an escort carrier division in Operation DRAGOON,[12] now had what was left of the "three Taffies."

Mindoro, the intermediate target, we shall come to presently.

4. *Japanese Plans and Preparations* [13]

By early November 1944 General Tomoyuki Yamashita, Commander Fourteenth Area Army, responsible for the defense of the Philippines, was convinced that Leyte could not be held. He and his staff estimated that by the middle of December MacArthur's

[12] See Vol. XI 279*n* for brief biography.
[13] MacArthur *Historical Report* II 404–07 and the following Japanese Monographs (see Preface): No. 4, No. 7, and No. 45.

control over Leyte would be sufficiently firm to permit his expansion from that island, probably to Luzon. He even anticipated an intermediate landing to obtain air bases for covering the main objective, but expected that MacArthur would select for this purpose a site such as Iloilo on Panay, rather than Mindoro, which Japanese engineers had surveyed and declared to be too rugged for an air base. The "Tiger of Malaya," already short of troops for the defense of Luzon owing to the waste of them in Leyte, had none to spare to hinder an Allied advance into the Visayas. But he made a remarkably accurate estimate that Luzon would be invaded between 7 and 10 January, either at Lingayen Gulf or Batangas Bay, and in ten-division strength. Actually there were six divisions plus a reinforced RCT and an armored group in the initial troop assignment.

General Yamashita even recommended to his superior officer, Field Marshal Hisaichi Terauchi, that no more reinforcements be sent to Leyte and that all available troops be assigned to the defense of Luzon. On 11 November Terauchi made the discouraging reply that the battle for Leyte must continue at all costs and preparations for the defense of Luzon be adjusted accordingly. He felt that to let the Americans secure even one good base in the Philippines would be tantamount to writing off the entire archipelago. On this basis Yamashita issued on 14 November a tentative operational outline for the Luzon campaign.

At that time there were almost 260,000 Japanese troops on Luzon, which was not far from the Sixth Army Intelligence estimate of 234,500 on 5 December.[14] The major units were seven infantry divisions and the 2nd Armored Division; all were below strength (two of them had lost about one third of their men en route to the Philippines) and short of equipment. There were also about 25,000 naval ground troops divided between Manila, Clark Field and Legaspi, under the command of Vice Admiral Denshichi Okochi. By the end of November, air strikes from Task Force 38 forced the Japanese to abandon Manila as a port of entry in favor

[14] Sixth Army Report III 27.

of San Fernando (La Union). Five destroyer escorts were at Manila on 13 December, but quickly withdrew to Camranh Bay, Indochina, on their own initiative, to escape Allied air attacks. After that only a few motor torpedo boats and subchasers were stationed in Luzon waters, mostly in Manila Bay. For naval defense the Japanese relied mostly on the new one-man "suicide boats," which began arriving in September, and whose total strength was built up to about 750, half of what had been planned.

Apart from these local defense units, the Japanese Navy was still a force to be reckoned with. Deployed from the Inland Sea to Singapore were superbattleship *Yamato*, five other battleships, four carriers, four heavy cruisers, about 35 destroyers and 43 submarines, ten of which were believed to be stationed at Formosa, available for immediate attack on an approaching naval force. Admiral Kinkaid warned Seventh Fleet that the enemy might combine his available naval strength for a major effort, or send small "Tokyo Express" task groups on high-speed sorties against our shipping.

Apparently Imperial General Headquarters had no such plan (probably because most of the ships were still being repaired), but depended for further defense of the Philippines largely on air power. Fourth Air Army and Second Air Fleet came under Yamashita's command early in the new year. He had 70 airfields in the Philippines from which military aircraft could operate. Major air bases on Luzon were at Clark Field and its satellites, and at Nichols, Nielson and associated fields in the Manila area. Principal secondary fields were located at San Fernando, Lingayen, Vigan, Baguio, Baler, Laoag, Aparri, Cabanatuan, Florida-Blanca, San Marcelino and Mariveles. But the number of planes immediately available to the enemy was not great.

Combined Army-Navy enemy air strength in the Philippines on 1 December is difficult to estimate, as the Japanese themselves at the end of the war did not know; estimates run all the way between 100 and 600 planes.[15] Kinkaid's Intelligence estimate of 405 is probably

---

[15] MacArthur *Historical Report* II 410–11, 430 (total of 233); Liaison Committee (Tokyo) for the Imperial Japanese Army and Navy answer to USSBS Memo

nearly correct. In any case, so many units were expended in the attacks (kamikaze and otherwise) on Mindoro and Lingayen convoys that Vice Admiral Shigeru Fukudome, commanding Navy air, said he had lost "practically all" his planes by mid-January; and when Japanese aircraft were finally evacuated from Luzon at that time only 47 planes of all types were left.[16] Several hundred replacements were sent to Luzon in December and January, but these too were expended, not only in attacks on ships, but by Allied air raids on Luzon fields during and after the Mindoro landings.[17] Nevertheless, through kamikaze tactics, the Japanese air forces inflicted damage on the Allied invasion forces all out of proportion to the numbers employed.

The attempted Japanese reinforcement of Leyte continued until Christmas, when Yamashita, having at last obtained consent of the higher command to bow to the inevitable, informed General Suzuki that he could expect neither help nor ships to evacuate his troops. which would have to shift for themselves.[18]

Field Marshal Terauchi's insistence on reinforcing Leyte, against Yamashita's better judgment, resulted in staggering losses for the Japanese Army, Navy and merchant service. Almost 80 per cent of the ships sent by Japan to Ormoc were sunk en route, and the partial sealing-off of Luzon by American air and submarine power rendered it exceedingly difficult for the enemy to send more supplies to Manila. In a situation analogous to that which prevailed off Ormoc, transports carrying reinforcements from China were sunk close enough to the Luzon coast for most of the troops to reach

NAV-3, 18 Oct. 1845. Admiral Fukudome estimated the strength in mid-December as 600–700 planes (*Inter. Jap. Off.* II 502–03). Cdr. Yamaguchi estimated strength on 15 December as about 100, and on 1 January 1945 as 70 or less. (Same, I 181–2.) Jap. Mono. No. 81, *Mindoro Battle* p. 8, gives Navy strength on 17 Dec. as 28 planes. Liaison Committee answer to USSBS NAV-3, 18 Oct. 1945 lists 80 kamikazes (Navy) at the Mabalacat fields on 1 Jan. 1945.

[16] *Inter. Jap. Off.* I 183, and Liaison Committee answer to USSBS NAV-3, 18 Oct. 1945. The remnants of 4th Air Army were ordered to Formosa 25 Jan. (Jap. Mono. No. 12, *4th Air Army Operations* p. 81). A few Navy planes lasted longer.

[17] The number of replacements is also uncertain; estimates vary from 255 to 660 in December.

[18] See Vol. XII 394. Suzuki had been warned of his fate as early as 18 Dec.

shore alive, but without arms or equipment. The Japanese command in Manila had to re-equip these survivors from stocks already depleted in the futile attempt to support Leyte.

In sharp contrast to most Japanese commanders, whose orders were full of "decisive battles" and "annihilation," General Yamashita's approach was realistic. He believed that the best he could do was a "strategic delaying operation." In order to pin down as many Allied troops as possible for as long as possible, he ordered three mountain positions to be prepared from which his forces could launch harassing attacks. The strongest was in the mountains north of the central plain, with headquarters at Baguio, which would also control the food-producing Cagayan Valley. The second position was in the mountains west of Clark Field, northwest of Manila, and the third in the mountains east of Manila. The capital was not to be defended; troops already there would withdraw to the mountains after blowing bridges. Owing to factors not under Yamashita's control his intentions for Manila were not carried out.

Late in November the Japanese began to transfer supplies, ammunition and essential base materials from Manila to these mountain positions. Shortages, poor transportation and operations of Filipino guerrillas hampered the operation, and by 9 January 1945 only a fraction of planned levels of supply had reached the hills. Some reinforcements reached Luzon during December, but they had suffered severe losses en route through the depredations of American submarines.

CHAPTER II

Mindoro[1]

December 1944–February 1945

1. The Plan

THERE was no urgency to liberate the inhabitants of Mindoro, since the Japanese held the island very lightly and did not interfere much with the natives. But the island was badly wanted by Allied forces as a steppingstone to Luzon. Possession of it would enable the Army Engineers to build airfields from which Southwest Pacific Air Forces could operate against enemy air forces on Luzon, and cover the Lingayen landings coming up in January.

Mindoro, whose greatest dimensions are 58 by 110 land miles, was so named by the Spaniards because of a reputed gold mine; and, although no gold was found, the name stuck. It is separated from Luzon by the 7½-mile wide Verde Island Passage, from the Sibuyan Sea by Tablas Strait, and from the Calamian Islands by Apo East Pass. All sea traffic from Mindanao, and from Leyte via the Surigao and San Bernardino Straits to central and northern Luzon, must pass close aboard this island, whose northern point, Cape Calavite, lies only ninety miles from Manila by sea. The greater part of Mindoro is wild and mountainous; Mount Halcon in the north,

[1] CTG 78.3 (Rear Adm. Struble) Action Report 15 Dec. 1944; Western Visayan Task Force Historical Report for 15 Dec. 1944–31 Jan. 1945, 1 Feb. 1945; CTG 77.12 (Rear Adm. Ruddock) Report of Operations of Heavy Covering and Carrier Group, 25 Dec. 1944; Carrier Unit (Rear Adm. Stump) Action Report, 25 Dec. 1944; CTG 77.3 (Rear Adm. Berkey) Action Report, 19 Dec. 1944; Sixth Army Report on Mindoro Operation, 22 Apr. 1945; R. R. Smith *Triumph in the Philippines*, chap. iii; MacArthur *Historical Report* II; Japanese Monograph No. 81 *Mindoro Battle* and No. 137 *General Outline* of same.

third highest in the Archipelago, rises 8481 feet above the sea. The 117,000 inhabitants are largely concentrated in narrow plains on the northern and eastern coasts.

The southeastern coast, the San José area, where there were level cane fields served by a narrow-gauge railroad, four nonoperational airfields, and ample sites for new ones, attracted naval planners. Ilin Island makes a sheltered seaplane base of Mangarin Bay and the nearby beaches are good for landing. Natural features, the proximity of the sea lane from Leyte to Lingayen, and minimum distance from Luzon, made this part of Mindoro the most suitable for landing and base development.

The move to Mindoro was one of the boldest during the Pacific War. To drive this wedge into the Central Philippines it would be necessary to bypass several important enemy-held islands, and, when established at the San José base, we would be almost surrounded by enemy airfields, yet 262 air miles from Dulag, our own nearest base in Leyte. And 260 miles was then beyond the normal range of land-based fighter planes. This did not worry General MacArthur, since the guerrillas already controlled large parts of Bohol, Cebu and Panay. But guerrillas were seldom able to stop enemy air operations.

Owing to the retarded air base development in Leyte that we noted and explained in Volume XII, Allied control of the air west and north of Leyte was far from complete on 5 December 1944. That was the reason why postponement to 15 December was imperative. Aside from tactical considerations, the original date left no time for amphibious rehearsals, or relief for ships in the New Guinea-Leyte shuttle, or (as Admiral Barbey pointed out) loading time for a 20 December landing at Lingayen, with which Mindoro was tied in. Postponement had the further advantage of giving the Army Engineers time to augment the overworked Tacloban airfield on Leyte by the Tanuan strip midway between Tacloban and Dulag, and the Bayug strip near Dulag.

Rear Admiral Arthur D. Struble, veteran of the Ormoc landings, and of the seizure of the outer islands in Leyte Gulf, was appointed commander of the Visayan Attack Force, as the expedition to this island was designated. Upon returning to Leyte Gulf from Ormoc 8 December, he raised his flag in light cruiser *Nashville*, General MacArthur's favorite ferryboat, and resumed planning. He drew his logistic support from Leyte, through Seventh Fleet Service Force representatives in Leyte Gulf. The Visayan Attack Force was divided into three groups: —

Mindoro Attack Group, under Admiral Struble's direct command. *Nashville*, 8 destroyer transports, 30 LST, 12 LSM, 31 LCI, 10 large and 7 small minesweepers and 14 other small craft, with 12 escorting destroyers.

Close Covering Group, commanded by Rear Admiral Berkey.[2] Two light cruisers, one heavy cruiser and seven destroyers.

Motor Torpedo Boat Group, consisting of 23 PT, under Lieutenant Commander N. Burt Davis.

In addition, Rear Admiral T. D. Ruddock [3] commanded a Heavy Covering and Carrier Group of battleships, cruisers, escort carriers and destroyers, to operate in the Sulu Sea in support. The inclusion of the CVEs, as we saw in the previous chapter, was Admiral Kinkaid's idea, as the one means of protecting the convoy during hours when the A.A.F. could not be present. Postponement of the target date enabled this group to rendezvous at Kossol Passage, on 5 December. It comprised battleships *West Virginia*, *Colorado* and *New Mexico*; light cruisers *Denver*, *Columbia* and *Montpelier*; escort carriers *Natoma Bay*, *Manila Bay*, *Marcus Island*, *Kadashan Bay*, *Savo Island* and *Ommaney Bay*; and 18 destroyers.

[2] See Volume XII of this History, p. 21*n*, for brief biography.

[3] Theodore D. Ruddock, b. South Carolina 1892, Annapolis 1914. Served in *Utah* through World War I and in *Tennessee* in 1921. After various sea commands and postgraduate study in ordnance engineering, became squadron gunnery officer of Desron 11, 1926-29. Testing ordnance at Dahlgren to 1932, gunnery officer *Nevada*, staff gunnery officer of DDs Battle Force 1934. Duty in Naval Gun Factory, Washington, 1935-38, Comdesdiv 6, 1939-40, duty in Buord to 1942, when he had a great part in expanding production. C.O. *Massachusetts* 1943-44, Combatdiv 4 in Marianas and Leyte Operations; wounded during fire support duty off Tinian. Duty in Bupers and on an Army-Navy committee at Washington 1945-46, Sup't, Naval Gun Factory to 1948; inspection duty to his retirement, 1951.

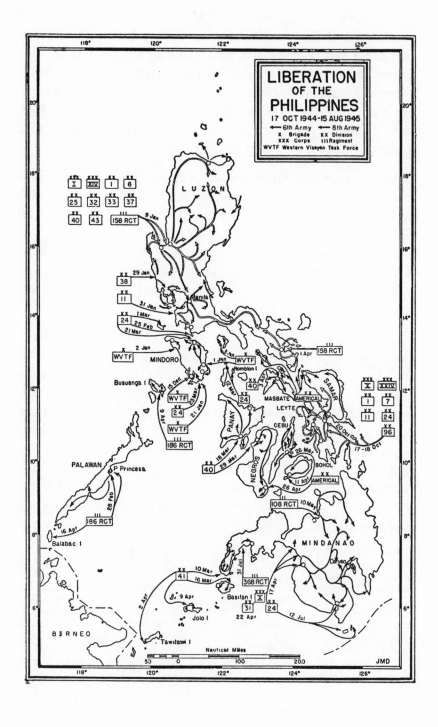

LIBERATION
OF THE
PHILIPPINES
17 OCT 1944-15 AUG 1945

6th Army   8th Army
X Brigade   XX Division
XXX Corps   III Regiment
WVTF Western Visayan Task Force

The carriers were Rear Admiral Stump's old Taffy 2. In anticipation of a series of air battles, they increased their complement of fighter planes from 16 to 24, at the same time reducing the number of torpedo bombers from 12 to 9. For the first time the CVEs were given an adequate screen — Captain J. G. Coward's Desron 54, which had delivered the initial torpedo attack in the Battle of Surigao Strait. Battleships and cruisers, included largely for their anti-aircraft fire, were screened by Captain R. H. Smith's Desron 22, of Ormoc Bay fame.[4]

Of ground forces embarked (their designation being the WESTERN VISAYAN TASK FORCE) the principal units were an RCT of the 24th Infantry Division and the 503rd Parachute Regiment. Brigadier General William C. Dunckel USA, who commanded them, was responsible for 11,878 combat troops, 9578 Army Air Force and 5901 service troops, these being provided to build airfields and other facilities. Over 16,500 men and 27,600 tons of equipment and supplies were landed during the assault, and an additional 5100 men with 16,800 tons of supplies were transported to Mindoro by VII Amphibious Force during the resupply phase of the operation.

The Japanese defenses were very inadequate. About 200 soldiers were in the San José area, and not more than 500 on the entire island. But the Japanese air forces held good cards in the shape of a dozen or more airfields in Luzon and the Visayas, all within range.

Since it was anticipated that the principal resistance to an Allied occupation of Mindoro would be offered by the Kamikaze Corps, an air plan was very carefully worked out. At a conference between Lieutenant General George Kenney USA and Rear Admiral Felix Stump on 7 December, it was agreed that V Army Air Force would augment combat air patrol in the Mindanao Sea during the passage and take complete responsibility at dusk every day. The escort carriers would provide fighter cover at other times and direct support at the objective area up to and including N-day (as Min-

---

[4] See Vol. XII chap. xvi.

doro D-day was called), 15 December. Then Army Air would take over support duties at the beachhead.

Admiral Halsey's Third Fleet and his famous Task Force 38, now under Vice Admiral John S. McCain, were brought into the picture in order to prevent the enemy from launching air attacks from Philippine fields during the approach, landing, and unloading. After a conference at Leyte a dividing line of responsibility was established between General Kenney's Southwest Pacific Air Forces and Admiral Halsey's Third Fleet.[5] This meant that Halsey was responsible for Manila Bay and all Luzon to the northward, leaving the Bicol Peninsula, Mindoro and the Visayas to be covered by General Kenney's land-based Army Air Forces. Halsey proposed to strike Luzon on 14, 15 and 16 December, refuel on the 17th and be available for strikes on 19, 20 and 21 December.

2. *The Approach, 12–14 December*

The first outfit to get going from Leyte Gulf, and the last to arrive at Mindoro, was an aggregation of tugs and barges known as Slow Tow Convoy. At 1500 December 11, Captain J. B. McLean, Comdesdiv 48, received an order from Admiral Struble to organize this unit and depart for Mindoro at 0600 next morning. As Captain McLean observed with considerable restraint, "Only limited preparations could be made." [6] His heterogeneous group comprised three destroyers, two destroyer escorts, six tugboats (one of the Australian Navy, one of the United States Navy and four of the United States Army), an Army aviation gasoline tanker and two LCTs. Other vessels that were scheduled never got the word, but some, not expected, joined. Each tug had a tow which made forming up difficult, especially since there was no voice communication between ships.

[5] The line followed lat. 14°30′ N, through the Philippine Sea to long. 121°50′ E, thence south to lat. 13°35′ N, thence west. Halsey Action Report.
[6] CTU 78.3.12 (Capt. McLean) Action Report Slow Tow Convoy 25 Dec. 1944.

In an effort to determine what the tugs were supposed to do with their tows, once they reached Mindoro, Captain McLean inquired: "What are your orders?" and received the following replies:

U.S.S. *Whippoorwill:* Turn tow over to PT unit.
H.M.A.S. *Reserve:* Deliver to PT Base.
FIRST ARMY TUG: We have no instructions. Sixth Army is to give them.
SECOND ARMY TUG: As far as we know, the Army will take them.
THIRD ARMY TUG: Don't know.
FOURTH ARMY TUG: Drop barge and return.
BOTH LCTs: Report to Senior Officer Present on arrival.
TANKER: Awaiting orders.

A semblance of order was finally established, but when Captain McLean tried to make a feint into Panaon Bay to deceive enemy air, he was blocked off by a resupply echelon returning from Ormoc Bay. No air attack developed and, in the early hours of 13 December, Slow Tow was overtaken and passed by Admiral Struble's Mindoro Attack Force, which had formed off Dulag, and Admiral Ruddock's battleships and escort carriers, from Kossol Passage.

It was an unlucky 13th for the main convoy, the Mindoro Attack Force. In accordance with the air plan, the escort carriers furnished in the morning a 12-plane combat air patrol (C.A.P.) over the Ruddock and Struble groups, which were fairly near to one another, and 35 Corsairs from land-based Marine Air Group 12 were maintained over Struble's convoys throughout the day. The forenoon watch was uneventful, but the presence of the force was discovered by a Japanese reconnaissance plane as early as 0900, and a few hours later kamikaze bombers with fighter escort took off from one of the Visayan fields to attack.[7] Shortly before 1500, as the convoy was about to round the southern cape of Negros into the Sulu Sea, a kamikaze Val sneaked in low from astern and crashed *Nashville* on her port side abaft Admiral Struble's cabin. That Japanese pilot was certainly loaded to kill. Besides crashing himself, he carried two bombs, both of which exploded. The ship was shaken

[7] MacArthur *Historical Report* II 411.

from stem to stern. Fires immediately broke out. Flag bridge, combat information center and communications office were wrecked. Ready ammunition from the 5-inch guns and 40-mm mounts started going off. No fewer than 133 officers and men, including the Admiral's and the General's chiefs of staff, Captain E. W. Abdill and Colonel Bruce C. Hill usa, and Colonel John T. Murtha usa commanding 310th Bombardment Wing, were killed or died of their wounds, and 190, including General Dunckel and several other members of his staff, were wounded. *Nashville* maneuvered radically until destroyer *Stanly*, detailed in the op plan for the special purpose of helping crippled ships, closed to render assistance, while *YMS-315* picked up men who had been blown overboard. Admiral Berkey temporarily took over tactical command, while Admiral Struble, General Dunckel and some fifty staff officers and war correspondents transferred to destroyer *Dashiell*. The damaged cruiser, escorted by *Stanly*, then returned to Leyte Gulf.

At 1705 December 13, shortly after Admiral Ruddock's group entered the Sulu Sea, bogeys appeared on radar screens closing from the northeast. These represented seven kamikazes with three fighter escorts which had taken off from Cebu at 1630. Combat Air Patrol intercepted them thirteen miles out, but three broke through. One was shot down by a screening destroyer, a second by *West Virginia;* but the third bore in on *Haraden*. Its right wing sheared the starboard end and after side of that destroyer's bridge; the fuselage, after clearing the starboard boat, struck the searchlight on No. 1 stack and exploded with its bomb load. The stack was carried away and burning gasoline splashed over the after part of the ship. Numerous small fires sprang up and steam shot out from severed uptakes, making it difficult for sailors to move about; but they managed to bring everything under control. *Haraden's* casualties were 14 dead and 24 wounded, and she too had to return to Leyte Gulf.[8]

About half an hour after *Haraden* was hit, the enemy started to

[8] *Haraden* War Damage Report 15 Jan. 1945. During this attack the escort carriers launched 30 fighters, ten of them to help repel the attack and 20 as relief for C.A.P.

work over Slow Tow Convoy astern, but Captain McLean's destroyers took very good care of their clumsy charges. Two enemy planes that managed to elude C.A.P. were so badly shot up by antiaircraft fire that they splashed, one so near the Army gasoline tanker that two of her men were blown overboard.

For 14 December the Japanese high command planned an all-out attack, with no fewer than 186 planes, on the Mindoro convoys, which they supposed to be heading for Negros or Panay. The plan, fortunately for Admiral Struble's force, miscarried; the dawn search, briefed to the effect that Binalbagan on the west coast of Negros was the American destination, missed the convoys, then well out in the Sulu Sea. At 0715, 29 Japanese Army planes (including 16 kamikazes) and 40 Navy planes (including 33 kamikazes) took off from the Clark Field complex. They unhappily encountered American carrier-plane sweeps from Task Force 38, and two thirds of them failed to return; those that escaped could not find the convoys and came down at Cebu and Davao.[9] Other TF 38 planes sealed off the Luzon airfields for the rest of the day. In addition, ten Marine Corsairs (F4U) from Leyte struck Masbate airfield, twelve others hit Naga airfield in southern Luzon, and the escort carrier planes had an active day sweeping San José airfield on Panay and Dos Hermanos strip on Negros (where they got nine enemy aircraft), besides maintaining C.A.P. and splashing a few planes that accidentally found Ruddock's battleships and cruisers. A second Japanese attempt to strike the convoy from Visayan fields was unsuccessful, and the Mindoro Attack Force was never spotted by the enemy until after the landings had begun.

During the night of 14–15 December, Admiral Berkey's Close Covering Group maintained a position about five miles ahead of the transports. "Black Cats" (night-flying Catalinas), sent from Leyte, patrolled twenty to thirty miles ahead and on each flank. At about 0300 December 15, one of them reported a surface contact approximately fifteen miles northwest of the Mindoro Attack

[9] MacArthur *Historical Report* II 411–12; Jap. Mono. No. 81, *Mindoro Battle*, says 85 planes were involved.

Group. After a check to make sure it was not one of our mine-sweepers, Admiral Berkey instructed the Catalina pilot to attack. Five minutes later he reported scoring one hit on a cargo transport of about 6000 tons. A couple of hours later, at 0455, destroyers *Barton* and *Ingraham* closed this target and took it under fire. The ship was soon enveloped in flames and left sinking. But "Black Cat" had seen a mouse, not a rat: the victim turned out to be an inter-island freighter of 150 to 500 tons.[10]

As the Attack Force approached the objective, the minecraft pulled ahead to sweep, but found no mines. The Japanese never did any serious mining of inner Philippine waters except off Cebu, since they counted on "annihilating" their enemies long before this defense line was breached.

3. The Landing, 15 December

The primary mission of Admiral Struble and General Dunckel was to establish a perimeter embracing the village of San José in southwestern Mindoro, and to begin airstrip construction. Between the Bugsanga River and Caminawit Point are four good landing beaches, two of which the joint commanders selected, designated Blue 1 and White.[11] The terrain behind these beaches is flat, covered by cane fields for two miles inland, and cut by numerous streams. Hilly country begins about three or four miles inland. The town of San José is easily accessible from either beach and San José air-field, least bad of the four abandoned airstrips in this area,[12] lay near the town.

At 0530 December 15, before first light, four fire support de-

---

[10] CTG 77.3 (Rear Adm. Berkey) Action Report.

[11] In addition to Blue 1 and White beaches, Beach Green north of the Bugsanga River mouth was used to land 170 men from destroyer transport *Crosby*, Beach Blue 2 was available in case extra landing area was needed, and Beach Red on Caminawit Point, a narrow sandspit about 2000 yards long, was the designated un-loading area for LSTs carrying men and equipment for the PT base to be con-structed on Mangarin Bay.

[12] There were eight nonoperational airfields on Mindoro, all in equally bad condition.

stroyers [18] left their screening positions in the Attack Group and stood in toward their assigned areas. Half an hour later, Admiral Berkey's Close Covering Group headed for a position to provide close cover for the assault forces. "Count" Berkey was at home in these waters, which he had surveyed for the Navy in 1935, and

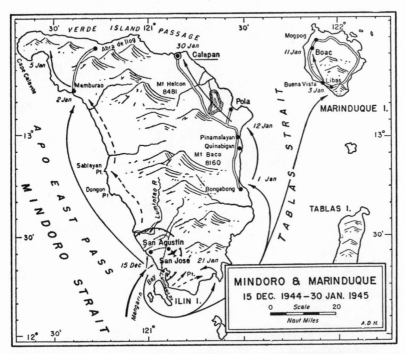

General Dunckel had once toured Mindoro in a Model T Ford. Admiral Struble deployed his Attack Group at 0640 and the amphibious craft maneuvered for position off Blue and White beaches. A few minutes later he set H-hour for 0730. A fire support destroyer then reported that many Filipinos and carabao were on the beaches; the natives to see the fun and the carabao doubtless anticipating a renewal of their long-denied sport, chasing and butting Yanks. The Admiral directed his ships to fire high air-bursts to warn them off, and signaled his ships: "Do not fire on natives or cattle. Report by name when on station. Hurry up." The last direc-

[18] *Fletcher, LaVallette, O'Bannon, Hopewell.*

tive was meant for the amphibious craft. At 0710 each destroyer
fired four warning shots and, much to the relief of all hands, both
men and beasts scattered inland. A couple of minutes later, the
pre-landing bombardment began.

The landing plan was simple, no opposition developed and the

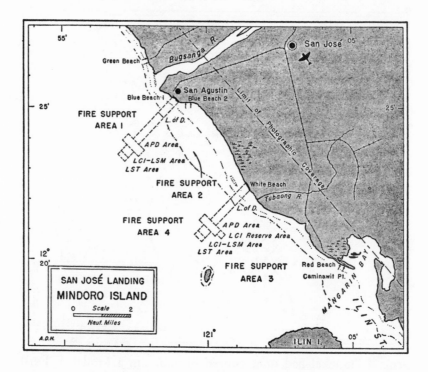

weather was perfect; so everything proceeded according to plan.
Wave 1 of 18 LCP(R) touched down at 0731; Waves 2 and 3,
composed of LCI, followed; then Waves 4 and 5, of LSM and LST.
The beaches were such that most soldiers went ashore standing up
and dry-shod, and all landing craft retracted.

For Admiral Struble, who had been through the Normandy operation in June, Mindoro was an amphibious group commander's
dream. General Dunckel, who had been an artillery officer at
Bougainville, also had a pleasant surprise. Ninety minutes after
landing, the infantrymen had pushed over a mile inland through

dry sugar cane, rice fields and scattered coconut groves, encountering only a small Japanese detachment on Caminawit Point. San José was occupied by the 503rd Airborne at noon. The terrain looked beautiful to men who had been slogging through Leyte mud for weeks, and were now out of the typhoon rain belt on good dry land. Indeed, the landing was almost too good. Some of the seasoned compaigners smelled a rat. He was coming, on wings. A Japanese reconnaissance plane had spotted the landing operations at about 0530; and shortly after, some 15 to 18 kamikazes with as many escorts took off from Davao and Clark Field.

At 0800 A.A.F. planes arrived over the Mindoro beachhead to relieve the carrier-based aircraft, and Admiral Stump's unit, with Admiral Ruddock's group, started back to Leyte.[14] Slow Tow Convoy was still coming up. Twelve minutes later the kamikazes began to bore in. One, a torpedo plane, headed for the carrier group. When about 300 yards on the starboard beam of *Ralph Talbot*, it disintegrated under her antiaircraft fire and flaming wreckage struck her deck. A few minutes later a second plane made a gliding approach out of the sun and was knocked down by C.A.P. At 0825 three more planes attacked. One came in low over the water through intense antiaircraft fire, but escaped; two headed for escort carrier *Marcus Island*. The first, hit by machine-gun fire, splashed about 20 feet on the carrier's starboard bow after striking a lookout platform with its wingtip and decapitating the lookout. The other, which ten seconds later dove on her starboard quarter, met the same fate. Damage to the carrier was superficial. At 0900 three more planes approached; one was shot down by *Savo Island's* C.A.P. within sight of the ship, the others driven off. Forty minutes later, three more were shot down by ships' antiaircraft fire.

Already there was action at the beachhead. A few minutes later C.A.P. tallyhoed about 20 planes approaching from the southward. Ten got by and came in low from both sides of Ilin Island. They spotted LSTs off Beach White on their way to the line of depar-

<hr>

[14] It was recalled at 1950 because bad weather over Leyte prevented A.A.F. planes from taking off.

ture, and at 0855 started diving from about 300 feet altitude. The LSTs and destroyer *Moale* (Commander W. M. Foster) opened fire and diminished their number, but the rest headed for *LST-738* (Lieutenant J. T. Barnett USNR), despite hits from her and the destroyer. One crashed the landing ship just above the waterline, breaking through into the tank deck, where high-octane gasoline ignited and ammunition exploded. The second made for her bridge but was shot down by *Moale*.

LST-738, however, was in a bad way. As the skipper observed the embarked soldiers to be "moving about the ship in a frightened state and suffering from smoke and burns," he ordered them to abandon ship and had the life rafts cast overboard. There followed a second large explosion, inflicting further damage; and when the situation was reported to the flotilla commander, Captain Richard Webb, he ordered *LST-738* to be abandoned. *Moale*, in the meantime, had, with some difficulty, closed to help fight the fire. No sooner was she in position alongside than a third explosion occurred in the LST, holing the destroyer's bow in several places, killing one and wounding ten of her crew. Attempts to fight the fire were discontinued and the landing ship was abandoned. She burned all day and was finally sunk by naval gunfire.

LST-472 (Lieutenant John H. Blakley USNR), a short distance away, was undergoing a similar experience, when off Beach Red. After one plane splashed to port and another clipped the port after gun tubs, she was crashed at deck level, just forward of the main superstructure. The plane's engine and burning parts were scattered across the ship; the bomb penetrated to the tank deck and exploded there. As if this were not enough, another plane following closely came in strafing. A Japanese pilot, hit by gunfire from another ship, tried to wing-over and hit the deck of *LST-472*, but overshot and splashed on her port beam. A minute or so later, a fourth plane came in strafing but did no damage; it was followed by a fifth, which dove onto the LST's bow, was taken under fire, and splashed. Blakley had on board NABU 5 and part of 113th Seabees.

Thus, within five minutes *LST-472* shot down or assisted in shooting down three of four attacking planes, a record that she had to pay for with her life. The explosion and resulting fire knocked out all her water mains, and the chemical fire-fighting equipment was inadequate. Destroyers *O'Brien* and *Hopewell* and *PCE–851* closed to help, but it was no use, and the ship was abandoned. Two large explosions then occurred. She burned until sunk by gunfire later in the day. This was a sad ending for one of the original work horses of VII 'Phib, participating in her thirteenth amphibious operation in twenty months overseas. Her casualties were fortunately light: 6 dead or missing; several wounded. Most of the equipment of the naval advanced base unit, including 250 tons of wheeled and tracked vehicles, was lost, making it impossible for the Seabees to build the planned base for motor torpedo boats.

Friendly planes reported to Admiral Berkey a "damaged enemy cruiser" in Mangarin Bay, and minesweepers sighted a destroyer hard on a rocky shoal between Ilin Island and Mindoro. Admiral Berkey guessed that the two were one and the same ship, and it turned out that she was Japanese destroyer *Wakaba*, which had grounded on an islet off the west coast of Semirara Island after being hit by a plane from carrier *Franklin* on 24 October. Destroyer *Walke* fired over one hundred 5-inch shells into the hulk, giving her gunners good target practice.

General Dunckel assumed command ashore at 1045. Fifteen minutes earlier the eight APDs, the nine LCI(R)s and the light transport unit of beaching craft were ready to depart for Leyte. The LSTs were being unloaded as quickly as possible in order to get them off and out to sea. "Unloading progressed rapidly under ideal conditions," reported Admiral Struble. "Not only were beaches excellent for the beaching of LSTs, but also the hard sand facilitated the carrying of supplies by vehicles to dumps. Beach parties, augmented by 1200 labor troops from the Army,[15] worked unceasingly in unloading the LSTs." They departed twenty-four

[15] These 1200 troops belonged to the 77th Division and were taken to Mindoro for the sole purpose of helping to unload, a scheme more often advocated than employed in amphibious operations. The troops returned to Leyte next day.

hours earlier than had been planned. Speed here was highly benefi-
cial because the Army planes that were furnishing C.A.P. over the
beachhead had to return to Leyte at 1335, bad weather then closed
in on the Leyte airfields, and the A.A.F. was unable to send relief
to Mindoro.

At Caminawit Point, Lieutenant Commander N. Burt Davis had
set up the advance base for his 23 PT boats by 1400.[16] By nightfall
15 December every landing ship but one had been unloaded and
Admiral Struble was ready to pull out for Leyte. The 27 LSTs,
together with all but two of the minesweepers and other amphibious craft, escorted by temporary flagship *Dashiell* and eight other
destroyers, sailed for Leyte Gulf shortly after 1900 N-day. Near
San José, American and Australian engineers were already at work
on another Allied airfield in the almost endless chain which now
stretched from Mindoro around the world to France, where at that
moment General Eisenhower was feeling the first impact of the
Runstedt offensive.

The Japanese propaganda version, naturally, was very different.
Lieutenant General M. Homma, in a broadcast to the Japanese people, advanced the theory that the Americans were "slipping away"
from a squeeze play on Leyte:

"The enemy was forced to make the Mindoro landing due to the
terrific pressure exerted by our victorious forces on Leyte Island.
We have the enemy in a position on Mindoro to deal him a stun-
ning blow. Douglas MacArthur, having many times escaped our
traps, will not this time slip away." [17]

MacArthur's forces were indeed slipping away, but in a direction
that meant no comfort for the enemy.

[16] Their first mission was on the night of 17 December. Two boats visited a
guerrilla hideout at Abra de Ilog on the north coast of Mindoro, where they were
met by Lt. Cdr. George F. Rowe usnr, the American liaison officer. After deliver-
ing sealed orders from General MacArthur and taking on board eleven American
aircraft pilots whom the guerrillas had rescued, they picked up two coast watchers
in Batangas Bay and returned to Mindoro. (Capt. N. Burt Davis's letter to writer
of 11 July 1958.)
[17] *New York Times,* 18 Dec. 1944.

4. *Air Attacks and Resupply Convoys, 16–24 December*

Slow Tow Convoy continued to serve as clown of the operation. This ungainly group arrived off the beachhead after dark on the 16th. Commander E. D. McEathron, commanding the minesweeping unit and at that time senior officer present, helped Captain McLean to herd the tows to an anchorage off Beach White; but the boat pool officer ashore, after being asked to send out a number of craft to take over the tows and beach them, in desperation did nothing, and signed off for the night! Nobody loved old Slow Tow; but some charitably inclined small Army craft and PTs came to its rescue, and by next morning watch had taken it in charge. The tugs reformed off Ilin Island and departed for Leyte within two hours.

On the slow return passage, air protection was furnished for only a short time but (miraculously as it seemed) not one plane attacked Slow Tow, whose members got a great laugh from a Radio Tokyo announcement to the effect that they had been "annihilated" by air and surface action.[18]

Admiral Stump's escort carriers in Admiral Ruddock's group were ordered to furnish air cover off the Mindoro beachhead for one more day, as foul weather at Leyte prevented most Army planes from taking off. Only eight Army planes turned up that morning, which was marked by several unsuccessful air attacks. A kamikaze which crash-dived the beach (after trying to fly into the bow doors of *LST–605*) killed four men, wounded eleven and burned up 21 drums of gasoline. Eight planes attacked the motor torpedo boats and other small craft, wounded five men (one fatally), but several were shot down by the C.A.P. Weather conditions improved, and at 1310 more Army planes arrived. The Ruddock group was then allowed to shove off for Leyte. It had done a fine support job, flying 864 sorties of all kinds (770 fighter,

---

[18] Capt. McLean Action Report.

94 torpedo) from 13 to 17 December inclusive, losing no planes to the enemy, two to "friendly" antiaircraft fire and seven operationally; but only one pilot went missing.

On the afternoon of the 17th, three planes attacked the PTs, two splashed when trying to hit these elusive targets, and one was shot down. On the 18th a kamikaze crashed *PT-300*, completely destroying her, killing or wounding all but one of her men, and seriously wounding the squadron commander, Lieutenant Commander A. P. Colvin. Another PT was straddled by bombs and three of her crew were wounded. This made the motor torpedo boat sailors rather jittery; they shot down a Marine Corps plane but managed to rescue the pilot. Thirteen enemy planes were over the Mindoro beachhead dropping flares on the night of 18–19 December.

Japanese air forces gave the liberators of Mindoro a short breather on 19 December; on the 20th they sent in a raid of 29 planes. The Army patrol of eleven planes shot down eleven, but lost three P-47s. Hill Field (named after the Colonel killed on board *Nashville*) was now operational; the San José airstrip was first used on the 26th. By that time the Japanese air forces were concentrating on resupply convoys.

An amphibious landing is only the first step in any overseas operation. Keeping the men supplied with food, clothing, matériel and implements of war is often the most difficult and important aspect of a successful campaign. To accomplish this, resupply convoys are formed and delivered to the new beachhead, on schedules dictated by needs and circumstances.[19]

The first resupply echelon for Mindoro, consisting of 25 ships, 14 LST and six chartered freighters, escorted by eleven destroyers, departed Leyte Gulf during the evening of 19 December. Captain T. B. Dugan, Comdesron 23 in *Charles Ausburne*, commanded. Two Oscars saluted the dawn of 21 December by making a hurried attack; they dropped small bombs harmlessly and made off. C.A.P.

[19] Resupply in the Bougainville operation is in Volume VI of this History, chaps. xix–xxi; that for New Guinea in Vol. VIII 54–6; and for France in Vol. XI chaps. ix, xvii.

then intercepted three "bandits" and shot one down. At 1631 radar contact was made on a group of enemy planes. At this time the C.A.P. consisted of twelve Army P-38s. The enemy made a deliberate but not well coördinated attack with 20 or more planes, eight of which C.A.P. shot down. Five planes of the first raid at 1718 broke through to attack the convoy. Although the screen had been well alerted and opened heavy antiaircraft fire, three Oscars passed over at 6000 feet without loss of control, picked out their targets and, diving vertically, crashed *LST-460*, *LST-749* and Liberty ship *Juan de Fuca*. The fourth, a Tojo, came down in a shallow glide and splashed close aboard destroyer *Foote*, slightly damaging her.[20]

Within two minutes it was all over, but in that short time the two LSTs had sustained fatal wounds. They and *Juan de Fuca* fell out of the formation. Captain Dugan ordered four destroyers and three other vessels to assist them, while the rest of his ships maintained formation and plugged stolidly along.

LST-460, carrying gasoline and ammunition and hit amidships, was soon blazing and exploding from stem to stern and became a total loss, lighting the sky for hours. *LST-749* (Lieutenant Ralph B. Flynn) was also hit amidships. The plane that crashed her carried two bombs, one of which exploded on the deck and the other in the provision issuing room, killing all men stationed there and tearing out the steering gear. Soon the entire after part of the ship was burning, but she continued to make headway as it was impossible to stop her engines. Destroyer *Converse* (Lieutenant Commander E. H. McDowell), had hoses rigged and was about to fight the fire when four twin-engined Japanese planes made a glide attack. Three were shot down by the destroyers, and the fourth retired, but during this attack the fires in *LST-749* gained such headway that she too had to be abandoned. Of the 774 soldiers and sailors on board the two LSTs, 107 were lost.

[20] CTU 78.3.13 (Capt. Dugan) Action Report Mindoro Resupply Echelon, 27 Dec. 1944. Japanese Monograph No. 12, *Philippines Air Operations Record, Phase Two*, states that 45 planes attacked shipping that day, lost 15 and claimed two sinkings.

The rescue of survivors was orderly, and excellent discipline was maintained by soldiers and sailors alike. Sergeant William A. Schnor of 240th Army Engineers had both feet cut off when the plane crashed *LST–749*. After his company officers had wrapped him in life jackets and lowered him into the water, he swam unaided about 200 yards to *Converse*. "His brave and cheerful demeanor was an inspiration to all those suffering and overburdened who knew his tragedy, and an indication of the deep wells of courage in the human spirit." [21]

The damage to *Juan de Fuca* was not serious; she could still maintain speed. All stragglers caught up with the convoy by dawn 22 December, and soon after that the LSTs went into Beach Red, Mindoro.

By 1620 December 22, when all twelve LSTs had unloaded and retracted, the first Mindoro resupply echelon got under way for Leyte. Within an hour, at dusk, this convoy was attacked by four kamikazes which orbited safely for five minutes, as they were mistaken for P–47s. All were shot down before inflicting damage. One made an almost vertical dive on destroyer *Newcomb* (Commander I. E. McMillian). As the skipper remarked, when it was all over, "An angel of the Lord tapped me on the shoulder and told me to look up." He ordered flank speed and hard right rudder and the kamikaze splashed only a few yards from the bridge.[22]

That day or the next saw the completion of a smart job by engineers of the United States and Australian Armies; the San José airfield was now officially activated. It was a great gain that Army planes no longer had to fly all the way from Leyte. The P–38s celebrated by shooting down 15 enemy planes on the 22nd; five when intercepting attacks on the convoy, and ten more over Mindoro.

---

[21] *Converse* Action Report 24 Dec. 1944.
[22] *Newcomb* Action Report; letters from Mr. Frank E. Shaffer, 11 Feb., 27 Apr., 1959.

5. Christmas Call by Admiral Kimura [23]

Unbeknown to anyone on Mindoro, the Japanese Navy already had a task group under way to bombard the beachhead. Field Marshal Terauchi urged a Mindoro counterlanding on General Yamashita, who wished to write the island off, but Imperial General Headquarters, feeling that Mindoro in American hands was a serious threat, insisted on doing something. The result was a half-hearted compromise: a bombardment mission by Vice Admiral Shima's Second Striking Force, followed by a small infantry raid to hamper our airfield development.

Shima did not head this "Penetration Unit," as it was called. Admiral Mikawa, Commander Southwest Area Fleet, placed it under the command of Rear Admiral Masanori Kimura, who had been Shima's squadron commander in the Battle of Surigao Strait.[24] It departed Camranh Bay, Indochina, Christmas Eve, on what turned out to be the Japanese Navy's next to last offensive sortie of the war. Wearing his flag in destroyer *Kasumi*, Admiral Kimura had with him heavy cruiser *Ashigara*, which had escaped undamaged from the Battle of Surigao Strait, light cruiser *Oyodo* (Admiral Ozawa's former flagship) and five other destroyers.[25] His orders were to sink any Allied shipping encountered off the Mindoro beachhead and to shell airfields and other installations around San José. This was sending a boy to do a man's job, but Kimura's force was the best that the Japanese Navy could assemble after the de-

[23] MacArthur *Historical Report* II 415–17; Jap. Mono. No. 81 *Mindoro Battle;* R. R. Smith, chap. iii; Craven & Cate V 399; data furnished by Air University, History Division; VPB–104 War Diary Dec. 1944; CTU 70.1.4 (Lt. Cdr. Davis) Action Report, enclosure to MTBs Seventh Fleet Action Report 1 Mar. 1945; letters of Capt. N. Burt Davis to writer, July 1958.
[24] Confirmed by Capt. Ohmae's letters in 1959. He adds, "since Rear Adm. Kimura desired to use the heavy cruiser *Ashigara* (Shima's flagship), Admiral Shima remained at Cape St. Jacques." This mission had originally been given to Desdiv 43 on 15 December, but the order had to be canceled for want of fuel.
[25] *Kiyoshimo, Asashimo, Kaya, Sugi* and *Kashi.* The first two were new 2050-tonners, the last three 1530-tonners.

struction and damage it had sustained in the Battle for Leyte Gulf two months earlier.

Commander in Chief Combined Fleet, Admiral Toyoda, may have intended to use his new 27,000-ton carrier *Unryu* in this raid, but she did not survive long enough. As she was steaming southerly toward Formosa Strait, either to join Kimura or to train new aviators at Lingga Roads, United States submarine *Redfish* on 19 December intercepted her in the East China Sea in broad daylight, scored two torpedo hits and had the satisfaction of seeing her go down.[26]

For two days Penetration Unit steamed unmolested across the South China Sea, eluding all United States submarines that might have sighted it.[27] Coming in under cover of foul weather, it achieved almost total surprise. Fortunately, at 1600 December 26, a Leyte-based Navy Liberator piloted by Lieutenant Paul F. Stevens, which was returning from a patrol to Camranh Bay, spotted it about 180 miles W by N of the San José beachhead; and reported the heavy cruiser to be battleship *Yamato*. But he counted the number of ships very nearly correctly and flashed the bad news promptly to the almost defenseless forces on Mindoro and to Seventh Fleet headquarters in Leyte Gulf.

Other sightings had already been made that day. A number of Japanese transports and freighters escorted by destroyers had been spotted off Subic Bay, Luzon. This convoy was being attacked by land-based planes from Mindoro when the news of the combatant ships came in. General Dunckel had to assume the worst, that the enemy was preparing to make a counterlanding behind the beachhead. But the two forces were not connected; the convoy off Subic Bay was reinforcing Manila.

Lieutenant Stevens landed at San José to make certain that General Dunckel got the word, refueled, took on four 500-pound

[26] *Imp. Jap. Navy in W.W. II* gives position as 250 miles NNW of Miyako Jima.

[27] R. R. Smith states that it was sighted by submarines on Christmas Day, but patrol reports of *Becuna* and *Hawkbill*, the only ones near its track, mention no surface ship contacts.

bombs, returned to shadow Kimura as he approached Mindoro, and stayed over him until 0400 next morning. That was a remarkable feat of endurance.

In the meantime the entire available strength of V Army Air Force at Mindoro — 92 fighter planes, 13 B-25 bombers, and a number of night-fighting P-61s — arose to meet the enemy. Kimura's ships were next sighted at 2030 by Lieutenant (jg) W. M. Cox usnr, pilot of a Liberator, some 50 miles northwest of San José. About half an hour later the air-surface battle began.

As a result of Stevens's contact report, Admiral Kinkaid sent three Catalinas and five tender-based Mariners up from Leyte Gulf and they got into the fight almost as soon as did the Mindoro-based Army planes. In addition, he quickly organized a task group of 14 ships to hasten to Mindoro. This consisted of heavy cruisers *Louisville* and *Minneapolis*, light cruisers *Phoenix* and *Boise*, and eight destroyers, under the command of Rear Admiral Theodore E. Chandler.[28] But Kimura had a head start, and was able to hit and run while Chandler's group was hundreds of miles away.

At the San José beachhead the situation looked much like that in Empress Augusta Bay on the night of 1-2 November 1943, but with no "Tip" Merrill in sight.[29] The only Allied naval vessels near the beachhead were a score of motor torpedo boats. Figuring that PTs in the hand were worth more than cruisers in the bush, General Dunckel looked for protection to them rather than to Chandler. He expected the enemy to attempt a night landing on the beach, coördinated with a paratroop drop on the two airstrips at San José, five miles inland. Disposing land forces accordingly, he gave responsibility for seaward defense to Lieutenant Commander Davis, who also had to protect the merchant ships present.

"Cancel or recall all patrols and assist in the defense of Mindoro," were the orders from Admiral Kinkaid to the motor torpedo boat

---

[28] On 8 Dec. 1944 Rear Adm. J. B. Oldendorf hauled down his flag in *Louisville* and Rear Adm. Chandler took over command of Crudiv 4. Oldendorf, as Combatron 1, and promoted to Vice Admiral, wore his flag in *California* until after the Lingayen operation.
[29] See Vol. VI 304-5.

commander. Davis accordingly set up a patrol line about three miles off the beach. He divided the nine most serviceable boats on hand into three groups as follows: —

1. Lieutenant Commander A. W. Fargo USNR: four boats stationed ten miles off Dongon Point to report the enemy's approach.
2. Lieutenant J. H. Stillman USNR: three boats posted one mile north of Ilin Island.
3. Lieutenant (jg) R. F. Keeling USNR: two boats in outer Mangarin Bay.

Two more, under Lieutenant P. A. Swart USNR, he recalled from their mission to guerrillas in northern Mindoro. Eleven PTs, unfit materially for offshore work, were stationed in Ilin Strait and inner Mangarin Bay.

Lieutenant Commander Fargo was the first to pick up the enemy, by radar, at 2048 December 26. He had the good idea to make radio contact on Lieutenant Swart, then off Cape Calavite, the northwestern point of Mindoro, and order him to shape a course converging with that of the enemy. At 2155, when about six miles off shore, Fargo's group was first taken under gunfire by the Japanese. Fargo picked up speed to 30 knots, zigzagged and laid small diversionary smoke-puffs, thus escaping all the enemy shots. But the greatest danger to the PTs came from Army aircraft shuttling between the Japanese ships and San José airfields. Fargo's men, knowing that these planes were "friendly," made vain efforts to signal them, and refrained from opening fire. The boats were strafed, the crews knocked flat by near-misses and at 2205 a bomb exploded close aboard *PT–77*, badly damaging her and wounding almost every member of the crew. Fargo detailed *PT–84* to escort her back to Mangarin Bay while the two remaining boats laid smoke to cover their retirement.

The Japanese Penetration Unit kept on coming down the coast and was sighted by Lieutenant Stillman's group off Ilin Island at 2215, about five miles distant. It looked like a fight; but Rear Admiral Kimura, cautious as Shima had been at Surigao Strait, stayed well outside the PTs' patrol line until 2240 when he turned his column shoreward. While under continual air attack, he bombarded San José town and airfield, and Beach Red, for 20 to 40 minutes.[30] A few Japanese planes based on Luzon turned up at the same time and attempted to bomb and strafe the town and airstrip, but these attacks were not pressed home, and the ships' shooting mostly went wild. Only superficial damage was inflicted on the airfield and no one was even wounded.

Kimura's ships closed Mangarin Bay briefly, tossed three salvos (fortunately overs) at Stillman's boats, reversed course shortly before midnight and retired to get beyond the range of land-based aircraft. Liberty ship *James H. Breasted*, while heading for the protection of Ilin Strait (whither she had been ordered some time before), was also taken under gunfire by the Japanese ships, hit on the port side and set afire. Lieutenant Commander Fargo saw a B–25 flying low over her; later investigation of the ship, when beached, revealed evidence of aircraft strafing and bombing, whether enemy or "friendly" was never ascertained. Nor did this exhaust the tale of confusion in Ilin Strait. Two boats of Fargo's group, ordered to thread the Strait and to attack any enemy ships encountered, ran aground on a coral reef halfway through. Both were salvaged next morning.[31]

Stillman reported to Davis at 0010 December 27 "that the enemy had apparently been forced to withdraw because of the continuous Allied air attack, and was now retiring at high speed up the beach to the northward, shelling as it went." That was correct. The frequent air attacks spoiled the Japanese gunners' aim by wrecking their control stations and knocking out a number of guns as well. But Kimura was not to be allowed to retire unscathed. When about eight miles north of Dongon Point, he encountered Lieutenant

[30] Jap. Monograph No. 81 *Mindoro Battle* states that the bombardment lasted from 2115 to 0010, obviously an exaggeration. Some American observers thought it lasted only 20 minutes; that the rest of the time all Japanese ships were firing at aircraft. Sixth Army Report on Mindoro p. 18 states that it began only at 2310.

[31] Details of this and the next PT action told the writer by Lt. (jg) H. L. Bennett USNR and Lt. (jg) F. A. Tredinnick USNR, C.O.'s of *PT–82* and *PT–77* respectively.

Swart returning from his PT mission at top speed, hoping to be in time for the fight. His wish was gratified. At 0050 these two boats found themselves two miles abeam of four ships, one of which spotted *PT-221* with a searchlight and opened accurate gunfire. She retired shoreward at 25 knots on a zigzag course, pursued for three or four minutes by 4-gun salvos. In the meantime the skipper of *PT-223*, Lieutenant (jg) Harry E. Griffin USNR, closed to attack. At 0105 he commenced firing both starboard torpedoes at a range under 4000 yards. The "fish" ran "hot, straight and normal," and three or four minutes later a flame shot up from a Japanese destroyer and she was observed to go dead in the water. This was 2100-ton *Kiyoshimo*, one of the newest and most powerful destroyers in the Japanese Navy.[82] According to survivors she had already been damaged by air attack, but this torpedo sank her.

At dawn 27 December, several PTs were sent to search for survivors of the night's action, or for evidence of an enemy landing. Three Japanese torpedoes ashore in Mangarin Bay were the only evidence on the beach that the enemy had paid a night call. During the afternoon, two PTs combed the waters south of Dongon Point, and picked up five Japanese survivors of *Kiyoshimo*.

The air-surface battle was over by 0200 December 27, when the Japanese ships were beyond range. One destroyer had been sunk and almost every enemy ship sustained damage; a very commendable score, considering that the airfield had been in operation for less than a week, that few pilots had been trained for night bombing, and that munitions were in short supply. The A.A.F. was ably assisted by the PBMs from Leyte. Twenty-six of our planes were lost (more by crash landings than by antiaircraft fire), but most of the pilots and crewmen were rescued, and no appreciable damage was done to airfield or to installations by the enemy bombardment.

Kimura's ships retired to Camranh Bay. His raid was a failure, in

[82] Erroneously reported in *Imp. Jap. Navy W.W. II* p. 251, which we followed in Vol. XII 356, as having been sunk in Manila Bay 14 Nov. 1944.

complete contrast to the bombardment missions that made nights hideous at Guadalcanal two years earlier. As with most hit-and-run raids, the psychological effect produced was more important than the damage inflicted; rumors that the Japanese had landed troops long persisted.

6. *Mindoro and Marinduque Secured, 27 December 1944–10 February 1945*

Admiral Chandler's cruisers and destroyers, dispatched from Leyte Gulf, reached Mindoro about twelve hours after the fight was over, although making 25 knots in a vain effort to get into it. They patrolled the west coast of the island for a night and a day, then headed back to Leyte Gulf, since it was clear that the enemy had no intention of returning.

Allied shore positions and convoys approaching Mindoro continued to be attacked from the air. On Christmas Eve a thousand-barrel gasoline storage tank was destroyed on Hill Field, and for the rest of the month Allied flight operations had to be sharply restricted.

During the last three days of 1944, Japanese air forces concentrated on a big resupply convoy, which was coming up from Leyte Gulf with man power and matériel for airfield construction. "Uncle plus 15," as this convoy was nicknamed,[88] formed off Dulag 27 December. It comprised 22 LST, 23 LCI, 30 PT, three Liberty ships, one aviation gasoline tanker, PT tender *Orestes*, two aircraft tenders, five Army freight and supply boats, one Army and two Navy crash boats, under the command of Captain J. B. McLean, who had nine destroyers in his screen. The 21st RCT of the 24th Division was embarked in the amphibious craft; *Orestes* acted as

---

[88] CTU 78.3.15 (Capt. McLean) Action Report "Uncle plus 15 Resupply Convoy" 28 Jan. 1945. The name "Uncle" was a synonym for D-day, and this convoy was due at the beachhead 15 days later.

flagship for Captain G. F. Mentz, Commander Diversionary Attack Group of LCIs and PTs, which was being moved to Mindoro with an eye to the future.[34]

Captain McLean expected trouble, and was not disappointed. From 0330 December 28, when his convoy rounded into Surigao Strait, and until it returned, it was either being attacked or had "bandits" on the radar screens. Attacks came at dawn, morning, noon, dusk and night. Flagship *Bush* sounded general quarters 49 times in 72 hours. Three days of hell and hard work for the sailors of 99 ships.

Sunrise 28 December came at 0659, and with it the depressing report that the weather at Leyte was so foul that no C.A.P. could come out. No air cover was furnished until after noon, and then only to meet an urgent need. But the weather was altogether too fair in the waters plowed by the convoy.

At 1012 two groups of three planes each from Cebu attacked. One plane was shot down in flames and another attempted to crash aviation gasoline (avgas) tanker *Porcupine*, but overshot and splashed. Almost immediately two others crashed Liberty ships *William Sharon* and *John Burke*. No kamikaze pilot ever obtained a more complete reward for his efforts than the one who landed on board the second of these ships, an ammunition carrier. A tremendous flash was followed by an enormous white cloud covering an area of several thousand yards. When the cloud cleared, it was as though *Burke* had never been. As she sank to the depths of the Mindanao Sea, other ships in the vicinity felt a severe underwater explosion, the last defiant growl of a vessel that went down with all hands: 68 merchant mariners, including the master, Herbert A. Falk.

William Sharon also was in a bad way, her entire superstructure aflame. Destroyer *Wilson* closed to assist, fought the fire, and took the entire crew on board. At 1111, "Flash Red" was sounded and

---

[34] Cdr. A. V. Jannotta USNR, Com LCI Flotilla 24, who relieved Capt. Mentz in command of TG 77.11, wrote the Action Report for 1–9 Jan. 1945, dated 12 Feb. 1945.

Wilson was forced to clear the Liberty ship. By that time the fire was fairly under control, and with another half hour's work might have been quenched. Unfortunately an LCM that she had in tow drifted against *Sharon's* weather side and had to be cut clear before the destroyer could close. With its engine still running, but no helmsman, the landing craft took off, pursued by 40-mm fire from *Wilson,* but when last seen was still traveling to an unrecorded end.

Fire-fighters from *Wilson* had just reboarded *Sharon* when the ammunition in her ready boxes began to go off, forcing the destroyer to clear for a second time. But her C.O., Commander C. J. MacKenzie, did not give up. He waited for the explosions to subside, then closed again, resumed fire-fighting, and within two hours had all fires out and the Liberty ship anchored in the middle of the Mindanao Sea. Salvage tug *Grapple* towed her back to Leyte, and Mindoro never got her cargo of gasoline, TNT, trucks, rations and beer, dearest of all commodities in the steaming Philippines.

The C.A.P., which arrived over Uncle plus 15 around noon, returned to Leyte at 1515 and no relief was provided. At about 1830, when the convoy was off the southern point of Negros, 20 to 30 enemy planes opened an attack which lasted an hour and three quarters. The planes split into two groups for a coördinated attack. Ships in the convoy opened fire and within the next half hour bagged three. Shortly after 1900, in bright moonlight, three more groups of planes closed the convoy on both quarters and astern, and an aërial torpedo hit *LST–750.* Seaplane tender *Half Moon,* sent to investigate, reported that she was "finished." After destroyer *Edwards* had confirmed this sad state of affairs, and had sent over a boarding party to search the LST for wounded (the others having been taken off by LCIs), she was ordered by the escort commander to be sunk. It took two torpedoes, which missed under, and about 150 5-inch hits, to send *LST–750* to the bottom.

This air attack was over by 2013, but there were bogies on radar screens all night. Captain McLean, believing the enemy would do his utmost to annihilate his convoy next day, begged Leyte and Mindoro by radio for continuous dawn to dusk air cover. Leyte was still blacked in, but Mindoro complied generously. Two P–61s reported before dawn; these were relieved by F4Us, P–38s and P–47s, and at one time as many as 36 fighter planes were over the convoy. The ships suffered no damage that day, but enemy aircraft were still about, and at dusk came the usual attack, with 20 to 30 planes. Combat Air Patrol, adequate throughout the day, was forced to depart at the critical hour of 1715 — and this was the night of full moon. Two P–61s came out later, and with the aid of the ships' gunfire splashed several enemy aircraft and kept the rest away. During the early morning of 30 December three more planes were shot down by the ships, and at 0710 Uncle plus 15 made Mangarin Bay, Mindoro. The PTs were immediately turned over to Lieutenant Commander Davis.

Captain McLean was naturally eager to unload his ships and head back to Leyte before dark. Events ran smoothly enough until 1540 when five Vals broke through the air cover and made a suicide attack that did the Kamikaze Corps proud. Destroyers *Gansevoort* and *Pringle*, tender *Orestes* and avgas tanker *Porcupine* were hit within a minute or two. *Orestes*, a converted LST, was crashed by a plane already in flames which bounced from the water into her starboard side, its bomb deflecting upwards and exploding within. The ship burst into flames, all power was lost, the fire mains were severed and the crew were picked up from the water by PTs and LCIs, two of which managed to quench the blaze and beach *Orestes* near the PT base at Caminawit Point. She was later towed to Leyte for major repairs and refit; but there was no return for 59 men killed and missing; 106 others, including Captain Mentz and key members of his Diversionary Attack Group staff, were wounded.

A second plane crashed the after deckhouse of *Pringle* but inflicted only superficial damage and this destroyer moved into the beach with the rest of the screen to render fire support against the air attacks.

Porcupine was anchored off Beach White when an enemy dive bomber came in low over the water on her port beam. She raised her quills, opening fire with all 20-mm guns, but was unable to divert the Val from its course. The kamikaze pilot dropped his bomb on the main deck and crashed in after it, impact and explosion rupturing fuel tanks and flooding the engine room with oil. The plane's engine went right through the hull, tearing a large hole underwater. Seven men were killed and eight wounded.

No sooner had *Porcupine* been hit than a third plane made for destroyer *Gansevoort* patrolling off Mangarin Bay. She turned up flank speed and fired continuously with all batteries, but the plane crashed her. Steering and electric power were cut and the ship began losing headway. Damage control parties could not gain access to the after part of the ship, as the main deck was blown upward on both sides forward of the after engine room. Destroyers *Wilson* and *Philip* were soon alongside, fighting the fires. *Gansevoort* was a mess, but the casualties were light. By 1640 the fires were out and Captain McLean ordered two LCMs and an Army tug to tow her toward the PT base, where she anchored in 15 fathoms. Presently she was given an unusual mission, to knock off the stern of *Porcupine* with a torpedo in the hope of extinguishing the fire before it reached the avgas stowed forward. But the water was too shoal for torpedoes to be effective, and in spite of one torpedo hit, the fire spread and the gasoline ignited, spreading across the water until it endangered the destroyer, which was towed to another anchorage. There, when abandoned, she was boarded without orders by volunteer officers and seamen from a PT boat, and their efforts saved a fine destroyer which otherwise would have been a total loss. *Porcupine* burned to her water line.

A couple of hours later, 30 December, Liberty ship *Hobart Baker* was hit by bombs and sunk off Mindoro beachhead. In the midst of all this excitement, Captain McLean, with his seven remaining destroyers, rounded up the return convoy, consisting of 21 LST, one Army supply boat and merchant ship *William S. Colley*. Their return passage to Leyte Gulf was relatively uneventful.

The losses from Uncle plus 15 created a critical supply situation at Mindoro beachhead, and a difficult problem for the Navy. Action reports of this and other convoys were read with keen interest and even anxiety by naval officers familiar with the Lingayen operation plan; for S-day at Lingayen was only a week ahead. As Ormoc Bay had proved to be a foretaste of Mindoro; Mindoro set a very unpleasant flavor for Lingayen. Not since the Anzio operation had the Navy experienced such difficulty supporting an amphibious operation after the initial landing.

On the last morning of 1944, Liberty ships *Simeon G. Reed* and *Juan de Fuca* were bombed and run aground on Barriage Reef off Mindoro. Army engineers ashore were counting on their cargo of bitumen, timber, installation materials and miscellaneous supplies. Construction was delayed until replacements arrived.

Destructive raids continued into the first few days of 1945. On the night of 1–2 January 1945, Liberty ship *John Clayton* received a bomb hit in her Number 3 hold, killing 6 men and wounding 11. She had to be beached to prevent sinking.[35] The last kamikaze to attack Mindoro, at 1730 January 4, made for Liberty ship *Lewis L. Dyche* (John W. Platt, master), which was loaded to the gunwales with ammunition. She blew up immediately, disintegrated, and went down with all hands, 71 merchant mariners. The explosion lifted right out of the water two motor torpedo boats which were a quarter of a mile away; they were badly damaged by the concussion and by falling debris, losing two men killed and ten wounded. A blown-up but unexploded shell from *Dyche* fell into a gun tub in *LCI(L)-621*, killing one man and wounding four; a minelayer and an oiler were also damaged.

Next day the Japanese found more alluring targets in the convoys heading for Lingayen Gulf, and laid off Mindoro for good. They had lost 103 planes shot down by fighters and antiaircraft fire over and around the beachhead, and at least that many kamikazes, there and on the convoy.

The American troops on Mindoro had been engaged in mopping up small enemy contingents. On New Year's Day, when two dry-weather runways on Hill and San José airfields were operational,

[35] Release of 27 May 1945 by War Shipping Administration; Seventh Fleet War Diary.

Eighth Army (General Eichelberger) took over, while General Krueger's Sixth Army pulled out — this time for Luzon. General Dunckel was relieved by Major General Roscoe B. Woodruff, commanding 24th Infantry Division, the transfer of command being marked by a party at paratroop headquarters, where PT sailors furnished the basis for refreshments — five gallons of torpedo alcohol.

A part of the halfhearted Japanese plan to neutralize Mindoro was an infantry raid to attack airfields under construction. This small force, variously estimated as between 113 and 400 men, assembled at Batangas, whence it was boated by landing craft to Calapan, the provincial capital, on the last day of 1944.[36] To counteract this effort and secure the island against possible surprise, General Woodruff laid on a series of minor shore-to-shore landings at various points on the east, west and northwest coasts of Mindoro. Twenty-five such movements were made in January and during the first ten days of February. The troops, varying in strength from a few men with supplies up to an infantry battalion, were lifted by LCI(L)s of Commander Jannotta's Diversionary Attack Group, escorted by a couple of PT boats.

The Japanese raiding force, with units of the Mindoro garrison, advanced from Calapan to Pinamalayan, where on 6 January it encountered a company of U.S. infantry and threw it for a loss. Reinforcements were sent up, Pinamalayan was recovered on the 11th, the Japanese fell back on their boats and retired to Calapan. Although they later succeeded in moving to Mansalay and infiltrating overland to San José, all attempts to raid the airfields aborted.[37]

General Woodruff made no attempt to liberate the whole of Mindoro, because the Japanese garrison was not strong enough to bother the natives. These, except for aborigines who stayed in the mountains, welcomed the Americans and furnished labor for build-

[36] Jap. Mono. No. 137 (cited note 1 to this chapter) p. 8, says 113. At Calapan it joined the major part of the Mindoro garrison of 373, which probably accounts for the larger figure.

[37] Details will be found in Western Visayan Task Force Historical Report of 1 Feb. 1945.

ing the PT base and the airfields. A perimeter defense, on the style of the Torokina one on Bougainville, was sufficient to defend the fields and the beachhead against infiltration or surprise attack.

On 2 January an infantry company, boated in LCIs, occupied the mountainous island of Marinduque, which commands the eastern entrance of Verde Island Passage between Mindoro and the Batangas area of Luzon, in order to deceive the enemy into expecting a major landing at Batangas. And on 9 January a reconnaissance party was landed on Pandon Island.

By 30 January no enemy forces capable of organized action remained in northwest Mindoro and further mopping up was left to the Filipino guerrillas, who as usual were glad of the opportunity. Lieutenant Commander Davis's PT boats maintained contact with them, and also with guerrillas at Batangas Bay, Luzon, who reported that area to be full of Japanese suicide boats. As higher authority was skeptical of their existence, Davis organized a raid with two of his boats, and two Army planes as air cover. The Lieutenant Commander himself with two or three sailors landed at Batangas, captured a suicide boat and took it in tow. On their way back to Mindoro both PT and tow were attacked by "friendly" planes, and the captive craft swamped; but Seventh Fleet accepted the evidence and due precautions were taken.[38]

A third airstrip on Mindoro, begun 2 January, was completed on the 26th; a heavy bomber strip was started next day and completed in early March. During January dumps were moved inland to the vicinity of San José and a two-lane road was constructed for hauling in supplies; an old narrow-gauge sugar railroad also helped. This work was done with considerable difficulty owing to material shortages occasioned by the heavy shipping losses to air attack.

Mindoro was a tough little operation from start to finish. There were 334 alerts of enemy air raids on the beach during the first 30 days. Compared with Leyte or Luzon, Mindoro may seem insignificant; but it marks a great step in the aërial aspect of the Philippines

[38] Letters of Capt. Davis 2 Aug. 1957 and 11 July 1958.

campaign. New airfields around San José could not guarantee that the Navy would sail into Lingayen Gulf unmolested, but the Army air forces based there probably saved that bloody passage from becoming a mass slaughter. And Mindoro proved to be a useful staging and assembly point for the expeditions to liberate the southern Philippines.

CHAPTER III

Fast Carrier Forces in Support[1]

10 December 1944–10 January 1945

1. New Carrier Tactics

VICE ADMIRAL John S. McCain,[2] the tough, wiry, sixty-year-old officer who relieved Marc Mitscher as CTF 38 on 30 October and became, as Admiral Halsey expressed it, his "strong right arm," had many problems on his hands. His carriers were not released from supporting the Leyte operation until 25 November, nearly a month later than the op plan provided. During the final strike of the Leyte campaign, 24 November, the kamikazes were so threatening as to suggest that with better training they might become lethal. The wing and part of the fuselage of a disintegrated suicider hit *Hancock's* flight deck and started a small fire; *Cabot* was damaged by the explosion of one which splashed close aboard, and *Essex* too was hit, but suffered only superficial damage.

[1] War Diary and three Action Reports by Com Third Fleet, Admiral Halsey: "Western Pacific Task Forces 31 Aug. 1944–24 Jan. 1945" (25 Jan. 1945); "Operations 1–29 Dec.," (10 Jan. 1945); "Operations 30 Dec. 1944–23 Jan. 1945" (23 Jan. 1945). Cincpac and Comairpac Monthly Analyses for Dec. 1944 and Jan. 1945; CTF 38 (Vice Adm. McCain) Action Report 30 Oct. 1944–26 Jan. 1945 (7 Feb. 1945), and War Diary; and those of his task group commanders. Sources for the typhoon are in Note to Section 2, this chapter.

[2] John Sidney McCain, b. Mississippi 1884; Annapolis '06. Served on Asiatic station and in various ships. Engineer officer *San Diego* 1915–18. Helped fit out *Maryland* and served as her navigator. Exec *New Mexico* 1926–28; course at Naval War College. C.O. *Nitro* 1931–33; head of planning div. BuNav. Qualified as naval aviator 1936 and became Com Fleet Air Base Coco Solo. C.O. *Ranger;* Com N.A.S. San Diego; Com Aircraft Scouting Force and Rear Adm. 1941; Com Aircraft Sopac May–Sept. 1942; Chief of Buaer to Aug. 1943, when became deputy CNO(Air) and Vice Admiral. For service in Leyte campaign as CTG 38.1 see Vol. XII. For later service as CTF 38 see Vol. XIV. Died 6 Sept. 1945.

Admiral Nimitz, Admiral Halsey and several thousand other sailors were worried about this Kamikaze Corps. Its pilots made no return trips, but almost one in every four found a target and did some damage, and one in thirty-three sank a ship.[3] Experts were set to work on the problem, and a tight censorship cloaked the whole dismal project. Officers and men returning to the continents of Australia and North America were warned not to mention the kamikazes, and mail was carefully scrutinized for any hint of them lest the enemy learn how much damage he was doing. From this point of view secrecy was effective; the Japanese air forces claimed a ship to every pilot expended, but never really knew the score. Not until April 1945, during the Okinawa campaign, when it was impossible to suppress the news any longer, did the Pentagon break one of the greatest news stories of the war. It so happened that the kamikaze story was revealed the same day (the 12th) that the death of President Roosevelt shook the Allied public; consequently it received comparatively little attention.

In early December 1944 Admiral Halsey wrote: "One fact is becoming increasingly evident. The Japanese air command, profiting by bitter experiences, has at last evolved a sound defensive plan against carrier attacks. He has coördinated and centralized his command responsibilities but decentralized and dispersed his air forces, taking advantage of dispersal opportunities he has previously rejected."[4]

The first countermeasure was to reorganize Task Force 38 into three rather than four task groups, each group consisting of a large number of carriers supported by a heavier screen. The new composition follows: — [5]

. [3] An USSBS Report (No. 62 on Japanese Air Power p. 76) states that during the Philippines campaigns 26.8 per cent of the kamikazes hit a ship and 2.9 per cent sank one. This was almost double the rate of their effectiveness later in the Okinawa campaign, but at that time there were many more of them, so the total damage was greater. Some 200 kamikazes were expended on Mindoro and the Mindoro convoys (calculations from Japanese sources after the war).

[4] Report for period 27 Oct.–30 Nov., 9 Dec. 1944.

[5] For complete task organization, see Appendix II.

TF 38 Fast Carrier Groups Pacific Fleet, Vice Admiral McCain in
HANCOCK
(*11–17 December 1944*)

TG 38.1 R. Adm. Montgomery		TG 38.2 R. Adm. Bogan	TG 38.3 R. Adm. Sherman
CV	YORKTOWN WASP	LEXINGTON HANCOCK HORNET	ESSEX TICONDEROGA
CVL	COWPENS MONTEREY	INDEPENDENCE CABOT	LANGLEY SAN JACINTO
BB	MASSACHUSETTS ALABAMA	NEW JERSEY IOWA WISCONSIN	NORTH CAROLINA WASHINGTON SOUTH DAKOTA
CA	SAN FRANCISCO BALTIMORE NEW ORLEANS	CL PASADENA ASTORIA VINCENNES MIAMI	CL MOBILE BILOXI SANTA FE
CLAA	SAN DIEGO	SAN JUAN	OAKLAND
	18 DD	20 DD	18 DD

Absent were *Enterprise*, the famous "Big E," under alteration for nighttime operating like *Independence*, and *Franklin*, *Intrepid* and *Belleau Wood*, undergoing major repairs. New *Essex*-class carriers were expected to join the fleet shortly.

Admiral McCain was a student of aircraft carriers and their tactics, and he had two exceptionally good men on his staff, Rear Admiral Wilder D. Baker and Captain "Jimmy" Thach, inventor of the Thach weave, his operations officer. Together they worked out some important tactical innovations to meet the kamikazes. Radar picket destroyers, equipped with the latest radar and aircraft homing devices, were stationed about sixty miles out from the task force on strike days on each side of the target-bearing line. Their job was to give advance warning of enemy aircraft approaching the fast carrier groups. Returning strike planes were required to make a full turn around designated picket destroyers (known as the "Tom Cats") on their return flight to the carriers, in order to permit "delousing" — the weeding out of kamikazes, who were apt to join returning American pilots with dark designs on their seagoing homes.[6] This separation of goats from sheep was effected by aërial "sheep dogs," the combat air patrol over the picket destroyers. A further advantage of this method was to keep radar screens clear of friendly aircraft on the line of most probable enemy approach. If planes adopted any but the standard approach, their enemy character was clearly indicated.

Equally important was a change in the complement of aircraft on board the big carriers. Formerly, each *Essex*-class carried (on an average) 38 fighters, 36 dive-bombers and 18 torpedo bombers. Now, their complement was 73 VF, 15 VB and 15 VT. The significance of this change, which the enemy soon appreciated, was that Admiral McCain had his Hellcat and Corsair fighters so modified as to be virtually all-purpose planes; they could carry up to two thousand pounds of bombs and fly a bombing mission unescorted, or intercept enemy strikes, or fly C.A.P. Under existing conditions, this virtually doubled the carriers' effectiveness.

On 1 December TGs 38.1 and 38.2 sortied from Ulithi; TG 38.3 was already at sea. A few hours later Admiral Halsey received word of General MacArthur's decision on 30 November to postpone the Mindoro landings ten days to 15 December. This news was received with cheers, since it enabled the carriers to return to Ulithi for ten more days' upkeep.

Task Force 38 again left Ulithi 11 December to make preliminary strikes on Luzon airfields, whence the Mindoro force might be threatened. At 1330 December 13, after fueling from Captain Acuff's oilers, the carriers headed west at 22 knots for their launching position off Luzon, lat. 16°15′ N, long. 123°45′ E, about 87 miles east of the coast of northern Luzon. This was north of those used in November. Here was tried, with good effect, another tactical innovation long talked about, for which never before had enough planes been available. This was the "Big Blue Blanket" (B.B.B.) keeping an umbrella of fighter planes over the Luzon airfields, day and night, so that enemy aircraft could not take off to

[6] Notes from conversation with Lt. Longstreth USNR of *Hornet*, Nov. 1945.

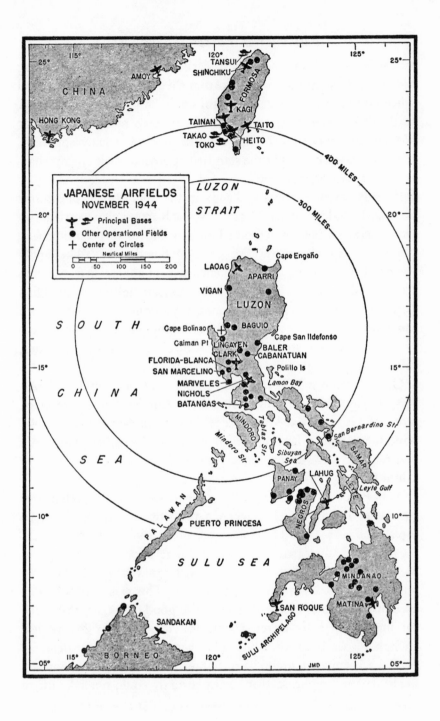

attack the Mindoro convoys. At certain moments when fighter squadrons were being relieved, bombers would come in and destroy grounded planes. This went on for three days, 14–16 December, and for a good part of the two nights. Many of the fields patrolled were found empty and inoperational; some previously reported were even found to be nonexistent.

Since the primary task was to blanket the airfield, no large-scale destruction resulted from the raids of 14–16 December; none had been contemplated. Out of 1671 sorties flown, 1427 were fighter planes and only 244 were bombers. Only 336 tons of bombs were dropped altogether, as compared with the 300 tons per day which had formerly been typical of Task Force 38 strikes. Nevertheless, by these raids Admirals Halsey and McCain accomplished what they set out to do. With the exception of the one Japanese strike that took off before 14 December, no Luzon-based aircraft attacked our Mindoro-bound shipping; those that did so came from the Visayan fields. And not one enemy plane penetrated the defensive air patrol of Task Force 38. The bag during these three days, according to Admiral Halsey, was 270, of which 208 were destroyed on the ground.[7] The cost to TF 38 was 27 planes in combat and 38 operationally. The bombers also sank three or four freighters, and one of two LSV (the Japanese LST) in Manila Bay.

A substantial proportion of the enemy planes shot down were destroyed by two interceptions. The first occurred on 14 December as eight fighters from *Ticonderoga* were making their last sweep of the day. They spotted 27 Oscars and Zekes near Vigan on the northwest coast of Luzon, probably flying in from Formosa. In the ensuing fight, *Ticonderoga's* pilots claimed to have sent 20 enemy planes flaming into the South China Sea but did not receive so much as a bullet hole in return. Again, at 0742 December 16, the first strike of the day from *Lexington* and *Hancock* encount-

[7] Japanese figures not available. Commo. Bates in *War College Analysis, Battle for Leyte Gulf*, I, comparing known Japanese air losses earlier in 1944 with American claims, worked out an average factor – 64% – to apply to claims in order to find out the number actually destroyed. This would mean 173 for the 14–16 Dec. strikes.

ered eleven enemy planes headed for the task force and splashed them all.

In a concise statement of the doctrine underlying the new tactics developed and applied during the Mindoro operation, Admiral McCain wrote: —

As never before, the offensive air strength of the fast carriers has had to be spread to cover the enemy in his large island systems and land mass dispersions. At the same time the force has found it necessary to concentrate its defense to a degree never before considered necessary. Before the innovation of suicide attacks by the enemy, destruction of 80 or 90 per cent of his attackers was considered an eminent success. Now 100 per cent destruction of the attackers is necessary to preserve the safety of the task force. New developments — the Jack Patrols,[8] Moosetrap exercises,[9] all-night C.A.P. and Tom Cats — are designed for this 100 per cent destruction. These new offensive and defensive requirements inherently conflict, and making the correct compromise is the continual task of the force commander.

As Admiral McCain wrote in his Action Report: —

The two cardinal principles which have evolved are: — (1) to defend the force with adequate patrols, (2) blanket the threatening enemy air opposition day and night with the most air power available. . . . More spectacular results at a higher price are always available, but any operations which consistently accept fast carrier damage cannot be continued without putting a definite end date on the operations of the fast carrier force. . . . Regardless of the attractiveness of other targets, responsible commanders must not be lulled into diverting so much of their strength from the "blanket" that the enemy's air is no longer thoroughly held helpless while it is being systematically destroyed.

Admiral Halsey had hoped, after completing the strikes of 16 December, to pull off his long-desired raid into the South China Sea, where survivors of the Japanese fleet from the Battle for Leyte Gulf had been reported. But Admirals King and Nimitz,

---

[8] "Jacks" were anti-snooper VFs stationed at each of the four cardinal points of the compass around each TG, at air altitudes not exceeding 3000 ft., within visual distance of the screen, as a defense against low-flying enemy planes.

[9] Large-scale task force training exercises simulating enemy tactics in order to show up weak spots in air defense.

feeling that our land-based air at Leyte was not yet sufficiently strong or reliable to risk moving the carriers from positions to cover Luzon, withheld their consent. And before Task Force 38 could do anything else, it encountered the worst storm of the year in the Philippine Sea.

2. *Weather Making Up, 15–17 December* [10]

This typhoon was comparatively small; but, owing to the fact that a number of deballasted destroyers ran smack into it, more damage was inflicted on the Navy than by any other storm since the famous hurricane at Apia, Samoa, in March 1889. Three destroyers capsized and six or seven other ships were seriously damaged, with the loss of almost 800 officers and men. As Admiral Nimitz said, this was the greatest uncompensated loss that the Navy had taken since the Battle of Savo Island.

For some reason that goes deep into the soul of a sailor, he mourns over shipmates lost through the dangers of the sea even more than for those killed by the violence of the enemy. He feels that the least he can do for those brave young men who went down doing their duty on 18 December 1944 is to set forth at length the causes and details of the catastrophe, in the hope that it may never recur.

Task Force 38 at this time was composed of seven *Essex*-class

[10] Ms. in Office of Judge Advocate General of the Navy, Washington, "Record of Proceedings of a Court of Inquiry Convened on Board U.S.S. *Cascade* by order of C. in C. Pacific Fleet, to Inquire into all the Circumstances Connected with the Loss of the U.S.S. *Hull*, etc., Dec. 26, 1944"; Admiral Halsey Report "Typhoon in Philippine Sea 17–22 Dec. 1944," 25 Dec. 1944; reports of individual ships; Cdr. G. F. Kosco (Aërological Officer Third Fleet Staff) "Highlights of the December 1944 Typhoon Including Photo, Radar Observation" (Fleet Weather Central Paper No. 10); and Fleet Weather Central "Report of Conditions Surrounding the . . . typhoon of 15–20 Dec. 1944." Capt. J. C. S. McKillip, Pacific Fleet Aërologist, helped me to interpret these data in 1945–46. This section was read by a task group commander and a destroyer squadron commander who were in the typhoon, and by Fleet Admiral Nimitz. Good articles are Hanson W. Baldwin's "When Third Fleet Met the Great Typhoon," in *N.Y. Times* Sunday Magazine Section 16 Dec. 1951, and Boatswain's Mate N. W. Tashman's "Typhoon: The Ordeal of a Ship" (*Melvin R. Nawman*) in same for 22 April 1945.

and six light carriers, eight battleships, four heavy and eleven light cruisers and about 50 destroyers. Captain Jasper T. Acuff's fueling group of the Third Fleet attending it comprised twelve fleet oilers, three fleet tugs, five destroyers, ten destroyer escorts and five escort carriers with replacement planes.[11] The fuel supply of many combatant ships was dangerously low after their three days' strikes on Luzon.

Rendezvous took place as planned at lat. 14°50′ N, long. 129°57′ E, in the eastern half of Philippine Sea, early Sunday morning 17 December. Fueling began promptly. There was a 20- to 30-knot wind from the NNE to NE, with a sea from the same direction, which made the transfer of oil difficult from the start. This fueling area, selected as the nearest spot to Luzon outside Japanese fighter-plane radius, lay in the normal track of typhoons. Weather signs on the 17th were not such as to arouse a seaman's apprehension, and the Pacific Fleet aërological service gave no hint of what was cooking; could not have done so, because Pacific Fleet had moved so fast and so near enemy-held areas that it had been impossible to establish enough weather reporting stations. The weather service did the best it could. Broadcasts summarizing all land stations' reports were made four times a day by Radio Kwajalein and eight times a day by Radio Manus. Search planes operating from the Marianas, Ulithi and the Palaus made weather reports. But these planes were not then much use to the Fleet, since they avoided bad fronts, and only in exceptional cases broke radio silence to send in their reports before landing. Consequently, most aircraft weather reports were at least twelve hours old before they reached a ship in the operating area. Weather map analyses were made four times a day by Pacific Fleet Weather Central at Pearl Harbor, whose forecasts were sent out twice daily to the Fleet by radio. Each aircraft carrier had her own weather man on board and flagship *New Jersey* had an experienced one, Commander G. F. Kosco, a graduate of the aërology course at Massachusetts Institute of Technology who had also studied hurricanes

[11] See Appendix II for list of ships and C.O.s.

in the West Indies. Yet none of these individuals or staffs were able to give Third Fleet due warning of the typhoon's approach.

The reason for the forecasters' failure lay in the nature of the beast. It was a small "tropical disturbance" that suddenly and unpredictably developed into a typhoon. The foul, Caliban-like birth of this little monster was unobserved by ship, shore station or search plane.

First hint of trouble reaching Fleet Weather Central was the report of a search plane pilot turned back by a "tropical disturbance" about noon 14 December, sixty miles SE of Samar. Nobody expected this to be serious, and actually it was not this disturbance that built up into the typhoon. Nothing alarming was observed by anyone on 15 or 16 December; and at 1414 December 17 Commander Kosco estimated that a "disturbance" — probably not the same — lay 450 miles east of *New Jersey*, moving NNW.

So this tight, young, wicked little typhoon came whirling along undetected toward waters where Third Fleet was trying to fuel. The sea was making up all day 17 December but the waves came from the same direction as the northerly wind (which was not above Force 8 — 30 to 40 knots), and that gave no indication of a typhoon. Wind and sea, however, had already rendered fueling difficult. Destroyer *Maddox*, a new 2200-tonner, required three hours' work to obtain 7093 gallons from oiler *Manatee*. The hose then parted and she had to cut the towline, narrowly avoiding a collision. Two hoses parted on *New Jersey* when she tried to fuel destroyers *Hunt* and *Spence*. Escort carrier *Kwajalein* (Captain Robert L. Warrack), one of the replacement-plane CVEs that belonged to an oiler group, was unable to transfer pilots by breeches buoy, and canceled air operations at noon. Her deck crews then concentrated on respotting and relashing planes, which were secured three ways with steel cables, the air having been let out of the F6F landing gears.[12] It was too rough for escort carriers to recover C.A.P. Two planes still aloft at 1500 were flagged off from their respective flattops and the pilots were ordered to turn their

[12] Lt. Peter M. Snyder USNR, report written for this History, 1947.

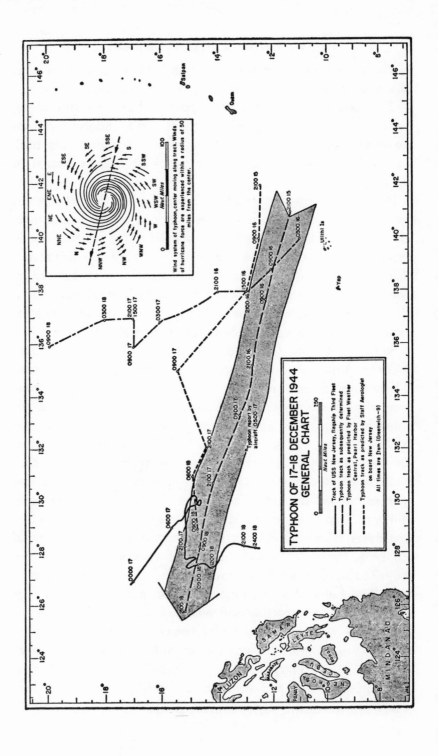

TYPHOON OF 17-18 DECEMBER 1944
GENERAL CHART

Track of USS New Jersey, flagship Third Fleet

Typhoon track as subsequently determined

Typhoon track as predicted by Fleet Weather
Central, Pearl Harbor

Typhoon track as predicted by Staff Aerologist
on board New Jersey

All times are Item (Greenwich −9)

Naut. Miles

0   250

Wind system of typhoon, center moving along track. Winds
of hurricane force are experienced within a radius of 50
miles from the center.

Naut. Miles

0   100

planes upside down and bail out. They were rescued by a destroyer.[18]

At 1251 December 17 Admiral Halsey ordered every ship to belay fueling as soon as practicable and steam northwesterly to fueling rendezvous No. 2, at lat. 17° N, long. 128° E, in order to resume at 0600 next day. He made this decision on the assumption by his weather man that the cyclonic disturbance was moving on a course to clear. Actually, the center at 1251 was about 120 miles SE of the Fleet's position, instead of 450 miles as Commander Kosco thought, and making right for it. But there were as yet no portents of a typhoon. This one was so young, small and tight that it had not yet thrown out signs to its periphery. Admiral Halsey was reluctant to abandon fueling because some of the destroyers urgently needed oil and he had to support the Mindoro operation (and the Lingayen one coming up) with a strike on Luzon two days later. He accepted the risk. One cannot quarrel with an officer who makes a mistake because of his single-minded devotion to his mission.

In obedience to Admiral Halsey's orders, Vice Admiral McCain ordered TF 38 to discontinue fueling at 1310 December 17 and set course 290° for the morrow's 0600 rendezvous. But he made an exception of destroyers *Spence*, *Hickox* and *Maddox*, then dangerously low on oil. The two first-named, unable to rig hoses, were ordered to remain with the oilers and seize their first opportunity to fill up.

By midafternoon of the 17th everyone concerned was making forecasts, but nobody got the position, course or strength of the circular storm correctly. The first to make a good guess seems to have been Captain Acuff, commanding the fueling and plane replenishment group. He conferred over TBS with the skippers of two escort carriers around 2257 December 17. All three agreed that fueling rendezvous No. 2, set by the Admiral for the 18th, would be directly in the typhoon track.[14]

---

[18] N. W. Tashman "Typhoon."
[14] *Aylwin* War Diary.

Admiral Halsey at 1533 December 17 again changed the fueling rendezvous for the morning of the 18th, to what we may call No. 3 position, at lat. 14° N, long. 127°30′ E. Immediately after he changed fleet course to 270°, which actually ran parallel with the typhoon track instead of, as the Fleet aërologist thought, at a wide angle from it. Nevertheless, as the Fleet on this westerly course was outstripping the typhoon by 3 to 6 knots, the glass rose and the sea moderated slightly, giving an illusion of improving weather.

Sunset that Sunday evening was not one to cheer the heart of a seaman, or to suggest hymn-singing, unless "For Those in Peril on the Sea." A sinister afterglow remained in the sky. The sea was deep black except where the wind whipped off wave crests into spindrift. On board carrier *Kwajalein*, then heading almost dead into the wind, "as each wave rolled under, the entire bow would come out of the water, hover for a few seconds, and then crash, taking the flight deck almost to sea level. Plates were clanging and snapping and ripples ran up and down the steel hangar deck. The forward lookouts, normally stationed in the catwalks, were ordered to secure." [15]

Zigzagging was canceled after sunset, owing to the mounting seas, and the Fleet continued to advance westward during the hours of darkness. At 2200 December 17, the glass read 29.76 on the flagship and a 28-knot wind was blowing from the N by E. Neither this barometer reading nor the strength of the wind nor the direction of the waves were such as to cause alarm, but they were enough to have suggested that someone try the old seaman's rule-of-thumb for locating a cyclonic storm center: "Face the wind, and the center lies 10 points (112°30′) to your right." If this simple rule had been practised at 2200 December 17 when the wind blew from 13°, it would have indicated that the storm center bore 125°, about SE by E, which was almost correct.[16] But

[15] Snyder Report.

[16] *New Jersey's* deck log shows that on the morning of the 18th the position of the typhoon center could have been plotted by this old method, not absolutely, but with sufficient accuracy to have avoided it in time. Captain Anderson, how-

Commander Kosco, the flag aërologist, still located the center hundreds of miles northeasterly.

Admiral Halsey now canceled No. 3 fueling rendezvous because the ships could not possibly reach it in time, and at 2221 set a new one (No. 4) for next morning, well to the northwestward, at lat. 15°30′ N, long. 127°40′ E. He hoped that at this position the wind would be on the starboard beam of fueling ships. At 2307 Admiral Halsey ordered all carriers and their escorts to change course from due West to due South at midnight in the hope of finding smoother water, and to NW at 0200 December 18 for fueling rendezvous No. 4. This move was unfortunate, as it took many ships straight into the path of the advancing typhoon.

3. *Typhoon, 18 December*

Between 1800 and 2400 that night Task Force 38 made good eighty-five miles in a westerly direction, slightly converging with the typhoon's course, but about three knots faster. At midnight, having reached lat. 15°17′ N, long. 127°50′ E, the task force changed course as ordered to the southward, and at 0200, when directly in the path of the typhoon, to the northwestward. Half an hour later, Commander Kosco "waked up and sort of thought something was wrong," but after checking reports and looking at the barometer he reflected that things didn't look too bad.

Maybe not, from a battlewagon, but it certainly looked ominous from escort carriers and destroyers. During the small hours of Monday 18 December, after the task force had commenced its 320° course toward fueling rendezvous No. 4, the weather became much worse, suggesting to Admiral Halsey at 0400 "for the first time" (according to the Court of Inquiry) "that the Fleet was confronted with serious storm conditions." But the barometer held

---

ever, points out that the Fleet was still beyond the circular wind pattern of the typhoon, so the rule did not apply; that it is a pure coincidence that if it had been tried, it would have worked!

almost steady at around 29.68 between 0500 and 0700. The Admiral spent about half an hour poring over weather maps with his aërologist, but came to no decision as to what, if anything, should be done. The wind still varied from N to NE. At about 0430 he began via TBS asking for estimates of the storm situation from Admiral McCain in *Yorktown* and Admiral Bogan in *Lexington*. At the same time Commander Kosco made a fresh estimate of where the storm center was located. All three were wide of the mark.[17] According to estimates made subsequent to these events, the typhoon center at 0500 December 18 was at lat. 14°34′ N, long. 129°10′ E, which bore about 90 miles ESE from the then position of the flagship *New Jersey*, and was moving at a speed of about 8.6 knots.[18]

At a few minutes after 0500 December 18, the Admiral canceled his No. 4 fueling rendezvous and did not set another, but ordered all groups to shape a course due South at their then speed of 15 knots, and to commence fueling as soon as possible. Assuming that his aërologist had estimated correctly, this course would have taken the Fleet into the southern quadrant of the storm. The wind at that time had not changed direction and its velocity was only 33 to 34 knots (force 7), which created the impression that nothing unusual should be anticipated. It was indeed a deceptive small typhoon which sneaked up on Third Fleet.

At 0701 Admiral McCain, following Admiral Halsey's order to commence fueling as soon as possible, ordered Task Force 38 to change course to 60°. A last, vain attempt to fuel was then made. Day was breaking but little light came through the heavy overcast and the hard, driving rain. Sea and wind were so high that fueling was both dangerous to attempt and impossible to achieve; and although Admiral McCain suggested that the neediest destroyers do it by the old-fashioned method, over the stern instead of along-

---

[17] Bogan said lat. 17° N, long. 131° E; McCain said lat. 12°30′ N, long. 131° E; Kosco said lat. 15° N, long. 131° E.

[18] The statement in Record of Court, F.F. para. 27, that the center at 0500 Dec. 18 was lat. 14°10′ N, long. 129°55′ E, was incorrect, based on the assumption that the typhoon was then making 12 knots' advance.

side, that would have required dismantling and rerigging hoses and other gear, which could not be effected in so rough a sea. This fueling course held the fleet on a collision course with the oncoming circular storm, the exact location and course of which, it must be kept in mind, nobody had yet ascertained.

The Fleet was now so spread out that weather records in the logs of different ships show varying conditions. The log of *Hancock*, remote from the center, notes only "scattered showers" prior to 0800, when "heavy continuous rain" started. Escort carrier *Kwajalein*, in Captain Acuff's group well to the eastward, had to heave to, and with both engines ahead full and wind 45° on the starboard bow, made a few knots' leeway. Salt water was blowing horizontally at bridge level. There seemed to be no separation between sea and sky. The sound of the wind in the rigging, especially in the large "bedspring" radar, was frightening. "The battle ensign was reduced to a small scrap showing two stars." [19] At 0744 Captain H. B. Butterfield of *Nehenta Bay*, another member of the replenishment group, spoke up over TBS and requested Captain Acuff's permission to leave formation with *Kwajalein* and *Rudyerd Bay* and their screen, owing to the pounding that they were taking. Permission was granted at 0753. Butterfield's initiative was commendable, but the course that he took in search of better conditions took him very close to the eye of the storm.[20]

Admiral Halsey was loath to give up his last attempt to fuel, so anxious was he to support the Mindoro operation; but by 0803 conditions were such that the risk was too great. So he canceled his last fueling directive and ordered the Fleet to resume course 180°. By 0830 all ships that could do so had complied. At 0913 Admiral McCain ordered course 220°.

Wind had now risen to 37–43 knots from a few degrees E of N, and the glass had fallen to 29.61. Still, this was no clear evi-

<hr />

[19] Snyder Report.
[20] Oiler *Mascoma*, which, owing to an engine breakdown on the 17th, had lagged behind the other ships, passed through the eye of the typhoon at about 0520, together with DE *Weaver*, her escort. Based on *Mascoma's* 0800 position reported, the eye was then at 14°27' N, long. 129°30' E.

dence of a serious typhoon. About 1000 when the barometer "started falling very, very rapidly," testified Commander Kosco, he began to feel that something nasty was coming, since this was the typical barometric nose-dive of a typhoon.[21] Also at 1000, for the first time, the wind was observed to be backing counterclockwise, sure sign of a typhoon, and that the sea was making up rapidly. According to *Wasp's* log, the sea was "very high" at 1030 and "mountainous" between 1130 and 1430. And by 1400 the wind had risen to 73 knots, almost hurricane force.

As the center of this tight, violently whirling cyclone approached, the weather became worse than the foulest epithet can describe. The eye of the typhoon passed so near several carriers as to show clearly on their SG radar screens. Photographs made of *Wasp's* radar screen — the first probably ever taken of the eye of a storm — have the appearance of an Edgar Allan Poe thriller. The seas took on those confused pyramidal shapes characteristic of hurricanes. Wind velocities were reported of over 100 knots in the gusts.

At 1149 December 18 Admiral Halsey directed CTF 38 to "take most comfortable courses with wind on port quarter." Seven minutes later, four minutes before noon, when the glass on board *New Jersey* read 29.55 and wind (then N by W) had risen to 51 knots, Admiral McCain directed TF 38 to steer course 120°. Both were sound decisions; the storm center was then about thirty-seven miles due north, and this southeasterly course took the Fleet away from it. But by that time the ships were strung out over some 2500 square miles of ocean and it was too late for some to escape. *Mascoma*, as we have seen, had already passed through the calm eye of the storm, saw blue sky for an instant, and was then buffeted from the opposite quarter; her barometer fell to 27.07.[22] This typhoon reached its greatest violence between 1100 and 1400

---

[21] Record of Court, 1st day's testimony, p. 15; *New Jersey* deck log. The rapid fall started as much as two hours earlier in ships nearer the center than *New Jersey*. The lowest recorded by *Wasp* was 29.1.

[22] Lower readings are mentioned in Record of Court, F.F. para. 27; but these were probably caused by a swing of the needle due to the heavy rolling.

December 18, depending on the position of the vessel concerned.

At 1345 Admiral Halsey issued a typhoon warning, to alert Fleet Weather Central to what was going on. This was the first reference to the storm as a typhoon in any official message. Unknown to Command Third Fleet, three of his destroyers had already gone down.

Here was a spectacle to excite the derision or pity of the gods. This mighty fleet, representing the last word in the energy and ingenuity of man on the ocean, was "running all over the sea trying to get behind the weather," as Joseph Conrad had written of his sinking ship in *Typhoon.* They were in a worse state than Phoenician galleys blown off shore, because too many of their skippers tried to fight the sea. Masters of merchant vessels had long since learned not to argue with a hurricane but to evade its center by the old rule of thumb; or, if conditions got too bad, heave-to, lie dead in the water and let the ship find her own way in the midst of the sea.[23] Yet, until just before noon, "no orders were issued to the Fleet as a whole to disregard formation keeping and take best courses and speeds for security." Fortunately, most unit and ship commanders had anticipated this order of 1149, and were doing just that.

By the afternoon of 18 December, Task Force 38 and its attendant fueling groups were scattered over a space estimated at 50 by 60 miles. Except in the case of the battleships, all semblance of formation had been lost. Every ship was laboring heavily; hardly any two were in visual contact; many lay dead, rolling in the trough of the sea; planes were crashing and burning on the light carriers. From the islands of the carriers and the pilothouses of destroyers sailors peered out on such a scene as they had never witnessed before, and hoped never to see again. The weather was so thick and dirty that sea and sky seemed fused in one aqueous

[23] "This basic fact of seamanship is not well understood among naval officers," remarked Admiral Halsey in his endorsement on *Buchanan's* report of this typhoon. "It should be in every seaman's bag of tricks." (12 Jan. 1945.) The C.O. of *Hickox,* Lt. Cdr. J. H. Wesson, knew it, however: "You cannot fight a typhoon," he reported, and saved his ship by heaving-to. So did Capt. Warrack of *Kwajalein* and many other C.O.'s.

element. At times the rain was so heavy that visibility was limited to three feet, and the wind so powerful that to venture out on the flight deck a sailor had to wriggle on his belly. Occasionally the storm-wrack parted for a moment, revealing escort carriers crazily rising up on their fantails or plunging bow under, destroyers rolling drunkenly in hundred-degree arcs or beaten down on one side. The big carriers lost no planes, but the extent of their rolls may be gauged by the fact that *Hancock's* flight deck, 57 feet above her waterline, scooped up green water. The battleships took the seas nobly, and *Miami* was the only cruiser to sustain damage.[24]

The light carriers had a particularly bad time because the rolling and pitching caused plane lashings on hangar decks to part, and padeyes to pull out of flight decks. Planes went adrift, collided and burst into flames. *Monterey* caught fire at 0911 and lost steerageway a few minutes later. The fire, miraculously, was brought under control at 0945, and the C.O., Captain Stuart H. Ingersoll, wisely decided to let his ship lie dead in the water until temporary repairs could be effected. She lost 18 aircraft burned in the hangar deck or blown overboard and 16 seriously damaged, together with three 20-mm guns, and suffered extensive rupturing of her ventilation system.[25] *Cowpens* lost 7 planes overboard and caught fire from one that broke loose at 1051, but the fire was brought under control promptly; *Langley* rolled through 70 degrees; *San Jacinto* reported a fighter plane adrift on the hangar deck which wrecked seven other aircraft. She also suffered damage from salt water that entered through punctures in the ventilating ducts.

Captain Acuff's replenishment escort carriers did pretty well. Flames broke out on the flight deck of *Cape Esperance* at 1228 but were overcome; *Kwajalein* made a maximum roll of 39 degrees to

[24] *Miami*, when turning N to NW at about 1425 Dec. 18, making revolutions for only 10 knots on the starboard and 5 on the port engine, took a series of heavy seas that buckled her shell, main deck and longitudinals from the stem to about frame 22.

[25] *Monterey* Action Report. These CVLs, converted from light cruiser hulls, were especially vulnerable to fire because the ventilating system took its air from the hangar deck. Consequently any fire in that deck might spread throughout the ship.

port when hove-to with wind abeam. Her port catwalks scooped up green water, but she lost only three planes which were jettisoned from the flight deck; it took one hour to get them over the side. Three other escort carriers lost in all 86 aircraft but came through without much material damage. Unable to head into or down wind, they steamed slowly with wind abeam, rolling horribly and occasionally backing engines emergency full to avoid collision with a cruiser or destroyer, since their course took them into the midst of one of the fast carrier task groups. *Rudyerd Bay* did so three times in as many hours. Total aircraft losses in the Fleet, including those blown overboard or jettisoned from the battleships and cruisers, amounted to 146.

Considering that in sailing-ship days guns often broke loose during storms and charged about the deck, it is not surprising that on so new a type as the aircraft carrier fittings and lashings should prove inadequate. But there was no flinching or failure on the part of the men. The carriers' crews showed complete disregard for their safety; in bringing these hurtling, exploding planes under control, and in mastering the fires, several men lost life or limb.

4. *The Ordeal of the Destroyers*

The destroyers had the worst experiences, and those of two ships of the *Farragut* class, the ten-year-old 1370-tonners, were frightful indeed. Lieutenant Commander J. A. Marks, skipper of *Hull*, had served in destroyers during bad Atlantic storms, but did not realize that this was a typhoon until about 0900 December 18. His ship, with destroyer escorts *Crowley* and *Lake*, was screening a fueling unit of four fleet oilers, *Monongahela*, *Neosho*, *Patuxent* and *Marias*. At about 1100 on the 18th, Commander F. J. Ilsemann, the unit commander in *Monongahela*, ordered a change of course to 140°. While this maneuver was being executed the wind increased to over 100 knots. As *Hull's* fuel tanks were 70 per cent full she did not take in salt-water ballast; events proved that it would have been well to have done so. When proceeding to her new station incident to the change of course, her helm failed to respond to any combination of rudder and engines. She lay in irons in the trough of the sea with the north wind on her port beam, yawing between courses 80° and 100°. The whaleboat, the depth charges and almost everything else on deck were swept off as she rolled 50 degrees to leeward, and before eight bells the rolls increased to 70 degrees. From two or three of them she recovered, but a gust estimated to be of 110-knot velocity pinned her down on her beam ends. Sea flooded the pilothouse and poured down the stacks, and at a few minutes after noon she went down. Of her complement of 18 officers and 246 men, only 7 officers and 55 men were ultimately rescued.[26]

It was noted in the Court of Inquiry that *Hull* had not taken in time the precaution of reballasting with salt water her partially empty tanks; but at that time it was neither ordered, nor considered necessary, for a ship of her class with that much fuel on board to reballast.

In these destroyers the fuel tanks were arranged roughly in this pattern: —

U.S.S. HULL

DISTRIBUTION OF FUEL AT TIME OF CAPSIZING

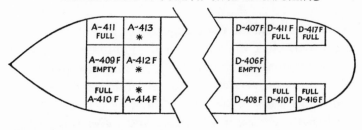

*A-412, 413, 414, filled to 13 ft. or 1st. Platform deck level

Half-empty tanks were a danger in a seaway, because when the ship rolled the center of gravity of the contents of each tank shifted to leeward and increased the roll. As a result of earlier typhoons

[26] For positions of rescue see chart. Exact time and position of sinking not known. Information on *Hull* from an interview of her surviving C.O., 1 Jan. 1945, and a later interview conducted by Adm. Nimitz; also Record of Court p. 96 Exhibit 11.

encountered by Third Fleet, destroyers were ordered, when encountering rough weather, to fill empty tanks with salt water. But the C.O. of a destroyer about to fuel would naturally hesitate to do this because the deballasting process takes as much as six hours, and might not have been completed when her turn came to fuel.

Dewey [27] (Lieutenant Commander C. R. Calhoun) was flagship of Destroyer Squadron 1, commanded by Captain Preston V. Mercer, formerly Admiral Nimitz's assistant chief of staff. Having been through 80-mile-an-hour winds in destroyer *Winslow*, he had given much thought to ship handling under such conditions. To Captain Mercer's "steadying influence, sound advice and mature judgment" the C.O. attributed the survival of his ship. She was in the screen of the logistics and plane-replenishment group, which included four oilers, seven destroyers and the three escort carriers whose story we have already told. Captain Acuff, the group commander, who wore his pennant in destroyer *Aylwin*, made no attempt to force station keeping. At 0744, as we have seen, he allowed Captain Butterfield to leave formation with the three escort carriers. As soon as he received Admiral Halsey's order of 0803 December 18 to break off attempts to fuel and steer south, Captain Acuff cast his screen loose and left the oilers to take care of themselves, for there was no use echo-ranging in a typhoon when sound gear will not work and submarines cannot operate.

Dewey began to lose lubricating oil suction around 0900. At about 0945, when the driving rain and spindrift had reduced visibility to less than a thousand yards, she narrowly missed colliding with *Monterey*. In avoiding this carrier she got herself into the same situation as *Hull:* in irons, broadside to wind in the trough of the sea, rolling heavily to starboard and unable to steer any

[27] War Diary and additional details in an unsigned, undated report by Lt. Cdr. C. R. Calhoun, read in Despac office March 1945; Capt. Mercer's testimony at the Court of Inquiry and subsequent conversations with him. Lt. Cdr. Calhoun's statement on microfilm gives 0800 position as lat. 14°57' N, long. 128° E, and *Aylwin's* was 15°04' 128°02'. *Dewey* changed from the fueling course of 60° to 180° at 0820. If the positions are correct (in view of conditions, they can be only approximate), this group continued some twenty miles farther on the 60° course than shown by track of *New Jersey* on our chart.

course but from E to ENE. Although *Dewey's* fuel tanks were 75 per cent full, the commanding officer, on the advice of Captain Mercer, not only jettisoned topside weights — a difficult and risky operation in that sea — but resorted to the desperate expedient of ordering her partially empty port tanks to be ballasted with 40,000 gallons of salt water and fuel oil from the starboard tanks. Even the feed water in No. 3 boiler on the starboard side of No. 2 fire room was run into a port tank to improve righting movement. At the same time, the skipper directed all hands to secure below on the port side, for which they needed little urging. She started rolling 60 degrees to starboard, hanging there and recovering slowly. A speed of about 3 knots was maintained with the starboard engine.

This procedure of ballasting the weather side was a terrific gamble, but it worked. If *Dewey's* reported position is correct, she was sculling around the eye of the typhoon when hove-to. Had the eye overtaken her, and the wind whipped around to the opposite quarter, she would have capsized immediately. A lucky ship, indeed!

Around 1100, when the glass read 28.84, wind was blowing hurricane force from the NNE and the sea had made up to condition 9. Several things then happened to *Dewey* at once. Sea water entering one of the mushroom ventilators short-circuited the switchboard in the steering-engine room, which severed steering control from the bridge. Lube oil suction had been completely lost, owing to the excessive list, so that the port engine had to be secured. Heavy seas crashed through engine room hatches, short-circuiting the main switchboard. This brought total loss of light and power. No 1 fire room began to leak. Lieutenant Commander Calhoun, finding his ship completely out of control, organized a bucket brigade to bail out the steering-engine compartment so that men on the hand wheel could keep the helm hard down. He caused submersible pumps to be rigged in various places to keep the ship clear of sloshing water, and organized a messenger service for transmitting orders, his bridge telephones having gone dead. It was impossible to exist, much less to stand, on deck. The after stack was invisible from the pilothouse; spindrift removed paint from topside surfaces as though it were a sand-blast.

Even worse was to come. At 1210 *Dewey* rolled 65 degrees to starboard, recovered, rolled 75 degrees and hung there. The barometer needle went off the scale at 27 and kept dropping; Captain Mercer believes that it reached 26.60. A lurch caused the skipper to lose his footing on the weather wing of the almost perpendicular bridge deck; he grasped a stanchion, and, before the astonished eyes of his quartermaster, hung there as on a trapeze. He was preparing to order the destroyer's mast to be cut away with an acetylene torch when No. 1 stack pulled out at boat-deck level and fell 'thwart ship, completely flattened; and although this loss caused flarebacks in No. 1 fire room and let in more sea water, it reduced the ship's "sail area" so that stability improved. Engineers maintained boiler pressure so that all pumps were soon working. By 1300 the center of the storm had passed, and by 1800 *Dewey* had full way on and was able very cautiously to wear around to a westerly course.

The factors that enabled this ship to survive were the prompt jettison of topside weights, ballasting with salt water, unremitting bailing and pumping, and the loss of the stack. She suffered one casualty that *Hull* did not, the drowning out of her steering engine, and dealt with it promptly.

Aylwin (Lieutenant Commander W. K. Rogers), Captain Acuff's flagship, water-ballasted her high side, and she too had the good luck to get away with it when the eye of the typhoon passed her close aboard. Around 1100, with steering control lost, engines stopped, and heading 220°, she rolled 70 degrees to port and then lay down on her side for twenty minutes. Steering control, regained intermittently, was employed to bring her stern to windward, using the bow's surface like a headsail to keep steerageway and pay off. This maneuver kept the wind at about 30 degrees abaft the starboard beam, but she frequently fell into the trough. From 1300, when lowest barometer reading — 28.55 — was observed, "ship did not roll *more* than 60 degrees." Engine rooms were abandoned when temperature reached 180° F., owing to failure of blowers. The ship's engineer officer, Lieutenant E. R. Rendahl USNR and Machinist's Mate 1st class T. Sarenski, standing watch in this terrific heat to protect the electrical circuits, stayed too long at their duty posts. When finally they could bear it no longer and crawled out on deck through the only exit, a hatch so narrow that they had to remove life jackets, they were immediately overcome by the change of temperature, collapsed, and before anyone could help them, were washed overboard and lost. At 1745 *Aylwin* got under way at 7 knots, with water sloshing around well above her floor plates; but she managed to control the flooding that night.

Hickox, a 2100-tonner of Desron 52, after six unsuccessful attempts to fuel on the 17th, was down to 322 tons, 14 per cent of her fuel capacity. Her C.O., Lieutenant Commander J. H. Wesson, began water-ballasting at 1750. By 1010 December 18 she had taken on 246 tons of sea water. Twenty minutes later, in avoiding a collision, she got herself in irons in the trough of the sea. Unable to tack or wear, Commander Wesson decided to ride it out with bare steerageway and set Condition "Affirm" — all buttoned up. Bridge lost steering control at 1130, owing to leaks in the steering-engine compartment, which took in water so fast that the sailors who tried hand steering had to be pulled out to save them from drowning. Only the best efforts of all hands kept *Hickox* from sinking. A bucket brigade worked in pitchy darkness with water and oil sloshing over the men in the heavy rolls. The engine room became a good imitation of Dante's Inferno. "With all vent systems out and with water entering through these systems, striking hot machinery and flashing into steam, the temperature and humidity rose to such a point that it was impossible to remain for more than a few minutes without collapsing." [28] After the steering-engine compartment had been partially bailed out and the leaks temporarily calked, the men rigged a lead to a submersible pump there from the switchboard power supply of No. 5 gun. In this

[28] *Hickox* Report of Storm Damage, 13 Jan. 1945.

situation *Hickox* handled herself very well, lying just out of the trough with the bow trying to head up, thus avoiding full, deep rolls. Despite frequent clogging of the submersible pump by seamen's clothing which had gone adrift, the flooded compartments were almost clear by 1745. Hand steering was resumed and, the worst of the typhoon having passed, *Hickox* complied with Admiral Halsey's order to the Fleet at 1800, to "come to a comfortable southerly course in search of fueling weather." [29]

Monaghan (Lieutenant Commander F. Bruce Garrett) was another *Farragut*-class destroyer that failed to stay afloat. She was operating independently of the task force at the height of the typhoon, with fuel tanks 76 per cent full. The skipper reported to Captain Acuff at 0925 December 18 that he was unable to steer the base course, and was then heading about 330° with the wind on starboard bow. Apparently he wore ship later, which took his destroyer as near to the track of the typhoon's center as *Hull*. At about 1100 her skipper attempted to ballast her weather side. *Monaghan's* senior survivor, Water Tender 2nd Class Joseph C. McCrane USNR, testified that he and his helper with great difficulty opened the ballast valves to the after tanks, but it was then too late to save her. Electric power and steering engine failed at about 1130. The engine and fire rooms' overheads began to rip loose from the bulkheads. *Monaghan* made several heavy rolls to starboard, hung there for a time, and shortly before noon foundered. Of her entire company only six enlisted men survived.

Spence (Lieutenant Commander J. P. Andrea), a 2100-tonner of *Fletcher* class, larger, newer and more stable than the others, formed part of Admiral Sherman's Task Group 38.3. Her fuel was down to 15 per cent capacity on 17 December. After an unsuccessful attempt to fuel from *New Jersey*, she was sent at 0800 December 18 to Captain Acuff's group in the hope of fueling at the first opportunity, since by that time she had only enough oil for 24

[29] As with his 1156 order, the Admiral meant "comfortable" in the nautical sense: the nearest course to south that a ship could steer without undue risk and strain. The actual course set by *New Jersey* at 1800 was 200° (about SSW), speed 11 knots.

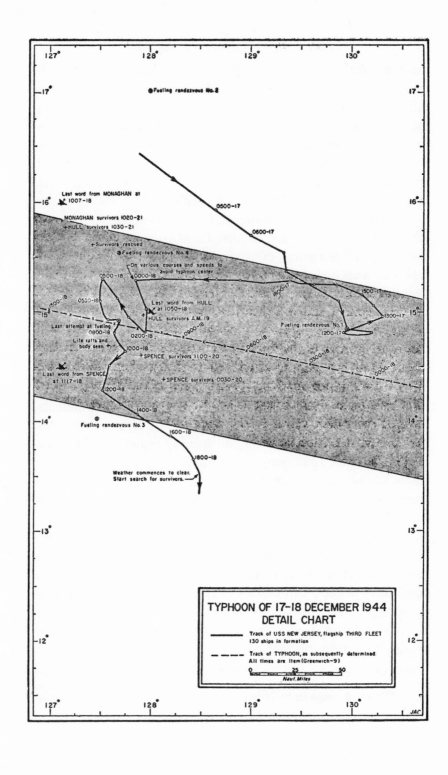

TYPHOON OF 17-18 DECEMBER 1944
DETAIL CHART

———— Track of USS NEW JERSEY, flagship THIRD FLEET
130 ships in formation

– – – – Track of TYPHOON, as subsequently determined.
All times are Item (Greenwich-9)

0   25   50
Naut. Miles

hours' steaming at 8 knots. The commanding officer began water-ballasting too late, after breakfast on the 18th, and Condition "Affirm" was never set. On a course heading southwesterly, she began rolling heavily to port. Water entered through ventilators and sloshed around below, short-circuiting the distribution board. The rudder jammed at hard right. At 1110 *Spence* took a deep roll to port, hung there a moment, recovered, rolled again, and then was swallowed up by the sea. Only one officer and 23 enlisted men were rescued.

Most successful in riding out the typhoon were the destroyer escorts. They rode the seas more easily than the destroyers, and were well handled by their young officers and men. *Robert F. Keller* (nicknamed "Killer Keller," as she was in the antisubmarine hunter-killer group with CVE *Anzio*) was saved by early reballasting of her almost empty fuel tanks, and "the superb seamanship" of her skipper, Cdr. Raymond J. Toner USNR.[80] A vivid account of the typhoon is given by the exec. of another destroyer escort in *Anzio's* screen: —

The wind was howling all through the ship — we were rolling probably 40 degrees — some men were doing their job in a matter of fact way — others were praying or sitting off by themselves, their faces white with fear. The spray covered the ship from the truck to the waterline. We realized that we were in a typhoon and we knew we were on the wrong side of it — would pass through the center if we stayed afloat that long.

At about 1230 the typhoon was reaching its height. We were completely at its mercy wallowing in the trough (this with 12,000 H.P.), port engine ahead one third, right full rudder. We tried every combination and this was the best — she would have broken in half if we had tried to run — provided we could have got on such a course which we couldn't have.

By 1300 we must have passed through the center for there was a momentary lull — the seas hit us from all directions and the ship was racked and twisted — but she survived. The respite from the wind was only a matter of minutes, then it howled, whined and finally got back to shrieking again. During the height of the typhoon there was a vacuum created throughout the ship — I suppose a sort of venturi action caused by the tremendous force of the wind. Standing in the pilothouse looking out at the bridge one could see for perhaps three feet. No one could have stood out there — the rain would have beat them to the deck or the wind lifted them bodily off their feet and hurled them off to leeward.

The greatest roll measured was 72 degrees. Just put that on paper — we were literally on our beam ends. By 1400 the barometer was back on the scale and we all began to hope that perhaps things might improve. The rain let up some — it blew perhaps 80 miles an hour instead of 120–130 and we began to be able to see first the pelorus, then the range finder and finally the mast.

Just listening to the voice radio kept one on edge. We were not the only one in trouble. The gunnery officers had one bad moment when a powder case broke and 60-lb. projectiles were rolling around amidst the powder. We all had our moments. I for one have never seen nature at work like this and I hope I never do again.[81]

Melvin R. Nawman lost her foremast, but she and all these gallant little ships came through with only superficial damage.

According to the Court of Inquiry, the commanding officers of *Hull, Monaghan* and *Spence* maneuvered too long in an endeavor to keep station, which prevented them from concentrating early enough on saving their ships. This was admitted by the C.O. of *Hull,* but the records of Third Fleet as a whole indicate that little effort was made to keep station after 0800 December 18. When, in the Court of Inquiry, Captain S. H. Ingersoll of carrier *Monterey* was asked whether he felt free to drop out of formation and handle his ship any way he saw fit, he replied that he did. It was the urgent need of these destroyers for fuel that got them in trouble; and although, in retrospect, it is clear that Admiral Halsey should have made no attempt to fuel on the 18th, he had no means of knowing where the center of the typhoon was, or even that it was a ty-

---

[81] Lt. Cdr. W. Reid Stanwood USNR to his father, 21 Dec. 1944, copy sent to me by his father's friend John Richardson.

phoon, until around 0900 that day. Under these circumstances it seems to this writer to have been too much to expect of junior destroyer skippers — Classes of 1937 and 1938, Naval Academy — to have pitted their brief experience against the lack of typhoon warnings and their own want of fuel. Let their successors, however, heed the stern, wise words of Fleet Admiral Nimitz: —

"The time for taking all measures for a ship's safety is while still able to do so. Nothing is more dangerous than for a seaman to be grudging in taking precautions lest they turn out to have been unnecessary. Safety at sea for a thousand years has depended on exactly the opposite philosophy."

Around 1500 on this blue Monday, 18 December, the wind began to moderate, and by nightfall was down to 60 knots; the sky brightened somewhat, and it became obvious that the eye of the storm had passed.

5. Rescue and Inquiry

Although Admiral Halsey at 1848 December 18 directed CTF 38 to organize a thorough search for men who had been washed overboard, he did not learn that any ship had been sunk until 0225 December 19, when word came from destroyer escort *Tabberer* that she was picking up survivors. He successively detached destroyers *Blue, Brown* and *Gatling*, escort carrier *Rudyerd Bay* with destroyer escorts *Robert F. Keller* and *Swearer*, and on 21 December *Nehenta Bay*, to search the waters into which survivors might have drifted. Continued day and night by plane and ship until noon 22 December, this search proved fruitful beyond anyone's expectation in recovering men alive from the tempestuous seas.

The report of Lieutenant Commander H. L. Plage USNR, C.O. of *Tabberer*, shows the difficulties of night rescue under these hazardous conditions.[32] Although the sea was so rough that search-lights merely touched the crests, and the boiling froth made it difficult to distinguish a man's head, she picked up ten *Hull* survivors before midnight December 18. Her method of securing them was to steam about 50 yards to windward of each man, check headway, and drift down toward him. While so doing she slung over her lee bulwarks two cargo nets, several life rings secured to lines, and a number of 21-thread manila lines with bowlines knotted in. One or more of the best swimmers then went overboard to help the survivors, with lines bent onto their life jackets. In a box search which continued all day 19 December, *Tabberer* recovered 28 more men; and when orders came from Admiral Halsey to continue searching all night, the destroyer escort's crew, who had had no sleep for thirty-six hours, gave a rousing cheer. They picked up a few more swimming survivors that night, and at 1057 on the 20th recovered ten *Spence* survivors from a raft, who, with four more swimmers, made a total of 55. On two occasions they used rifle fire to drive away sharks which were making passes at the survivors, but not one of the men rescued was injured while being taken on board. All but one, it was observed, wore kapok life jackets, not the pneumatic abominations recently issued; and the whistles and flashlights with reflectors attached to these life jackets were a material aid in attracting attention.

Destroyer escort *Swearer* also did good rescue work, recovering nine *Spence* survivors between 0320 and 1520 December 20th. Destroyer *Brown* picked up 12 *Hull* survivors at 1030 December 21, 66 miles northwesterly from where the first ones had been recovered by *Tabberer* on the morning of the 19th. *Brown* also recovered the six lone survivors from *Monaghan* — who had been sighted by escort carrier planes — on 21 December.

Prompt action was taken by the Navy to ascertain the facts and take measures to prevent recurrence. A court of inquiry presided over by Vice Admiral John H. Hoover, consisting of himself, Vice

[32] *Tabberer* letter, 29 Dec. 1944; article by Warren Moscow in *N. Y. Times* 20 Jan. 1945.

Admiral George D. Murray and Rear Admiral Glenn B. Davis, with Captain Herbert K. Gates as judge advocate, was convened on board destroyer tender *Cascade* in Ulithi Lagoon on 26 December 1944. After sitting for several days and examining over fifty witnesses, this court placed the responsibility for storm damage and losses on the shoulders of Admiral Halsey. No negligence was imputed to him; his mistakes, said the court "were errors in judgment committed under stress of war operations and stemming from a commendable desire to meet military requirements." [33]

In my opinion — after rereading the testimony fourteen years later, and examining the meteorological data then available to Admiral Halsey — the court was not fair to Commander Third Fleet. It assumed that the typhoon sent out warnings long before there were signs of anything more than a normal tropical disturbance.

The court recommended measures to reduce topside leakage on destroyers, and other alterations to improve stability. Improvements were recommended in the Navy's meteorological service, such as maintaining weather ships in the typhoon area, establishing weather stations on rocks like Parece Vela [34] and a new weather central at Guam, and providing for properly staffed weather reconnaissance planes to make accurate and prompt reports. Most of these improvements were carried out during the next six months. On the first day of 1945 a fleet weather central was established at Leyte; and in February, a more important one at Guam. Tended weather stations were established at Pulo Anna on Current Island (about halfway between the Palaus and Morotai), Geferut Island (one of the northern Carolines) and at Angaur, Peleliu, Ulithi and

[33] Adm. Nimitz's endorsement 22 Jan. 1945 on Court of Inquiry's Record. Adm. King concurred (his endorsement, 21 Feb. 1945) altering "commendable desire" to "firm determination," and adding after "judgment": "resulting from insufficient information."

[34] A reconnaissance of Parece Vela in Apr. 1945 found that the Japanese had razed the pinnacle rock which "appeared a sail" to the old Spanish navigators, and had constructed a circular concrete block structure about level with high water and 120 feet in diameter. Apparently they had done nothing with it, and Vice Adm. Hoover recommended that it be used as a combined weather-reporting and loran (long range navigation) station. Report to Cincpac Conference at Guam, 17 Apr. 1945.

Saipan and, as soon as they were secured, Manila, Iwo Jima and Okinawa. The weather central already established at Chungking set up additional stations in China (as we describe in Chapter XIV). Further coverage of the Philippine Sea was provided in May 1945 by three PCEs specially equipped as weather ships, and by planes taking competent observers on special weather-reporting flights.[35]

After its rough treatment by the typhoon, Task Force 38 could not carry out the strikes scheduled for 19–21 December on enemy airfields on Luzon. On the 19th all ships not searching for survivors were fueled. Next day they steamed westward in preparation for strikes on the 21st. In so doing they overtook the tail of the typhoon, then moving slowly over northern Luzon, and by the morning of the 21st it was apparent that weather over the big island would make air operations impossible. So, leaving a few ships to continue the search for survivors, Third Fleet returned to Ulithi for repairs, rest and replenishment.[36]

Admiral Halsey felt that despite the typhoon the month of December was marked by "unparalleled success" in paralyzing enemy air effort over Luzon and disrupting counterattacks at their source. "The increased number of days afforded for repairs and reconditioning of materiel and personnel were put to excellent use." [37] Temporary repairs to all ships damaged in the typhoon were completed by Service Squadron 10 at Ulithi by 29 December. Next day the indefatigable Fast Carrier Force again sortied to render air support in the liberation of Luzon.

Admiral Nimitz, who kept Christmas at Ulithi, heard about events of the typhoon at first hand, discussed them with numerous officers of the Third Fleet and pondered them deeply. After the Court of Inquiry had rendered its report, the Admiral issued a

---

[35] "Analysis of Typhoon Warning Service Western Pacific Nov. 1944–Nov. 1945" Nov. 1945. In spite of these new facilities, Third Fleet ran into another destructive typhoon in June 1945.

[36] Action Report Western Pacific Task Forces 24 Aug. 1944–26 Jan. 1945 pp. 16–17.

[37] Halsey Action Report on Operations 1–29 Dec. 1944 (10 Jan. 1945).

Fleet Letter full of sound seamanship. Its most pregnant paragraphs
follow: —

A hundred years ago, a ship's survival depended almost solely on the
competence of her master and on his constant alertness to every hint of
change in the weather. To be taken aback or caught with full sail on
by even a passing squall might mean the loss of spars or canvas; and to
come close to the center of a genuine hurricane or typhoon was syn-
onymous with disaster. While to be taken by surprise was thus serious,
the facilities for avoiding it were meager. Each master was dependent
wholly on himself for detecting the first symptoms of bad weather, for
predicting its seriousness and movement, and for taking the appropriate
measures, to evade it if possible and to battle through it if it passed
near to him. There was no radio by which weather data could be collected from over all the oceans and the resulting forecasts by expert
aërologists broadcasted to him and to all afloat. There was no one to
tell him that the time had now come to strike his light sails and spars,
and snug her down under close reefs or storm trysails. His own barometer, the force and direction of the wind, and the appearance of sea and
sky were all that he had for information. Ceaseless vigilance in watching and interpreting signs, plus a philosophy of taking no risk in which
there was little to gain and much to be lost, was what enabled him to
survive.

Seamen of the present day should be better at forecasting weather at
sea, independently of the radio, than were their predecessors. The general laws of storms and the weather expectancy for all months of the
year in all parts of the world are now more understood, more completely catalogued, and more readily available in various publications.
An intensive study of typhoons and Western Pacific weather was made
over a period of many years by Father Depperman at the Manila Ob-
servatory, and his conclusions have been embodied in the material
available to all aërologists. What Knight and Bowditch have to say on
the subject is exactly as true during this war as it was in time of peace
or before the days of radio. Familiarity with these authorities is something no captain or navigator can do without. The monthly pilot
charts, issued to all ships, give excellent information as to the probable
incidence and movements of typhoons. Stress of the foregoing is no be-
littlement of our aërological centers and weather broadcasts. But just
as a navigator is held culpable if he neglects "Log, Lead, and Lookout"
through blind faith in his radio fixes, so is the seaman culpable who re-
gards personal weather estimates as obsolete and assumes that if no

radio storm warning has been received, then all is well, and no local weather signs need cause him concern. . . .

The safety of a ship against perils from storm, as well as from those of navigation and maneuvering, is always the responsibility of her commanding officer; but this responsibility is also shared by his immediate superiors in operational command, since by the very fact of such command the individual commanding officer is not free to do at any time what his own judgment might indicate. . . .

It is most definitely part of the senior officer's responsibility to think in terms of the smallest ship and most inexperienced commanding officer under him. He cannot take them for granted, give them tasks and stations, and assume either that they will be able to keep up and come through any weather that his own big ship can; or that they will be wise enough to gauge the exact moment when their task must be abandoned in order for them to keep afloat . . .

In conclusion, both seniors and juniors must realize that in bad weather, as in most other situations, safety and fatal hazard are not separated by any sharp boundary line, but shade gradually from one into the other. There is no little red light which is going to flash on and inform commanding officers or higher commanders that from then on there is extreme danger from the weather, and that measures for ships' safety must now take precedence over further efforts to keep up with the formation or to execute the assigned task. This time will always be a matter of personal judgment. Naturally no commander is going to cut thin the margin between staying afloat and foundering, but he may nevertheless unwittingly pass the danger point even though no ship is yet *in extremis*. Ships that keep on going as long as the severity of wind and sea had not yet come close in capsizing them or breaking them in two, may nevertheless become helpless to avoid these catastrophes later if things get worse. By then they may be unable to steer any heading but in the trough of the sea, or may have their steering control, lighting, communications and main propulsion disabled or may be helpless to secure things on deck or to jettison topside weights. The time for taking all measures for a ship's safety is while still able to do so. Nothing is more dangerous than for a seaman to be grudging in taking precautions lest they turn out to have been unnecessary. Safety at sea for a thousand years has depended on exactly the opposite philosophy.

C. W. NIMITZ [38]

[38] Fleet Adm. Nimitz Letter 14CL–45 on Lessons of Damage in Typhoon, 13 Feb. 1945. The whole is printed in U.S. Naval Institute *Proceedings* LXXXII (Jan. 1956) pp. 83–88.

To sum up: Fundamental causes of the heavy loss in this typhoon were (1) Admiral Halsey's commendable zeal to support the Army in the forthcoming landing on Luzon, by weakening the Japanese air forces on that island; (2) the typhoon being so new, small and tight as to send out no unmistakable signs to the Fleet until it was almost upon it; (3) the desperate need of certain destroyers for fuel, which led their commanding officers to neglect ballasting until it was too late.

6. TF 38 Back to Battery,
29 December 1944–9 January 1945 [39]

On 28 December Fleet Admiral Nimitz and Rear Admiral Forrest Sherman stopped at Ulithi on their way back from Leyte and conferred with Admiral Halsey. At that time Cincpac gave his approval to Halsey's long-desired South China Sea incursion, but only after TF 38 had finished covering the Lingayen landings. In the light of recent experience the plane complement of certain carriers was changed, the better to meet combat conditions. Two squadrons of Marine Corsairs were placed on board *Essex*.[40] She and *Wasp* now carried 91 fighter planes and 15 Avenger torpedo bombers each. In order to improve and extend night search and introduce night striking, a night-flying carrier task group consisting of *Independence*, newly converted *Enterprise* and six destroyers was formed on 5 January 1945.[41] On that date "Big E," flying the flag of Rear Admiral M. B. Gardner, joined Task Force 38. During daylight this TG 38.5 operated within the screen of Rear Admiral Bogan's TG 38.2 but pulled out as an independent group when directed by the task force commander.

[39] Com Third Fleet Action Report for 30 Dec. 1944–23 Jan. 1945; Cincpac and Comairpac Monthly Analyses for Jan. 1945.

[40] This was the first use of the Marine Corps air arm by TF 38.

[41] See Vol. VII chap. xviii for an account of the first night carrier strike on Truk in Feb. 1944. Despite the success of that operation, night bombing ran into many difficulties and encountered much opposition even within aviation circles, hence had not been developed as fast as its enthusiastic advocates had hoped.

Admirals Halsey and McCain sortied from Ulithi 30 December in command of Third Fleet and Task Force 38, the most powerful naval striking force that the world had ever known. The year 1944 had been one of victory from the Marshalls to the Philippines; they were determined that 1945 would see the final and complete liquidation of Japanese sea power, and they had their wish. But the immediate road ahead was rough. Halsey's schedule called for air strikes on Formosa, 3 and 4 January; fueling on the 5th; a strike on Luzon next day and on Luzon or Formosa on the 7th; fueling on the 8th; and striking Formosa again 9 January, which was D-day in Lingayen Gulf. Then, if circumstances permitted, he could enter the South China Sea.

As TF 38 headed northwest, training activities occupied every day and a part of each night. An anti-snooper patrol screen operating out of Saipan and Leyte warded off possible discovery by enemy search planes. January 2 was spent fueling from Captain Acuff's logistics group. The task force reached its initial launching point, 140 miles from the nearest Formosa airfields, in the early morning of the 3rd. Complete surprise was achieved.

In this two-day strike, southern Formosa and the Pescadores Islands were assigned to Admiral Bogan's Group 2; central Formosa, the Sakishima Gunto and Okinawa were covered by Admiral Sherman's Group 3; northern Formosa by Admiral Radford's Group 1. Blanket tactics, as employed in the December strikes on Luzon, were planned, except for the long-range strikes on the Nansei Shoto.

Upon arrival at the launching point, TF 38 ran into the first installment of the almost continuous foul weather which was to hamper its air operations throughout January. A heavy front lay between the ships and Formosa. Planes of the pre-dawn launch of 3 January had to make their way through almost solid overcast, and a number of pilots were unable to reach the target. No blanket tactics were possible; the weather, in fact, rendered them unnecessary as the Japanese did not attempt to fly. In the afternoon the weather again closed in so thick that all strikes and searches had to be recalled. The carriers retired to the southeastward, to be out of range of Luzon-based aircraft. Next day the strikes again had to be curtailed, and retirement in the afternoon became the only practicable course. On 5 January, while Admiral Oldendorf was catching it from kamikazes off the west coast of Luzon, TF 38 fueled at sea. The results of the two days' bombing strikes were largely unobserved and have never been reported. It is a guess that about 100 enemy planes were eliminated. But 22 American planes were lost.[42]

Nevertheless, these strikes paid off. They did help the Luzon Attack Force; no planes from Formosa participated in the fierce attacks on our ships in Lingayen Gulf during the following week.[43]

According to Admiral Halsey's plan and at General MacArthur's request, a strike on Luzon airfields was laid on for 6 January. Despite foul weather an estimated 32 enemy planes were shot down or destroyed, but there were plenty of holes in the "blanket" through which enemy aircraft leaked out to attack Admiral Oldendorf's bombardment groups in Lingayen Gulf.[44]

By the 7th the pilots had a new set of air photographs to help them choose targets, and the weather cleared up so that the camouflaged dispersal areas revealed by the photographic interpreters could be located. In accordance with a request from Admiral Kinkaid, TF 38 struck Luzon again on the 7th rather than Formosa. Admiral Halsey sent the pilots a personal message demanding "extra effort in support of our comrades of the Southwest Pacific in their Luzon attack," [45] and they covered Luzon up to Lingayen Gulf. Although the weather deteriorated in the carriers' launching area during the afternoon, making flight operations hazardous, Task Force 38 kept an air blanket over the principal Luzon fields until 2100.

[42] Admirals Halsey and McCain each estimated 85 for 3 January and the same number for 4 January. The number lost in combat is McCain's.

[43] "No assistance at all from Formosa" said Col. Matsumae, senior staff officer, Fourth Air Army Manila, in his interrogation (USSBS No. 249 p. 9) on 27 Oct. 1945.

[44] Capt. R. N. Hunter (formerly C.O. of *Kadashan Bay*) "Naval War College Staff Presentation on Lingayen Gulf." See also Chap. iv sec. 3 for the air attacks of 6 January.

[45] Halsey War Diary for Jan. 1945.

The enemy seemed unwilling to challenge the carrier planes; he was saving his planes for what he considered a more worthy object. Throughout the entire day of the 7th only four Japanese aircraft were observed to rise in order to give battle, and they were promptly shot down. TF 38 claimed to have destroyed 75 others on the ground; its own losses were heavy — 28 planes, 18 of these operational. With the assistance of 143 sorties [46] from the eleven escort carriers with Admiral Oldendorf, and of the Army Air Force, these strikes accomplished their object of protecting the fleet at Lingayen Gulf, for a time, from kamikaze attack. Only about half as many Japanese planes were observed in Lingayen Gulf on the 7th as on the 6th, and after the 7th, air opposition to the amphibious operation was sporadic. And the Japanese air forces on Luzon were almost wiped out. About 130 Japanese planes, kamikazes and escorts, were expended in the attacks on Allied ships.[47] No new planes were sent in to Luzon after about 9 January, and no assistance was received from Formosa.

Upon completing his Luzon raids, Admiral Halsey rendezvoused with Captain Acuff's service group on 8 January, about 160 miles east of Cape Engaño.[48] A fast run-in was made during the night of 8–9 January, and at 0530 on the 9th, when slightly over a hundred miles off the nearest point of Formosa, a pre-dawn launch was made and the strikes began.

On 9 January, when Seventh Fleet was engaged in landing Sixth Army on Luzon, TF 38 supported them by hitting Formosa, 360 miles to the northward. Bad weather again plagued the pilots. Planes of Rear Admiral Sherman's TG 38.3, assigned to the Ryu-

---

[46] This includes only direct-support missions. The CVEs actually made 435 sorties on 7 Jan.; the total of TF 38 was 757.

[47] MacArthur *Historical Report* II 430. Col. Matsumae in USSBS Interrogation No. 249 pp. 3–9 gives higher figures.

[48] On 8 Jan. Adm. Halsey transferred destroyer *Hailey*, Cdr. P. H. Brady, from TG 38.2 to Capt. Acuff's fueling TG 30.8. Cdr. Brady then sent a dispatch to Com Third Fleet, ". . . would appreciate greatly your advising me of any operational, administrative, or material deficiencies, or any other reasons for *Hailey* being detached from TG 38.2 to TG 30.8 in exchange for *Trathen*. Have inquired of screen, task group, and task force commanders. None of them knows why this ship was detached." To which Halsey replied same day: "Relax. Com Third Fleet still loves you. Wanted to give 30.8 a radar jammer" (*Hailey* War Diary).

kyus, ran into a heavy weather front; after reaching the Sakishima Gunto they were unable to locate enemy airfields and turned back. Later in the day two strikes from "Ted" Sherman's TG 38.3 and one from "Jerry" Bogan's TG 38.2 succeeded in reaching Formosa, and another got through to Miyako Jima. "Raddy's" TG 38.1 also made three strikes each from two fleet carriers, and one each from his two light carriers. "We hit the field at Hieto," wrote one of the pilots from *Hancock*, "finding mostly dummy planes, and wasting our energy on two steam rollers that were repairing the field." [49]

The total number of sorties 9 January was 717, and 212 tons of bombs were dropped. Enemy reaction was slight. The only four planes which rose to intercept were shot down, and an estimated 42 — some of them doubtless dummies — were destroyed on the ground. Better results were obtained against shipping. Destroyer escort *CD-3*, a PC and five *Marus* were sunk; destroyer *Hamakaze*, ten others and three *Marus* damaged. The price of these strikes was ten aircraft, five pilots and eight crewmen.

On the same day, the B-29s based at Kunming attacked Kiirun Harbor and other shipping around Formosa, and 72 of the B-29s newly based in the Marianas dropped 122 tons of bombs over Japan, one third of them on the Musashino aircraft plant outside Tokyo. In Europe, the R.A.F. and the A.A.F. bombers had been within range of German aircraft factories since the beginning of the war and had pounded them intensively since 1943, forcing Goering to disperse his plants in small units or install them underground. Distance prevented the American air forces from doing this in Japan until 1945.

Third Fleet's direct support of the Lingayen operation ended with these 9 January strikes on Formosa. In one week, 3–9 January, TF 38 had flown a total of 3030 target or combat sorties and dropped 9110 bombs, aggregating approximately 700 tons, losing 86 planes, 40 of them operationally.[50] There is no question but that

[49] Report by Lt. J. J. Cote USNR made for this History, 1947.
[50] CTF 38 Reports.

these operations, combined with the all-out effort of the Army Air Force and the escort carriers, saved hundreds of American lives in the Lingayen landings.

Admiral Halsey now pulled off his long-desired incursion into the South China Sea; but before we come to that, we shall have to tell the story of the landings at Lingayen, and of progress ashore during the first week of the invasion.

CHAPTER IV

Preliminaries to the Lingayen Landings

15 December 1944–9 January 1945

1. *Staging and Rehearsal* [1]

MARSHALING the forces for an operation such as this is no mean task. Once the plans are issued, the wheels of the military machine start to turn in their appointed orbits, geared to surprise the enemy at H-hour on D-day. To arrest this machine when once set in motion is a problem that no military commander cares to face. This had to be done in the case of Mindoro and Lingayen because of the postponement of the one for ten days and the other for three weeks. Yet almost everyone was grateful for the extra time. While the hard-worked ships of TF 38 obtained rest and replenishment at Ulithi, men in the amphibious forces took things easy for a few days and then worked rehearsals into their revised schedule.

Rear Admiral Kiland,[2] who was to transport and land the 37th

---

[1] Com Seventh Fleet (Adm. Kinkaid) Action Report 3–27 Jan. 1945, 15 May 1945; CTF 79 (Vice Adm. Wilkinson) Action Report 5 Feb. 1945; CTF 78 (Vice Adm. Barbey) Action Report 12 Feb. 1945; CTG 77.2 (Vice Adm. Oldendorf) Action Report "Bombardment and Occupation of Lingayen Gulf 28 Jan. 1945"; CTG 77.3 (Rear Adm. Berkey) Action Report 1–31 Jan. 1945, 7 Feb. 1945; Sixth Army *Report of Luzon Campaign* Vols. I–IV. For the Japanese side, the Mac-Arthur *Historical Report* II is supplemented by the interrogation of Col. Matsumae, USSBS No. 249 (27 Oct. 1945); Capt. R. Inoguchi and Cdr. T. Nakajima *The Divine Wind* (Roger Pineau trans., 1958), and "Action Record of Kamikaze Special Attack Force," a full translation of Appendices A & B of *Divine Wind*.

[2] Ingolf N. Kiland, b. South Dakota 1895, Annapolis '17. Service in *Sterett*. Helped fit out *Elliott* and served as her exec. C.O. *Young* 1921; M.S., Columbia, 1923; served in *Oklahoma* 1924–27. In charge of Optical School at Wash. Navy

Infantry Division at Lingayen, proceeded to Bougainville to pick them up, together with General Griswold and XIV Corps Headquarters personnel, while Rear Admiral Royal[3] went to Cape Gloucester, staging point for the 40th Infantry Division. By 15 December all transports sent to Bougainville were loaded, and Vice Admiral Wilkinson had already arrived in *Mount Olympus* to embark General Griswold and staff. He had commanded the initial landings at Empress Augusta Bay in 1944, and General Griswold was the victor of the Battle of the Perimeter.[4] Seldom in the brotherhood of arms has there been a more congenial team than that of Wilkinson and Griswold, and it was a good omen that once more they were to work together.

Memorable was the little ceremony attendant on General Griswold's departure from Bougainville on 15 December. It was a typical South Pacific winter day, hot and bright. A few scattered clouds floated in the pale blue sky; a cool northwest breeze from the Bismarck Sea tempered the noontime heat. From the shade of coconut palms lining the beach, one could gaze out over Empress Augusta Bay, where "Tip" Merrill's cruisers had won a memorable victory, and over which troops and supplies had been brought in to the Torokina perimeter. Now the roadstead was crowded with transports, in which were already embarked the 37th Division and XIV Corps headquarters. LSTs with bows open and LCIs with ramps down lined the beach. The crews had knocked off work at midday; an atmosphere of somnolence lay thick over the scene. An occasional sailor walked slowly up the beach, contemplating the hundred-odd ships that lay at anchor and wishing that he too could

Yard to 1929. Gunnery officer on staff of Com Cruisers Scouting Force to 1932; Inspector of ordnance, Ford Instrument Co., to 1934. C.O. *Schenck,* navigator *Arkansas;* exec. Dahlgren Naval Proving Ground 1937–40. Exec. *Savannah;* C.O. *Crescent City* Dec. 1941–Nov. 1942. Comtransdiv 2 to Feb. 1943 (see Vol. VI 98–99). Duty with CNO to Oct. 1944. Com Group 7 Amphibious Force Pacific Fleet in Lingayen and Okinawa campaigns, and in supporting armies of occupation in China and Korea after the war. Com Training Command, Pacific, Dec. 1945–Aug. 1947. Assistant CNO for logistics to 1950; Comamphibpac 1950–53; Comfive to 1957, when retired as Vice Admiral.

[3] For brief biography, see Vol. XII p. 140*n.*
[4] See Vol. VI chap. xxv,

leave Bougainville with those lucky GIs who, he imagined, would be enjoying a Christmas liberty in Manila.

All days had been more or less alike on Bougainville since fighting ceased; but today, General Griswold's departure would bring a bit of pageantry to vary the afternoon routine. He was to board ship at 1400, and the commanders of the various units remaining on the island had decided to make it a memorable occasion, to honor a soldier whose popularity knew no barriers of rank or service. He had already paid a farewell visit to the cemetery, where lay many of his comrades in arms under white crosses and stars, and stood for a few minutes in silent prayer.

A small crowd gathered at the docks near the Torokina fighter strip, built by Seabees a year before at the cost of many lives, but now so little used that grass and weeds were thrusting up through holes in the Marston matting. An honor guard, consisting of a company of soldiers from the Americal Division, came down the dusty road in khaki battle dress and drew up at attention in line of platoons. A platoon of sailors in faded blue dungarees and white hats took station alongside the soldiers. A small Army band was there, too. Soon Admiral Wilkinson's barge drew up to the pier. Under the brilliant sunlight, it seemed like a messenger from the peacetime world of naval reviews and regattas. The fresh gray paint, the shining brightwork, the flaked and flemished lines, the new ensign fluttering from the stern staff, the crew of smart, lanky sailors in clean, well-pressed uniforms with squared white hats, made the Admiral's barge a symbol of naval smartness and efficiency.

Forty or fifty officers were lined up along the pier to shake the departing General's hand. Prominent among them were Lieutenant General Savige of the Australian Army, who had relieved General Griswold; Major General Ralph Mitchell USMC, commander of the North Solomons Air Force; Commodore "Mike" Moran, commander of the motor torpedo boats; Commander Earle H. Kincaid of the "Bougainville Navy."

A cloud of dust heralded the command jeep rolling down the

road built by Seabees. As the General alighted from this appropriate chariot, the platoons of soldiers and sailors came to attention and the band struck up a well-known but somewhat inappropriate tune which celebrated Casey's famous waltz with a strawberry blonde. General Griswold briefly inspected each rank of soldiers and sailors and then, relaxing, strolled down to the pier between a double file of officers, shaking hands with every one and pausing long enough to give a word of farewell. While "the band played on," he stepped on board the Admiral's barge. The coxswain struck two bells, and as the boat pulled away from the pier heading toward *Mount Olympus*, a sailor broke a major general's flag — two white stars on a scarlet field — from the jackstaff. The music ceased and officers and men broke ranks. Their leader had gone. That brilliant chapter in American military history, which opened at Guadalcanal in early August 1942, was now a closed book.

Already, on 15 June, Admiral Halsey had bade farewell to the South Pacific, to penetrate Japanese home waters with Third Fleet. Similar rites were being enacted at many other places in the Pacific as the tide of Japanese empire ebbed. For many who took part, they produced a strange but deep emotion. There was a peculiar feeling about leaving one of these primitive islands where friends and comrades had died. You might be sick of the magnificent scenery, hate the steaming climate, and loathe the squawks of the white cockatoos; but something of you had been left behind, irrevocably; and you hated to think of the jungle taking over roads and airstrips, encampments and buildings, which had cost so much effort and so many lives. As Virgil makes Aeneas deplore the city he had left and lost forever: *iam seges est ubi Troia fuit* — "now corn grows where Troy was."

Mount Olympus, with Admiral Kiland's amphibious group in company, sailed to Huon Gulf, where Admiral Royal's group, carrying the 40th Infantry Division, joined. On a beach between Lae and Salamaua, at the foot of the Markham River Valley, Admiral Wilkinson's TF 79 and General Griswold's XIV Corps conducted a rehearsal for the Lingayen landing. They arrived at Seeadler Harbor, their final stop, on 21 December.

Admiral Barbey's TF 78 (the San Fabian Attack Force) had also benefited by postponement of the Lingayen landing. It embarked General Swift's I Corps (6th and 43rd Infantry Division) at Sansapor and Aitape. As neither place had a harbor — only an open roadstead — loading was restricted to morning hours when the sea was comparatively calm, and even on some mornings the surf rose too high for loading. Thus, two weeks were required to embark two infantry divisions and their assault equipment in 44 transport types and 137 LSTs. Each division held a rehearsal, but no supplies or equipment were unloaded since there was no time for reloading. Very seldom in the Southwest Pacific was the Army able to conduct a proper dress rehearsal as had been done in England before OVERLORD and in North Africa before the invasion of Sicily. As a result, off-loading at the target area and handling supplies over the beaches continued to be a problem until the end of the war. But, as we shall see, it was very well done at Lingayen.

The San Fabian Attack Force kept Christmas at their New Guinea rehearsal areas and were well under way toward Luzon before the end of 1944.

Of Rear Admiral Conolly's Luzon Attack Force Reserve, the 25th Infantry Division, loaded at Nouméa and held rehearsals near Tetere on Guadalcanal. After spending Christmas Eve in Purvis Bay, with its convenient Ironbottom Bay club, the ships weighed anchor Christmas afternoon and shaped a course for Manus. The 158th RCT embarked at Noemfoor, New Guinea, rehearsed on 2 January 1945 at Japen Island, Geelvink Bay, and refueled at Mios Woendi. Other elements of the Sixth Army were embarked at Leyte and at six different points between the New Guinea bird's tail and his head — Milne Bay, Oro Bay, Finschhafen, Lae, Hollandia, Biak and Noemfoor. Thus, the troops for the Lingayen landing were lifted from sixteen different bases in the South and Southwest Pacific, all but one of which — Nouméa — the Allies had wrested from the Japanese.

2. *Oldendorf's Eventful Passage, 2–6 January*

As in the assault on Leyte, Admiral Oldendorf in battleship *California* took charge of all operations en route to Lingayen Gulf and until Admiral Kinkaid arrived with the amphibious forces. He commanded a fleet of 164 ships: four of the six battleships which had taken part in the Battle of Surigao Strait, together with *Colorado* and *New Mexico*, 6 cruisers and 19 destroyers, an escort carrier group of 12 CVE, 14 destroyers and 6 destroyer escorts, a minesweeping and hydrographic group of 72 miscellaneous ships, over half of them motor minesweepers; 10 destroyer transports carrying the underwater demolition teams; 2 fleet tugs, a seaplane tender and 11 LCI gunboats.[5] These made rendezvous at Leyte Gulf on or shortly after New Year's Day, to form cruising disposition for the final passage.

Commander Loud's Minesweeping and Hydrographic Group and the salvage and LCI units sortied from Leyte Gulf on 2 January because of their slow speed. That afternoon three Sallys dropped bombs which missed, but the convoy's position was evidently reported, because at 0728 January 3 a Val, one of two which had taken off from Sarangani, made a suicide dive on oiler *Cowanesque*. Part of the Val landed on her deck, killing two men, but the material damage was negligible. This crash was the first in a series which made the kamikaze raids of the past two and a half months seem just a warming-up.

The Japanese still had plenty of planes. Their aircraft factories, undisturbed as yet by bombing, as the German works had been, largely replaced the heavy losses in the Leyte campaign.[6] But losses of aviators were not so easily overcome — since pilot training

[5] For complete composition of forces see Appendix I.

[6] Figures vary. USSBS *Japanese Air Power* p. 29 states that the peak production month was Sept. 1944 with output of nearly 2000 planes and by Jan. 1945 it was down to 1383; it estimates that total aircraft on hand on July 1944 was 5500 planes of all types. But a list furnished by Capt. T. Ohmae, prepared by Japanese Dept. of Commerce and Industry, states that peak production month was June 1944 with 2857 planes.

lagged far behind aircraft production, and in the final analysis it is "capacity in the cockpit" that counts. The main reason why the Japanese organized this Kamikaze Corps was the growing inability of their pilots to get through our fighter plane protection and hit ships with conventional bombs and torpedoes. Unable to create "cockpit capacity" by short cuts, Japan employed quantities of planes by adopting the kamikaze technique, which required more guts than training.

At the same time the Japanese air forces continued conventional bombing on land targets. As late as 4 January 1945 one Japanese bomber broke up a squadron of Navy Venturas parked at Tacloban, Leyte, completely demolishing eleven aircraft.[7]

Admiral Oldendorf's main force passed through Surigao Strait into the Sulu Sea, where it formed two groups around a nucleus of escort carriers. These furnished a C.A.P. of 40 fighter planes, augmented by as many Army planes as could be maintained; at one time the total amounted to 68 aircraft. Fighter direction for the van was in escort carrier *Makin Island,* and for the rear in *Natoma Bay.* Yet this apparently air-tight defensive formation failed to stop all suicide attacks, or even at times to give adequate warning. One kamikaze was splashed 500 yards astern of *Makin Island* at 1700 January 3. On that day, and the next two, between 15 and 20 enemy planes were destroyed near the formation. From Japanese sources, however, we learn that the C.A.P. prevented the situation from being far worse. About 120 Japanese army planes from Clark and as many or more from Nichols and other Luzon airfields were committed against the expeditionary force during the first week of January. "In view of the very heavy Allied fighter cover," said Colonel Matsumae, senior staff officer of the Fourth Air Army, "our planes could not penetrate to the convoy and had to go around, either to the north over Cape Bolinao or to the south of Corregidor, and attack from the west."

At 1712 January 4, when the formation was debouching from

[7] Letter of ARM2c Jack W. Martin to Y1c Don R. Martin of my staff, Dec. 1945.

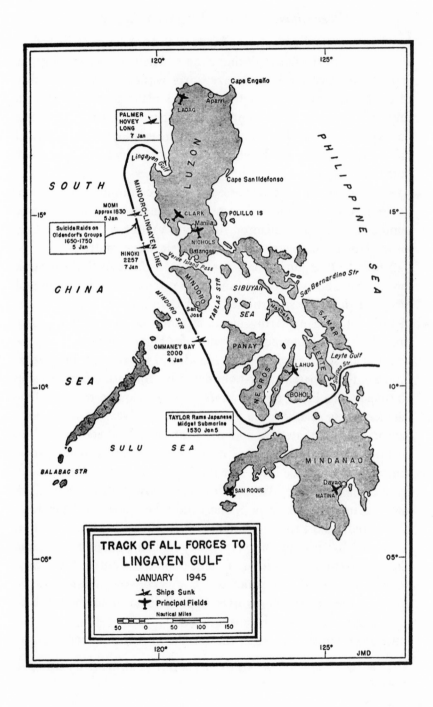

TRACK OF ALL FORCES TO
LINGAYEN GULF

JANUARY 1945

Ships Sunk
Principal Fields

Nautical Miles

50   0   50   100   150

Sulu Sea by Apo East Pass, escort carrier *Ommaney Bay* was struck a fatal blow by a plane that seemed to drop plumb out of the sky; 17 lookouts and the most modern radar equipment failed to pick up this twin-engined bomber as it dove, and *New Mexico* was the only ship to open fire on it.[8] The carrier's first warning that she was the intended victim came from the plane's strafing, a split second before it side-swiped her island and crashed the flight deck. One bomb penetrated to the hangar deck and exploded, another passed through to the second deck and started an oil fire in the forward engine room, producing volumes of heavy smoke which soon permeated the ship. With no pressure on the fire-fighting mains, the conflagration got out of hand. All efforts of destroyers to get near enough to apply hoses were frustrated by intense heat, heavy smoke and exploding ammunition. *Ommaney Bay* gradually lost headway. Beginning at about 1745 the most seriously wounded men were strapped into cots, covered with kapok life jackets and lowered into the water, with two able swimmers to take care of each float. Captain Young ordered Abandon Ship at 1750 and himself went over the side at 1812. Six minutes later the torpedo warheads exploded in the hangar deck aft, the resulting debris killing two members of the crew of nearby destroyer escort *Eichenberger*, which was recovering survivors. Another kamikaze, coming in shortly after, missed escort carrier *Lunga Point* by 50 yards. A torpedo by destroyer *Burns*, as ordered by Admiral Oldendorf, sank the burning and exploding *Ommaney Bay*. She lost 93 killed and missing and 65 wounded; seven survivors were later killed by kamikazes on the ships in which they were embarked.

Next day, 5 January, when Oldendorf's ships (which had now overtaken the minesweeping group) were steaming within 150 miles of the Japanese airfields on Luzon, they were again spotted by search planes. Their reports convinced the Japanese high command that Lingayen was the American destination. As the two re-

[8] This must be the attack mentioned in Japanese Monograph No. 12 p. 117. The plane had taken off from Sarangani at 1705, according to *The Divine Wind* p. 218 — which, however, gives the wrong date. This plane surprised the CVE, because the nearness of the Cuyo Islands and Panay blacked out her radar.

cently developed American airfields on Mindoro were neutralized by wet weather, the expeditionary force had to depend on its own efforts for defense. At 0758 C.A.P. intercepted 15 to 20 enemy planes about 35 miles from the formation, shot nine down and turned the others back. At noon, a raid of undetermined size — probably the 15 kamikazes with 2 escorts which left Mabalacat at 1125 — was intercepted and turned away about 45 miles from the ships.

About 1430 a patrolling airplane sighted two Japanese 1260-ton destroyers, *Momi* and *Hinoki,* which were trying to get from Manila to Formosa. The aviators passed the word to the nearest squadron commander, Loud of the minesweepers, who sent destroyer *Bennion* (Commander R. H. Holmes), the heaviest ship in his group, with Australian sloop *Warrego* and frigate *Gascoyne,* to intercept; *Bennion,* as a fighter-director ship, was able to use two planes of C.A.P. as air spot. At 1550 she sighted the ships on the horizon, about twelve miles away. They headed south at top speed, about 27 knots. *Bennion,* leaving her Australian consorts astern, bent on 30 to 32 knots in pursuit. After a stern chase for more than an hour she opened fire at a range of 18,200 yards; the Japanese ships made smoke and increased speed. *Bennion* worked the range down to 14,000 yards, turned broadside and fired full salvos. Neither side managed to hit the other, at least not seriously, and *Bennion* had to break off at 1640 to rejoin the minesweepers, which reported a heavy air attack coming in. The chase was then taken up by 19 Wildcats and 16 torpedo bombers from the escort carriers. It took them over an hour to locate their quarry, but they got a torpedo into *Momi* which sank her. *Hinoki* made good her escape to Manila, again sortied, ran afoul of Admiral Barbey's force and got herself sunk on the 7th.[9]

The last and heaviest air attack of 5 January came in on "Oley's" group at 1650 when it was about a hundred miles off Corregidor. Sixteen kamikazes with four escorts, which took off from Mabala-

[9] *The Story of the Bennion* (offset book pub. Nov. 1947). It was formerly assumed that these two vessels belong to the Mindoro Penetration Unit, but they did not.

cat at 1557, broke through C.A.P. Only two of them returned to base, but their sacrifice produced crashes on two heavy cruisers, an escort carrier and a destroyer escort, besides near-misses on several other ships.

Heavy cruiser *Louisville,* now flagship of Rear Admiral Chandler, had been known as a lucky ship since her commissioning in 1931. Her crew called her "Lady Lou" or "Man of War," since her mascot was a picture of the famous Kentucky stallion of that name. But her luck began to run out. A single-engined kamikaze dove on her from ahead, crashed and badly damaged the forward face of No. 2 turret. Fires broke out immediately but were quickly brought under control. One man was killed and 59 wounded, and Captain Hicks was badly burned; but *Louisville* carried on. A second kamikaze crashed H.M.A.S. *Australia* with a bomb whose explosion killed 25 men and wounded 30, but inflicted slight material damage. H.M.A.S. *Arunta* was near-missed so close as to be stopped dead, and to lose two men killed. Escort carrier *Savo Island* escaped, owing to expert handling by Captain Ekstrom. He promptly applied hard right rudder, directed the 24-inch searchlight full at the plane's cockpit during the last 1500 feet of its dive, and his antiaircraft gunners scored many hits during the plane's final approach. It splashed after its wing had clipped the carrier's radar antenna.

Manila Bay was not so fortunate. Two Zekes came in about 50 to 100 feet above the water at high speed, weaving and strafing. At a distance of about a thousand yards from the ship they pulled into sharp, climbing turns, turned over on their backs, then straightened out and dove from an altitude of about 800 feet. The first hit the carrier's flight deck at the base of the island structure, and the bomb penetrated, exploding in the radar transmitter room and the upper part of the hangar. This messed things up, but only two planes caught fire and quick work by damage control handled them in short order. The second plane splashed about 30 feet from the ship. *Manila Bay* lost 22 dead or missing and had 56 wounded, but she was ready for limited air operations twenty-four hours after the hit, completed repairs under way, and by S-day (9 January) she was able to conduct a "fairly full schedule."

Destroyer escorts *Goss* (Lieutenant Commander C. S. Kirkpatrick USNR), *Stafford* (Lieutenant Commander V. H. Craig USNR) and *Ulvert M. Moore* (Lieutenant Commander F. D. Roosevelt, Jr. USNR) occupied adjacent stations, screening escort carrier *Tulagi*, when the kamikaze attack reached the formation. Each shot down one plane, but a third got through and crashed *Stafford*. A hole 12 by 16 feet was opened in her starboard side, and the No. 2 fire and engine rooms were flooded. She lost two dead and twelve wounded. Destroyers, a DE and tug *Quapaw* stood by her, and they with *Stafford* had to "steam and stumble around off the west coast of Luzon" for five days until they could join a convoy returning to Leyte, beating off sundry enemy air attacks and having hairbreadth escapes from being taken for Japanese by friendly ships and planes.[10]

Another kamikaze headed for destroyer *Helm* in the screen. It clipped off her aftermast, smashed a searchlight and tumbled into the water, inflicting slight wounds on six men.

At 1715, Commander Loud's minesweeping group came under attack and three kamikazes splashed close aboard three of the sweepers, not damaging them. A fourth hit *LCI(G)*–70, killing 2 men, seriously wounding 6, and knocking 8 more overboard. The radar screens did not justify an All Clear until 1840.

Altogether, 5 January was a lively day for the Lingayen-bound task groups. And snoopers were over them at intervals during the night, acquiring useful data for the kamikazes' big day, the 6th.

3. *"One Helluva Day" in Lingayen Gulf, 6 January* [11]

By 0345 January 6, Oldendorf's and Loud's task groups were abreast of Cape Bolinao, which sticks out from Luzon like the

---

[10] *Stafford* Action Report 27 Jan. 1945; letter of her exec., Lt. Carl H. Williams, 7 Dec. 1958.
[11] See Appendix IV for list of ships hit and casualties.

thumb of a mitten. They then broke up into small groups to execute the op plan. Escort carriers under Admiral Durgin operated in a designated area northwest of Lingayen Gulf; fire support groups proceeded to San Fernando Point and off Santiago Island to prepare for their scheduled bombardments. Captain W. L. Freseman's destroyers, *Barton, Walke, Radford* and *Leutze,* steamed ahead in order to render support to Commander Loud against coastal batteries that might interfere with the slow-moving sweepers. Thus, by sunrise 6 January (S-day minus 3), four vitally important groups of ships had arrived at Lingayen Gulf, somewhat banged up but all present and full of fight — excepting *Ommaney Bay,* 200 fathoms deep in the Sulu Sea.

Just as "Oley" began his preliminary bombardment and minesweeping, the first air attack began, by about ten enemy planes. C.A.P. shot down five with a loss of one, and no ships were damaged. A good omen, not fulfilled; before noon, kamikaze activity reached a new high. Between 1122 and 1143 they began to attack in force. One splashed close aboard destroyer *Richard P. Leary,* after a wing had brushed the shields of two 5-inch guns. At noon, when battleship *New Mexico* — flag and guide of the San Fabian Fire Support, carrying important passengers — was bombarding the shore around San Fernando, she was crashed on the port wing of her navigating bridge by a Japanese plane already in flames. Rear Admiral Weyler and the Royal Navy observer, Admiral Sir Bruce Fraser, who were on the starboard side, were not hurt. Lieutenant General Herbert Lumsden (Winston Churchill's personal liaison officer at General MacArthur's headquarters); Captain R. W. Fleming the battleship's commanding officer, his communications officer, an aide to General Lumsden, and *Time Magazine* correspondent William Chickering, all on the port wing of the bridge, were instantly killed. There were 25 other fatalities and 87 men wounded. Damage to the ship's superstructure was serious but she continued shooting.

Destroyer *Walke,* attacked by four planes in rapid succession at noontime, knocked down two which splashed in flames close aboard, but a third crashed the port side of her bridge, fatally wounding her thirty-three-year-old, Philippine-born captain, Commander George F. Davis. Being in the path of the plane when it crashed, Davis was drenched with gasoline and for a moment burned like a living torch. The sailors near him smothered the flames and he conned his ship, exhorted officers and men to save her; and, still on his feet, saw his guns in local control destroy a fourth kamikaze. When the fires were under control and the safety of his ship assured, he consented to be carried below. But his burns were too terrible to be borne, and a few hours later he died.

A plane that crashed destroyer *Allen M. Sumner* killed 14 men and injured 29, and damaged her deckhouse and torpedo mounts, sheering off several torpedo warheads en route. Her after magazine flooded, and was not cleared for three days.

A few minutes after noon, two Zekes, flying about 25 feet above the surface, attacked the minesweeping group. As one headed for *Long* (Lieutenant Stanley Caplan USNR), she bent on 25 knots and commenced firing all guns which could be brought to bear. At 1215 the Zeke crashed her port side above the waterline, starting extensive fires. She was abandoned, owing to a misunderstanding of the skipper's permission given to men trapped on the fo'c'sle to leave. Tug *Apache* put the fires out, but before a salvage party could be collected, at 1730, another enemy plane crashed *Long* and broke her back. The C.O. and salvage party returned on board next day, but she capsized and sank. *Hovey* rescued all her crew, of whom 35 were wounded by burns and one died. Destroyer transport *Brooks* of the same group was hit at 1252 January 6, losing 3 killed and 11 wounded in the crash. Destroyer H.M.A.S. *Warramunga* closed, got her fires out in half an hour, and towed her clear of the gulf.

This was a gruesome day for all hands in Lingayen Gulf, and it might have been worse but for Admiral McCain's fast carrier planes roaming over the Luzon airfields. On the previous day General MacArthur had requested Admiral Halsey to send aircraft across the dividing line between his and General Kenney's areas of responsibility, and Commander Third Fleet was only too happy to oblige. Task Force 38 fueled that day, and by dawn 6 January had reached launching position, 120 miles southeast of Cape Engaño. Targets were assigned to all three task groups. Unfortunately weather prevented their spreading a "B.B.B." over Clark and Angeles airfields, and heavy overcast protected the fields of northern Luzon from attack. Only 14 planes were destroyed in the air and 18 on the ground, and the cost for that to TF 38 was 17 aircraft.[12] Photographs taken near the end of the day indicated 237 enemy planes operational, the greatest concentration being well dispersed and camouflaged in the vicinity of Clark Field. At Admiral Kinkaid's urgent request, Halsey decided to devote 7 January to the same business.

Back in Lingayen Gulf, minesweeping proceeded on schedule 6 January, except for the lethal hit on *Long*. The two fire support groups bombarded Santiago Island, Cape Bolinao and the San Fernando area in order to knock out "Japanese coastal batteries," which were mostly not there. At 1519 Admiral Oldendorf directed both his groups to thrust into the Gulf to support minecraft and to bombard targets of opportunity. The rigging of paravanes delayed the start, and after penetrating the Gulf about twenty miles, and firing a few shots at the railroad that runs along the eastern shore, this mission had to be called off owing to another serious kamikaze attack.

At 1720 five kamikazes with one fighter escort from Mabalacat caught up with this fire support column, then steaming at the low speed of 5 knots to commence night retirement. Approaching from astern, two made for destroyer *Newcomb*, flagship of Captain Smoot. The 20-mm crew on her fantail splashed one, but the other whizzed past at deck level, then banked left and crashed battleship *California* at the base of her mainmast; the fuselage hit the deck between the mast and No. 4 director. At the same time *California* was sprayed by shell fragments from a nearby destroyer that was trying to shoot down the plane; her casualties from both sources, mainly

[12] CTF 38 (Vice Adm. McCain) Action Report 30 Oct. 1944–26 Jan. 1945.

enemy, were 45 killed and 151 wounded. *Newcomb* also received damage from "friendly" 40-mm bullets and 5-inch shell fragments, losing 2 killed and 15 wounded.

Admiral Oldendorf felt obliged to issue a stern warning: —

"A day which was characterized by brilliant performance on the part of many ships was seriously marred by indiscriminate, promiscuous and uncontrolled shooting. Ammunition was wasted, death and injury to shipmates inflicted, and material damage caused to our ships. All hands are enjoined to make certain that their guns are fired at the enemy and not at their shipmates."

Light cruiser *Columbia*, "the Gem of the Ocean" as her crew called her,[18] that afternoon became the target of two kamikazes. The first, at 1424, passed between her masts, sprayed her deck with gasoline which providentially did not ignite, and splashed close aboard. The second, three hours later, crashed her main deck on port side turret No. 4 with tremendous force. Plane, pilot and engine penetrated the deck and the bomb went through two more decks before exploding. Several fires blazed up, and all power including steering control was lost aft; but prompt flooding of the magazines for turrets Nos. 3 and 4 saved the ship from a magazine explosion. Nine compartments were flooded, causing her to settle 5 feet by the stern. By 1800 all fires were out, and at 1828 "the Gem's" forward 20-mm gunners shot the tail off a plane trying to crash H.M.A.S. *Australia*. Her damage control did a wonderful job; by 2027 steering control was regained aft, and despite her flooded compartments and loss of two main battery turrets, *Columbia* completed fire support assignments with her two remaining turrets. Casualties were 13 killed and 44 wounded.

H.M.A.S. *Australia* received a crash on her starboard side forward at 1734, adding another 14 killed and 26 wounded to her already high casualties of the previous day. One gun mount, too, was

---

[18] *Battle Record and History of U.S.S. Columbia 1942–1945* (Baltimore: Horn-Shafer Co., n.d.), lent to me by Lieut. Robeson Peters USNR, is one of the best ship's histories of the war. *Man of War. Log of the U.S. Heavy Cruiser Louisville* (Phila.: Dunlap Printing Co., 1946) is another excellent one.

knocked out, but, like her neighbor "the Gem," she kept fighting.

Louisville, which had also been crashed the day before, now took another and more serious blow. The kamikaze hit her at 1730 on the starboard side abreast the bridge structure, tearing apart the bridge, sky control and a 40-mm mount. Rear Admiral Theodore E. Chandler, as he stood on flag bridge, was frightfully burned by the flaming gasoline. He helped handle a fire hose and took his turn with the enlisted men for first aid; but as the flames had scorched his lungs all efforts to save him failed, and next day he died. Thirty-one shipmates went with him, and 56 more were wounded; but for an ample supply of blood plasma most of those, too, would have died. "Lady Lou" was so extensively damaged that for the first time in her life — this was her thirteenth birthday — she was unable to complete her assignment. Admiral Oldendorf's flagship *California* took over her bombardment and fire support duties on D-day, and she departed 10 January with a returning convoy.

Destroyer *O'Brien* (Commander W. W. Outerbridge) was covering a group of minesweepers at 1427, passing *Barton* (Commander E. B. Dexter) on opposite courses close aboard, when two Zekes dove almost vertically out of a cloud. One missed both ships, splashing about ten feet ahead of *Barton;* but a second crashed *O'Brien* on her fantail, ripping off a section of her topside and flooding two compartments, yet inflicting neither casualties nor damage to her power plant. *Barton*, the flagship of Captain W. L. Freseman (Comdesron 60), then relieved *O'Brien* and escorted the minecraft into the Gulf. Her conduct, wrote Commander Outerbridge, "was to me most impressive and inspiring. Her task was the most hazardous I have ever seen a vessel undertake." No more so, however, than those of the minecraft themselves, who bore the brunt of the attack this day, owing to their distance from supporting ships. Destroyer minesweeper *Southard* (Lieutenant Commander J. E. Brennan USNR) was crashed on port side of No. 2 fire room at main deck level at 1732, rupturing main and auxiliary steam lines and starting a fire. Damage control got that out inside half an hour. *Breeze* towed her clear of the Gulf, where, lying-to twelve miles off San Fernando Point, her crew effected repairs during the night, and by the end of morning watch had her under way, ready for another day's work. Six men only were wounded. She brought the number of ships sunk or damaged by the kamikazes between 3 and 6 January up to 25, of which three suffered two or more attacks.[14]

The normal C.A.P. over this bombardment force on 6 January consisted of 24 planes from Rear Admiral Durgin's escort carrier group then operating off the Gulf, the rest being required for support missions. They flew 126 sorties over the beaches. Sailors in the Gulf felt that they should have had more plane protection; but, as Durgin observed, "Fighters must intercept at a distance to prevent ships from getting hit." Mountains so blanked the ships' radar that there was no time after detection to vector C.A.P. into an intercept position. Durgin complained that his planes were detained long after they were scheduled to return to their carriers, where flight schedules were so tight that unexpected delays fouled up launching and recovery. And in the interceptions, our Wildcat (FM-2) showed up inferior to the improved Japanese Zeke, not only in speed and maneuver, but in climbing ability at altitudes above 5000 feet; and we had not enough Wildcats. Admiral Oldendorf reported, "Too much is expected of these escort carriers. They are gamely and courageously led and can be counted on for the last measure of devotion"; but, if required to function every day as they did on 6 January, they will deteriorate.

Not only Admiral Oldendorf, but all responsible officers in the forces at Lingayen, were seriously alarmed when they contemplated the results of this 6th day of January, three days before the landings. The score of one ship sunk and eleven damaged, with a rear admiral USN, a lieutenant general of the British Army, and some hundreds of others killed, was the worst blow to the United States Navy since the Battle of Tassafaronga on 30 November 1942. It was the more difficult to bear because the recent naval victory at Leyte Gulf had made men believe that Japan was licked. In

[14] See Appendix IV.

the kamikazes she had sprung a tactical surprise that might prolong the war another year. But Admiral Oldendorf never seriously considered withdrawal. He realized that to retire would crown the efforts of the suicide plane with success. In a message to Admiral Kinkaid at 2110 he pointed out that if the transports on S-day received similar treatment the troops might be slaughtered before they could land. He urged that the A.A.F. and TF 38 be asked to do their best to interdict Luzon airfields, that Third Fleet proceed into the South China Sea in order to be in a better position to protect the Lingayen convoys, and that existing plans be reconsidered. Admiral Kinkaid understood what "Oley" meant, was equally concerned about the situation, and did everything asked, except for urging Admiral Halsey to enter the South China Sea.

Kamikaze aviators were inspired by their "Song of the Warrior": —

> In serving on the seas, be a corpse saturated with water.
> In serving on land, be a corpse covered with weeds.
> In serving the sky, be a corpse that challenges the clouds.
> Let us all die close by the side of our sovereign.[15]

As the sun set over the South China Sea on 6 January these corpses could point with ghostly pride to their most effective kamikaze attack up to that time, and the most effective of the war in relation to the number of planes involved — 28 kamikazes and 15 fighter escorts.[16] Off Okinawa the Navy would be faced with an even more intensive suicide effort, but by that time the cream of the kamikaze crop had destroyed itself and the Allied Navies had additional means of protection.

4. Turn for the Better, 7–8 January

Inside Lingayen Gulf the brightly moonlit night of 6–7 January was uneventful until about 0430, when the minesweepers caught it.

[15] *O.N.I. Weekly* III 3998 (13 Dec. 1944).
[16] *The Divine Wind* pp. 219–20. But MacArthur *Historical Report* II 432 says that 58 kamikazes and 17 escorts were involved.

Chandler picked up a couple of low-flying planes on her radar, and sighted them fitfully in the moonlight. Two or three of them closed her and *Hovey*. *Chandler* opened fire; one plane burst into flames and splashed, but not before dropping a torpedo which hit *Hovey* and sent her to the bottom of the Gulf within three minutes. *Chandler* stood by and recovered 229 officers and men, including survivors from the previously stricken *Brooks* and *Long;* but 22 of *Hovey's* complement and 24 of the survivors were lost.

At 0655, thirty-five minutes before sunrise, Admiral Oldendorf formed his bombardment and fire support ships into two columns. An hour later they entered Lingayen Gulf, "paravanes streaming," which in modern warfare corresponds to the "colors flying and trumpets sounding" of Elizabethan days. Commander Loud had reported the main channel to be well swept, but continued sweeping all day and found ten more mines.[17]

Naval bombardment both by the San Fabian and the Lingayen Groups opened at 1030 January 7. That afternoon, under cover of the bombardment, six underwater demolition teams, commanded by Lieutenant Commander Owen B. Murphy USNR of *Humphreys,* began to go ashore in specially equipped landing craft from the APDs.[18] They worked over the five beaches selected for the landing, compiling information on surf and other conditions. Only one beach put up machine-gun and rifle fire, and that was quickly smothered by the fire support ships. No underwater or other obstacles, and but one mine, were found. Heavy surf was reported on beaches adjacent to the town of Lingayen, which did not enjoy the protection from the easterly monsoon that the San Fabian beaches had from the Caraballo Mountains.

Since sunrise it had been a comparatively easy day for all hands and the few enemy planes that appeared were shot down before

[17] Adm. Kinkaid Action Report has a story of Filipinos with *bancas,* who, having recovered in Lingayen Gulf some 350 mines, took them apart to provide themselves with explosives. Nobody now believes this yarn, which was probably told to the Admiral in order to explain the faulty Intelligence estimate of five mine fields in the Gulf.

[18] Detailed accounts of earlier UDT operations will be found in Volumes VIII and XI of this History.

doing any damage. But at 1835, when the fire support ships were heading out of the Gulf for night retirement, death suddenly came out of the air to minesweeper *Palmer*. The Japanese seem to have picked on minecraft because they were usually isolated and had no good antiaircraft support. A Japanese plane, a Dinah, dropped two bombs which hit *Palmer's* port side amidships near the waterline, then turned as if to attack another ship and splashed. The ship flooded abaft her forward engine room, the after engine room bulkhead gave way and she sank within six minutes. *Breeze* and *Hopkins* rescued 123 officers and men from the water but *Palmer* lost 28 killed or missing and 38 wounded.

The events of 8 January, S-day minus one, opened with four enemy snoopers approaching the escort carrier disposition during the mid-watch. Two were shot down by Army land-based night fighters and the rest retired. Just before sunrise, the first kamikaze raid of the day came in and concentrated on plucky, twice-hit *Australia*. Lookouts in *California* reported five planes going for the Australian heavy cruiser at 0720. The leading one was seen to splash only 20 yards from the ship — it actually skidded into her side; the other four were overzealous Wildcats, from the escort carriers' C.A.P., chasing him in. Unfortunately their friendly character was not recognized and one, hit by antiaircraft fire, had its hydraulic system punctured, which made its landing wheels drop, giving it the appearance of a "pants-down" Japanese Val, a type favored by the kamikaze because it was obsolete. The wounded pilot bailed out and was picked up by a destroyer. The other three Wildcats, although shot up, managed to return to their carriers.

That incident was barely over when a second kamikaze went for *Australia*. It was shot down but skidded into her side below the bridge, where the bomb went off, blowing a hole 8 by 14 feet and flooding two compartments. There were no casualties. After this fourth suicide attack on *Australia*, Admiral Oldendorf offered to relieve her of further duties that day, but the sailors from "down under" would have none of that, and carried out the rest of their assignment after effecting temporary repairs.

At 0800, a few minutes after the shore bombardment began, the pilot of *Colorado's* spotting plane reported a procession of fifty to 100 people near the beach on the southern shore of the Gulf, carrying American and Philippine flags. Admiral Oldendorf directed the battleships not to fire into this area and sent one of *California's* planes to drop leaflets advising all friendly people to clear out. After allowing a reasonable time for them to comply, bombardment was resumed.

Admiral Oldendorf later observed that the new Japanese tactics of withdrawal from beach areas made much of his bombardment unnecessary. His observation was entirely correct. His ships sacrificially served the invasion by acting as bait for the kamikazes, which expended themselves before S-day; but the bombardment itself was not needed. Lieutenant Colonel Russell W. Volckmann, leader of the guerrillas in Northern Luzon, recovered some documents from a crashed Japanese plane which gave away General Yamashita's plan to concentrate his defense in the mountains. When, in late December, Colonel Volckmann received instructions from General MacArthur indicating that invasion was imminent, he radioed to MacArthur, "There will be no, repeat no, opposition on the beaches," [19] hoping to prevent a pre-landing bombardment and save lives. But nobody in Southwest Pacific staff appears to have given this any attention. The Navy never got the word; it expected to have to deal with heavy coastal defense guns, double-purpose and antiaircraft batteries. Actually the only batteries along Lingayen Gulf were two 300-mm howitzers, two batteries of 150-mm howitzers and about a dozen other guns of that caliber or smaller. And most of these were on the eastern shore.[20]

After the day's bombardment and during the night of 8–9 January, preceding S-day, Admiral Oldendorf maneuvered near the mouth of the Gulf, awaiting the arrival of the attack forces under

[19] R. W. Volckmann *We Remained* (1954) pp. 181–82. Sixth Army G-2 Report says that more than 50 guerrilla radio stations were in contact with GHQ SW Pac, which would seem to have been enough for checking.
[20] Jap. Monograph No. 4 p. 15.

Admirals Kinkaid, Wilkinson and Barbey. Prospects for a successful landing were favorable, with the beach area evacuated by the enemy, no underwater obstacles or mines, and a friendly reception committee ashore. The kamikazes had shot their bolt — but nobody in the expeditionary force knew that.

5. *Attack Forces Move Up, 2–9 January*

Passage of the assault forces to Lingayen was accomplished in much the same manner as the one to Leyte in October. Admiral Barbey's two San Fabian Attack Force transport groups, his own for Beach White and Admiral Fechteler's for Beach Blue, rendezvoused at sea near the Palaus on 3 January, with two escort carriers and the 148 vessels of Admiral Wilkinson's two tractor groups which had departed Manus on 27 December. The combined force then steamed in three groups with an interval of about 14 miles between, together with some tankers destined for Mindoro. All arrived during the afternoon of 4 January at Leyte Gulf, picked up additional amphibious craft which had been loaded there, and were joined by Admiral Berkey's Close Covering Group (light cruisers *Boise, Phoenix, Montpelier, Denver* and eight destroyers), with General MacArthur and staff embarked in *Boise*. The formation now stretched over 40 miles of ocean. It passed through Surigao Strait on the night of 4–5 January and followed the same route employed by Admiral Oldendorf a few days earlier.

At 1509 January 5, when passing tiny Apo Island, between Negros and Siquijor, *Boise* received this message from *Phoenix:* — "Torpedoes on course south, headed toward you." The intended victim maneuvered radically at high speed and avoided the torpedoes, which came from a midget submarine. One midget broached to be bombed by a plane of the antisubmarine patrol and rammed, depth-charged and sunk by destroyer *Taylor;* the other escaped. That night a group of about 15 enemy planes passed over the formation, but fire was withheld and the ships escaped notice. And on

5–6 January the Japanese were too busy trying to annihilate Admiral Oldendorf's group to bother the amphibious forces.

Shortly before daybreak on the 7th, when the attack forces were passing through Mindoro Strait, a bomb splashed on *Boise's* quarter, and as day broke a Nick approached this cruiser — which had General MacArthur on board — but was driven off. At 0739 oiler *Suamico* joined Berkey's group to fuel his destroyers, and stayed with the disposition until afternoon. In the meantime another Nick was driven off by C.A.P. The next attack on Barbey's force came at dusk when it was in the South China Sea about 45 miles off the Lubang Islands. Light cruisers' antiaircraft fire accounted for two planes, one of which disintegrated in the air so that flaming debris straddled *Phoenix*. One got through and crash-dived *LST–912*, killing four men but inflicting slight damage.

Admiral Barbey, having heard of the two Japanese destroyer escorts encountered by *Bennion* off Manila Bay on the 5th, formed cruising disposition during the night of 7–8 January with a screen of cruisers and destroyers flung out five miles on van and both flanks, while Army night flyers from Mindoro kept watch overhead. Shortly after 2100 one of these planes reported a surface contact. The Admiral directed his right flank destroyers, *Charles Ausburne, Braine, Shaw* and *Russell,* to "close and destroy." They opened fire at 10,000 yards, closed to 1100 yards, and at 2255 sank destroyer escort *Hinoki*, which had escaped on 5 January, and, after being patched up at Manila, was trying to get to Camranh Bay.[21] The disposition was shadowed all night by enemy planes which dropped flares near the cruisers, but the Army C.A.P. shot down four and the rest did no harm.

Daybreak, finding the disposition about 55 miles off Palauig Point in Zambales Province, heralded renewed attacks on the assault forces. For an hour and a quarter the 5-inch 38s were barking and machine guns chattering. The escort carriers were under almost continuous attack. At 0749, a quarter hour after sunrise, a

[21] Although O.N.I. and *Imp. Jap. Navy W. W. II* do not concur in the sinking of *Hinoki*, the above has been verified by 2nd Demobilization Ministry Japanese Navy, in memo. prepared for this History in 1947.

plane was observed heading toward *Kadashan Bay*. Captain R. N. Hunter ordered full left rudder and opened fire on it — an Oscar carrying two small bombs. Hit by the automatic weapons, it began to show small bursts of flame and smoke, but kept on coming for the carrier's bridge. When very close its nose dropped, and at 0751 it struck *Kadashan Bay* at the waterline, tearing a hole 9 by 17½ feet in her side. Miraculously nobody was killed and only three men wounded, but the gasoline system was ruptured and by the time fires and flooding were brought under control, the ship was down five feet by the bow. *Marcus Island* took care of her planes, and *Kadashan Bay* was ordered back to Leyte with the first return convoy.

Attack transport *Callaway*, flagship of Captain H. J. Wright and manned largely by coastguardsmen, was the next target. A plane hit the starboard wing of the bridge at 0755 and landed on the fiddley above the blowers. Fragments of plane and bridge whipped about, the flaming gasoline spread, 29 of the crew were killed and 22 wounded. But not one of the 1188 troops on board was even scratched; and as the material damage was superficial, *Callaway* carried out her assigned mission.

The rest of the MacArthur-Barbey-Berkey passage to Lingayen was uneventful. During the mid-watch 9 January the ships approached their transport areas in the southern part of the Gulf. At 0646 signal "Deploy" was hoisted and the San Fabian Attack Group made ready for a hard day's work.

Task Force 79, Admiral Wilkinson's Lingayen Attack Force — except for the tractor groups, which had gone ahead with Barbey — departed Seeadler Harbor on the last day of the old year. Escort carriers *Kitkun Bay* and *Shamrock Bay* were detailed to provide air cover. About ten miles separated Admiral Kiland's Group Able from Rear Admiral Royal's Group Baker; Wilkinson's flagship *Mount Olympus* with General Griswold and XIV Corps Staff on board sailed in the van with Admiral Royal who acted as O.T.C. Early 5 January, two hundred miles east of Leyte Gulf, two oilers joined, fueled all escorts and remained with the disposition until 7

January, when they topped off everyone who needed it and put into Mindoro. Off Leyte Wilkinson's disposition was joined by Admiral Kinkaid's flagship *Wasatch* with Commander Seventh Fleet embarked, and by seaplane tender *Currituck* flying the flag of Rear Admiral Frank Wagner, Commander Aircraft Seventh Fleet. Making good a speed of 12 knots, Wilkinson's disposition gradually overhauled Barbey's. Manila Bay was passed without incident. At 1800 January 8, off the butt end of Cape Bolinao, Berkey's Close Covering Group dropped back from Barbey's force and *Boise* with her distinguished passenger joined Wilkinson's force. General Mac-Arthur promptly signaled his "greetings to men of all ranks."

As the sun sank into "China 'cross the Bay," the soldiers and sailors steaming north witnessed one of those sunsets that poets wrote about in happier times. The sea was smooth, and the orange and scarlet glow suffused over a cloudless aquamarine sky seemed too brilliant to be real. A gentle breeze rippled through the convoy, cooling the steel plates of the transports and giving all hands a refreshing breath as they came on deck during the second dogwatch. Men laid it away in memory's locker as one of those rare impressions of natural beauty that survive when the horrors of war are forgotten.

Task Force 79 was not allowed to forget them long. Mother nature was in a peaceful frame of mind but the enemy was not. Bogeys were in the air half an hour before sunset, and presently in came six kamikazes hoping to paint the ships' decks the same color as the setting sun. C.A.P. got four and antiaircraft fire opened on two and drove them off temporarily. But one pilot was not to be balked. He jockeyed into position at an altitude of about 6000 feet and dove directly on *Kitkun Bay*, Rear Admiral Ofstie's flagship. Every vessel within range fired, but the plane kept on coming. Quick ship handling on the part of Captain Handly almost evaded the dive but the kamikaze crashed her port side at the waterline at 1857, exploding so close aboard as to blow a hole 9 by 20 feet, half of it below water. Fire and engine rooms were partially flooded, all controls except steering were lost, and within a few minutes the carrier had a 13-degree list to port. Seventeen men were killed and 36 wounded. And at 1903 another kamikaze splashed just astern of H.M.A.S. *Westralia*, temporarily deranging her steering gear.

As soon as this attack was over, to quote Joseph Conrad's *Typhoon*, "The coppery twilight retired slowly, and the darkness brought out overhead a swarm of unsteady big stars, that, as if blown upon, flickered exceedingly and seemed to hang very near the earth."

Kitkun Bay was taken into tow by fleet tug *Chowanoc*. Next morning she was able to steam under her own power at 10 knots and join Admiral Durgin's escort carrier group off Lingayen Gulf.

All Barbey's and Wilkinson's ships arrived at their designated rendezvous points on schedule in the early hours of S-day, January 9. They then turned south to their transport areas in lower Lingayen Gulf. Wilkinson's tractor group entered the Gulf at 0245. The final approach to the transport areas was uneventful, and by 0700 the transports were all in their prescribed positions.

Preliminary operations were now over; the long-dreaded, last two hundred miles of approach had been made with far less loss and damage than had been anticipated. The bluejackets in their boundless optimism guessed that for them the tough part of the Luzon operation was over. On the whole it was, for the Navy.

PART II

Luzon Liberated

January–February 1945

CHAPTER V

The Lingayen Landings[1]

9 January 1945

Moonrise, 0245; Sunrise, 0721; Sunset, 1846.

1. *Lingayen Attack Force Lands*

SHIPS of the Luzon Attack Force were now all together for the first time since the landings on Leyte three months before. As they steamed into the Gulf, Admiral Wilkinson's Lingayen Attack Force favored the western side and Admiral Barbey's San Fabian Attack Force the eastern. Both arrived off their respective beaches simultaneously.

It was an unusually clear night and the sky was bright with stars. It seemed cool to sailors used to the sweaty nights of New Guinea, yet a cotton shirt was all the clothing needed topside. The temperature, the early morning breeze and the last-quarter moon suggested late spring in Northern climates rather than the jungle nights of recent experience; this sail in darkened Philippine waters reminded sailors from New England or Puget Sound of those far-off shores on which they had grown up. Almost everyone was anxious, those on the bridge particularly so; for the word had gone around that kamikazes generally aimed at the bridge.

American bluejackets approached the landing beaches in Lingayen Gulf simply as men doing a job that their country had called on them to perform. Most of them were fundamentally religious

[1] Sources in Chap. IV note 1, plus CTG 79.1 (Rear Adm. Kiland) Action Report 20 Jan.; CTG 79.2 (Rear Adm. Royal) Action Report 1 Feb.; Comtransdiv 20 (Commo. D. W. Loomis) Action Report 25 Jan.; Comtransron 14 (Commo. C. G. Richardson) Action Report 24 Jan.; CTG 78.6 (Rear Adm. Fechteler) Action Report 14 Feb. 1945.

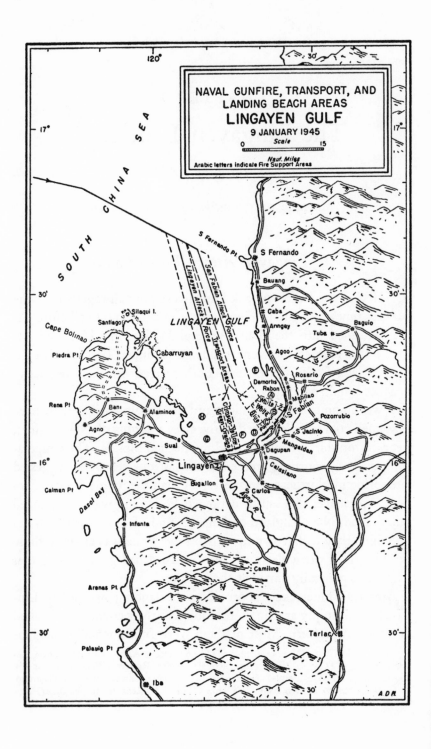

NAVAL GUNFIRE, TRANSPORT, AND
LANDING BEACH AREAS
LINGAYEN GULF
9 JANUARY 1945

Scale
0   15

Naut. Miles
Arabic letters indicate Fire Support Areas

and sentimental. All they now asked of God was to let them return home alive and unharmed. They were conscious of being part of a vast war machine in the Pacific, but they also lived in the dream world of an idyllic future, generally with some chosen girl. Killing or getting killed, indeed war itself, still seemed strange, abnormal, to the average young American. He had to "remember Pearl Harbor" or actually see a Japanese plane kill shipmates to feel angry. But sailors usually manage to adjust themselves to their environment, since they are part of a ship, that matchless means of building morale and group loyalty.

As S-day, 9 January, dawned, ships could be seen in every direction, and presently, at about a quarter to seven, the eastern and western shores of the Gulf could be dimly seen. The mountain ranges (Ilocos and Zambales) that parallel these shores were covered by low-hanging clouds, creating the illusion that the mountains themselves were thrice their real height.[2] As yet the flat southern shore of the Gulf was invisible. Although there was very little wind, cumulus and cirrus clouds drifted over the Gulf, making a partial overcast.

At 0700 the combatant ships began hurling high explosives at supposed enemy installations. The two amphibious force commanders, Wilkinson and Barbey, were working their ships into position to discharge the assault troops. The "ordered confusion" of an amphibious operation was more orderly here than usual, because almost every responsible officer was a veteran and the planners had done their part very well. By 0715 all Wilkinson's ships began boating the infantry men of General Griswold's XIV Corps. At one minute before eight bells Admiral Kiland, and ten minutes later, Admiral Royal, sent Wilkinson "affirmative" to his query as to their ability to meet H-hour, 0930.

The enemy was not napping. A few minutes after 0700 one of three kamikazes which had left Nichols Field at 0650 picked on destroyer escort *Hodges* but misjudged the target angle, knocked down her foremast and radio antennas and splashed without in-

[2] Mt. Santo Tomás is 7407 feet above sea level.

flicting a single casualty. Another was being driven away from Admiral Wilkinson's flagship *Mount Olympus* by antiaircraft fire. The third spotted light cruiser *Columbia*, already twice hit. She was only 4000 yards from the beach and completely surrounded by landing craft, unable to maneuver. The kamikaze crashed her forward main battery director and his bomb exploded on impact, carrying the director over the side. Five more directors and 5-inch mount No. 2 were also knocked out. The casualties were 24 killed or missing and 68 wounded; yet, already shorthanded from her earlier losses, *Columbia* quenched the fire that sprang up, completed her bombardment schedule half an hour after the hit and then stood by for call fire. Her valiant C.O., Captain Maurice E. Curts, could not be stopped as long as his ship could fight, and "The Gem" had a remarkably bold and efficient crew.

At 0842 Admiral Fechteler informed Admiral Barbey that he was ready to land the 6th Infantry Division over the Blue beaches as scheduled. Barbey as group commander had already told Barbey as San Fabian Attack Force commander that he was ready to boat General Wing's 43rd Division.

Admiral Wilkinson's landing beaches had been chosen in preference to others which had more shelter, for two reasons: Just behind them was an airstrip constructed by the Japanese, and the little beaches of Port Sual on the west flank would be useful for post-assault landings. All lay open to "the high winds which often lash Lingayen Gulf into a white-capped fury," and immediately behind them lay "numerous swamps and fish ponds, intertwined by many streams and several fair-sized rivers, which could only be traversed over a series of easily defended causeways and bridges." [3] Such disadvantages caused the Japanese, when they invaded Luzon in December 1941, to regard these beaches as unsuitable for an amphibious assault, and they assumed that the Americans would take the same view. [4]

Admiral Royal's group drew a 2500-yard stretch of beach which

[3] Sixth Army Report I 7.
[4] MacArthur *Historical Report* II 434. Cf. the Utah beaches in Normandy Vol. XI pp. 93–109.

ran from the eastern end of the airstrip west to the center of Lingayen town. This gave him four adjacent beaches, each 625 yards wide, designated Green 1 and 2 and Orange 1 and 2, upon which to land General Brush's 40th Infantry Division. One thousand yards east of this area, Admiral Kiland had a slightly shorter stretch (divided into Crimson 1 and 2 and Yellow 1 and 2), to land General Beightler's 37th Infantry Division. The lines of departure were respectively 4000 and 4500 yards off shore.

These two landings followed the pattern established at Leyte, with a more liberal use of the amphtrac, the LVT. These were tracked amphibious craft which could surmount coral reefs, waddle up the beach, and protect the troops they carried from rifle and machine-gun fire. At 0900 the signal flags for Wave No. 1 were two-blocked and the movement toward the eight beaches began. As soon as the first three waves of amphtracs were safely past the LSTs, which were anchored inshore of the big transports, a series of big splashes marked the LSTs dropping off the pontoon causeways lashed to their topsides. The LCI gunboats, which preceded the amphtracs by 300 yards, and kept "as perfect a line as the Rockettes" (according to a participant),[5] began saturating the beach with their projectiles when 2700 yards from shore. Bombardment ships then shifted gunfire to both flanks of the beachhead. This was the pattern for assaulting well-defended beaches, and a proper precaution even though these were not so defended.

On Admiral Kiland's Yellow and Crimson beaches, LCVPs — the conventional ramped landing craft — acted as guides to Wave 1, consisting of 13 amphibious tanks, and Waves 2, 3 and 4, consisting of 84 LVT carrying assault troops. Waves 5 through 13, which added up to 165 LCVP, 12 LCM and four LSM, landed between 0941 and 1031. In addition, 15 dukws from LSV *Ozark*, carrying two battalions of supporting artillery, remained on call at the line of departure and landed before noon.

The wind was almost flat calm that morning in the Gulf, with a gently heaving ground swell and fair visibility despite smoke and

[5] Notes from Mr. Philip A. Crowl, 1959.

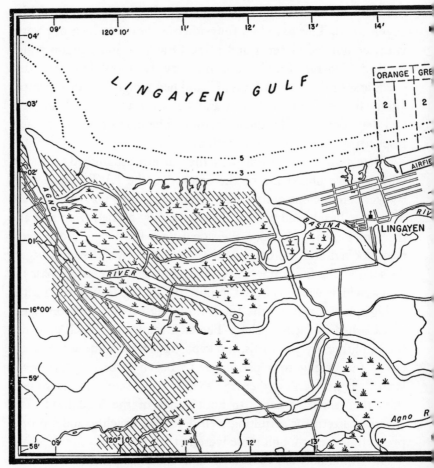

dust kicked up by the bombardment. Beach defenses were not manned; "practically no opposition" was offered by the enemy, either to the boats as they swarmed landward, or to the soldiers as they ran across the beaches or alighted from the amphtracs. Here was the first large-scale application of the new Japanese tactics to counter an amphibious landing, first tried at Peleliu.[6] Even at Leyte the Japanese had fought to maintain beach positions; but at Lingayen there was no defense except on the left flank, and very little opposition in the center. By 16 January, when XIV Corps was al-

[6] See Vol. XII 36-43.

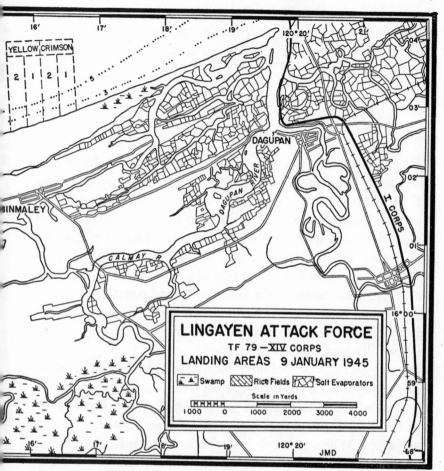

LINGAYEN ATTACK FORCE
TF 79 — XIV CORPS
LANDING AREAS   9 JANUARY 1945
Swamp   Rice Fields   Salt Evaporators
Scale in Yards
1000   0   1000   2000   3000   4000

ready thirty miles inland — after losing but 30 men killed — only eight Japanese prisoners had been taken and a hundred or so killed. On the left flank, I Corps lost 220 killed and 660 wounded during the first week, but almost all these casualties were incurred after the landings.

By 0940, ten minutes after designated H-hour, the first three or four waves had hit all eight beaches and assault troops were rapidly advancing inland.

After the assault waves landed, Commander R. A. Montgomery led seven mortar- and gun-equipped LCIs along the shore east of

Beaches Yellow and Crimson, laying down a barrage ahead of the advancing troops, who were spreading out in that direction. At 1032, the Army asked for no more of this, as no enemy had yet been encountered.

2. *San Fabian Attack Force Lands*

Rear Admiral Barbey's task was potentially the more hazardous. There were Japanese-prepared positions in caves and tunnels in the hills behind the eastern shore, and troops to cover General Yamashita's yet incomplete concentration in northern Luzon. To protect this left flank of Sixth Army's beachhead was the object of Admiral Barbey's San Fabian Attack Force and General Swift's I Corps.

Dan Barbey worked on two levels, as Kelly Turner was wont to do: overall commander of the attack force and commander of one attack group, Rear Admiral Fechteler taking the other. And Rear Admiral Dick Conolly was due to arrive on S plus two day to land the first follow-up echelon of troops.

Starting on the west, Admiral Fechteler's beaches, Blue 1 and 2, began 3500 yards east of the Dagupan river mouth, and about five miles east of Beach Crimson of the Lingayen Attack Force. Each Blue beach was 1000 yards long. Admiral Barbey's were split into two groups, White 3 which was about 3500 yards northeast of Blue 1, and White 1 and 2 the same distance northeast of White 3. Line of departure for all five beaches was set 4000 yards off shore. It could have been much closer but for depths too shoal for transports to maneuver.

Admiral Fechteler's Beach Blue landings were unopposed and uneventful. Surf and beach conditions were generally good, only one boat being lost by swamping. The last organized assault wave was dispatched to the Blue beaches at 1038; and immediately thereafter control vessels shifted to their stations for the unloading phase, about 700 yards off their respective beaches. Things went smoothly also on Admiral Barbey's Beach White, where the first two waves

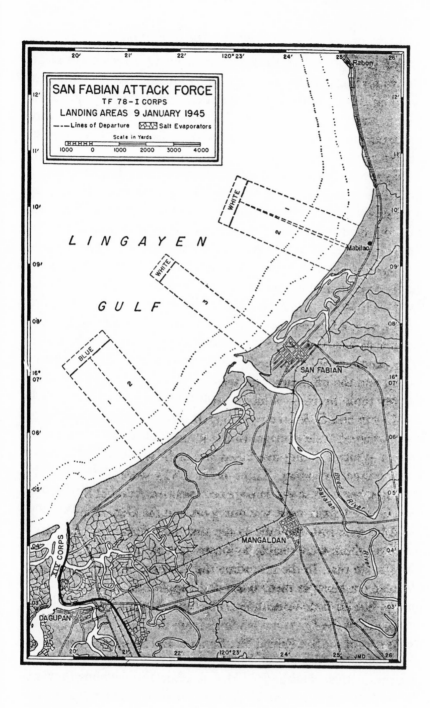

SAN FABIAN ATTACK FORCE
TF 78-I CORPS
LANDING AREAS 9 JANUARY 1945
- - - Lines of Departure   Salt Evaporators
Scale in Yards
1000   0   1000   2000   3000   4000

LINGAYEN

GULF

WHITE

WHITE

BLUE

Rabon

Mabilao

SAN FABIAN

MANGALDAN

DAGUPAN

XIV CORPS

Bued River

Pastran River

JMD

were composed of LVTs, led as usual by LCI rocket craft. The third wave on all beaches, consisting of LCVPs, and the sixth wave on Beach White 2, lost their bearings, owing to difficulty in finding their control vessels in the smoke caused by the bombardment, and ran up the wrong lanes. Otherwise, everything went off according to plan.

No opposition was encountered on any of these beaches, or up to 300 yards inland. The few Japanese defenders of this section threw a little mortar fire, largely harmless, into the beachhead, and subsequently fired their artillery emplaced along the ridges behind the narrow coastal plain. But the enemy batteries were merely biding their time until they found profitable targets in their sights; it was no use wasting ammunition on landing craft, always difficult to hit.

At 0931 destroyer *Jenkins*, operating in a fire support area north of Beach White 1, observed a splash about 25 yards on her port beam, and, a few seconds later, received a hit from a 75-mm shell. Three of her crew were killed and ten others injured. *Jenkins* at 0932 commenced counter-battery fire, destroyer *Converse* lent a hand, and the offending gun was silenced. Enemy artillery on the ridges took Beaches White 1 and 2 under fire at about 1000. *LSM-127* and *LSM-219* were hit, six men killed and 31 wounded, but sustained little damage. In the afternoon *LSM-269* was hit on Beach White 2, losing five killed and eight wounded, but was able to continue unloading. Three other LSTs were hit on the same beaches, but with slight damage or casualties. Admiral Barbey notified General Swift what was going on, and the General promised to send his men into the hills to dig out these fieldpieces, which the ships off shore were unable to locate. It took the Army about four days to do that. In the meantime the Japanese artillery took intermittent pot shots at men, boats and supplies on Beaches White 1 and 2, but hit little or nothing. This was the sum total of Japanese resistance to the Lingayen landings from the shore side.

As part of the San Fabian Fire Support and Bombardment Group, battleship *Mississippi* and H.M.A.S. *Australia*, "bloody but unbowed," lay off Dagupan to deliver call fire if needed for the 6th

Infantry Division, which had landed on the two Blue beaches. At 1302 two Vals belonging to the noon flight of four kamikazes and four escorts from Tuguegarao headed for these ships. *Mississippi* commenced firing her forward machine guns but the pilot that had her number kept coming, leveled off in a shallow glide, passed over the forecastle, struck the battlewagon on the port side below bridge level, continued in a straight line until he landed against an antiaircraft gun and toppled over the port side. Minor blast and fragment damage resulted and several blister compartments were flooded, but casualties were heavy. In this brief moment of action 23 men were killed or died of wounds and 63 others were wounded.

No sooner had this plane crashed *Mississippi* than her gun crews shifted fire to the second Val which was heading for *Australia's* bridge. The pilot just missed; his wing caught a foremast strut which swung him into No. 1 stack and overboard. There was little material damage other than the top of the stack being sliced off, and no casualties.

After this, her fifth encounter with the kamikazes, H.M.A.S. *Australia* snuggled up to Rear Admiral Sowell's flagship *West Virginia* for additional antiaircraft protection. Upon departing Lingayen Gulf with the first returning echelon, her C.O., Captain J. W. Armstrong RAN, received the signal from Rear Admiral Berkey, his former group commander: "Sorry the Hell Birds concentrated on you. My deep regrets for losses in the stout ship's company." To which Armstrong replied: "Thank you very much. There is still a lot left in us. At least we acted as cockshy and attracted flies from others." [7]

3. *Unloading and Progress Ashore, S-day*

Beach and shore parties were landed immediately after the assault waves and at about 1100 general unloading began on all beaches. At this point, where the confusion inherent in landing on a

[7] *Australia* Action Report 17 Jan. 1945.

hostile shore is apt to be worse confounded, the experienced Wilkinson and Barbey had drafted plans to prevent the usual jam. Landing craft were scheduled for cargo trips as soon as conditions ashore permitted, and transports closed the beach to facilitate the turnaround. The surf was very moderate for the Gulf of Lingayen, not more than four feet high, which did not interfere with the installation of pontoon causeways. The gentle gradient which caused LSTs to ground 75 to 300 feet from the water's edge had been anticipated and arrangements made accordingly. Pontoon causeways were launched promptly and by early afternoon unloading slots for LSTs were in operation at both sets of beaches. As a result, 15,463 tons of supplies and equipment were landed over Wilkinson's beaches on S-day, and about the same were placed on Barbey's.

In the San Fabian sector, Beaches White 1 and 2 were good for beaching LSTs but White 3 proved a washout and was abandoned, all pontoon causeways being sent to the Blue beaches. All attack transports (APA) carrying 450 tons each, attack freighters (AKA) carrying 1500 tons each, and ordinary transports (AP) carrying 300 tons each, as well as the LSDs, were unloaded on S-day. LSMs and LCTs were used in addition to the transports' own landing craft. Pontoon barges were used to carry cargo from the transports to a fleet of landing craft that shuttled to and fro from points near the beach. This required a double handling of cargo, but saved time.

At 1930 Admiral Wilkinson designated Commodore D. W. Loomis to herd the first echelon of empty ships back to Leyte Gulf. Very few unloaded ships remained off the beachhead overnight. This return echelon, including 21 large transports, 5 LSD and one LSV, escorted by nine destroyers and three destroyer escorts, was joined by the three battle-damaged cruisers and escort carrier *Kadashan Bay*. "Count" Berkey's Close Covering Group patrolled off Cape Bolinao west of the convoy lanes, and air cover to the convoy after it cleared the Cape was provided by shore-based aircraft. If

these ships could steam safely as far as Mindoro they would have little else to worry about.

Lieutenant General Walter Krueger, commanding Sixth Army,
followed the progress of his troops ashore with satisfaction as reports reached Admiral Kinkaid's flagship, in which he was embarked. Infantry men of the I and XIV Corps had plenty of air support from the escort carriers and from A–20s of the V A.A.F. based
on Mindoro. Over each Corps area, a direct support group consisting of eight carrier-based fighters and twelve torpedo bombers, augmented by a special strike group of nine torpedo bombers, to
which the A–20s were later added, struck pre-assigned targets such
as road intersections, ammunition and supply dumps, military buildings and gun positions. At 0930 Admiral Kinkaid's air controller,
embarked in *Wasatch*, had a strafing group of 16 torpedo-bombers
hitting targets of opportunity 3000 yards inland from the beaches.
In addition, the planes in Wilkinson's sector bombed and rocketed
the northeastern slopes of the Zambales Mountains and some planes
of the direct support groups attacked enemy small craft near Santiago Island.

The only enemy resistance encountered during S-day was on the
extreme left, the northeastern flank. This was the only hot spot of
the beachhead. One battalion was held up by heavy enemy fire
coming from a point on the coast about 1500 yards north of Mabilao. Nevertheless, General Wing's 43rd Division, to which this battalion belonged, by the close of the day had made the biggest bulge
of the beachhead, some 8000 yards deep, and was in touch with
General Patrick's 6th Division on its right. That Division met no
opposition, advanced rapidly, and by dusk had reached points 900
yards inland.

In General Griswold's XIV Corps area, General Beightler's 37th
Division probed inland unopposed; it secured the town of Binmaley
and two important bridges, which afforded the best outlets from
the soggy beachhead to the central plain of Luzon. General Brush's
40th Division on the extreme right (west) flank met no opposition

and quickly seized the 5000-foot Lingayen airstrip, which was found to be in excellent condition. It then secured the town of Lingayen, with its much-battered Grecian style provincial capitol, a relic of the days when Americans ruled the Philippines. At the end of S-day, this division had a beachhead 6000 yards deep and 9000 yards wide. It was almost too easy; the soldiers were given no foretaste of the tough days ahead for them.

CHAPTER VI

Progress of the Operation[1]

9–11 January 1945

1. Hot Night in the Gulf

THE SUN set on S-day, 9 January 1945, at 1846. A smoke plan then went into effect, with much better success than when it was first tried in Leyte Gulf. Smoker LCIs anchored to seaward and windward of the transports, and smoker LCVPs were stationed to windward of individual ships. Before sundown they all lighted their smoke pots so that, by the time C.A.P. retired, shortly after sunset, an effective blanket lay over the transport area. The smoker LCIs moved shoreward before dawn in order to take advantage of the early offshore breeze. This procedure, repeated twice daily, proved effective in averting air attack on the larger ships during those critical periods, but it was no help to screening destroyers and other escorts. They were not under the blanket, and they caught it.

The first unwelcome visitor arrived four minutes before sunset, made a lunge at destroyer *Bush*, and was splashed by machine-gun fire 25 feet short of her fantail. During the next hour more kamikazes came in; and although not one made a hit, our efforts to hit them boomeranged. Some gun crews were too "trigger-happy" to withhold fire when hearing a target overhead, despite the fact that all they could accomplish was to draw the enemy's attention to

[1] Same sources as in Chap. IV, Note 1, especially the Barbey, Wilkinson, Royal and Kiland Action Reports; CTG 77.9 Report of Reinforcement Group Participation in Amphibious Operations for Capture of Luzon, 20 Jan. 1945; *Sixth Army Report* III and MacArthur *Historical Report* II; notes from Mr. Philip A. Crowl, 1959.

themselves. Three men on *LSM–66* were wounded by falling shell fragments, and worse would befall a battleship.

At 1905 *Colorado*, when working up to flank speed with rudder hard over, was hit at sky control level by a shell, later identified as a "friendly" 5-inch 38-caliber. As she had only the one air defense station, this accidental hit wiped out her key air defense men and seriously affected the ship's combat efficiency. After the casualties had been removed from the bloody shambles that had been sky control, all hands learned that 18 shipmates were dead or dying and another 51 wounded. The only heavy ships in Lingayen Gulf still undamaged were *West Virginia*, *Pennsylvania*, *Portland* and H.M.A.S. *Shropshire*.

Shortly after midnight a Japanese 320-mm howitzer, located in a ravine between Damortis and Rosario and sited to enfilade Beaches White 1 and 2, opened up; and, as the Army Engineer historian remarked, "The society for the improvement of foxholes sprang into life within a few seconds." Since the fire support ships could not locate "Pistol Pete," as this gun was nicknamed, it continued intermittent fire for several nights, inflicting surprisingly little damage.[2]

During the same night of 9–10 January the Japanese pulled the suicide boat out of their bag of tricks. Port Sual, protected by a point of land stretching down from the north and in the southwest corner of Lingayen Gulf, was the concealed anchorage for no fewer than 70 of these 18½ feet long fast plywood boats. Each carried two 260-pound depth charges, one light machine gun and a few hand grenades, with a crew of two or three men, chosen from the Japanese Army, to destroy Allied shipping in Lingayen Gulf. Although their intended victims spotted less than half of them, Japanese postwar sources state positively that all 70 sortied and "nearly all" were lost in their initial attack on the night of S-day. The first group headed out of Port Sual shortly after 0200 January 10. When approaching Admiral Wilkinson's transports at low

[2] *Surf and Sand: The Saga of the 533rd Engineer Boat and Shore Regiment* (1947) p. 141.

speed, hoping to slip through his inner screen undetected, three
boats at 0320 registered on the radar screen of destroyer *Philip*
(Commander J. B. Rutter), who recognized what they were and
gave the alarm. An hour later another boat, when only 25 yards
from *Philip*, was hit by her 20-mm gunfire and immediately ex-

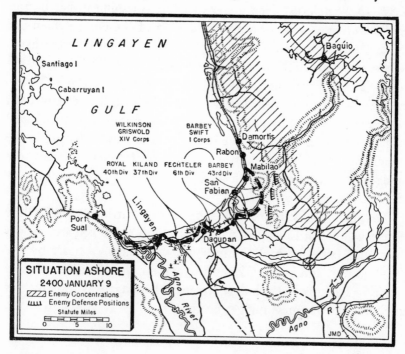

ploded. *Leutze* destroyed two midgets around 0440 and was still
"repelling boat attacks" at 0455. Others headed at high speed for
the nearest target. Some ten ships in all were attacked and a few
were damaged. The midgets approached from astern, and when
nearly alongside heaved a depth charge with a shallow setting over
the stern and attempted a quick getaway. These simple tactics were
effective, because if a boat succeeded in approaching undetected it
was so close to its intended victim that no guns could be brought
to bear.

As a result of this initial attack, *LCI(M)-974* was sunk, transport
Alcyone was attacked but escaped damage and eight others were

damaged. The force of an explosion close to transport *War Hawk* opened a hole in her 12 feet long extending below the waterline, which flooded her No. 3 hold and reduced maximum speed to 10½ knots. *LST–925* reported a hole below the waterline and her starboard engine out of commission. The charge which damaged *LST–1028* exploded deep under the ship, smashing in her bottom and lower side, with consequent flooding of the engine room and other damage as well. *LCI(G)–365* was so seriously hurt that it was recommended she be abandoned.[3] Two other LSTs were damaged. The toll was high, but not nearly so high as Radio Tokyo reported — 20 to 30 Allied vessels sunk. Four of the enemy craft were reported sunk by gunfire from the ships and a fifth is believed to have been destroyed by the explosion of its own charges in the attack on *War Hawk*; but, according to Japanese sources, the midget-boat regiment, which sortied that night 70 strong, was "incapable of further operations."[4]

That being so, it is not surprising that no further attacks of the sort developed at Lingayen. Similar boats later attacked at Batangas Bay with fair success. But the lesson was taken to heart by the Pacific Fleet, and in the Okinawa operation one of the reasons for securing Kerama Retto before the main landings was to deny this anchorage to Japanese midget boats.

2. *Unloading Problems and Departing Convoys*

Before dawn of 10 January, routine General Quarters were sounded, the usual smoke screen blanketed the transports, sailors

---

[3] For exploits of *LCI(G)–365* at Eniwetok see Vol. VII 302.

[4] MacArthur *Historical Report* II 436; but an accurate account of this attack is impossible to obtain. It was a dark night, very few people saw anything, there was a great deal of confusion, and many conflicting stories and rumors. Usually, under such circumstances, the number of attackers is exaggerated, but in this instance, if the Japanese statements to MacArthur's historical staff are correct, it was greatly underestimated. Rumors went around next day that some Japanese who had been picked up in the water were suicide swimmers who had explosives attacked to their backs with the mission of blowing up ships. These proved to be unfounded; the swimmers were crews of the suicide boats.

shook a leg, scrambled to battle stations and spent the next hour waiting for the kamikazes. The cool air topside cleared the heads of men who had slept in crowded compartments below decks, but the smell of chemical smoke on an empty stomach about evened things up. No one talked much — just waited for something to happen, which is the way you spend a good nine tenths of your time in a war.

As usual the kamikazes kept their dawn rendezvous with death. Destroyer *Dashiell* had been patrolling off Santiago Island during the night. At 0711, when she was about nine miles northeast of the island, a Val tried to crash-dive her but was frustrated by high speed and radical maneuvers. Destroyer escort *LeRay Wilson*, on antisubmarine station northwest of the Gulf, was not so lucky. Visibility to the westward was low, and it was still so dark that another DE, about two and a half miles away, was invisible. At 0710 a twin-engined plane was observed broad on the port beam, distance about 1000 yards, heading directly for the ship and very low over the water. It was immediately taken under gunfire. When about 200 yards from *Wilson*, its engine and port wing were set afire, but after veering slightly it smashed through the port flag-bag and past two 20-mm guns, smacked the stack and torpedo tubes and sliced off two other 20-mm's. Part of the plane fell overboard; the rest was strewn over *Wilson's* superstructure and the torpedo deck. She was badly damaged, six of her crew were killed and seven wounded, two of them diagnosed as "probably fatal."

American amphibious forces almost always enjoyed the good fortune of a day of calm and moderate weather when landing on a coast where weather is generally bad and the surf high. On S-day, 9 January, surf conditions had been almost ideal, but now a shift of wind built up a heavy ground swell so that pontoon causeways began to buckle and broach and boat service had to be halted in the afternoon. Sailors who had landed at Salerno, Omaha Beach, Munda or Kwajalein would have considered Lingayen "duck soup," but Lingayen Gulf provided some special problems. The beaches are composed of hard, firm sand, excellent for vehicles, but in Wilkinson's sector they were bordered by a low bluff six to twelve feet high, and the exits — as those from Utah Beach in Normandy — proved to be very soft. The shore party had insufficient steel matting, hence there were frequent delays owing to trucks getting mudbound and having to be dragged out by bulldozers. Most amphibious operations in the Pacific were hampered by old or obsolete hydrographic information; in this instance, the data on the charts, based on a survey of 1903, proved to be reliable but in such small scale as to provide few details; for instance, there was an uncharted shoal between the two-fathom and the three-fathom line; this was undetected by the UDTs, and it hampered the LSTs.[5] And off the beaches there were underwater holes into which many vehicles fell and drowned their engines.

On S-day, pontoon causeways had been installed and six LST unloading slots established at the meeting point between the Green and Orange beaches, with five more to the east of Beach Crimson. On 10 January the surf began to break them up, and by the afternoon it was not possible to unload an LCM without undue risk of broaching. One LSM did broach on Beach Blue, and one LST, clumsily handled when retracting, fouled the stern anchor cable on an adjacent LST and ended up parallel to the beach, forcing others out of position and wrecking the causeways that they were using. Admiral Royal's beachmaster and the senior Seabee officer assigned to that group applied themselves to the difficult task of salvaging and resetting broached causeways. Four, reëstablished by 1400 January 11, were used for the discharge of high priority airfield equipment over the Orange and Green unloading slots.

There was also trouble on Beach Crimson. But by the morning of 12 January the surf had abated to an average height of four feet, so that three unloading slots could be maintained. Admiral Barbey's sector was better off, with natural protection from the surf.

During this unloading phase of the Lingayen operation, old problems were encountered to a degree not anticipated. We find the usual complaint about labor parties assigned for unloading boats

[5] Notes made by III 'Phib beachmaster, Capt. H. E. Bramston-Cook USNR.

"melting away"; in this instance to visit Filipinos and swap government property for souvenirs. By S-day plus 1 the natives were streaming into the beachhead like a swarm of locusts, to fraternize, beg and pilfer. By 11 January supplies littered the beach down to and below high water mark. A shortage of trucks developed because the Army advanced inland at unexpected speed. Both shore parties had a few dukws available and employed them for unloading the LSTs. The 37th Division shore party took many cargoes ashore by this means from LSTs in the stream.

Admiral Royal's attack group had a skillful and energetic beachmaster, Lieutenant Commander W. W. Sullivan USNR. The III 'Phib beachmaster, Captain Bramston-Cook USNR, complained bitterly of the unloading of Admiral Kiland's attack group, but this group unloaded an average of 5700 tons of vehicles and cargo daily during the first four days,[6] which compares favorably with other amphibious operations, especially in view of the surf, which held everything up for many hours.

By 1400 January 10 the airstrip at Lingayen was ready for emergency landings, and the headquarters company of 308th Bomber Wing arrived next day. By late afternoon, one slow and one fast convoy were ready to depart for Leyte. Commodore C. G. Richardson, at about 1800, took out the fast one, consisting of 17 transport types and two LSD, with a screen of three damaged destroyers and three smaller escorts. One of the big ones, attack transport *Du Page*, nosing up the Gulf to get into formation, secured from general quarters. No sooner had the men gone below to relax and thank their lucky stars they were on the way out, when the clang of General Quarters sounded again and back they went to battle stations. Enemy aircraft were reported in the vicinity. At 1915 a Nick was spotted almost dead ahead, flying at 800 feet altitude. After reducing altitude to about 60 feet the kamikaze pilot commenced a steep bank, slammed into the port wing of the transport's navigation bridge, and continued on a destructive course aft. Burn-

---

[6] Kiland Action Report. *Surf and Sand* pp. 136–45 has a good description of the trouble in landing supplies over the White beaches.

ing gasoline started serious fires and the casualties were very heavy
— 32 killed and 157 wounded. But *Du Page* was able to continue
with the convoy.

The slow convoy, under the command of Captain T. B. Dugan,
consisting of about 32 beaching craft and screened by four destroyers and six other escorts, also got under way that evening, fortunately in a less spectacular manner than Commodore Richardson's
outfit.

The damaged escort carrier *Kitkun Bay* joined early next morning. Planes could still take off from her so that she furnished C.A.P.
on 11 January, but as the damage to the carrier prevented recovery
they had to land at Mindoro that night.

3. *Reinforcements Arrive; Kamikazes Return* [7]

The night of 10–11 January passed uneventfully, as did the following dawn; no sign of enemy in the sky or sea. Not one kamikaze
put in an appearance that day.

Rear Admiral Richard L. Conolly, Commander Amphibious
Group 3, was now bringing up the first reinforcement echelon. The
details of this are interesting as an example of meticulous planning
and using every ship to best advantage. Owing to the inclusion of
50 LST and ten Liberty ships in this echelon there had to be a slow
convoy, which was placed in charge of Commander A. A. Ageton,
best known as an authority on celestial navigation. He now commanded LST Flotilla 3, which sailed from Hollandia 30 December.
Other groups departed various points in New Guinea or joined at
Leyte.

Rear Admiral Conolly in *Appalachian*, after embarking the 25th
Infantry Division and 158th RCT in his big transports at Nouméa
and Noemfoor and holding a rehearsal at Guadalcanal, departed

---

[7] There appear to be no Japanese records on this concluding phase of kamikaze
activity in the Philippines. All the data in *The Divine Wind* are from Allied
sources.

Manus 2 January, accompanied by a small escort carrier group (*Saginaw Bay* and *Petrof Bay*) under Rear Admiral G. R. Henderson. This fast convoy overtook Ageton's slow one on 10 January in order to simplify air coverage on the run-in to Lingayen Gulf. The escort carriers now peeled off and joined the one remaining CVE (*Marcus Island*) of "Count" Berkey's group to furnish C.A.P. and antisubmarine patrol for convoys entering and departing. This duty lasted until 17 January when Army Air Force planes based at Lingayen relieved the CVEs.

Admiral Conolly's convoy ended an uneventful passage at the transport area on the eastern side of Lingayen Gulf at 0700 January 11, where it split into three groups. Two transports and 10 LST reported to Admiral Wilkinson; 4 transports and 28 LST and 12 APD to Admiral Barbey; the 15 transports which floated Sixth Army Reserve reported to Admiral Kinkaid for later assignment. The 158th RCT was landed near Mabilao and went right into action with I Corps; the 25th Division landed in the San Fabian area.

These landings went smoothly except for a slight collision between two transports, and a mishap to an LCVP from attack freighter *Warren*, which was preparing to unload her troops and supplies over Beach White 2. This landing craft was one of two which carried beachmaster Lieutenant (jg) R. Y. Bussey USNR and his party ashore. The first boat took a wrong course from the coxswain of a returning LCVP, with the result that Bussey and several bluejackets jumped ashore right in the enemy's lap, at the town of Damortis. When the Japanese opened up with small-arms fire the Americans ran back to their boat, to find that it was hard and fast aground. The enemy then brought mortar, machine-gun and three-inch gunfire into play, not only on the beachmaster's boat, but on the second LCVP, which lay about a thousand yards off the beach. All weapons of the stranded LCVP were turned on the enemy, but that was like trying to kill an elephant with a peashooter. The hull of the boat was peppered with holes and a shell exploded on the engine house, whose occupants jumped overboard and started swimming out to sea, followed by enemy gunfire.

By this time the LCVP off shore had gone to get help. Destroyer *Russell* and two APDs [8] soon arrived to search for survivors of the stranded craft, assisted by two planes which spotted the men in the water and remained overhead to distract the enemy by diving at him while the rescue work went on. By noon 20 survivors, eight of them wounded, had been recovered; eleven, including beachmaster Bussey, were missing.

The remainder of 11 January was routine. Surf conditions improved and unloading speeded up. On orders from Admiral Kinkaid, Rear Admiral Royal wound up his amphibious business and was detached from the Lingayen Attack Force. Next day Vice Admiral Barbey was designated S.O.P.A. Lingayen Gulf by Admiral Kinkaid. At 1243 General Swift left his comfortable quarters on board flagship *Blue Ridge* and assumed command of I Corps ashore. Three hours later Vice Admiral Wilkinson escorted Major General Griswold to the quarterdeck of *Mount Olympus* and wished him good luck as he departed to assume command of XIV Corps on the beach. At sunset a fast and slow convoy, 38 ships, got under way for Leyte, escorted by 21 vessels ranging from destroyers to submarine chasers.

At sunrise on the 12th, when Admiral Halsey and TF 38 were knocking out Japanese teeth off Indochina, the kamikazes returned. First ships to catch it were destroyer escorts *Gilligan* and *Richard W. Suesens*. The former was part of the outer, and the latter a unit of the inner antisubmarine screen for western Lingayen Gulf. The attack began a few minutes after first light broke over the mountains. A twin-engined Betty approached from the dark western horizon on a low horizontal run, but was picked up by *Gilligan's* radar when eight miles distant. At 0658, when less than 1000 yards away, it was sighted. The ship changed course to put the plane on her starboard beam, and bring the maximum number of guns to bear.

We have found many instances in this history of individual

[8] A minor mystery here: One APD was *Lloyd;* the other, states *Warren's* Action Report, was *Cofer;* but it was really *Newman.*

bravery by bluejackets; here now is one of a contrary nature which may be a caution against deserting one's battle station. A range-finder operator, under fire from a plane's machine guns, and seeing the plane heading directly towards him, leaped from his platform to the main battery director, throwing it off the target and knocking the operator down. Other bluejackets did their duty nobly, but this episode prevented the DE from getting off more than 14 rounds of 5-inch. The No. 3 director and No. 40-mm gun crews, under the direction of Lieutenant W. K. Stewart USNR, delivered a large volume of fire at the enemy plane, which was headed directly for them, and they were still shooting when the kamikaze crashed and exploded. "When the flames cleared away, their stations had completely disappeared. The only survivor was the assistant gunnery officer, who was found in the water badly wounded." [9] A tremendous gasoline explosion followed, with flames 100 feet high extending from the torpedo tubes aft to the fantail, while the main deck was covered with blazing wreckage. Casualties were surprisingly low: 12 men killed or missing and 13 wounded. By 0715 the fires were under control and wreckage cleared from the main deck.

Destroyer transport *Goldsborough* closed, and had just put two LCVPs over the side to render medical assistance to *Gilligan* when the enemy came in again. *R. W. Suesens*, which was searching for men blown overboard from *Gilligan*, at 0729 picked up a bogey coming in from over the land. Emergency full speed was rung up, and full right rudder, which kept the plane under fire of the entire starboard battery, together with the 20-mm guns on the port side, during its approach. This maneuver forced the pilot to make a large semicircle, and probably killed him. The plane passed about five feet over the top of the after 40-mm gun and splashed so close aboard that the ship's fantail passed over the wreckage. Eleven men in *Suesens* were wounded.

There is an interesting exchange of ideas in the endorsements on the report of this action by the C.O. of *Suesens*, Lieutenant Commander R. W. Graham USNR. Rear Admiral Forrest B. Royal

[9] *Gilligan* Action Report 12 Jan. 1945 and oral information at the time.

started the sequence by observing that "full power, and evasive course, combined with rapid and accurate gunfire, proved to be an effective defense against suicide dives." Vice Admiral Wilkinson agreed in general, but remarked that owing "to the high speed of the plane as compared with the relatively slow speed of the ship, even at full power, an evasive course is inconsequential." Admiral Kinkaid had the last word: "A skillful pilot, intent on crashing a ship, is almost certain to succeed if unopposed by antiaircraft fire, regardless of what maneuvers the ship attempts. Therefore, the chief advantage of maneuvering is to unmask the maximum number of guns, and to present a narrow target in range, since an error in judgment by the pilot is more likely to result in overshooting than in a deflection error."

Everyone was searching for the answer, or any answer, to this kamikaze problem, the most debated question in the Fleet. On one point all were agreed: the best defense for a ship after an attack started was concentrated, accurate and rapid gunfire. But, owing to the suddenness of most onslaughts, often unheralded even by radar in operations close to shore, it was very difficult to concentrate enough gunfire on the kamikaze in time to stop it before the impetus of the plane carried it to the target, even with a dead man at the controls. This was illustrated by the attack on *Belknap* on the morning of 12 January.

A slow convoy of beaching craft bound for Leyte was off Santiago Island at dawn that day with Commander M. H. Hubbard in destroyer *Isherwood* as O.T.C. Three Zekes, using land cover and a solid overcast, approached the convoy undetected. The first kamikaze attracted antiaircraft fire from one side of the disposition, while the other two attacked the opposite flank. A steep dive aimed at transport *War Hawk* was stopped, but the plane dropped its bomb 100 yards on her port bow and splashed just ahead of her, no damage resulting. The next plane selected *LST–700* as target, passed over her at 0815 and splashed close aboard. The C.A.P. that belonged to a nearby task unit, flying over to help, attacked the third Zeke. It dropped low and leveled off to escape, but was lethally hit by ships' gunfire. The pilot made a desperate but unsuccessful attempt to crash the nearest vessel before his plane splashed.

After several ships inside the Gulf had been unsuccessfully attacked, the All Clear signal was sounded at 0748. Immediately after, four Tonys penetrated to the center of Admiral Wilkinson's transport area by following in a Navy Catalina. They broke formation, dove towards destroyer transport *Belknap*, and were taken under fire by all guns that would bear. After making a complete circle around the ship, one plane turned, dived and started strafing. One of the two bombs which it carried under its wings was knocked loose and fell into the sea about 500 yards short of *Belknap*, and the barrage of 20-mm and .50-caliber shells set the plane on fire. But the momentum of its drive carried it forward, and at 0753 it crashed *Belknap's* No. 2 stack. Then the remaining bomb exploded. By this time another kamikaze was diving on the ship from dead ahead. *Belknap* fired her No. 1 gun at it until the range was fouled by a destroyer which crossed her bows; but she got the Tony. Her stack was completely demolished and her casualties were 38 killed or died of wounds and 49 wounded.

After this attack things quieted down in Lingayen Gulf, but later the same day (12 January) ships of the Second Supply Group were mussed up a bit off the west coast of Luzon. This convoy, under the command of Comdesron 5, Captain W. M. Cole, consisted of over 100 ships, mostly LSTs and merchantmen, which had been loaded at ports all the way between Finschhafen and Leyte. On the afternoon of 11 January the convoy arrived off San José, Mindoro, where it was joined by 23 PTs of Squadrons 28 and 36, under the overall command of Lieutenant Commander F. D. Tappaan USNR, with their tender *Wachapreague*. The passage of this Second Supply Group was uneventful until the afternoon of 12 January, when it was given the Lingayen treatment. At 1250, when the convoy was off Bataan, a kamikaze made an undetected approach and crashed the starboard side of Liberty ship *Otis Skinner*. The plane's fuselage penetrated the ship, tearing a 15 by 35 foot hole, and exploding after going through the second deck. Miraculously there were no casualties other than slight burns.

A few hours later, about 1830, the convoy underwent a worse attack by about six kamikazes. One crashed the deck of S.S. *Kyle V. Johnson*, lighting a large fire and killing 129 men. A second plane was shot down close aboard *LST-778*, but she sustained neither damage nor casualties. The third and fourth planes picked on S.S. *David Dudley Field* and *Edward N. Westcott*. Both splashed just short, but *Field* sustained minor engine-room damage while *Westcott* received substantial damage from flying debris; six of her merchant seamen and seven of her Naval Armed Guard crew were wounded. Another plane was splashed near the rear of the convoy and the sixth retired without attacking.

That night two returning convoys formed up and prepared to leave Lingayen Gulf, under Rear Admiral Conolly in *Appalachian* as O.T.C. The fast convoy consisted of 21 transport types, one LSD and *Mount Olympus* with Vice Admiral Wilkinson embarked, screened by five destroyers and seven APD. Its return passage to Leyte was interrupted by only one attack, early in the morning of 13 January. Leading the inboard column on the starboard side of the convoy and directly ahead of *Mount Olympus* was attack transport *Zeilin*, flying the flag of Commodore H. W. Graf. At 0815 Flash Red was signaled to the convoy, and all hands went to general quarters. At 0821 a single-engined plane was sighted by *Zeilin* about 1000 yards away, coming out of low-hanging clouds on her port quarter. The plane banked to the left, making the men on *Mount Olympus's* flag bridge feel certain their number was up; then straightened out and headed for *Zeilin* in a 40-degree dive. It bore through the fire of the after 40-mm battery and the port automatic weapons; its right wing struck the port kingpost and boom serving No. 6 hatch, swung inboard under the radio antenna and crashed the starboard side of the housetop. Only ten seconds elapsed from the time the plane was sighted until it crashed. Fortunately, there was no big explosion and the ship's ability to operate was not impaired; but 8 men were killed and 32 wounded.

Commander M. H. Hubbard's slow convoy of 43 ships, mostly beaching craft, which had been attacked on the morning of 12 January, was in for another on the 13th. It was about sixty miles west of Manila at 0810 when a Zeke went after *LST-700*, which had narrowly escaped the previous morning. This time she was not so lucky. The LST opened fire and made some hits, but not enough, for the enemy flew low over her port side and crashed the weather deck. Main and auxiliary engine rooms flooded; she went dead in the water and casualties were 2 killed and 2 wounded. *LST-268* took her in tow, while *LST-911* stood by to render medical assistance and *YMS-47* to assist in pumping. The towline parted twice, and the consequent slowing down of the convoy to three knots was a risk which proved to be justified. The damaged ship was delivered to Mindoro the following morning. Commander Hubbard's reaction to the attacks is interesting: "It is noted that the Japs expended four airplanes and four trained aviators to kill three men and damage one ship of an empty convoy!" He regarded them as very stupid. The fact is that, after S-day, kamikaze attacks were delivered by individual glory seekers, without plan or orders.

The rest of the passage to Leyte was quiet. Snoopers appeared at dawn 14 January but did not attack. One P-47 of the C.A.P. splashed near Sequijor Island off Cebu, but the pilot in his raft reached that island, whence he was rescued by a "Dumbo." The natives of Sequijor told him that he was the first American to set foot there in three years, and raised an American flag in honor of the event.

On the morning of 13 January trouble recurred in Lingayen Gulf. Admiral Durgin's escort carriers were then operating off the mouth of the Gulf as part of the Luzon Defense Force.[10] A message received from V Army Air Force at Leyte that there might be a raid by land-based bombers from Formosa, with fighter cover from

[10] This Luzon Defense Force, comprising TGs 77.2, 77.3 and 77.4, was formed on 10 January with Admiral Oldendorf as over-all commander.

northern Luzon, and another message to the effect that units of the Japanese Fleet were moving up the west coasts of Borneo and Palawan under cover of heavy weather, caused Captain J. I. Taylor of escort carrier *Salamaua* to stack his local C.A.P. as high as 20,000 feet. At 0858 an unidentified kamikaze, diving almost vertically on this escort carrier, hit her before guns could be brought to bear. The plane, carrying two 250-kilogram bombs, one under each wing, plunged through the flight deck. One bomb exploded and started fires on the flight deck, hangar deck and spaces below. The second bomb failed to explode but went through the starboard side of the ship at the waterline. Fifteen men were killed and 88 wounded. Power, communications and steering were lost. The after engine room flooded and the starboard engine was put out of commission, but in the following ten minutes the ship's antiaircraft gunners managed to splash two enemy aircraft. *Salamaua*, after temporary repairs and screened by two destroyers, joined Captain Seay's slow convoy of beaching craft, which left Lingayen Gulf that evening and returned to Leyte.

This was the last successful kamikaze attack in Philippine waters. The reason became clear after the war. By 12 January the Japanese had expended every aircraft they had in the Philippines. Admiral Fukudome began evacuating his planes to Formosa on the 8th, when Rear Admiral Ohnishi, organizer of the Kamikaze Corps, reluctantly departed. Ground crews were sent off to join the infantry defending Luzon, and the surviving pilots, kamikaze and others, flew north as best they could. Only 47 aircraft, and possibly double that number of pilots, escaped; and after 15 January only ten Japanese planes were left on the entire island of Luzon. Reorganized at Tainan airfield, Formosa, the kamikazes were next heard from on 21 January when they attacked TF 38; but for the most part, from 13 January to the Iwo Jima operation, they remained grounded. For the Allies they now seemed but a horrible dream. Unfortunately, like other bad dreams, this one recurred.

4. *Assault Operations Concluded, 13–17 January 1945*

General MacArthur and staff went ashore from *Boise* at 1415 January 13 and set up headquarters at a schoolhouse in Dagupan. A few minutes later, General Krueger descended the gangway of flagship *Wasatch* and stepped into Admiral Kinkaid's barge for his last taste of the sea before assuming command of Sixth Army ashore.

The next two days, 14 and 15 January, passed uneventfully.[11] Vice Admiral Barbey left for Leyte Gulf on the 15th, but Admiral Kinkaid in *Wasatch* remained off Lingayen until 27 January. In the meantime a full-fledged land campaign was under way. The Japanese had shot their bolt temporarily, as far as air attacks were concerned; fortunately so, since the resupply convoys that were shuttling to and fro between Leyte and Lingayen had small and weak screens. Battle damage, operational requirements at Leyte and Mindoro and commitments for forthcoming operations had reduced the supply of escorts. Schedules had to be arranged on a "break off" and "pick up" basis. Four resupply echelons arrived Lingayen Gulf between 14 and 27 January, and three more between 8 and 18 February.

The keeping of this schedule presented a complicated and difficult problem in shipping procurement and loading. Distances involved in the turnaround in some cases exceeded 5000 miles. Almost all Cincpac shipping used in the assault phase could make one more round trip, but the barrel had to be scraped for resupply and reinforcement. Many of these ships had been fleeted up from Guam, Guadalcanal, and even Pearl Harbor to odd places such as Emirau

---

[11] Except for a bad accident in CVE *Hoggatt Bay* at 1424 January 15. Lt. Cdr. E. N. Webb, skipper of *VC-88*, had just made a normal landing of his Avenger when one of its 100-pound bombs exploded, demolishing the plane, killing Webb, his two crewmen and seven of the deck crew and wounding nine other sailors. But within three hours the flight deck had been temporarily repaired and was ready for launching and recovery.

and Finschhafen. Schedules were so tight that no time was available for routine maintenance and upkeep.

Sixth Army, by 16 January 1945, controlled a beachhead almost 30 miles deep and about the same distance wide, with four infantry

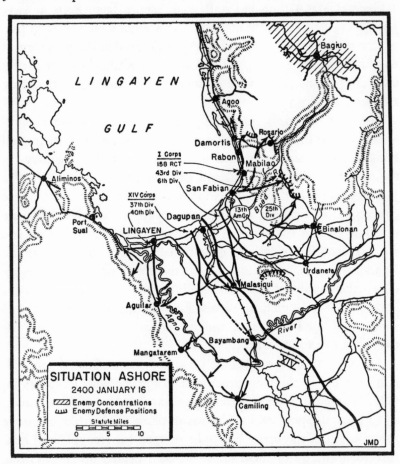

divisions and one RCT. The enemy had left himself wide open in this area. Only on the Sixth Army's left flank did General Yamashita try to hold the south flank of his Damortis-San Fernando position and prevent the Army's advance to Rosario, which he rightly estimated would seal off his forces in the mountains of eastern Luzon. By exception, Lieutenant General Nishiyama, commanding the 23rd Division which faced Sixth Army, planned a big banzai attack on the central part of the beachhead for the night of 16–17 January. It went completely awry. One of four noisy raiding units, mounted in two tanks, penetrated our lines a short distance and set fire to a gasoline dump, but was thrown back with heavy loss.

The battleships, cruisers, destroyers and escort carriers under Admirals Oldendorf, Durgin and Berkey, which had operated together as the Luzon Defense Force since 10 January, now dispersed. Oldendorf's fire support ships, newly designated the Lingayen Heavy Covering Group, were no longer wanted for call-fire owing to the lack of enemy opposition and the prompt landing of divisional artillery. The Army was able to take care of its own gunfire needs and the naval shore fire control parties that accompanied Army units had practically nothing to do. Until 15 January, about 20 different destroyers answered calls for gunfire from time to time. Rear Admiral Oldendorf and Captain Bates, his chief of staff, called on General MacArthur at his Dagupan headquarters on the 16th. The General embraced the Admiral and declared that he could never have landed his troops without naval gunfire support — a polite exaggeration — ; the Admiral promised to deliver more of the same whenever called upon; but no more was needed. There was less naval gunfire support in this operation than in any other in the Pacific since 1942. Such as there was, consisted largely of area neutralization and illumination by destroyers.

Eight escort carriers, with a screen of 14 destroyers and DEs, returned to Ulithi under Rear Admiral Durgin, who then reported for duty in the Iwo Jima operation. Six escort carriers, with a similar screen under the command of Rear Admiral Stump, remained with Seventh Fleet until the end of January, operating with Rear Admiral Berkey's Close Covering Group off northwestern Mindoro "for mutual protection and to economize in the use of destroyers and destroyer escorts."

During the twelve days that they supported the Lingayen landings the CVEs launched 6152 aircraft sorties, of which 1416 were in direct support of infantry. They claimed destruction of 92 Japanese planes, but lost only 2 Wildcats in combat. On 17 January Lieutenant General Kenney became responsible for all air operations in and over Luzon, and the CVEs were no longer needed.

Admiral Kinkaid released Admirals Wilkinson and Conolly from duty with Seventh Fleet on 18 January. They headed for Ulithi in their flagships, and on the 22nd flew to Guam, where Nimitz, a five-star Fleet Admiral since 19 December 1944, had established his forward headquarters on 2 January, Pearl Harbor being now too far in the rear.[12] After a brief leave, Wilkinson and Conolly began to plan the landings on Kyushu that were never necessary.

The amphibious phase of the Luzon campaign was over, but Seventh Fleet still had plenty to do. With the help of Admiral Halsey and Third Fleet, Admiral Kinkaid set out to secure a difficult sea lane, the Mindoro-Lingayen line, upon which the success of the Luzon campaign and the lives of thousands of American soldiers depended.

[12] Adm. King was promoted Fleet Admiral 17 December. Cincpac had all important documents duplicated, packed in 75 crates, each 6 ft. by 3, weighted so they would sink in case of accident and shipped to Guam. His staff and subordinates were divided into five groups. One day a Douglas transport plane took the lowest echelon to Guam. Next day a second took the next higher echelon, and so on. Thus, Cincpac-Cincpoa headquarters moved 3500 miles to the Marianas without interruption. *Time*, 26 Feb. 1945, p. 28.

CHAPTER VII

Third Fleet Cuts Loose[1]

10–27 January 1945

1. The Mindoro-Lingayen Line

THE Navy's chief problem in the Philippines during the first month of 1945 was protection of the 300-mile route from San José, Mindoro, to the southern entrance of Lingayen Gulf. This was not only the shortest route to the beachhead, but the only one practicable as long as the enemy held northern Luzon and Manila.

Although the Japanese no longer were capable of cutting this lifeline, it had to be assumed that they would make the effort. Admiral Kimura's sortie to shell Mindoro on 26 December was freshly remembered, and a repeat performance was to be expected against the stream of transports and freighters plying back and forth between Mindoro and Lingayen Gulf. Consequently an attempt was in order to neutralize or destroy all means of counterattack still possessed by the enemy between Tokyo and Singapore.

Across the South China Sea, 715 miles from Manila, Camranh Bay in Indochina afforded the battered and reduced Japanese Fleet a fine harbor. About 900 miles to the southward and 1400 miles from Manila lay Singapore, now center of the oil production region of the Netherlands East Indies, which the Japanese had overrun in 1942. Hong Kong, also in Japanese possession, is 609 miles from

[1] Com Third Fleet (Admiral Halsey) Action Report 30 Dec. 1944–23 Jan. 1945 and War Diary for Jan. 1945; CTF 38 (Vice Adm. McCain) Action Report 7 Feb. 1945; Cincpac Analysis "Fast Carrier Operations in the China Sea 10–16 Jan. 1945"; Report written for this History in 1947 by Lt. J. J. Cote USNR of Air Grp. 7 in *Hancock;* General MacArthur *Historical Report* II and *Imp. Jap. Navy in WW II* for the Japanese side; Craven & Cate Vol. V.

Manila. The island fortress of Formosa lies only 345 miles north of Lingayen, and southern Kyushu is only another 725 miles farther north. Scattered throughout was a network of airfields from which kamikaze as well as bombing planes could operate.[2] Looking at the situation on the map, these centers of enemy air power were linked together like a long and deadly snake, with its head in Hokkaido and tail in Timor, in comparison with which the liberated parts of the Philippines suggested a rabbit ready to be devoured. Something had to be done — scotch the snake or kill it.

Allied naval authorities had more respect for the striking power of Admiral Toyoda's Combined Fleet than it deserved, as the Japanese had concealed the extensive damage suffered by ships which survived the Battle for Leyte Gulf. It was supposed that Combined Fleet was divided into two main sections, one in the South China Sea with *Ise* and *Hyuga*, and the other in the Inland Sea, with battleships *Yamato, Nagato* and *Haruna,* and one or two carriers. Either section, if it broke loose, might raise havoc with the supply line. As the Inland Sea was too far away to be struck even by B–29s, the alternative was Admiral Halsey's long-desired raid of TF 38 into the South China Sea. But Intelligence made a mistake as to the deployment of Combined Fleet. By New Year's Day of 1945, *Ise* and *Hyuga* were in Lingga Roads near Singapore and Camranh Bay sheltered nothing bigger than escort vessels and auxiliaries.

The actual organization and location of the Japanese Navy and Air Forces on 1 January 1945 was as follows: — [3]

Combined Fleet, Admiral Toyoda, at Tokyo

Second Fleet, Vice Admiral S. Ito, in Inland Sea

Batdiv 1   YAMATO, NAGATO, HARUNA; KONGO had been sunk
Cardiv 1   (Rear Admiral K. Komura, in Inland Sea) AMAGI, KATSURAGI, RYUHO; Air Group 601, 48 aircraft
Desron 2, in Inland Sea: Light cruiser YAHAGI and destroyers ASASHIMO, KASUMI, USHIO, ISOKAZE, HAMAKAZE, YUKIKAZE, SHIGURE, HATSUSHIMO, FUYUZUKI, SUZUTSUKI.
Heavy cruiser TONE, at Kure for the Training Squadron

[2] At that time it was estimated the Japanese had 280 operational planes in the Netherlands East Indies, 170 in Indochina, Burma and Thailand, and 500 in China, Hainan and North Indochina; total 950.
[3] From a letter to Dr. K. Jack Bauer from Capt. T. Ohmae of 4 Mar. 1959.

Fifth Fleet (disbanded 5 February), Vice Admiral K. Shima,
at Singapore or Lingga Roads

Heavy cruiser ASHIGARA
Desron 31: Light cruiser ISUZU, destroyers HINOKI, SUGI, KASHI, KAYA, KIRI, TAKE,
MAKI; DEs No. 22, 29, 31, 43

Units of Second Fleet at Lingga Roads

Crudiv 5 Heavy cruisers MYOKO, HAGURO, TAKAO
Cardiv 4 Battleships ISE, HYUGA

Sixth Fleet, Vice Admiral S. Miwa, at Kure

Tender CHOGEI and 44 submarines

(Transferred from Philippines to Formosa 9 January)
First Air Fleet, Vice Admiral T. Ohnishi

About 50 aircraft

Third Air Fleet Vice Admiral K. Teraoka, in Japan

About 200 aircraft

Eleventh Air Flotilla, Rear Admiral C. Yamamoto, in Kyushu

About 200 Navy and 54 Army aircraft

Sixth Air Army, on Honshu

About 50 aircraft

Japan's logistic situation was fairly desperate. Imports of oil from
Malaya, Borneo, Indonesia and Burma, in the fiscal year of 1 April
1943 to 31 March 1944, were only 34 per cent of the wartime peak,
and no more rice had come in from these sources. Imports of coking
coal from Manchuria, South China and Karafuto (Sakhalin Island)
fell to only 36 per cent of the wartime peak, and those of iron ore
to 33 per cent. Thanks to wartime stockpiling, these shortages were
not yet reflected in basic war industries. Aircraft were still being
built at 69 per cent, shipping at 47 per cent, and army munitions
were being put out at 72 per cent of the wartime rates.[4]

Imperial General Headquarters contemplated no all-out offensive
against the Mindoro-Lingayen line. On 20 January, just as the
Halsey raid into the South China Sea ended, the Emperor approved
and I.G.H. promulgated a new "Outline of Army and Navy Operations". This anticipated a "final decisive battle," to be waged on
Japan proper. Formosa, the Bonins, a part of the Chinese coast and

[4] MacArthur *Historical Report* II, 534, notes.

Southern Korea were designated as the new outer defense sphere —
what a retreat from the "defense perimeter" of 1942 that ran
through Midway, the Gilberts and the Solomons! Forces in the
Philippines were to resist as long as possible, in order to delay the
enemy and give time for the fortification of strongpoints in Formosa, Iwo Jima, Okinawa, Shanghai and South Korea. "When
[significantly, not *if*] the enemy penetrates the defense zone, a
campaign of attrition will be initiated to . . . delay the final assault
on Japan," but ground forces at these key points were not to be
reinforced. Preparations for the decisive battle in Japan itself were
to be completed by the early fall of 1945.[5]

Thus, the raid into the South China Sea was unnecessary to protect the Mindoro-Lingayen line. But a second object of this bold
operation, the attrition of Japanese shipping, was brilliantly fulfilled.

This was not the first visit of United States naval aircraft to
Camranh Bay. In late November 1941, when Japan and the United
States were tottering on the brink of war, the then Chief of Naval
Operations (Admiral Harold R. Stark) ordered Commander in
Chief Asiatic Fleet (Admiral Thomas C. Hart) to reconnoiter the
Manila-Camranh Bay line. This order, because of an alarm from
British sources of an imminent Japanese movement south, was in-
tended to determine the precise location of Japanese ships. Admiral
Hart complied, and between 30 November and 4 December 1941
United States Navy Catalinas operated over this vulnerable route,
sighting 21 transports and other ships in Camranh Bay.[6] If Admiral
Hart had then commanded forces even faintly comparable with
those under Halsey in 1945, Japanese expansion might have ended
then and there.

[5] MacArthur *Historical Report* II 544.
[6] Summary of testimony of Vice Adm. Wilkinson before Congressional Pearl
Harbor Investigating Committee and *Attack*, Part 4 p. 1773, Part 15 pp. 1768–69;
Adm. Hart ms. "Narrative of Events 8 Dec. 1941–15 Feb. 1942"; Craven & Cate
I 191.

2. Halsey's Plan and Supporting Air Operations

During the autumn of 1944, Admiral Halsey was constantly watching for an opportunity to raid the South China Sea, and had proposed to do so on 21 November, but received a decided negative. At Ulithi around Christmas time he had an opportunity to talk it over with Admiral Nimitz, and on 28 December Cincpac gave Commander Third Fleet the green light, "if major Japanese fleet units were sighted." Halsey issued his already prepared plan on 28 December and at 0900 January 9 sent out the "execute."

Rear Admiral R. W. Christie, Commander Submarines Seventh Fleet,[7] provided lifeguard service for Third Fleet. Submarine *Angler* would be at Tizard Reef to look out for fliers who might be forced down, *Rock* would be on the watch thirty miles east of Camranh Bay off Hon Lon Island, and *Kraken* on 14 January would stand by south of Hainan. Vice Admiral C. A. Lockwood, Commander Submarines Pacific Fleet, sent other boats to strategic areas in the South China Sea and around Formosa.

Halsey chose to enter the hitherto forbidden sea northabout, by Luzon Strait, so that he could take a whack at Formosa on the way and give strategic support to Admiral Kinkaid's amphibious forces on Lingayen S-day. Foul weather was anticipated, and would not be wholly to our disadvantage since it might blanket some of the numerous enemy air bases to the north, west and southwest of Halsey's route.

The XX Army Air Force, under the direct command of the Joint Chiefs of Staff, through General H. H. Arnold, planned, with its

[7] Ralph W. Christie, b. Mass. 1893, Annapolis '15. After serving in *New Jersey*, specialized in submarines and became C.O. of *C-1* in World War I. Helped fit out tender *Camden;* C.O. of *R-6;* studied ordnance engineering at Annapolis and M.I.T., where graduated M.S. 1923. C.O. *S-1* and *S-17*, in charge of submarine base at Cavite 1925–26. Two tours of duty at Naval Torpedo Station, Newport. Torpedo repair officer of tender *Argonne* 1928–30, C.O. *Narwhal* 1933. Helped fit out *Ranger* and her navigator to 1936, when became head of torpedo section Buord. Comsubdivs 15 and 20, 1939–42. Com Subs SW Pac Mar. 1943. Com Puget Sound Navy Yard Feb. 1945–7. Com U. S. Naval Forces Philippines 1948–49, when retired as Vice-Admiral.

B–29s, to take over Halsey's former task of keeping Formosa pounded down.

These new Superfortresses, first of the "very heavy" bombers, were of conventional mid-wing design and cost approximately six hundred thousand dollars. Five officers and six enlisted men were the flying crew of a B–29, but seven more officers and 67 more enlisted men were required, as reliefs and ground crew, to keep one unit in combat and operation. A B–29 combat group comprised three squadrons of seven units each, together with five reserves. Four combat groups constituted a wing, with total combat strength of 112 planes and 140 complete crews.[8] Each B–29 was equipped with the latest radar and remote-control automatic gun turrets, operated by a central fire-control system. A pressurized cabin allowed it to fly up to 30,000 feet. With cruising speeds in excess of 300 miles per hour, a 1500-mile tactical radius of action, and a maximum carrying capacity of ten tons of bombs, the B–29 became one of the most powerful striking weapons of World War II. It will be recalled that a primary reason for occupying the Marianas in June 1944 was to supply a base of operations for B–29s within striking distance of the heart of Japan. This was done; but not until 24 November 1944 did the 21st Bomber Command, the Marianas-based B–29s, no fewer than 111 of them, fly their first raid against Japan, directed at an aircraft engine plant near Tokyo. The damage they inflicted was disappointingly small, and the same may be said for the first few months of B–29 operations. Not until March 1945, with Iwo Jima secured and incendiaries substituted for ordinary bombs, did these great aircraft become horribly effective.

The less spectacular operations of the India- and China-based B–29s, the 20th Bomber Command, are more pertinent to the Philippines Campaign. This command, which had been hitting industrial targets in Japan since June 1944, also coöperated with Third Fleet in striking Formosa in October. Its operations were sharply restricted by logistics. Fuel had to be moved to advanced bases by

---

[8] Craven & Cate V 55, 539. By the end of the war 1437 B–29s and 42 F–13s (the recce. plane used by XX A.A.F.) had been delivered in the Pacific Theater.

tanker aircraft flying over "the Hump" through extremely variable weather. Maintenance and repair facilities in the forward area were inadequate. Vast preparations had to be made for each major strike launched from Chinese bases, hence it was impossible to make them frequently.[9] General Kenney's Far Eastern Air Force, having recently moved most of its bombing planes to Morotai, Leyte and Mindoro, was also coöperating. Thus, all available air and surface forces were mobilized to protect the Mindoro-Lingayen line, while Third Fleet was busy in the South China Sea.

During the month of January, tactics and strategy unfolded more like a running battle than a planned operation. General Mac-Arthur, following his request that the B–29s hit Formosa on 9 January, requested "Hap" Arnold, Commanding General of the Army Air Forces, that both Formosa and Okinawa be attacked by XX Army Air Force through 17 January, to the limit of its capabilities, in order to keep enemy air away from the Lingayen beachhead. General Arnold promptly ordered Major General C. E. LeMay's 20th Bomber Command to do it. Lieutenant General Wedemeyer, Commander U.S. Forces China Theater, was asked to furnish as much logistical support as possible to help carry out these strikes,[10] and General Arnold ordered that all other operations scheduled by the XX A.A.F., which might conflict with this directive, be canceled. It was estimated that with Wedemeyer's logistic support, two attacks of 50 to 60 aircraft each with eight- to ten-ton bomb loads,

[9] The XIV Army Air Force with headquarters at Kunming, China, and later the X A.A.F. when it moved from India to Luichow, China, were faced with the same problem, but their fuel was brought in by C–54s directly from Calcutta. By January 1945, 46,000 tons of cargo a month were being flown over the Hump. An amazing achievement, it was merely a drop in the bucket for the needs of the Chinese and their Allies. "The attainment of air supremacy in China was an uphill fight. In spite of the reopening of the Burma Road and the completion of the pipeline to Kunming, the supply position of the XIV Air Force was never better than critical." (Gen. H. H. Arnold Third Report 12 Nov. 1945.)

[10] When General Stilwell was relieved in the fall of 1944, American Army administration in the China-India-Burma theater was split. Lt. Gen. D. I. Sultan, who had been General Stilwell's deputy, was given command of the India-Burma theater, while Lt. Gen. A. C. Wedemeyer, formerly Chief of the War Department Strategical Planners, was appointed Com U. S. forces China, succeeding General Stilwell as Chiang's Chief of Staff. The India-Burma theater then engaged in a major offensive against the Japanese in Burma.

could be launched by the 20th Bomber Command on the air installations of Formosa. In the meantime, approximately 48 bombers of the same command based near Calcutta were to attack drydock and repair facilities at Singapore, which they had been doing at intervals since 5 November 1944.

Owing to bad weather, General LeMay did not pull off his first B–29 strike against Formosa until 14 January, but he repeated it on the 17th. These two strikes, together with the one on 9 January and a raid on the Omura aircraft plant in Kyushu on the 6th, were the limit of the China-based B–29s' capacity to strike the enemy that month. Other B–29s of the 20th Bomber Command based at Calcutta hit Bangkok on 2 January, Singapore on the 11th and 31st, and Saigon on the 27th.

Although the 21st Bomber Command – operating from Isely Field, Saipan, which General LeMay took over on 20 January – was getting prepared for a massive assault on Japan later in 1945, it flew six daylight missions in January against aircraft manufacturing plants in Japan. General Chennault's XIV A.A.F. sank fifteen enemy ships during January, totaling 13,500 tons, and damaged others. Its greatest success occurred between 16 and 20 January, when over a hundred enemy planes were destroyed on the ground in and near Shanghai. The XI A.A.F., based in the Aleutians, flew 15 missions during January against the northern approaches to Japan, while General Kenney's Far Eastern Air Forces flew 7717 sorties against the enemy and dropped 6440 tons of bombs on targets ranging from Bougainville on the east to Lombok in the west, and from Formosa on the north to Timor in the south. Thus, very few segments of the enemy snake lacked attention.

3. *Into the South China Sea, 10–20 January*

On the night of 9–10 January, Third Fleet passed through Luzon Strait into the South China Sea, while the fast fueling group under Captain Acuff steered a southerly course through Balintang Chan-

U.S.S. *Nashville* hit by kamikaze off Negros, 13 December
An LCI(G) in foreground

Destroyer U.S.S. *Barton* repelling air attack off Mindoro

Kamikaze Shows His Hand

LST-472 burning after kamikaze hit, 15 December
Destroyer U.S.S. *Hopewell* assisting

Official U. S. Army Photogra

Troops landing from LCI at Beach White, Mindoro

Mindoro Operation

U.S.S. *Langley* taking a deep roll

Deck crew wrestling with TBM on flight deck of U.S.S. *Anzio*

The Great Typhoon

U.S.S. *Spence*

U.S.S. *Monaghan*

Victims of the Typhoon

Rear Admiral Theodore E. Chandler USN

Vice Admiral McCain, wearing his "lucky cap"

Rear Admiral Russell S. Berkey USN

Two Great Task Force Commanders

H.M.A.S. *Australia* after Kamikaze Attacks

U.S.S. *Pennsylvania, Colorado, Louisville, Portland* and *Columbia*
Entering Lingayen Gulf

Vice Admiral Theodore S. Wilkinson usn
At "Camp Crocodile," Guadalcanal

Vice Admiral Daniel E. Barbey usn

General of the Army Douglas MacArthur USA, and his
Chief of Staff, Lieutenant General R. K. Sutherland USA

General MacArthur Goes Ashore

Lieutenant General Walter Krueger USA

First aid after a Kamikaze Attack

Landing craft approach beach opposite Lingayen town

The "ordered confusion" of an amphibious landing

S-day at Lingayen

Broached landing craft and congested supplies

U.S.S. *Mount Olympus* (left) and transports under air
attack, 12 January. Tug *Chickasaw* in foreground

Admiral William F. Halsey

Official U.S. Coast Guard Photograph

Reception Committee, Lingayen

Friendly approach, Nasugbu

Old Friendships Renewed

Corregidor during the air drops
The white dots are parachutes. Note PT boats patrolling for rescue

A PT approaches to rescue paratroops

Corregidor, 16 February 1945

A U. S. Army tank enters Fort Santiago, Manila

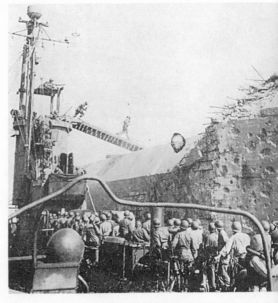

Official U. S. Army Photogra

Soldiers assaulting Fort Drum, El Fraile
from an LSM

Medieval Remains and Modern Methods

U.S.C.G.C. *Spencer*, Command Ship at Palawan and Cebu

U.S.S. *Columbia*

Magellan Monument at Mactan

Assault waves at Cebu, 26 March 1945

Amphibious Operations of 1521 and 1945

Colonel Wendell W. Fertig
at his Mindanao headquarters

Amphibious Engineers' LCM(G)
firing on Balumis, 21 April 1945

Photo courtesy Colonel Robert Amory

Liberating Mindanao

Commander J. P. Graff USN, beachmaster for
Balikpapan, transferred from flagship *Wasatch* to
PC-610 en route

LCI(R)-338 firing rockets at Balikpapan
1 July 1945

The Invasion of Borneo

Front row, left to right: General MacArthur, Lieutenant General Sir Leslie Morshead, General Kenney, Rear Admiral Royal, an Australian soldier.

General of the Army Douglas MacArthur and Party at Labuan, 10 June 1945

Rear Admiral Ralph W. Christie USN

U.S.S. *Bowfin*

Rear Admiral Forrest P. Sherman USN

Rear Admiral Milton E. Miles USN

nel. Neither was discovered by the enemy, but night fighters from carrier *Independence* shot down three Japanese planes flying from Luzon to Formosa.

Bad weather prevented the scheduled topping-off of destroyers on 10 January. After reaching the rendezvous for next day, Vice Admiral McCain set a fueling course downwind to the southwest-ward and every ship got its share of Captain Acuff's black gold. Good luck and an alert and efficient C.A.P. prevented discovery of the Fleet in this vulnerable situation. Fueling was completed by noon 11 January, when Admiral Halsey reorganized his forces for the smash hit on Indochina.

Heavy cruisers *Baltimore* and *Boston* and five destroyers were now detached from Radford's TG 38.1 and assigned to Bogan's Group 2. This increased Bogan's strength to one light and three large carriers, two battleships, two heavy cruisers, three light cruisers, one antiaircraft cruiser and twenty destroyers.[11] Halsey's battle plan, based on the expectation of finding Japanese battle-ships in Camranh Bay, was to split Bogan's group on the morning of 12 January into two parts — one composed of the carriers and their screen; the other, in anticipation of surface action, of cruisers and battleships with the double mission of bombarding Camranh Bay and sinking enemy ships damaged by the carrier aircraft.

At 1400 January 11 Admiral Bogan's reinforced group started its run-in toward Camranh Bay, and Admiral Halsey sent off a mes-sage to the entire Task Force: "You know what to do — give them hell — God bless you all. HALSEY." Combat Air Patrol was furnished by TG 38.1 (Radford) and 38.3 (Sherman), which trailed Bogan. Captain Acuff's fueling group remained jockeying around lat. 13°30' N, long. 115°50' E, very much on the alert against enemy air attack.

The spearhead, however, was the night-flying carrier group, consisting of *Independence*, *Enterprise*, and six destroyers. This TG 38.5, commanded by Rear Admiral M. B. Gardner, launched a pre-dawn search of the coast at 0330 January 12. These pilots pro-

[11] For composition of forces, see Appendix II.

vided the rest of TF 38 with precise information of enemy locations; and instead of returning at dawn they stayed aloft and fought all day. All nearby bays were searched for *Ise*, *Hyuga* and other capital ships — in vain. At the time it was feared that they had been

so expertly camouflaged as to escape notice; but, months later, it was learned that these ships were safe in Lingga Roads.

By 0600 January 12 Bogan's group was within 50 miles of Camranh Bay, and the other two day-flying groups, Sherman's and Radford's, were close behind. Forty minutes later Admiral Halsey activated his special surface strike group of battleships and cruisers, and at 0731, about half an hour before sunrise, air strikes were launched from all three carrier groups, from about lat. 11°31′N, long. 110°01′E.

There then came a comic interlude that might have been tragic. Lifeguard submarine *Rock*, operating off Hon Lon [12] to salvage splashed aviators, was mistaken by picket destroyer *English* for a Chinese junk or Japanese sailing vessel. The story is amusingly told by Commander J. J. Flachsenhar, C.O. of *Rock*, in his report for 12 January: —

0500. Heard a ship request permission on VHF from CTG 38.2 to destroy a sailboat. Said that sailboat had fired two flares. We realized that he may have seen us, but believed that if he did, either he or the task group commander would realize his mistake. We were still not sure our contact was friendly. We certainly didn't expect a destroyer to open fire at a range of over 9000 yards without challenging, on a sailboat which was making 14 knots into the wind, in a submarine patrol zone, and which he couldn't see.

0510. Heard ship receiving permission to destroy sailboat.

0514. Contact on SJ commenced closing rapidly from 150° T. Attempted to identify ourselves on VHF and by challenging with SJ. Instructions prohibited use and nullified value of IFF. Certainly didn't want to challenge an American ship by light at five miles which couldn't tell the difference between a submarine and a sailboat.

0522. Contact commenced firing at range 9300 yards. Splashes were very close but short. Submerged. Fired two green flares from signal gun, although realized that this was disclosing our presence to the Japs. Was still confident that contact, if friendly, could be identified by sound.

0523. Manned battle stations submerged, rigged for depth charge, went to 300 feet. Surface ship was not sending challenge, and was pinging. . . . Apparently the flares didn't work, or ship didn't recognize them. At this point began to give up hope that our friend had read any of the letters, including the one on depth-charge settings in submarine patrol zones.

0615. Screws and pinging faded out. Started up to periscope depth.

0640. At periscope depth, fairly light, all clear. 0651, surfaced.

. . . . . .

[12] A prominent lighthouse at entrance of Nhatrang Bay on the Indochina coast, about 60 miles north of Camranh Bay.

0730. First air wave started in; an inspiring sight but a little nerve-wracking after the morning's experience as they passed directly overhead, tested their guns, and put on a good show for us. Recovered aviator later said there were 850 planes involved in today's operation. . . . Makes quite a sizable number of planes passing over and back, and we didn't appear to miss many. The CD and IFF were left on continuously and were invaluable. We had colors rigged on deck and at the gaff.[18]

Flying conditions that day were only average; showers were frequent. Even under this handicap the 850 available planes in TF 38 flew 1465 sorties, 984 of them sweep-and-strike missions which ranged the Indochinese coast for some 420 miles, together with 481 sorties for C.A.P. between Tourane and Saigon. Admiral Halsey expended 92 per cent of his air striking effort on shipping, and got a full bag. But the surface strike group was doomed to frustration; there being no enemy fleet in Camranh Bay to engage, it turned back and rejoined TG 38.2. Groups 1 and 3 now drew up from their rear positions and joined Bogan's group at 0800.

Although the Japanese Navy had had the good sense, or luck, to depart Camranh for safer waters, plenty of merchant mariners under the Rising Sun were on the receiving end. A fifteen-ship convoy found off Quinhon was "severely mauled" by two successive strikes from "Ted" Sherman's group, which sank the main part of it — nine fully loaded tankers — as well as an escort, light cruiser *Kashii*.[14] Another oiler, two DEs and a patrol craft were sunk out of a convoy off Cape Padaran. Similar treatment was given to a convoy of seven ships and four escorts off Cape St. James. Two freighters, three oilers and three DEs and an LSV (Japanese-type LST) were sunk or beached, and the fighters in this strike started to strafe survivors running across the sand dunes until ordered to desist by the strike coördinator. Near Saigon the disarmed French

18 *Rock* Report of 5th War Patrol. The times are How, used at Perth, one hour earlier than Item. *English* Action Report admits firing on "unidentified" vessel at lat. 11°46′ N, long. 109°44′ E, at 0625.

14 MacArthur *Historical Report* II 534n. But *Imp. Jap. Navy W.W. II* says eight ships sunk of which only two were tankers, plus two DEs and the CL sunk, three damaged.

cruiser *La Motte-Piquet*, although still flying the tricolor, was mistaken for Japanese and sunk. Shipping was attacked all along the coast. Two freighters and a tanker were sunk at Saigon, another oiler sunk off the coast, and others were damaged. Of the damaged ships (two to four DEs, three LSVs, a minesweeper, a patrol craft, five freighters and two tankers), many were beached and later wrecked by a storm. Docks, airfield facilities and oil storage ashore were also heavily hit.

In these strikes Admiral Halsey's claim of ships sunk was unduly modest. He claimed 41 ships sunk, totaling 127,000 tons. Actually TF 38 planes sank 44 ships totaling about 132,700 tons. Of these, 15 ships of about 16,700 tons were combatant vessels of the Japanese Navy and 29 ships of 116,000 tons belonged to the merchant marine. An even dozen of the sunk *Marus* were oil tankers. Admiral Halsey did not exaggerate in calling this "one of the heaviest blows to Japanese shipping of any day of the war," and stating that "Japanese supply routes from Singapore, Malaya, Burma and the Dutch East Indies were severed, at least temporarily."

Enemy air opposition to this strike was meager. Fifteen enemy planes were shot down, 20 float planes in Camranh Bay destroyed, and an estimated 77 destroyed on the ground. The total cost to Task Force 38 for the entire day's operations was 23 planes, but very few pilots. Most of those shot down in Indochina were rescued by friendly natives and returned via Kunming.

At 1931, three minutes after sunset, Task Force 38 changed course to 70° and steamed away from Indochina at 20 knots, heading for a rendezvous with Captain Acuff's oilers near lat. 14° N, long. 114° E, on 13 January. The ships held this northeasterly course at high speed, both to confound enemy searches and to escape an approaching typhoon. Fortunately, for once, the "heavenly wind" worked to the detriment of the Japanese; this storm hovered over the Indochinese coast well to the southward of Task Force 38. But the sea rose, making fueling impossible for some ships and hazardous for all. Only with great difficulty and much delay were most of the destroyers fueled on 13 January. The oilers remained in company with the task force to complete fueling next day.

Fleet Admiral King, in Washington, now stepped into the picture. On 13 January he "directed that the Third Fleet be maintained in a strategic position to intercept enemy forces approaching the Lingayen Gulf area from either the north or south." Fleet Admiral Nimitz passed the word to Halsey, who was already in position to comply. He operated north of his 13 January fueling rendezvous, and continued air search to locate heavy ships. And Nimitz told Halsey that if he did not find any more important targets, he could at his discretion strike Hong Kong.

Next day, 14 January, the wind and sea continued unfavorable for fueling, but by persistent efforts and good seamanship the remaining destroyers were fueled and all heavy ships were brought up to a minimum of 60 per cent capacity, taking most of the black gold left in Captain Acuff's six fast oilers. Fueling completed, around lat. 16°48′ N, long. 116°08′ E, Acuff's group set a southeasterly course to rendezvous off Mindoro with relief tankers approaching through Surigao Strait. The three fast carrier groups now began a northerly run to launch strikes against Formosa. The northeast monsoon was blowing strong, raising a heavy sea and compelling TF 38 to reduce speed to 16 knots. This was the same monsoon that kicked up an annoying sea in Lingayen Gulf.

Weather conditions did not improve as TF 38 headed for Formosa. At 0300 January 15, Vice Admiral McCain recommended to Admiral Halsey that the day's strikes be canceled and that the task force reverse its course. Halsey reviewed weather reports and the tactical situation and decided, since a reversed course would not take his ships beyond enemy air range, and since he wished to hold down Formosa, to continue to run north. At the same time he sent out planes to search the Pescadores, Amoy, Swatow, Hong Kong and Hainan, in the hope of finding the elusive *Ise* and *Hyuga*.

Before sunrise 15 January, the ships arrived in their launching position about 250 to 260 miles ESE of Hong Kong and 170 miles from southern Formosa. *Enterprise* night fighters had been searching since 0400. First strikes were launched about 0730, half an hour before sunrise. Six fighter sweeps were sent against airfields on the China coast, and ten more against airfields on Formosa; eight strikes attacked shipping at Takao and Toshien. Takao Harbor appeared to be full of shipping, but low ceilings prevented the pilots from making the most of this situation – and intense antiaircraft fire did not improve matters. Nevertheless destroyer *Hatakaze* and high-speed transport No. 14 were sunk at Takao, and a tanker was disabled and ran ashore. Other strikes were diverted to Mako in the Pescadores, where better weather prevailed, and there the old destroyer *Tsuga* was sunk. In addition, a Japanese weather station and radio installations on Pratas Island were bombed by eight night-flying planes from *Enterprise*.

The aircraft bag, however, was meager: 16 planes shot down and 18 destroyed on the ground. TF 38 lost 12 planes operationally or in combat.

At 1644 January 15 the carriers shaped a course to a striking position east of Hong Kong, to complete the devastation of shipping off the China coast. At 0732 January 16 the first strikes were launched from lat. 20°15′ N, long. 115°08′ E. Once again weather handicapped the aviators; the torpedo planes fared ill as their low-level attacks exposed them to intense antiaircraft fire and many of their torpedoes, with depth settings too deep, nosed into harbor mud. Hong Kong bore the brunt of this attack, but Hainan and Canton were also hit. Fighters swept airfields along the coast from Liuchow Peninsula north to Swatow, with disappointing results. Admiral Halsey claimed to have sunk five ships aggregating 13,000 tons on the 16th and damaged an additional 75,000 tons, but the postwar record indicates that the score was one freighter and one 10,000 ton tanker sunk, three tankers and a freighter heavily damaged; they, too, were probably a total loss.[15] The day's bag of enemy planes was 13, but Third Fleet operational losses were 27 planes, and combat losses 22, mostly from antiaircraft fire. At Hong Kong, according to Vice Admiral G. D. Murray (Comair-

[15] *Imp. Jap. Navy in W.W. II*; JANAC, however, gives greater losses.

pac), the Japanese used effective antiaircraft tactics which had never before been encountered.

Radio Toyko now informed the world that TF 38 was bottled up in the South China Sea and broadcast dire threats of what would happen to it. "Tokyo Rose" (so Admiral McCain told a correspondent after it was all over) said, "We don't know how you got in, but how the hell are you going to get out?"

That was Admiral Halsey's immediate problem. The weather on 17 January was bad, sea fairly rough and flying conditions undesirable. Fueling began about 1000 in the vicinity of lat. 16°23′ N, long. 116°37′ E, about 190 miles west of Cape Bolinao. Station keeping was so difficult that the task force was only partially fueled, and the oilers stayed in company all night as TF 38 steamed north at eight knots in search of smoother water. With the NE monsoon blowing up to 40 knots, seas broke over *Nehenta Bay's* flight deck, already weakened in the December typhoon, and carried away a part; but she was still able to launch and recover planes.

Halsey advised Nimitz that after finishing fueling on the 18th he intended to disembogue by Balintang Channel and to strike Formosa and Okinawa next day from the eastward. But 18 January proved even worse than the 17th. Fueling was impossible, and by noon TF 38 again had to reverse course and sail south in search of protected waters. Since fleet aërologists predicted that foul weather would continue at least through 19 January, Halsey decided that he had better fuel under the lee of Luzon that day and then leave South China Sea by Surigao Strait; and he so informed Nimitz.

Cincpac, squeezed between his commitments to carry out existing strategic plans (Iwo Jima and Okinawa coming up), and Admiral Halsey's tactical problems, decided that in this instance strategy outweighed tactics. He replied to Halsey that, although Commander Third Fleet must make the final decision, he strongly recommended that TF 38 withdraw via Luzon Strait, waiting for good enough weather to avoid storm damage and permit the offensive use of carrier aircraft. Since the enemy still held Mindanao, the passage of TF 38 through Surigao Strait would give him definite information that Halsey was well out of his way, and might invite trouble. And Nimitz wished to give the Japanese Navy no chance to pull another undetected move as Kurita had done when he sortied from San Bernardino Strait in the Battle for Leyte Gulf. Cincpac concluded his message by assuring Halsey that he was proud of his recent success and had confidence in his judgment.

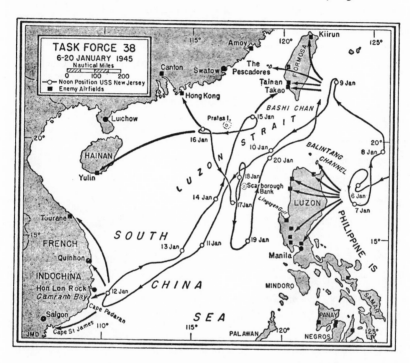

Halsey followed these orders precisely. After fueling on 19 January south of Scarborough Bank, about 180 miles west of Luzon, he shaped a course for Balintang Channel, while Captain Acuff's now depleted oilers headed south for Surigao Strait.

By the afternoon of 20 January TF 38 was heading east into Balingtang Channel, a destroyer division sweeping ahead of the three task groups. Bogeys were almost constantly on the screen, but no attack developed; and about 15 enemy planes which were evacuating air personnel from Luzon to Formosa were shot down.

Two hours before midnight the transit was complete and TF 38 continued to its launching position for the 21st.

During these eleven days, 10–20 January, Third Fleet had logged 3800 miles in the South China Sea without incurring any serious mishap. As Nimitz well said, when endorsing Halsey's Action Report, "the sortie into the South China Sea was well-conceived and brilliantly executed. A most important element in the success of this operation was the plan for logistic support of the Fleet, whose execution left little to be desired. It is regretted that more important targets were not within reach of the Task Force's destructive sweep." These "more important targets" were the capital ships of the Japanese Navy which had retired well out of range of Third Fleet aviators. Imperial General Headquarters would have found some relief from the menace of impending total defeat, had it known the anxiety that this "fleet in being" was creating at American headquarters.

4. *Strategic Discussions, 11–19 January* [16]

The crowded timetable for major operations in 1945 must constantly be borne in mind: Lingayen Gulf 9 January, Iwo Jima 19 February, Okinawa 1 April, Kyushu 1 November. Thus, in January 1945 Admiral Nimitz had two big operations to execute presently, and at the same time he had to support General MacArthur and Seventh Fleet until the Philippines were strategically self-sufficient. It is natural to consider one's own job the most important, particularly in matters of strategy. Thus, the distribution of naval forces between the Philippines campaign and those coming up was the occasion of a firm though courteous discussion between General of the Army MacArthur and Admiral Kinkaid on the one side, and Fleet Admiral Nimitz on the other. Fortunately the restrained tone of the dispatches permitted a compromise with no bitter aftertaste.

[16] Message file of the late Vice Adm. Wilkinson, which he entrusted to me shortly before his untimely death in 1945. All messages are paraphrased.

Upon receipt of Admiral Kinkaid's operation plan of 30 December, Admiral Nimitz noted that it contemplated the continued use of Pacific Fleet battleships, cruisers, destroyers and escort carriers which had initially been borrowed for Leyte. Since these loans had tripled or quadrupled the striking power of Seventh Fleet, it was now accustomed to high living and had no desire to return to the starveling days of New Guinea. Kinkaid proposed to hang on to what he had, and this somewhat shocked Nimitz. In a dispatch to General MacArthur, Cincpac referred to the agreement made by Rear Admiral Forrest Sherman with the General at his Tacloban headquarters on 5 November 1944, to the effect that after the Lingayen operation was well in hand he would release Pacific Fleet fire support ships in time to arrive at Ulithi by 19 January and replenish, in order to meet the target date for Iwo Jima, which the J.C.S. had ordered to be seized as soon as possible after the Lingayen landings. He therefore requested Admiral Kinkaid to delete from his op plan all Pacific Fleet ships then allocated to his command.

Admiral Kinkaid, in reply, observed that his 30 December op plan, which had stirred up Cincpac, was merely an addendum to his Lingayen plan, providing for reinforcement of the initial assault troops and any contingent operations which might be required to protect their movement to the beachhead. He expected to release ships of the fire support group on the scheduled date if the situation at Lingayen permitted. General MacArthur now stepped into the breach and assured Admiral Nimitz that the controversial op plan had been drafted merely to cover possible contingencies; that he shared the Admiral's desire to invade Iwo Jima on the date already announced, and would do everything in his power to help. But he wished to observe that if he stripped down Seventh Fleet, as it were, to the skivvies of New Guinea, it would be too weak to protect Lingayen beachhead from enemy surface attack and barely sufficient to provide escort duty to and from the beachhead. The General invited Cincpac to suggest some other method for him to carry out the liberation of Luzon, as set forth in the J.C.S. basic directive.

Admiral Nimitz answered, in effect, that Third Fleet would continue its efforts to destroy surviving major units of the Japanese
Fleet, the early accomplishment of which would best solve the
problem of protecting the Luzon beachhead. He expressed his
gratification over the General's assurance that he would do everything within his power to help Cincpac invade Iwo and Okinawa
on the planned dates. His previous dispatch, he said, was intended
to ensure that Kinkaid would not count on detaining ships of Pacific Fleet to help establish a new beachhead or on starting some
new operation in the MacArthur bailiwick.

On 17 January Nimitz notified King (with MacArthur, Halsey,
Kinkaid and Spruance as information addressees) that *Ise* and
Hyuga had been located at Lingga Roads, that the four big Japanese battleships were in the Inland Sea, and that enemy air strength
in Formosa and Okinawa had been so augmented that those islands
should be Halsey's next targets. At the same time, Third Fleet
would be ready to intercept any heavy ships that might sortie from
the Inland Sea with designs on the Mindoro-Lingayen line. But he
conceded that Seventh Fleet might keep four of his battleships for
an additional three weeks.[17] And Cominch approved.

Admiral Kinkaid was far from happy over this arrangement.
Next day he pointed out to Admiral Nimitz that he needed more
cruisers and that, in view of kamikaze tactics, Nimitz's proposal to
leave him only enough destroyers to bring the total under his
command up to 50 was insufficient to protect the Luzon Defense
Force, the merchant shipping at Lingayen, Mindoro and Leyte, and
to escort the transports about to lift five reinforced divisions and
an airborne division from New Guinea and Leyte to Luzon. He insisted that he would need a minimum of 58 destroyers until 29 Jan-

---

17 In the same dispatch Admiral Nimitz stated that he would conduct the Iwo
bombardment by employing Rear Admiral P. K. Fischler's Batdiv 5 (*Texas, Arkansas, New York*), just then reporting to the Pacific Fleet from duty in the Atlantic, plus *Nevada, Tennessee* and *Idaho*. But before he was through he had to call
upon *Washington* and *North Carolina* for additional bombardment support, forcing them to divide their time between regularly assigned missions with the fast carriers and support of the amphibious operation. It was literally true that there was
not a ship to spare.

uary, when the scheduled landing near Subic Bay would come off. Until that was over, he felt that he should be allowed to retain at least 26 Pacific Fleet destroyers, which made no allowance for possible combat losses or for upkeep. General MacArthur concurred, but was even more concerned over Cincpac's intention to recall two of the six battleships then with Seventh Fleet for repairs. The reader will recall what a pasting *California* and *New Mexico* had taken. The General felt that this would leave Seventh Fleet in a weak position between two Japanese naval forces and doubtfully superior to the northern one, which included *Yamato.* He pled strongly to retain all six battleships until the situation had been clarified; or, if the two battleships were returned for repairs, to have them replaced by two others.

The final outcome of these discussions was a decision by Admiral Nimitz on 18 January. He then informed General MacArthur that he concurred generally with his ideas and those of Admiral Kinkaid, but did not share the General's opinion that the enemy was capable of concentrating six battleships for a quick attack on Seventh Fleet. Nor did he consider the Japanese capable of inflicting disaster on Philippines operations if the United States Pacific Fleet were employed offensively. Cincpac observed that if a local naval defense force capable of meeting all heavy ships left in the Japanese Fleet were retained continuously on station, further major operations in the Pacific would have to be postponed indefinitely. The best naval protection for the Philippines, as well as for our exposed island positions elsewhere in the Pacific, would be offensive operations against Japan. He repeated his request for the immediate return of the two damaged battleships so that their fighting efficiency might be promptly restored, but sweetened this demand by approving the temporary retention by Seventh Fleet of cruisers *Portland* and *Minneapolis* and 22 of the destroyers that Kinkaid wanted.

Admiral Kinkaid, to protect the Mindoro-Lingayen line, now allotted four light cruisers, seventeen destroyers, six escort carriers and four destroyer escorts to a task group, to be alternately commanded by Rear Admirals Berkey and Stump. This group operated west of Mindoro and sufficiently far off shore to reduce the possibility of enemy air attack and at the same time remain within supporting distance of the line of communications. He announced that he intended to employ this group to support Admiral Struble's forthcoming landing on the Zambales coast on 29 January, and Rear Admiral Fechteler's at Batangas two days later. The escort carriers would then be replenished and returned to Pacific Fleet. The CVEs were not to be called upon to furnish air cover for convoys except in emergency, since it had been agreed that, from 17 January on, air cover for convoys in Philippine waters would be furnished by General Kenney's land-based Far Eastern Air Forces.

General MacArthur stated his position for the last time on 19 January. He informed Admiral Nimitz that he wished to retain a strong naval force in the Philippines only during the short but critical period between the withdrawal of Third Fleet and the installation of Far Eastern Air Forces on Luzon. So far, it had been possible to base near Lingayen only a few fighter squadrons, inadequate to deal with enemy ships. He requested to be informed when Admiral Nimitz wished *California* and *New Mexico* to be withdrawn, and remarked, with a trace of sarcasm, that his retention of these two veterans of the Pacific Fleet could hardly affect the success of the massive offensive being planned by Cincpac.

Admiral Oldendorf and the two controversial battlewagons finally left Leyte on 22 January. The other four stayed with Seventh Fleet until 14 February, 1945.

Five months later Admiral Raymond Spruance, over-all commander for Iwo and Okinawa, wrote that "the planning for and the actual execution of the Iwo Jima operation were affected to a considerable extent by the operations in the Philippines which immediately preceded it, and by the necessity of preparing for the Okinawa operation which was to follow. The Philippines operations necessitated last-minute changes and reduced the total number of ships which had been previously allocated to the Iwo Jima operation. This applied primarily to battleships, cruisers and destroyers for the Joint Expeditionary Force, although other forces were also affected to a lesser extent." [18]

There can be no question that the Philippines campaign was a thorn in the side of those eager to get on with the Pacific War as rapidly as possible. In retrospect, and with the full knowledge of the Japanese Navy's condition in January 1945 — which contemporaries did not have — it appears it would have been a mistake to have retained massive surface forces in Philippine waters.

5. *Fast Carriers Strike Formosa and Retire, 20–27 January*

Admiral Halsey, although well aware of what was going on between Nimitz and MacArthur, went right ahead with his plans. Once more he led Third Fleet in a series of strikes to support the Philippines Campaign. This time TF 38 paid dear for success.

At 0100 January 21, three hours after completing its passage through Balintang Channel, TF 38 changed course to 345° and began to approach the launching position for Formosa, about 120 miles east of Takao. By 0650 all three task groups were launching pre-dawn fighter sweeps to neutralize airfields in Formosa, the Pescadores and the Sakishima Gunto. Strikes were launched regularly throughout the day with emphasis on shipping in the morning and airfields in the afternoon. Flying weather was the best of the month so far. A total of 1164 sorties was flown; 104 enemy aircraft were claimed destroyed on the ground; Takao, Tainan and Kiirun were heavily hit. Because of shoal water in Takao harbor, it was difficult to distinguish between damaged ships resting on the bottom, and others still afloat, but at the end of the day conditions at Takao harbor looked like those at Manila. By postwar check, ten *Marus*, including five tankers, were sunk, and in the Pescadores destroyer *Harukaze* was damaged. Only three enemy planes were encountered over Formosa and two were shot down.

[18] Com Fifth Fleet Report of Iwo Jima Operation 14 June 1945.

At sea it was a different story. Kamikaze came to life, and for the first time since November delivered a damaging air attack on ships of the fast carrier task force.

At noon 21 January, TF 38 lay about one hundred miles east of the southern coast of Formosa. Rear Admiral Radford's Group 1 was approximately twelve miles south of Bogan's Group 2; Sherman's Group 3, which first caught it, was farther north. Four destroyers were being fueled from battleships *North Carolina* and *Washington* at a speed of 16 knots. Presently four kamikazes with three escorts, from Tainan, Formosa, came in on them. At 1206 a single-engined aircraft was sighted from carrier *Langley*, flying down-sun at her from astern in a low glide. It was taken under fire but managed to drop two small bombs, one of which hit the forward part of the carrier's flight deck, ripping a hole 10 by 14 feet and lighting small fires which were quickly brought under control. Within three hours *Langley* had effected temporary repairs and was recovering her aircraft. Her casualties were 3 dead and 11 wounded.

Two minutes after *Langley* was hit, a kamikaze dove out of the sun and clouds and crashed the nearby carrier *Ticonderoga*. It penetrated the flight deck and the 550-pound bomb exploded between the hangar and gallery decks. An intense fire flared up among closely spotted and gassed planes which were about to take off for the next strike. It spread to the second and third decks. Rear Admiral Sherman [19] maneuvered Group 3 around *Ticonderoga* to give her close support while she adopted the most advantageous course for fire-fighting.

[19] Frederick C. Sherman, b. Mich. 1888, Annapolis '10. Service in various ships until 1915, when C.O. of submarines *H-2* and *O-7* through World War I. Commanded Subdiv 9 1921–24; gunnery officer *West Virginia* 1926–29; various shore duties until 1932. Navigator *Detroit*, Comdesdiv 1 1934; became naval aviator at Pensacola, exec. *Saratoga* 1937, and of N.A.S. San Diego to 1938. C.O. Patwing 3, 1939; senior course at Naval War College, C.O. *Lexington* 1940 (see Vols. III and IV). After her loss in the Battle of the Coral Sea he became assistant chief of staff to Cominch with rank of Rear Admiral until the end of 1942, then Comcardiv 2 of the Fast Carrier Forces Pacific Fleet (details in Vols. V, VI, VII, VIII). Com Fleet Air West Coast Mar.–Aug. 1944, when became CTG 38.3 (details in Vol. XII). Com 1st Carrier Task Force Pacific Fleet with rank of Vice Admiral July 1945; Com Fifth Fleet 1946; retired 1947; died 27 July 1957.

While Sherman was handling this bad situation a raid of 13 enemy planes (7 kamikazes, 6 escorts) approached Radford's Group 1 from the Babuyan Islands in the south. They had taken off from Tuguegarao, Luzon, and must have been the last Japanese combatant planes left on the big island. Eight fighters from *Cowpens* were vectored out to intercept. They destroyed a majority of the enemy formation and the rest retired.

The second raid of the day from Formosa, eight kamikazes with 5 escorts, approached Group 3 at 1250. Some were intercepted; six were shot down, two escaped and dove at *Ticonderoga*. One fell victim to antiaircraft fire, but a few seconds later the other crashed the damaged carrier's island structure. Flaming gasoline engulfed the island and many planes spotted on deck were damaged, but by 1415 all fires were under control and steps were taken to correct the nine-degree list which had developed. By 1800 the list had been reduced to three degrees, compartments had been freed of smoke, and vigorous efforts were being made to restore her fighting trim. But her casualties were 143 killed or missing and 202 wounded, and she lost 36 planes. Her C.O., Captain Dixie Kiefer, was badly wounded, but recovered.

At 1310, less than twenty minutes after *Ticonderoga* received her second blow, destroyer *Maddox* (Commander J. S. Willis) received the kiss of death. She, in company with *Brush* (Commander J. E. Edwards), was on picket duty some thirty-five miles nearer Formosa than TF 38, reporting planes flying toward the carriers, recovering splashed pilots and controlling C.A.P. A Japanese Zeke pilot pulled the old trick of joining a returning flight of American planes. The Tom Cat destroyer failed to delouse him, and at the proper moment he peeled off and dove on *Maddox*, crashing amidships. A split second later his bomb exploded, but the fire that resulted was immediately brought under control. Damage was moderate, but casualties amounted to 7 killed and 33 wounded.

That was the extent of enemy counterattack, but there was more trouble ahead for TF 38. At 1328 a torpedo plane returned on board Vice Admiral McCain's flagship, carrier *Hancock*, part of Admiral Bogan's Group 2. The pilot made a normal landing but a 500-pound bomb fell out of his bomb bay as he was taxiing up the deck and exploded. Heavy fires broke out on the flight, gallery and hangar decks. The ship's company quenched the fire on the hangar deck within fifteen minutes of the explosion; by 1405 all fires were under control, and at 1510 emergency repairs were completed on the flight deck. But the casualties were heavy: 52 killed and 105 wounded.

That evening Admiral Halsey formed a special task group consisting of two light cruisers and three destroyers, including *Maddox*, to escort *Ticonderoga* back to Ulithi.

The rest of TF 38 headed north for strikes against the Ryukus next day, 22 January. At 0200, en route to Okinawa, seven night-flying torpedo-bombers were sent on a strike against Kiirun Harbor, Formosa. They claimed to have destroyed a large ship moored to a wharf. This turned out to be a 10,000-ton tanker. Three planes failed to return.

The primary objective at Okinawa was to obtain photographic coverage in anticipation of the campaign to capture that island, but it was also desired to destroy shipping and bomb airfields. A rather bewildering array of targets was selected; the Sakishima Gunto, Ie Shima, Okinawa, and two islands in northern Amami O Shima.

Pre-dawn searches were launched about 0615, half an hour before sunrise, from about lat. 24°40′ N, long. 128°10′ E. A total of 682 sorties were flown of which 47 were photographic. There was no enemy air opposition and some 28 planes were destroyed on the ground. Admiral Halsey claimed that "the job of destruction of 10 October was supplemented and completed," but there was plenty left for Fifth Fleet to do before the landing there in April.

At 2000 January 22, TF 38 started south, fueled on the 23rd and returned to Ulithi for a well-earned rest.

Third Fleet support of the Luzon campaign is impressive. During January some 300,000 tons of enemy shipping was sunk or destroyed,[20] and the number of aircraft destroyed is claimed to have been 615. The cost to the United States was 201 carrier aircraft, 167 pilots and aircrewmen, and 205 sailors who were killed in the kamikaze crashes of 21 January.[21] Both ships and men had proved their ability to carry on in almost continuous bad weather. As the fearless Admiral Halsey wrote, "The outer defenses of the Japanese Empire no longer include Burma and the Netherlands East Indies; those countries are now isolated outposts, and their products are no longer available to the Japanese war machine except with staggering and prohibitive losses en route."

In *New Jersey* he arrived Ulithi on the afternoon of 25 January and at 1630 Admiral Spruance and members of his staff came on board for a conference. Next afternoon, 26 January, Halsey gave a farewell party at Commodore "Scrappy" Kessing's club on Asor Island; and at midnight Admiral Raymond A. Spruance assumed tactical command of the Fleet, which under him was numbered the Fifth. He had a wonderful reputation to live up to, and that he did.

In his parting message to the Fleet, Halsey expressed his admiration and gratitude:

"I am so proud of you that no words can express my feelings. This has been a hard operation. At times you have been driven almost beyond endurance but only because the stakes were high, the enemy was as weary as you were, and the lives of many Americans could be spared in later offensives if we did our work well now. We have driven the enemy off the sea and back to his inner defenses. Superlatively well done. HALSEY."

[20] In Jan. 1945 the Japanese merchant marine lost 248,000 tons of freighters and 182,000 tons of tankers. This was the most destructive month of the war except Oct. 1944, when total losses were 522,000 tons, but the most destructive of all for tanker tonnage. USSBS *War Against Japanese Transportation* pp. 116–18.

[21] Pilot and plane losses from Cincpac Monthly Analysis for Jan. 1945; 103 planes were lost operationally and 98 in combat; 31 aviators operationally and 136 in combat.

CHAPTER VIII
Luzon Liberated[1]
17 January–30 June 1945

1. Southward Drive and Subsidiary Landings, 17 January–3 February

IN his pleas to the Joint Chiefs of Staff in 1944 to be allowed to liberate Luzon, General MacArthur predicted that his forces could capture Manila about two weeks after the initial landings. On 12 January 1945 (Lingayen S-day plus 3) MacArthur, now a five-star General of the Army, called Vice Admiral Kinkaid, Vice Admiral Wilkinson and Lieutenant General Walter Krueger to a conference on board cruiser *Boise,* off the beachhead. He stressed the urgency of occupying Manila as early as possible in order to free the Allied prisoners and internees who were slowly starving to death. He emphasized that our losses so far had been small and predicted that the enemy would evacuate Manila rather than defend it. Such indeed was Yamashita's intention; but, as we shall see, his orders were not carried out.

Krueger demurred from MacArthur's wish for a dash on Manila, although before the operation began he had hoped to celebrate the General's 65th birthday (26 January) in the capital. "Too precipitate an advance," he believed, would cause Sixth Army to outrun

[1] Seventh Fleet and VII 'Phib War Diaries; CTG 78.3 (Rear Adm. Struble) Action Report of Zambales Landing 4 Mar. 1945; Letters from Adm. Struble 11 Apr. 1947 and 2 May 1947; CTU 77.3.1 (Rear Adm. Riggs) Action Report 10 Feb. 1945; CTG 78.2 (Rear Adm. Fechteler) Action Report 8 Mar. 1945; Comdesron 49 (Capt. B. F. Brown) Action Report 6 Feb.; *Sixth Army Report* I; R. R. Smith chaps. viii, xxviii; Lt. Gen. Walter Krueger *From Down Under to Nippon* (1953) chap. xxiv; Robert Sherrod *History of Marine Corps Aviation in World War II* (1952); Maj. B. C. Wright *1st Cavalry Division in World War II* (1947).

supply from the Lingayen beaches, and expose it to flank attacks from the Zambales and the Ilocos mountains. Actually the enemy had no substantial forces on the Sixth Army's Zambales flank, but Yamashita had established his headquarters at Baguio and was capable of making harassing raids on the Ilocos flank, or even counterattacking Lingayen beachhead. The bulk of Major General Swift's I Corps had to be used to contain Yamashita, while XXIV Corps pressed southward to Clark Air Centers near San Fernando, the hub of a complex of airfields around the old prewar Clark Field.

But the real drag on the pace of advance, as General Krueger admitted after the war, was the fact that Sixth Army was inexperienced in "overland movement by large forces." It had practised tough fighting in New Guinea and on Leyte, but always so near a beachhead that it was able to depend on the Navy for the major part of its supply line. It had "practically no stocks of Bailey bridging, floating bridge equipment and similar vital engineer items," nor was there any way of getting them in time for this operation. "Our greatly overtaxed means of transportation" wrote Krueger, "were not, in fact, materially relieved until the bulk gasoline pipeline was laid from Lingayen Gulf to Dau, . . . the railroad to San Fernando . . . rehabilitated, and the port of Manila opened again." [2] In particular, he felt that it would be impractical to dash to the capital until after arrival of the first big reinforcement echelon (32nd Infantry and 1st Cavalry Divisions) due at Lingayen 27 January.

Although the Japanese hardly fired a shot on the XIV Corps front they obstructed the advance by blowing bridges, ripping up the railway and building road blocks. Krueger drove his Army Engineers to the utmost, but by 29 January XIV Corps had advanced only to San Fernando. On that day the Navy bore a hand by landing XI Corps (38th Infantry Division and 34th RCT) on the coast of Zambales Province, about 45 miles across a mountain

[2] Krueger pp. 321–22. Compare the situation in the European campaign in Sept. 1944, when Gen. Patton's column outran the capacity of his crosscountry supply line, despite the short distance from English ports of supply to the Normandy beachhead.

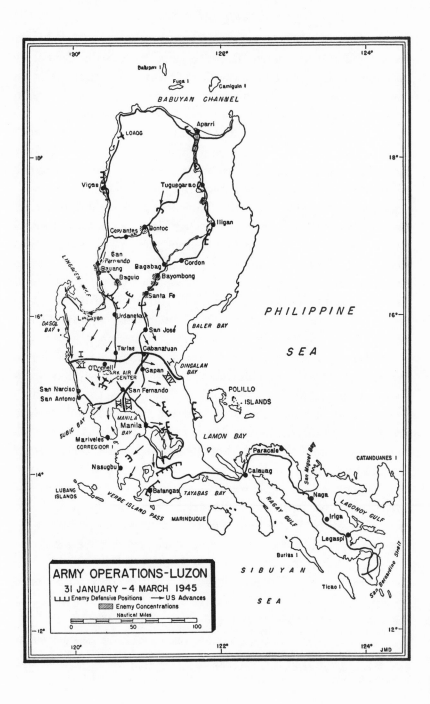

BABUYAN CHANNEL

PHILIPPINE

SEA

BALER BAY

DINGALAN
BAY

POLILLO
· ISLANDS

LAMON BAY

CATANDUANES I

RAGAY GULF

LAGONOY GULF

SIBUYAN

SEA

Burias I

Ticao I

ARMY OPERATIONS-LUZON

31 JANUARY – 4 MARCH 1945

⊔⊔⊔ Enemy Defensive Positions   ➤ US Advances

▨ Enemy Concentrations

Nautical Miles

0   50   100

Aparri

LOAOG

Vigas

Tuguegarao

Iligan

Cervantes   Bontoc

San
Fernando   Cordon
Bauang   Bagabag
Baguio   Bayombong

Santa Fe

Lingayen   Urdaneta

San Jose

Tarlac   Cabanatuan

O'Donnell
CLARK AIR
CENTER   Gapan

San Narciso   San Fernando
San Antonio

Mariveles   MANILA   Manila
CORREGIDOR I   BAY

Nasugbu   Paracale

Calauag   Naga

Batangas   TAYABAS BAY   Iriga

MARINDUQUE   Legaspi

LUBANG
ISLANDS   VERDE ISLAND PASS

LINGAYEN GULF

DASOL
BAY

SUBIC BAY

San Miguel Bay

San Bernardino Strait

120°   122°   124°

JMD

range from San Fernando. This target had been selected at the *Boise* conference on 12 January as the means of providing a western pincer to operate in conjunction with the straight-arm of XIV Corps.

This MIKE VII Operation, as the Zambales landing was called, took place over beaches in front of the little towns of San Felipe, San Narciso and San Antonio. The main objective was to seal off Bataan Peninsula so that Japanese forces in Manila could not hole up there and make a prolonged resistance, as General Wainwright's troops had done in 1942. Since the Zambales landing was uncontested, it need not occupy us long. It was given to Rear Admiral Arthur D. Struble,[3] commanding Amphibious Group 9 of the VII 'Phib from flagship *Mount McKinley*, to land XI Corps, Major General C. P. Hall. The Army part of the plan was handled at Tolosa, Leyte, by Lieutenant General R. L. Eichelberger, Commanding Eighth Army, to which XI Corps then belonged.[4] Admiral Struble, who had to prepare the tactical plans, had only two weeks for the job.[5] He could not get the allotted transports into Leyte Gulf until a couple of days before the expedition was scheduled to depart.

The Zambales landing was formidable in size but uncontested by the enemy. Some 30,000 troops were landed on B-day (29 January); two transport divisions together with several Liberty ships and the usual array of beaching craft were employed. Air cover was furnished by General Kenney's planes from Leyte and surface cover by light cruiser *Denver* and two destroyers under Rear Admiral R. S. Riggs.[6] There were 14 destroyers and DEs in the screen,

[3] See Vol. XII 119*n* for brief biog.

[4] This was done to relieve Sixth Army staff of the planning. XI Corps reverted to Sixth Army the day after landing.

[5] Adm. Barbey's staff had been working on a previously ordered landing at Vigan (Ilocos Sur), only to get the word on 14 January that Vigan was canceled and Zambales substituted.

[6] Ralph S. Riggs, b. Texas 1895; Annapolis '18. Served in *Minneapolis* and *Manly* in World War I, at the end of which commanded all the "Eagle" subchasers. In *Utah* for 4 years, aide to Com CL Divs., Scouting Fleet, Yangtze Patrol, and to Combatdiv 1 in *Texas*. C.O. *Zane* 1933; duty in Bunav, navigator *West Virginia*, C.O. *Arctic*, aid to Ass't Secnav, Comdesdiv 2 in *Aylwin* 1941–42. Comdesron 14 in *Bailey* in Battles of the Coral Sea, Midway and Komandorskis, chief of staff to

eleven big and 19 small minesweepers under Lieutenant Commander J. R. Keefer, and an APD embarking an underwater demolition team. Rear Admiral Berkey's Close Covering Group, which guarded the Mindoro-Lingayen line, furnished C.A.P. over the landing area and was near enough to help in case of trouble.

No trouble developed. On the basis of Intelligence reports that very few Japanese were about (actually there were only 46), and that Filipino guerrillas were in control, Admiral Struble ordered the two fire support destroyers to close the beaches at first light B-day and report what they saw before opening bombardment. Destroyer *Young* (Commander D. G. Dockum) reported the presence of many natives with their boats, and *Isherwood* saw a small Japanese tanker wrecked just north of Beach Blue. To give this peaceful scene a touch of the ludicrous, a *banca* manned by enthusiastic Filipinos closed destroyer *Picking*, its occupants crying "Liberty! Liberty!" to the startled bluejackets, who would have appreciated a little liberty themselves. Lieutenant A. F. Tadena of the Philippine Resistance Army boarded *Young,* and two guerrillas who had been enlisted men in the U.S. Navy boarded *Sproston*, to report that the entire area was in friendly hands and that American and Philippine flags were already flying ashore; the nearest Japanese were a few thousand troops concentrated at Olongapo on Subic Bay. So the Admiral canceled the bombardment and the landing went off peacefully. It was all over by 0945 January 29. The 34th RCT secured San Marcelino, where work immediately began to put the airstrip in condition for landings and takeoffs by the Army Air Force.

That evening, four destroyer transports under Commander W. S. Parsons, which had come up empty, embarked a reinforced infantry battalion of the 38th Division from the Zambales beach and, with the new LSV *Monitor* carrying trucks and armor, landed early 30 January near the mouth of Subic Bay on Grande Island, abandoned by the enemy. Their object was to secure the Bay

Comdespac July 1943, C.O. *South Dakota* Mar.–Nov. 1944, then Comcrudiv 12 to end of war. Comcrudiv 14 1946, General Board, Ass't C.N.O., retired 1951.

and eventually to reactivate the old American advanced naval base of Olongapo on its southern shore.[7] An interesting incident of this landing was the rescue of a U.S. Army staff sergeant who, taken prisoner when Corregidor fell in 1942, had been on board a Japanese transport sunk off the Bay on 15 December 1944. He swam ashore and concealed himself until he saw the task unit, when a native boat brought him on board.

Commander Parsons reconnoitered Olongapo shortly after the landing on Grande Island, arriving in time to see troops of the 38th Division walk into the town. Transport *Cavalier*, when forming up at 0133 January 31 for return passage, suffered a violent underwater explosion, believed to be from a Japanese submarine's torpedo. It jammed her propeller and she was towed to safety by minecraft *Rail*.

A third minor amphibious operation, designed to establish a line of advance on Manila from the southwest, was the landing of the 11th Airborne Division (Major General J. M. Swing) by Rear Admiral Fechteler's Group 8 of VII 'Phib on the beaches at Nasugbu, Batangas Province, on the last day of January. Operation MIKE VI (the code name of this landing) was ordered by General MacArthur on 15 January and mounted by Eighth Army on the shore of Leyte Gulf, not far from where Admiral Struble was assembling the Zambales force. The 11th Airborne was lifted by a transport group under Commander W. V. Deutermann which comprised 4 APD, 44 LCI, 16 LSM and 10 LST, and screened by Desron 5, Captain William M. Cole. Rear Admiral Riggs doubled for fire support after he was through at Zambales. Batangas Bay, south of Nasugbu, reconnoitered by Lieutenant Commander N. Burt Davis's Mindoro-based PTs, had been found to contain a nest of Japanese midget explosive boats; but the objective here was the town of Nasugbu, western terminus of a road network that leads into Manila.

Owing to numerous swamps and rice paddies in the low country,

[7] The SWPac Amphibious Training Center, started at Port Stephens, Australia, in 1943, was transferred from Milne Bay to Subic Bay in March 1945.

mountains and ravines inland, and two large bodies of fresh water
(Lakes De Bay and Taal), movement within this region is confined
to roads and crests of ridges. Fortunately for the Americans an all-
weather highway leads uphill and inland from Nasugbu to Tagaytay Ridge, which runs at about 2000 feet elevation along the north-

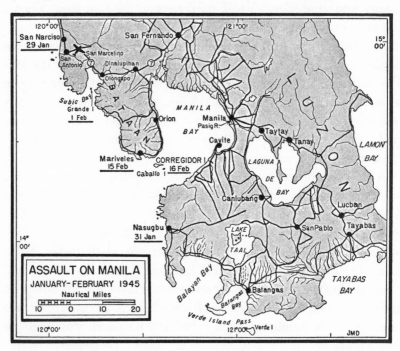

ern shore of Lake Taal, and supports Tagaytay City in the center.
Manila, thirty miles northeasterly, is clearly visible from this ridge.
From Tagaytay, a two-lane concrete highway runs north past the
former United States Naval Base at Cavite, then along the shore of
Manila Bay and into the city.

The morning of 31 January, called "X-ray day" at Nasugbu, was
warm with a 10- to 15-knot northeasterly breeze. The sea lay
calm under an almost cloudless sky. The soldiers in the high-speed
transports had to transfer into LCP(R)s for the landing, but the
LCIs went directly in to the beach.

Admiral Fechteler had chosen a 600-yard stretch of shore about

1500 yards south of the Wawa River, designated Beach Red, for his landing. The minesweepers accomplished their mission rapidly and reported no mines present. As the amphibious craft anchored in their assigned areas, Captain Cole's screen got ready to soften up the landing area, where the enemy was believed to be present in some force. There was no reply; but as no friendly natives came out to welcome the invaders, a regular assault landing was executed, with rocket and gunboat fire, and air strafing furnished by A–20s of the A.A.F. Machine-gun fire on the left flank was silenced by two LCIs and destroyer *Claxton*. The beaches were too sloping to be satisfactory, but the 188th RCT (the paratroops) were all ashore a little after noon. They pushed up the road toward Manila and captured a strategic bridge on the Pasig River before dark.

Owing to the beach gradient, about 6 LST and several LCI could not be unloaded until high water at midnight; hence several destroyers, DEs, PCs and LCIs anchored or patrolled off the beachhead the night of 31 January–1 February. It was a perfect tropical night. A full moon rose at 2120. An hour and a quarter later *PC–1129* reported small boats to be about. At 2300 destroyer escort *Lough* (Lieutenant Commander Blaney C. Turner USNR) picked them up, identified them as enemy, and notified the nearest U.S. ship to them, which happened to be *PC–1129*. Before this patrol craft could do anything about it she was surrounded by the midgets, like an old-time trading schooner by native canoes, and one of them blew a six-foot hole in her side. That was too much for a PC to take; she rolled over and sank. All the crew but one were subsequently picked up.

Lough at 2300 saw about 1000 yards ahead of her a line of 25 to 30 small boats extending from east to west. They showed no wake, looked like a swarm of waterbugs in the moonlight; and, being built of wood, did not register on her radar screen. The destroyer escort bent on 20 knots, approached the sinister-looking formation down-moon, and enfiladed it with 20-mm and 40-mm fire. The boats then attempted to surround the DE as they had the PC, but she was too nimble for them. *Claxton*, when trying to increase the light on the scene with star shell, dodged a torpedo that one of the midgets sent her way. After *Lough* had diminished the midget fleet by at least six units, the rest retired without penetrating the inner and more vulnerable screen of LCIs. After daylight Admiral Fechteler organized a search of the coast through Talin Bay which bagged another couple. The commander of these midget craft, which were based at Balayan on the bay of that name, notified Tokyo that he had sunk eight enemy ships.

The troops who landed on 31 January, urged on by General Eichelberger in person, pushed ahead fast toward Tagaytay; but there was trouble on the beach. The LST flotilla, having unloaded, was unable to retract before high water, which arrived after midnight. So the same force of destroyers and small craft was kept on duty off shore, with Admiral Fechteler as O.T.C. In the small hours of 1 February he encountered two motor torpedo boats and briefed them on the midgets, but owing to a communications failure they were unable to advise him of their night movements. *PT–77* and *PT–79*, when hunting for midgets, unfortunately encountered *Conyngham* and *Lough*, which had been ordered to shoot up suspicious-looking craft making no signals. One boat did flash the letters "PT," but, as it kept on coming, the C.O. of *Lough* suspected an enemy ruse and let go with both 40-mm and 5-inch guns at a range of 1200 yards. The PTs tried to escape at top speed, and might have succeeded had not *PT–77* grounded on a reef. A shell from *Lough* hit her there and killed the squadron commander, Lieutenant J. H. Stillman USNR. *Lough* and *Conyngham* then shifted gunfire to *PT–79* and managed to sink her, with the loss of the C.O., Lieutenant (jg) M. A. Haughian USNR, and two petty officers. Thirty men, survivors of both boats, swam ashore, evaded seizure by the Japanese with the aid of guerrillas, and were picked up by two PTs from Mindoro on 3 February.[8]

[8] R. J. Bulkley "PT History" p. 541; Rear Adm. Fechteler, *Conyngham* and *Lough* Action Reports. The Admiral had had an agreement with PT commanders about signals, hence it was natural for him and his captains, especially after the previous midget attack, to assume that any small craft approaching without signals was hostile.

After 8000 men and 4200 tons of supplies had been landed at Nasugbu on X-ray-day and the following, a second convoy arrived 4 February. Resupply convoys came along at short intervals.

2. *On to Manila, 27 January–15 March*

By the time these subsidiary landings were completed, Sixth Army drive on Manila was gathering momentum. On 27 January, as we have seen, the reinforcements that General Krueger wanted, 32nd Infantry and 1st Cavalry Divisions, were landed by the Navy on the Lingayen beaches. The 32nd was sent to help I Corps on the Army's left (eastern) flank, while the troopers were attached to XIV Corps and moved forward to Cabanatuan. There, reinforced by a tank battalion, they formed a flying column to dash for Manila along Highway No. 3 as soon as General MacArthur gave the word.

The General, exceedingly anxious about the American civilians and P.O.W.s in Manila prisons, was becoming impatient with the slow advance of XIV Corps. Prodded by his remark (after a personal reconnaissance) that Sixth Army was showing insufficient drive and initiative, General Krueger on 30 January ordered XIV Corps, then about to take Clark Air Center, "to advance aggressively southward" and cross Pampanga River within two days. At the same time he ordered I Corps to attack vigorously on the left flank and capture San José (Nueva Ecija), an important road and railway center. XI Corps, which had landed at Zambales three days before, was ordered to push across the base of Bataan Peninsula and join hands with XIV Corps. At the same time 1st Cavalry Division (Major General Verne D. Mudge), with 44th Tank Battalion, covered by Marine Corps aircraft, spearheaded the dash to Manila.[9] The troopers were given additional stimulus by a personal message from General MacArthur to General Mudge: —

[9] Sherrod pp. 294–302; Maj. C. W. Boggs USMC *Marine Aviation in the Philippines* (1951) chap. iii.

"Go to Manila. Go around the Nips, bounce off the Nips, but go to Manila. Free the internees at Santo Tomás. Take Malacañan Palace and the Legislative Building."

The drive started at dawn 1 February, and before the end of the day XIV Corps took Clark Air Center and the nearby Fort Stotsenberg. The Navy participated in this drive, through the Marine Corps aviators. These were the old "Airnorsols" group, which at Bougainville, under Major General Ralph J. Mitchell usmc and in conjunction with the 37th Infantry Division, had made an intensive study of close air support for ground troops, an aspect of combat aviation to which the Army Air Force had been somewhat indifferent. We have already seen that units of Airnorsols, at Admiral Halsey's suggestion, were fleeted up to Leyte in 1944 to help the ground troops there.[10] But on Leyte the Marine flyers were attached to General Kenney's Far Eastern Air Forces and unable to practice their principle that close support air missions, to be effective, must be "talked onto a target" by the front line commander. This contrasted with the cumbrous Army system of relaying the demand and the information through successive echelons and leaving the decision to a distant air controller.

Two Marine Air Groups, the 32nd (Colonel Clayton C. Jerome usmc) and the 24th (Colonel Lyle H. Meyer usmc) were assigned to the Luzon operation. They had to find and activate their own airstrip. It was built for them by Seabees on top of a paddy field near Magaldan, about fifteen miles east of Lingayen. By 27 January they were ready to make their first strikes. The technique of their support was worked out in a conference at 1st Cavalry headquarters. Here the principals were one of the instructors in the new doctrine from Bougainville, Captain Francis R. B. Godolphin usmc (a name to conjure with among old troopers), and Lieutenant Colonel Robert F. Goheen usa, 1st Cavalry intelligence officer, who had been Godolphin's student at Princeton, and eventually became president of that university. Thus it happened that Colonel Jerome was prepared to provide an "air alert" from dawn to dusk

[10] Vol. XII Chap. xvi.

over the 1st Cavalry Division. And an air liaison party with radio-equipped jeep was assigned to each brigade to stay with the Brigadier throughout the drive.

The troopers jumped off at one minute after midnight 1 February, with 1st Brigade in the lead. Beginning at dawn, the Marine Corps flyers ranged ahead on the flanks of the column, looking for enemy movements and roadblocks. Next day, when the troopers were held up by a strong Japanese position, Marine Corps SBDs were called down, made several strafing runs without firing a shot as they were very close to 1st Brigade's front line, yet diverted the attention of the enemy so that the squadron easily overran his position. On 3 February Marine flyers reported the Novaliches bridge over the Bulacan River on the outskirts of Manila to be intact. The troopers dashed ahead and reached it just in time for a Navy bomb disposal officer to cut the already lighted demolition fuze and save the bridge.

Late in the afternoon of Saturday 3 February, nine Marine fighter planes buzzed the Santo Tomás camp in Manila, where some 3700 emaciated Allied prisoners were interned. The Japanese guards pretended to ignore them but some of the internees saw an object drop from one of the planes. It proved to be a pair of pilot's goggles with a note attached: "Roll out the barrel. Santa Claus is coming Sunday or Monday." [11] Soon shouting was heard, then the roar of engines, and an unmistakable American voice just outside the compound was heard yelling, "Where the hell is the front gate?" Then Santa Claus's reindeer, in the form of a tank named "Battling Basic," upset the Marines' timetable by crashing through the front gate to liberate the inmates.

The troopers, who had entered the city at 1835, dashed on after liberating Santo Tomás to seize the other objectives given them by General MacArthur. One squadron occupied the ground of Malacañan Palace and fought off a Japanese effort to recapture it later that night. Another column of dismounted cavalry headed for the Quezon Bridge across the Pasig River in the heart of the city. En

11 Wright *1st Cavalry* p. 125.

route they were held up for a while at the University of Manila, across the street from Bilibid Prison. After a sharp fight at the University, 3767 internees, including 267 American hostages, were liberated. As it now lacked only half an hour to midnight General Chase decided to take the Legislative Building later. The 37th Division, entering from the northwest along Route 3, was not far behind the 1st Cavalry. It entered Manila 4 February, captured Bilibid Prison releasing 1024 Allied prisoners of war, and reached the Pasig River.

Speedy liberation of these Allied prisoners in Manila had always been one of General MacArthur's objects in pressing for a Luzon rather than a Formosa campaign; and the several thousand men, women and children whom his troops released on 3–4 February felt sure that they would all have starved to death or been massacred if another strategic plan had been adopted, and Manila left to "wither on the vine." That this was no fanciful apprehension may be seen by the fate of the American prisoners in Palawan and the Australian prisoners in North Borneo, which we shall mention in due course.

By 4 February it became clear that General MacArthur's hope of a quick evacuation of the rest of Manila was not to be fulfilled. General Yamashita had not planned to defend Manila; he intended to let it go by default, along with the central plain of Luzon. In December 1944 he decided to pull out the bulk of his forces and set up headquarters at Baguio, leaving in Manila a small army defense force to maintain order, protect supply movements and to blow bridges. But the Japanese Navy moved into Manila as the Japanese Army moved out. Vice Admiral Denshichi Okochi, Commander Southwest Area Fleet, strengthened the defenses of the city during the second half of December and set up a separate naval defense force, placing it under the command of Rear Admiral Sanji Iwabachi, commander of the 31st Special Naval Base Force. When Admiral Okochi evacuated Manila with General Yamashita he placed this defense force, some 16,000 men strong, under General Yokoyama of the Shimbu Army Group, one of the three major

Luzon defense forces up in the hills, hoping to obtain unity of command.

But unity of command did not work with the Japanese. Admiral Iwabachi insisted that he would not come fully under Yokoyama's command until he had finished various tasks assigned to him by Admiral Okochi. Yokoyama made plans for a delaying action based on the assumption that there were only 4000 naval troops in the city. He called several conferences to iron out the difficulties, only to find that Iwabachi felt that Manila should be defended to the bitter end, and would obey no orders to do otherwise. To make the best of a bad situation, Yokoyama assented and placed the 3750 troops of the Japanese Army defense force under Iwabachi's command.

Word of this squabble presumably never reached General Yamashita at Baguio until it was too late to assert his authority. On 15 February he censured Yokoyama for letting the Navy defy his orders and advised him to order all troops out of Manila immediately. By 17 February, when Iwabachi got the word, it was too late; all possible withdrawal routes had been cut off by Krueger's Sixth Army. And as surrender was out of the question to a man of the Admiral's kidney, he fought to the bitter end. Manila was fanatically defended from house to house by upwards of 20,000 troops, three fourths of them naval. In the month-long battle that resulted, the Japanese defense forces were wiped out almost to a man; but the beautiful city was wrecked, and Intramuros, the old Spanish walled town, was reduced to rubble.

Major General Swing's 11th Airborne Division, which landed at Nasugbu on 31 January and advanced rapidly to the Tagaytay Ridge, was held up on 4 February by strong opposition at the Paranaque River. They were now on the isthmus between Laguna De Bay and Manila Bay, with little room to maneuver. They ran into strong Japanese defenses at Nichols airfield, which lies directly behind the Lunetta, the waterfront boulevard whence in days of peace one observed the gorgeous sunsets over Corregidor. It took them many days to beat down these defenses and Admiral Iwabachi's fighting sailors. One company commander facetiously signaled his division headquarters, "Tell Halsey to stop looking for the Jap Fleet; it's dying on Nichols Field."

With the support of XIV Corps artillery, the 11th Airborne overran the airfield on 12 February. By General MacArthur's command Manila was never bombed. But artillery fire, necessary to dig out the Japanese, and their own demolitions, did almost as much damage as the bombers might have inflicted. Not until 4 March, with the capture of the shell of the Finance Building, was the city cleared of Japanese. By that time it was a shambles — a more complete picture of destruction than Cologne, Hamburg or the City of London. But at least it was free. Even before the fighting ended, General MacArthur caused a provisional assembly of Filipino notables to be summoned to Malacañan Palace — where his father, General Arthur MacArthur, had lived when military governor — and in their presence declared the Commonwealth of the Philippines to be permanently re-established. "My country had kept the faith," he said; "your capital city, cruelly punished though it be, has regained its rightful place — citadel of democracy in the East." [12]

3. Clearing the Bay and Harbor, 3 February–18 April [13]

Steps had already been taken to secure the entrances to Manila Bay. On 3 February, General MacArthur ordered General Krueger, in addition to other operations, to effect this by the seizure of Corregidor and positions around Mariveles, on the southern end of Bataan Peninsula. "The Rock," he informed Krueger, should be taken by a shore-to-shore amphibious operation or parachute drop, or both. On 5 February XI Corps, moving east from Subic Bay,

[12] Willoughby & Chamberlain *MacArthur 1941–51* p. 268.
[13] Sixth Army Report; CTG 77.3 (Rear Adm. Berkey) Action Report 27 Mar. 1945, Rear Adm. Struble Action Report 29 June 1945; R. R. Smith chs. xvii, xviii; Krueger, ch. xxviii; Comdesron 49 and Comdesdiv 46 Action Reports.

made contact with XIV Corps, thus sealing off the Bataan Peninsula.

General MacArthur first set D-day (as the Corregidor assault day was actually called) for 12 February, but it was later postponed to the 15th to give XI Corps a little more time. Admiral Barbey designated Rear Admiral Struble to command the assault. The landing force for Mariveles was the 151st RCT under Major General Chase, who had recently transferred from the 1st Cavalry to command the 38th Infantry Division. These troops were transported from Subic Bay in APDs, LCIs and landing craft. And the 503rd Parachute RCT (then at Mindoro) was scheduled to be airdropped on Corregidor on the 16th, to be followed by a BLT, from the 24th Division, landing on the south side of the Rock. With a scant week for planning, Admiral Struble and the other commanders were rushed; but the operation went off very much as planned, against strong enemy opposition.

Troop allocations were made on Intelligence estimates that placed about 6000 Japanese on the Bataan Peninsula and 850 on Corregidor. Both were wide of the mark. Postwar studies indicate that there were no more than 1400 Japanese troops on Bataan, and very few in or near Mariveles. On the Rock, however, there were over 5000 troops, mostly naval.

First requirement was a careful minesweeping by six AM and 15 YMS, under Lieutenant Commander James R. Keefer USNR, covered by Rear Admiral Berkey's light cruisers and destroyers. They were to conduct bombardments coördinated with bombings by V A.A.F. aircraft based on Mindoro. Minesweeping began on 13 February with "Count" Berkey's Support Group bombarding designated targets in and around Mariveles, Corregidor and the islets (La Monja, Caballo, El Fraile and Carabao), across the entrance to Manila Bay. There was no Japanese reaction to these operations, a condition which "exceedingly perturbed" Berkey, as he expressed it, because he had hoped that the enemy would be forced to reveal his strong points. "Juicy targets were placed under the Nip's nose, but he declined to take a crack at them." On completion of the day's work, which included cutting numerous mines, the ships returned to Subic Bay for the night.

When they returned on St. Valentine's Day they met a reception that was anything but loving. The sweepers went to work promptly between Corregidor and Caballo. Cruisers and destroyers opened bombardment at 0840. At 0933, when the sweepers reported they were being fired upon from Corregidor, *Boise* was ordered to locate and destroy the offending battery. A few minutes later the minecraft noticed shots coming from Caballo; when the craft worked into the mine field south of that islet, the Japanese there really opened up, and also fired from caves on the south side of Corregidor, from Carabao Island, and, later, from a nearby strong point on the mainland. Their gunfire, fortunately inaccurate, was answered by the sweepers and by Berkey's cruisers and destroyers. Most of the racket had ceased by 1018, and the sweepers, after destroying 76 mines, turned at 1130 to other areas.

Destroyers were sent to destroy floats and buoys in Mariveles Harbor in order to clear the way for the sweepers. At 1300 *Fletcher*, when preparing to send in a boat to sink the one remaining buoy, was hit on her forecastle by a 6-inch shell. This caused extensive damage forward and started a fire, soon brought under control. The offending battery was located in a cave or tunnel on the face of a Corregidor cliff; *Phoenix* and two destroyers were soon "on." Other batteries on the Rock took minecraft under fire when they started sweeping off Mariveles. Destroyer *Hopewell* was ordered into a position to cover them, but at 1359 *YMS-48* was hit and set on fire. The sweepers were then ordered out, while the covering ships took several batteries on Corregidor under fire. At 1413 *Hopewell* received four hits that destroyed her fire control gear and inflicted enough damage to cause her to be sent to Manus for repairs. She had 7 killed and 12 wounded. *Fletcher* assisted *YMS-48* under cover of a smoke screen, picked up the crew and sank the burning vessel with gunfire.

Minecraft were now sent right into Mariveles Harbor, covered by destroyers *LaVallette* and *Radford*. About 1730, after one sweep, they formed up for a second run. The two destroyers eased in astern to sink loose floaters and others as fast as their moorings were cut. At 1800, when a short distance inside the harbor and in water that had been swept twice, *LaVallette* had a mine explode under her. *Radford* was trying to get a line on her when she also bopped a mine. Both ships retired under their own power, but with extensive underwater damage in the forward fire room and machinery spaces, and between them they lost 9 men killed and 27 wounded. Salvage vessels were now signaled, and the damaged destroyers retired to Subic Bay.

Admiral Struble, then en route with the landing force, was intercepted by Admiral Berkey. After a conference over TBS they agreed, as a safety precaution, to call forward the reserve fire-support group of H.M.A.S. *Shropshire* and U.S.S. *Minneapolis* and *Portland*, with six destroyers, under Commodore H. B. Farncomb RAN. Admiral Struble also agreed to change H-hour from 0900 to 1000 to allow more minesweeping in Mariveles Harbor.

At daybreak 15 February, the support group, less the two mined destroyers, took station 500 yards apart on a line running northward from La Monja islet and reaching almost to the Bataan shore. As the light increased these ships opened a deliberate fire on targets on the north side of Corregidor, while the cruisers' off-side 5-inch batteries trained on the Mariveles shore for bombardment and close support if necessary.

By 0900 three sweepers had looped around Mariveles Harbor with negative results. Gunfire on Corregidor was then lifted to make way for an air strike on the island. Japanese batteries had opened up once or twice but were so promptly smothered with gunfire that they were soon silenced.

As the shore-to-shore landing force from Subic Bay approached Mariveles, Japanese on the Rock took pot shots at landing craft, but the covering cruisers and destroyers soon stopped that. The first wave landed on a beach in Mariveles Harbor at 1000, exactly on time. Opposition from the beach was negligible. One 5-inch shell from Corregidor landed close aboard an LCP(R) and caused some casualties, but otherwise the landing continued as planned until the seventh wave, when *LSM-169*, waiting to go in, hit a mine. There were several casualties to the troops embarked, and a fire burst out. This was brought under control, and the LSM beached, unloaded, and was towed back to Subic Bay. There was no further enemy interference; the final assault wave beached at 1135.

As the LSTs were not unloaded by nightfall, they were left at the beach until the next high water, at 0115 February 16, with a tight screen and patrol covering the entrance. Anchored across the harbor mouth were a number of LCS(L), the new converted LCI armored support craft, armed with machine guns of three different calibers, and with rockets. At about 0315 on February 16, a number of Japanese 17-foot suicide boats succeeded in making an undetected approach and sank three of these support craft. *LCS(L)-27* sank five of the midgets; then a sixth blew up close aboard and put her out of action. About 30 of these boats had been sent to Mariveles from Corregidor during the night of 15–16 February. One was spotted and blown up by *Conyngham* about a mile and a half southwest of Mariveles at 0700 on the 16th. Two others were seen and destroyed by *Young* and *Nicholas*.

The troops found little opposition ashore at Mariveles, but beat off a light enemy attack the first night. Patrols were now sent up the east and west coasts of Bataan, and on 18 February contact was made with another force that was making its way southward from the direction of Manila. The Bataan operation was reduced to mopping up and to driving Japanese survivors into the mountains, where they were no longer a threat.

The combined parachute-amphibious assault on Corregidor was set for 16 February. The logical drop zone was Kindley Field at the northern end of the tail of this tadpole-shaped island. But a drop on that point would have forced the paratroops to fight uphill, against positions dug in and connected by tunnels. The maximum elevation on the bulbous end of the island is 538 feet, but the highest part of the island, known as Topside, is relatively flat. It was so covered with splintered trees, wrecked buildings and bomb craters that only two small areas were suitable for parachutists: the old parade ground, about 325 by 250 yards, and a tiny golf course only slightly larger. These two Topside spots were picked for the air-drop, in order to achieve surprise and give the paratroops an excellent position for beating off counterattacks. This was admittedly a very risky operation; winds were tricky, and the planes could be over the target only long enough for six to eight men to jump in one pass.

In order to soften up the island and to keep the Japanese off Topside, the Army Air Force since 22 January had dropped over 3200 tons of bombs on the Rock, one of the heaviest bomb saturations in the Southwest Pacific. And it was also subjected to naval bombardment, as we have seen. At 0630 February 16 gunfire support ships took station for a final bombardment which was completed at 0746. Not one enemy replied. Naval bombardment was followed by an air strike at 0800, and at 0830 the paratroops began tumbling out of their transport planes. Most of them landed on Topside, but some hit the water, where they were picked up by waiting PT boats, and others were carried to the face of the cliff between Topside and the bay. One such miss proved to be fortunate. Captain Itagaki of the Japanese Navy, who commanded at Corregidor, had his attention called to landing craft approaching from the direction of Mariveles and so occupied an observation post near the waterline. Suddenly some 25 paratroops, blown over the cliff by the wind, began dropping into and all around his post. Completely surprised, the Japanese were quickly overpowered and Itagaki was killed.

With their commander gone, the defense showed neither spirit nor cohesion. That was doubly fortunate, as the defenders outnumbered the attackers three to two. On Topside, too, complete surprise was achieved and the slight opposition was quickly overcome.

At 1030 a battalion of the 34th Infantry was scheduled to land in a cove on the south side near the base of the tail and take Malinta Hill, which, next to Topside, is the most dominant feature of the island. The troops had been staged through Mariveles from Subic

Bay and lifted in 25 LCM of the Engineer Special Brigade. At 0852 *Picking* and *Young* took positions off the selected beach, and *Wickes* north of the island, for preliminary bombardment. Fire was opened at 0942 and continued until 1020. Two minutes later, guns on Caballo Island opened on the approaching landing craft and were promptly taken under fire by the destroyers. The first wave hit the beach at 1030 under a hail of small arms and mortar fire. A tank and a bulldozer, when rolling out of their respective LCMs, exploded land mines and were disabled. Every boat making the beach was hit, one in the third wave 40 times, by enemy fire.[14] But the landings continued and the destroyers closed in for gunfire support as soon as they could make contact with naval gunfire liaison officers ashore. A second wave of paratroops dropped on Topside at 1230. Rate of jump casualties was so high that a third group due to drop on 17 February was flown to Subic Bay instead and transported to the island by boat.

The Japanese in a maze of tunnels and caves put up fanatical resistance and had to be dug out or sealed in. For ten days, Desdiv 46 kept two ships on station to support the troops. They closed to a few hundred yards from the shore where they could see the Japanese run between salvos and report their movements. The destroyers proved useful in sealing off caves; moving in close and spotted from ashore, they fired single 5-inch and 40-mm shots directly into the mouths of caves where Japanese were reported. By 26 February most of the island had been cleared and the destroyers withdrew.

It had cost us 225 killed and missing, 405 wounded and 240 injured in drops. Of the enemy, more than 4500 dead were counted and 20 captured, about 200 were killed when trying to escape by swimming and an estimated 500 were buried alive in caves.

In order to make the entrance to the Bay completely secure, the other islets and the southern shore had to be cleared of the enemy. On 2 March troops of the 11th Airborne Division mopped up

---

[14] William F. Heavy *Down Ramp* (Washington 1947) p. 154, but R. R. Smith chap. xviii says that there was no opposition to the first four waves.

about 1350 Japanese at Ternate on the mainland just inside the South Channel.

General of the Army Douglas MacArthur returned to Corregidor that day and presided over an impressive flag raising on the Rock, which he had left under such different circumstances on 12 March 1942.

Caballo off Corregidor was the first of the small island targets to be taken, on 27 March. After reconnaissance showed up defenses on the high ground near its center, they were bombed from the air and bombarded by destroyers and rocket-equipped PTs; artillery on Corregidor also helped. A BLT of the 151st Infantry then landed in ESB boats which loaded at Corregidor — one of the shortest shore-to-shore amphibious operations of the war. The Japanese were holed up in three hills near the center of Caballo. The surface of the island was overrun that day, but about 200 Japanese pulled back into pits and tunnels under a hill, and there seemed to be no way of getting them out. After four days' effort the engineers tried pouring diesel oil into a tunnel and igniting it, but they could not get enough oil up the hill to do the job properly. A few days later someone thought of pumping the oil up. The Navy came through with a pump, and two pontoon units were filled with oil; this rig was set up from an LCM. And on 5 April 2500 gallons of oil were pumped into the pits and ignited by white phosphorous mortar shells, with "gratifying results." This was repeated for two days, but some of the enemy managed to live through it — and not until 13 April did a patrol enter a hitherto inaccessible tunnel to kill the lone survivor.

Next on the list was El Fraile, about five miles south of Corregidor. This isle was surmounted by Fort Drum, built by the United States Army years before, with walls 25 to 36 feet thick, tapering to 20 feet at the top — shaped like an old-time battleship. Before World War II, the fort housed four 14-inch guns mounted in turrets, and four 6-inch. These had been knocked out by the Japanese in 1942 and never replaced, but the site presented a formidable problem. It was accessible only by a ramp on the eastern side, whose approaches were thoroughly covered inside the fortress. So the oil technique was repeated. In the second week of April, *LSM-51* and *LCI-547*, under Commander Samuel H. Pattie, closed the islet on the opposite side from the entrance to Fort Drum, and troops went ashore over a bridgelike ramp which, when rigged, looked like a drawbridge crossing a medieval moat. While GIs kept the gunports covered, an oil-line was run ashore from the LCM, 3000 gallons of oil were pumped down a ventilating duct, and a 600-pound charge of TNT lowered down another. *LSM-51* then pulled off a short distance to watch the fireworks, and in due course was rewarded by seeing chunks of concrete and steel plates hurled hundreds of feet into the air and flames and smoke pour out of every gunport. Explosions continued for days afterward. On 18 April, a reconnaissance party entered the wrecked fort and found 65 dead Japanese.

Carabao Island was the last obstacle. After a two-day aërial and naval bombardment, troops were landed there on 16 April. The Japanese had already withdrawn to the mainland.

Since 9 March Commodore William A. Sullivan, the Navy's salvage expert, had been working on the problem of clearing Manila Harbor. He had done it at Casablanca, Palermo, Naples, Cherbourg and Le Havre; but Manila, he told the writer, was the worst. There were hundreds of sunken ships there, and the Japanese were much more efficient demolitioners than the Germans. Sullivan turned-to immediately, and with the aid of the Army Engineers' Special Brigade, two battalions of Seabees, and several salvage ships and minecraft, raised some wrecks, destroyed others, and, for future action, buoyed many more. Sullivan's quick method was to have divers seal up a sunken ship, blow in air to displace water, and, when the hulk surfaced, tow it to a place where it could be dealt with later. Minesweepers *Scuffle* and *Cable* with 15 YMS and LCVP fitted with sweeping gear, all under Commander Eric A. Johnson USNR, worked from 24 February to 15 April covering the harbor and bay; they swept 615 square miles of water and destroyed 584 mines, including those that exploded accidentally. One of Commodore Sullivan's particular problems was the tampering with wrecks by natives, owing to a rumor that some of the sunken ships contained millions of silver pesos which the Japanese had taken out of the Bank of Manila. He dealt with this by attaching signs to the wrecks: "This ship has been booby-trapped." [15]

The first ship had entered the harbor 15 March and tied up to No. 7, Manila's "glamour pier," as Commodore Sullivan called it. By the end of that month, the harbor could handle 50,000 dead-weight tons of shipping per week; in April the capacity rose to 70,000 and in May to 90,000 tons. Floating mines continued to be a menace for some time; two Liberty ships were badly damaged by them. By 1 May, 350 of the sunken vessels had been removed and the waterfront was progressively cleared until, in mid-August, 24 Liberty ships could berth simultaneously.

4. *Liberation Completed, 31 March–30 June*

Although the task of finally liberating Luzon was done by the United States Army, aided by Filipino guerrillas, the Navy took a leading part in one more small amphibious operation. This was to land troops at Legaspi on the Bicol Peninsula, near the southeastern tip of the Luzon tail. General MacArthur's instructions of 5 February 1945 ordered Sixth Army to free this peninsula of the enemy and to clear the northern entrance of San Bernardino Strait, in conjunction with Eighth Army approaching it from Samar. Troops were wanted on Bicol Peninsula to contain and overcome one of the principal foci of enemy activity. Possession of San Bernardino Strait would greatly shorten the passage from Leyte Gulf or beyond to Manila, in comparison with the Surigao Strait route. San Bernardino Strait was swept on 31 March by *Sentry, Scout, Salute*

[15] *Engineers of the SW Pacific* VI 357; conversation of writer with Commo. Sullivan at Manila, 1 May 1945.

and *Scrimmage* under Lieutenant Commander T. R. Fornick USNR. with negative results; and next day they swept Albay Gulf and waters around Legaspi.[16]

General Krueger designated the 158th RCT, Brigadier General Hanford MacNider USA, to secure Legaspi on 1 April. Admiral Barbey chose Captain Homer F. McGee, commanding LCI Flotilla 7, as naval commander of the expedition. McGee's group consisted of destroyers *Bailey* and *Bancroft* and DEs *Day* and *Holt* for bombardment and support; two SC, two LCS, one LCI and one LCI(R) for control and close support; three APD, nine LCI, five LST and four LSM for lifting the troops, and the minesweepers already mentioned. The assault shipping was loaded at Subic Bay and staged through Lemery in Balayan Bay. They departed Lemery 30 March, steamed through San Bernardino Strait and arrived off Legaspi at 0815 April 1. Air strikes and sweeping were going according to plan when, at 0837, an enemy battery opened up from a hill 12,000 yards inland. Counterbattery fire silenced it and the first wave landed at 1000, on time and against only light opposition. Troops met only sniper fire until about 500 yards inland where they found a road block. But the beachhead was reported secured at 1020; General MacNider promptly assumed command ashore, and mopping up of the Bicol Peninsula followed rapidly. This was the last amphibious movement conducted by VII 'Phib on Luzon.

By mid-February almost all the big transports had been returned to Pacific Fleet and the Liberty ships to War Shipping Administration to serve at Iwo Jima and Okinawa. From such troop-lift as Seventh Fleet still retained, Rear Admiral Barbey organized task units and directed them by movement orders. For instance, 32 separate movements were listed for 15 February 1945, the principal ones being these: twelve LST from Leyte to Finschhafen; four merchant ships and 24 LST escorted by three destroyers arrived Leyte from Hollandia; transport division 9 with six destroyers and DEs departed Leyte for Ulithi to return to Pacific Fleet; and 12 LCI departed Hollandia for Leyte. Rear Admiral Struble was con-

[16] CTU 78.4.7 (Lr. Cdr. Fornick in *Scuffle*) Action Report 2 Apr. 1945.

ducting a landing at Mariveles; Rear Admiral Fechteler was planning for the Palawan and Rear Admiral Royal, S.O.P.A. Lingayen, for the Zamboanga landing, target date 10 March. It was a regular jigsaw puzzle. The merchant ships were controlled by the Army, but the Navy provided escorts and routing. Rear Admiral Barbey's staff handled this very efficiently, as they had been used to the same thing on a smaller scale in New Guinea.

Even after Manila was liberated General Yamashita had about 170,000 troops on Luzon.[17] They were split into several parts: the biggest portion, known as the Shobu group, was in northern Luzon where Yamashita had his headquarters and commanded in person; the second most important, known as the Shimbu group, commanded by Lieutenant General Yokoyama and responsible for southern Luzon, was ordered to dig into the mountains east and northeast of Manila. And there were several smaller pockets of troops elsewhere: the Kembu group of about 30,000 men in the Zambales mountains, a nuisance to us on the Clark Airfield complex; another group on the Bicol Peninsula, dealt with by the troops who landed at Legaspi; one in the heights south of Lake Taal; one on the Bataan Peninsula. Yokoyama's Shimbu group, which had 80,000 men at the start and controlled two major dams and reservoirs whence Manila derived most of its water supply, resisted fanatically. But it was finally reduced to a point where it was losing ten men by disease and starvation to every one in combat, and at the end of the war, in August 1945, only 6300 of Yokoyama's soldiers were left to surrender.[18]

As a by-product to operations against the Shimbu group, Sixth Army was given the additional mission to secure Balayan and Batangas bays south of Manila Bay, facing the Verde Island Passage. Plans were being made at Southwest Pacific Area headquarters for a big staging base, landing craft assembly plant and hospital center at Batangas in preparation for the expected invasion of Japan

[17] Krueger p. 271. Up to that time Sixth Army had lost 3591 killed and missing, 13,164 wounded. The 11th Airborne and Navy losses would bring the total killed up to about 4000.
[18] R. R. Smith chap. xxi. p. 69.

in the fall of 1945. To secure this area, a part of the 11th Airborne Division which had been landed at Nasugbu advanced overland from Manila, with the 158th RCT, and occupied Batangas on 12 March.

General Yamashita's Shobu group, in the mountains of northern Luzon, which at peak strength numbered 150,000 men, gave the most trouble. "By any standard," writes the U.S. Army historian, "the Shobu group accomplished the delaying mission Yamashita envisaged for it." [19] The I Corps was not enough to reduce it. At one time four reinforced U.S. infantry divisions, one division plus one regiment of Filipinos built around Colonel Volckmann's guerrilla outfit, and a battalion of the 11th Airborne, were employed against the Shobu group. An important step in this campaign was the capture of Baguio on 27 April.

By 30 June, although Yamashita still had 65,000 men under the Rising Sun, his particular planet had set; the Allies controlled all Luzon that had any strategic or economic value. On that date, Eighth Army took over from the Sixth the mission of destroying the Shobu group, which, mostly holed up in the mountains, retained only a nuisance value. General Yamashita and about 50,500 of his men finally surrendered after the close of hostilities on 15 August.

For the Sixth Army the campaign for the liberation of Luzon had lasted 173 days (9 January–30 June 1945), during which it lost 8297 killed or missing and had 29,557 wounded.[20] Losses to the U.S. and Australian Navies in the Luzon campaign, mostly due to kamikaze attack, were more than 2000.[21] At Okinawa, in the campaign which started on 26 March, the relative score of suffering by Army and Navy would be reversed, owing to Japan's intensive use of kamikaze tactics.

[19] R. R. Smith chap. xxviii.
[20] Krueger p. 318. R. R. Smith states that between 30 June and 15 Aug. the "Filipino-American forces engaged in northern Luzon" lost an additional 440 killed and 1210 wounded.
[21] Kinkaid Action Report pp. 80–83; this is an approximation.

PART III

Central and Southern Philippines

February–August 1945

CHAPTER IX

Palawan and Zamboanga

March–April 1945

1. *Plans and Procedures*

GENERAL of the Army Douglas MacArthur was far from satisfied with the liberation of Leyte and Luzon. From the time of his 1942 promise to return to the Philippines, he had envisaged expelling the enemy from the entire Archipelago.

The MUSKETEER II plan of 26 September 1944 provided that after General Krueger's Sixth Army had liberated the greater part of Luzon, General Eichelberger's Eighth Army, having followed the Sixth into Leyte, would occupy the central and southern islands of the Archipelago, and continue on to free the Dutch East Indies from the Japanese. And in his PRINCETON I plan of 31 October the General laid the groundwork for three series of operations: one called VICTOR for the Visayas; a second, called OBOE, to be conducted by Australian troops, starting with Mindanao; and a PETER series providing for the reconquest of the Dutch East Indies. When the heavy fighting on Leyte showed that no fixed timetable for these operations could be set months in advance, plan PRINCETON II was issued on 20 November. This had essentially the same objectives without specific target dates. Finally, in February 1945, the General's MONTCLAIR plan placed Mindanao in the VICTOR series and Borneo, Java and the rest of the Dutch East Indies in the OBOE operations for the Australians to execute.

The Joint Chiefs of Staff did not see eye to eye with General MacArthur in all this. At the Yalta Conference, on 1 February 1945, General Marshall told the British Chiefs of Staff that the

J.C.S. did not contemplate employing major United States forces to mop up in the Philippines or the Dutch islands; he assumed that the Filipino guerrillas and the newly activated Army of the Philippine Commonwealth could take care of the rest of their country, and that Anglo-Australian forces would recover the N.E.I.

It is still somewhat of a mystery how and whence, in view of these wishes of the J.C.S., General of the Army Douglas MacArthur derived his authority to use United States Forces to liberate one Philippine island after another. He had no specific directive for anything subsequent to Luzon. He seems to have felt that, as Allied theater commander in the Southwest Pacific, he had a right to employ the forces at his command as he thought best for the common cause; certainly he went ahead with his plans. And as Seventh Fleet and Eighth Army were not urgently required at Iwo Jima (invaded in February 1945) or Okinawa (invaded at the end of March), the J.C.S. simply permitted MacArthur to do as he chose, up to a point. He sent his plans, as they came out, to Washington, and if no objection was raised from the Pentagon, went ahead and executed them. But he finally did reach a point where the J.C.S. pulled him up short. That was a plan for moving Australian troops into Java and restoring the rule of the Royal Netherlands' government. This needed more shipping than he then had, and the J.C.S., at Yalta in February, told him he could have no more. They approved the three invasions of Borneo, but vetoed the Java plan in April 1945, to the bitter disappointment of our Netherlands allies and the chagrin of the General.[1]

The series of amphibious operations that followed were conducted under MacArthur's over-all command by Eighth Army and Seventh Fleet. Lieutenant General Robert L. Eichelberger of Eighth Army had already distinguished himself in the New Guinea campaign.[2] In him, states one of MacArthur's biographers, the theater commander "had found his Stonewall Jackson. What 'Old Jack' meant to Lee in swift and sure obedience and energy, the tall,

[1] Lt. Grace P. Hayes "History of the J.C.S." II 365-7.
[2] See Volume VIII of this History.

fearless Buckeye meant to the Southwest Pacific commander in chief." [3]

With Admiral Kinkaid the reader of these volumes is already familiar. He, too, was highly appreciated by General MacArthur; the more so because, while accepting a subordinate rôle under the theater commander, and the Navy's primary duty to serve the Army, Kinkaid always spoke his mind. The postponement of invading Mindoro and Lingayen is a case in point; MacArthur would not hear of it at first, but gave in to the irrefutable arguments of the Admiral. Kinkaid was a methodical fighter and a first-class organizer, rather than a spectacular leader of the Paul Jones or Nelson type; and that was just what MacArthur wanted and valued.

The Admiral moved his headquarters ashore to Tolosa on the gulf shore of Leyte on 4 February 1945, and there supervised the series of amphibious operations that we are about to describe. All were conducted under the immediate command of the veteran Commander Amphibious Force Seventh Fleet (Com VII 'Phib), Vice Admiral Daniel E. Barbey. His headquarters were on board flagship *Blue Ridge*, which moved from San Pedro Bay to Subic Bay 7 February, and there remained except for occasional visits to Manila Bay. Barbey, in turn, designated one of his amphibious group commanders for the larger operations. Whilst, in general, no shortages of troops, ships or materials existed, there were so many of these operations that the planners had a jigsaw puzzle of providing amphibious shipping and follow-up support. And from each of the larger operations stemmed a host of small shore-to-shore lifts, arranged locally between the Army and Navy commanders on the spot, or using Army boats of the Engineer Special Brigades. It would be hopeless to attempt to detail all these activities; in the following chapters we shall confine ourselves to the main stream of events.

These events fall into a fairly regular pattern. An amphibious group of Seventh Fleet, under Rear Admirals Fechteler, Royal, Noble or Struble, is mounted at Leyte Gulf or Mindoro and, cov-

[3] Frazier Hunt *The Untold Story of Douglas MacArthur* (1954) p. 382.

ered by Rear Admiral Riggs's or Berkey's light cruisers, steams to the objective without incident, since enemy aircraft no longer operate over Philippine waters. A landing is made from LVT or LCVP, with follow-up waves of LCT and LST, against only token opposition, or none; the Japanese tactics first noted at Peleliu – withdrawing from the beachhead to make a last-ditch defense in the mountains – are now doctrine. The liberating forces are greeted enthusiastically by the populace and the guerrillas. Amphibious craft retire, but Seventh Fleet keeps cruisers and destroyers on hand for call fire as long as necessary, and maintains a supply line to Army units ashore. These proceed to expel the enemy from his interior line of defenses and hunt him down in the jungle fastnesses. The mopping-up process is usually not complete by the time of the surrender of Japan in August 1945, but in the meantime the inhabited parts of the island have been liberated, civil government of the Philippine Commonwealth [4] set up, and life in the Archipelago has resumed some semblance of normality. That is, where the "Huks" are not operating.

The operations that follow were short and swift; and, in comparison with Leyte and Lingayen, not very arduous. After it was all over General Eichelberger figured that Eighth Army had conducted 14 major and 24 minor landings in 44 days; and "Uncle Dan" Barbey of VII 'Phib hung up a record for amphibious operations that is not likely to be challenged for some time.

A brief resumé of the major operations is on opposite page.

2. *Palawan* [5]

As soon as Sixth Army penetrated Manila, General MacArthur on 6 February issued the first of his orders for the VICTOR series. Eighth Army would seize the Puerto Princesa area on the island of

[4] The Philippines did not formally become an independent republic until 4 July 1946, but President Osmeña's Commonwealth government enjoyed complete autonomy from the time that it occupied the Malacañan Palace in Manila, in March 1945.

[5] Rear Adm. Fechteler (CTG 78.2) op plan and Action Report; Eighth Army Report of the Palawan and Zamboanga Operations; R. R. Smith "Triumph in the Philippines"; R. L. Eichelberger *Our Jungle Road to Tokyo* (1950).

Palawan (VICTOR III), target date 28 February, and go into Zamboanga on Mindanao and parts of the Sulu Archipelago (VICTOR IV), target date 10 March. The early designation of these objectives was dictated in part by the desire of Far Eastern Air Forces to exten᷐ their range of operations, Palawan being some one hundred a᷄ᷗ fifty miles closer to Indochina than our hitherto nearest fields.

SUMMARY OF OPERATIONS IN SOUTHERN PHILIPPINES AND BORNEO, 1945

			Commanders		
Target of Operation	Code Name	D-day 1945	Naval Attack Group	Covering Group	Military
Palawan	VICTOR III	28 Feb.	Fechteler	Riggs	Haney
Zamboanga	VICTOR IV	10 Mar.	Royal	Riggs	Doe
Panay and W. Negros	VICTOR I	18 Mar.	Struble	Riggs	Brush
Cebu	VICTOR II	26 Mar.	Sprague	Berkey	Arnold
Bohol	VICTOR II	11 Apr.	Deutermann	none	Arnold
S.E. Negros	VICTOR II	26 Apr.	Deutermann	none	Arnold
Mindanao	VICTOR V	17 Apr.	Noble	Riggs	Sibert
Tarakan	OBOE I	1 May	Royal	Berkey	Morshead
Brunei Bay	OBOE VI	10 June	Royal	Berkey	Wootten
Balikpapan	OBOE II	1 July	Noble	Riggs	Milford

	Major Units Engaged		Objective Secured
Target of Operation	Naval	Military	1945
Palawan	8th 'Phib Group	41st Div.	22 April
Zamboanga	6th 'Phib Group	41st Div.	15 August
Panay and W. Negros	9th 'Phib Group	40th Div.	4 June
Cebu	TG 78.2	Americal	18 April
Bohol	TU 78.3.3	164th Inf.	20 April
S.E. Negros	TU 78.3.3	164th Inf.	12 June
Mindanao	8th 'Phib Group	X Corps	15 Aug.
Tarakan	TG 78.1	Aus. I Corps	30 May
Brunei Bay	TG 78.1	9th Aus. Div.	1 July
Balikpapan	8th 'Phib Group	7th Aus. Div.	22 July

Planes operating thence could seal off the South China Sea and cut Japanese sea lanes along the China coast. And aircraft from Zamboanga Peninsula could spearhead the attack on important Japanese oil installations in Borneo.

General Eichelberger designated the 41st Division, Major General Jens Doe, to conduct both of these operations. Rear Admiral W. M. Fechteler, Commander Amphibious Group 8, who had landed the 41st on Biak in May of 1944, was assigned the naval command. Anticipating General MacArthur's orders, Admiral Fechteler's informal conferences on the forthcoming operation between VII 'Phib and Eighth Army planners began 5 February at Mindoro. Upon the arrival there of the 41st division four days later, agreement was quickly reached as to beaches, landing plan and composition of the assault echelon. By 18 February the necessary repair and resupply arrangements had been completed and the assault shipping assembled at Mindoro.

This outer group of the Philippines consists of Palawan Island, heavily forested and mountainous, about 225 miles long and 30 miles wide, and a number of small islands at each end. The Palawan coastal plain is narrow and the coast is fouled by sand banks, coral reefs and mangrove swamps. At gaps in these obstacles there are good harbors, of which Puerto Princesa, about in the center of the southeastern coast, is the best.

Intelligence estimated on 15 February that there were 2735 enemy troops in the Palawan group, including 1800 around the Puerto Princesa area, which was fairly accurate. Selected as initial landing force was the 186th RCT under the command of Brigadier General Harold H. Haney. His combat team had a strength of 5700 troops, augmented by 2300 service troops.

There being no beaches at Puerto Princesa suitable for landing craft, the initial assault waves had to go ashore in LVTs from beaching craft, and the LSTs and LSMs were not to beach until a hydrographic party could locate proper slots for them. Admiral Fechteler, taking no chances on reports that these shores were undefended, arranged a preliminary bombardment by Rear Admiral

Riggs' Crudiv 12, consisting of light cruisers *Denver*, *Cleveland* and *Montpelier*, and four destroyers. A rehearsal was held at Mindoro on 24 February, and two days later the group sortied, proceeding to Puerto Princesa by a circuitous route, so that if Japanese coast watchers spotted it they could not guess its objective.

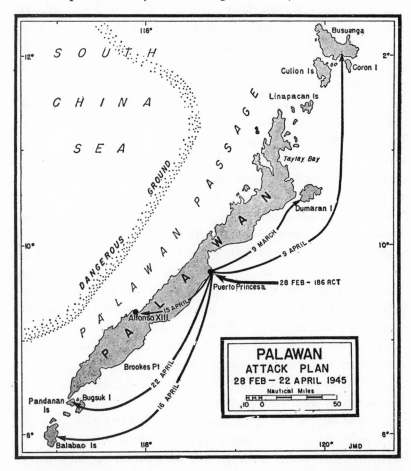

Off Puerto Princesa at 0650 February 28, designated H-day, the group deployed for entrance. The scheduled bombardment began at 0715 and at 0730 minesweepers, which had been sent ahead, reported "negative." All elements reached initial positions on time and at 0820 LVT of the first waves began rumbling out of their parent LSTs. There was no opposition ashore, landings proceeded as scheduled, and the troops fanned out to their initial objectives. General Eichelberger watched the show from a B–17. The main difficulty was to find beaching points to take LSM and LST. This problem was never solved, and unloading was therefore delayed. It would have been even slower, reported Admiral Fechteler, "except for the very efficient performance of the Army Shore Party and Boat Company." [6] These were of the Engineer Special Brigades with which the Navy had closely coöperated since the New Guinea campaigns.

H-day objectives were achieved by 1300, and at 1530 a company was landed by shore-to-shore movement at the mouth of the Iwahig River, but met only scattered small-arms fire. By 1540 No. 3 phase line had been reached and patrols continued to advance. As the day progressed, it became evident that the enemy had pulled out and into the hills. No defensive positions were found in Puerto Princesa itself, but evidence was uncovered of particularly cruel treatment of prisoners. About 150 American soldiers, who had surrendered or been captured in 1942, were kept in a stockade at Puerto Princesa and used in airfield construction. Upon receiving report of the approach of an Allied convoy on 14 December 1944 — the convoy actually destined for Mindoro — the Japanese commander of the 131st Airfield Battalion caused these prisoners to be herded into two air-raid shelters which they had constructed, soaked them with gasoline and then set them afire by tossing lighted torches into the crowded shelters. Those who tried to escape were shot down by rifle and machine-gun fire. Three prisoners only managed to escape, through a tunnel which led to the open face of a cliff overlooking the sea, where they were picked up and sheltered by natives. The bones of the victims were found by the forces of liberation and given a proper burial. [7]

The cruisers were released at 1800, and at 1900 empty amphibious shipping and craft were formed into a return echelon. Admiral

[6] Fechteler Action Report.
[7] Eighth Army Report and Eichelberger *Jungle Road* p. 206.

Fechteler remained at the objective until 3 March and set up a destroyer screen outside the harbor with close support craft inside. At 0530 March 1 the reinforcement echelon, consisting of 19 LST, accompanied by PT tender *Willoughby* (Lieutenant J. P. E. Brouillette) and PT Squadrons 20 and 23, under tactical command of Lieutenant James H. Van Sticklen USNR, arrived. The boats were ready to begin patrols that night.

Not until 2 March, when the troops reached the foothills, was the first enemy resistance encountered. For several days thereafter the troops were engaged in routing out enemy pockets while the Japanese withdrew farther into the mountains and to the west coast. Near Puerto Princesa an all-weather airstrip was in operation by 20 March. It had been an easy operation except for the slow unloading, owing to poor beaching conditions.

Even the PTs found slim pickings on Palawan. Starting their patrols the night of 1–2 March they ranged from one end of the long island to the other without finding one target. Eventually they smoked out a Japanese garrison on Pandanan Island, off the southern end of Palawan, and strafed it repeatedly. Return fire gradually slackened and then ceased. On 22 April a landing party from a PT found the island deserted, and patrolling from Palawan ended on 28 April.

On 6 March General Eichelberger ordered General Haney to seize Busuanga and Culion Islands north of Palawan and on the 15th he issued oral orders to secure Balabac Strait to the southward. Because of reported mine fields in these waters, the movements were postponed until exploratory sweeps could be made, by *Scuffle* and three YMS, between 1 and 4 April. In the meantime, on 9 March, a reconnaissance party landed on Dumaran Island and found no Japanese. One month later, a company landed on Busuanga Island by shore-to-shore movement, killed ten Japanese and scattered a few others. Culion Island, in the same group, contained no enemy.

To complete the mop-up of outlying points, small parties were landed on Balabac Island 16 April, and on Pandanan, where the PTs earlier were resisted, on 22 April. Both islands were occupied without incident, and by that day the entire Palawan group may be called liberated.

The Air Forces profited by Palawan. The concrete airstrip was reconditioned, enlarged and covered with steel matting, owing to the poor quality of Japanese concrete. It had parking space for 175 planes, which were used to cover later operations in the Southern Philippines and Borneo. Heavy bombers also used it, as a staging field for strikes against the Asiatic mainland in April and May.[8]

3. *Zamboanga* [9]

Overlapping the Palawan operation, but distinct from it, was VICTOR IV. This took the form of a landing by the remainder of the 41st Division at Zamboanga, at the tip end of the tapering peninsula of that name, which forms the western part of the big island of Mindanao. The peninsula is bordered by a cultivated coastal plain, four miles wide, around a spine of mountains.

On 20 February 1945 Rear Admiral Forrest B. Royal, Commander Amphibious Group 6, was relieved of his duties as S.O.P.A. Lingayen Gulf and given the naval command for Zamboanga. After conferring with Admiral Barbey at Subic Bay, he arrived at Mindoro 22 February in his command ship *Rocky Mount*. There he embarked Major General Jens Doe USA and continued to Leyte for conferences at Eighth Army headquarters. After landing planes had been drafted the principal commanders returned to Mindoro, where rehearsals were held on 5 and 6 March.

Intelligence indicated that there were about 4500 (later raised to 8300) Japanese troops on the Zamboanga Peninsula, and that strong defensive positions existed in the vicinity of the town. As the shoreline here was marked by fringing reefs and coral heads, initial land-

---

[8] *Engineers in the Southwest Pacific* VI 370; Craven & Cate V 502.
[9] CTG 78.1 (Rear Adm. Royal) op order and Action Report; Eighth Army Report of the Palawan and Zamboanga Operations; Eichelberger *Jungle Road;* Sherrod *Marine Corps Aviation.*

ings again had to be made in LVTs. Four contiguous beaches, each 350 yards long, were selected opposite the Calarian airstrip – three miles northwest of Zamboanga town. The first objective was the airstrip, 600 yards inland.

Because of the suspected strength of the defense, a prolonged bombardment was planned beginning 8 March. The XIII A.A.F. began pre-landing bombing on the first day of the month, and Marine Air Groups 12, 14 and 32 were assigned for close support of the 41st Division.

Rear Admiral Berkey's *Phoenix, Boise* and six destroyers, given the bombardment assignment and that of covering minesweeping and hydrographic reconnaissance, arrived off the beaches at sunrise (0622) 8 March. Minesweeping began at once. The scheduled operations were carried out with no interference except by small-arms and 75-mm fire, which was silenced as soon as it revealed itself. At 0845, a lone Japanese plane was shot down over the airstrip by the Marine C.A.P. on station. At 1320, a heavy explosion was heard in the town of Zamboanga. This later proved to have been Japanese demolitions blowing up the inner end of the jetty.

The same pattern of operations was repeated 9 March. Minesweepers were harassed by light artillery and mortar fire but sustained no casualties. Two squadrons of PTs arrived with their tender *Oyster Bay* and began prowling around Basilan Island, 12 miles south of Zamboanga. At 1050 an Army B-24 was seen to explode over the target, apparently hit by a bomb from another bomber; a Kingfisher from *Phoenix* landed on the water near the beach and recovered the lone survivor of this freak accident. Minesweeping was completed at 1816 and the group retired for the night.

On 10 March, J-day, Admiral Royal's group arrived off Zamboanga. At 0636 he ordered "Commence the Approach," when all vessels and small craft proceeded to their assigned stations under cover of the final bombardment, which had already began. An hour later came the order "Land the Landing Force." At 0915, preceded by a rocket barrage from LCI(R)s, the first LVT wave hit the beach. Others followed at three-minute intervals. Activity at the

beaches assumed the familiar appearance of orderly confusion, with
landing and beaching craft touching down, discharging their troops
or cargoes, and retracting. At 1004 a Japanese battery somewhere
inland commenced intermittent artillery fire, which caused a few

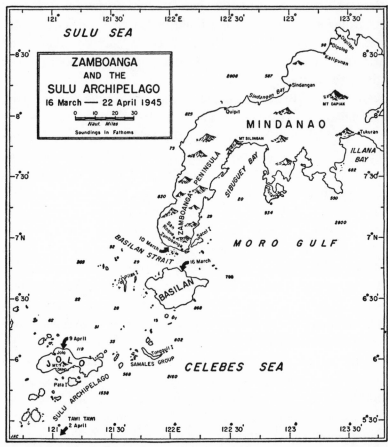

casualties in two LCI. Most of the shells fell in the water between
the line of departure and the beaches, as usually happens in amphibious operations. From the shore the water looks almost completely
covered with boats, but actually the chance of hitting one is slight.

General Doe landed at 1000 to take command ashore, and General Eichelberger, who had come up in *Rocky Mount* to watch the
show, inspected progress. At noon Admiral Berkey's group began

to deliver gunfire support as called for by the control parties with the troops. One LST received an enemy mortar hit on her bridge, with some casualties, and another LST was holed. *Rocky Mount* retired at sunset with Berkey's cruisers, leaving an area screen and LSTs at the beach to continue unloading during the night.

Fighter cover over the objective was furnished by Marine planes operating from Dipolog airstrip near the northern point of the peninsula and 145 miles from Zamboanga. During 8–10 March, two companies of the 24th Division were flown in from Mindanao to help defend this guerrilla-held strip and to protect the Marines' air operations. Ground elements of Marine Air Group 12 landed at Zamboanga itself on J-day and on 14 March the first Corsair landed on a temporary strip. The Marine Air Groups Zamboanga ("Magzam" for short), under Colonel Clayton C. Jerome USMC, were built up to almost 300 planes. Except for a detachment of Army P-61 night fighters and a few Navy PBY rescue planes, air operations here were entirely under the Marine Corps — and, as such, unique in World War II.

On shore the troops advanced rapidly against sporadic rifle and machine-gun fire. A formidable network of pillboxes, trenches and wire entanglements were deserted by the enemy; only occasionally were the troops held up by strong points. By nightfall the beachhead had been expanded to 3500 yards and included San Roque village, a mile and a half northeast of the beaches. Some rifle fire and artillery fire was directed against our positions throughout the night.

On 11 March mortar and artillery fire continued to fall on the beaches and one enemy shell fired a fuel dump. About 1111 *Boise*, using plane spot, placed accurate salvos on the Japanese artillery positions, after which their harassing fire died down. Troops ashore occupied the San Roque airstrip and the town of Zamboanga. On 12 March they advanced towards Pasananca, in the foothills about three miles inland, near which was the water reservoir for the city. It was there that the first strong resistance was met, in the normal Japanese pattern at this stage of the war.

Heavy fighting took place in the hills as our troops slowly advanced, supported by Marine Corps planes and by gunfire from Admiral Berkey's cruisers and destroyers. The fire support cruisers were released on 12 March as they were required shortly off Cebu. Destroyers then took over fire support missions and continued to deliver call fire until 18 March. Not until the 24th were the Japanese driven from their strong points in the hills north of the town.

On 16 March, a shore-to-shore landing in company strength was made on Basilan Island, 12 miles south of Zamboanga. Two days later a similar landing was made on Malamaui Island, another and smaller island just off Basilan.

The PTs found many fruitful targets around Zamboanga. Working independently at night and with bombing planes in the daytime, they destroyed a number of small craft, including two enemy PT boats and a number of suspected suicide craft. Biggest haul was at Jolo City, on the island of Jolo, 80 miles southwest of Zamboanga, on 15 March. *PT-114* and *PT-189* destroyed eight small craft, while two Mitchell (B-25) bombers set off an ammunition dump and set fires to other supply dumps. Guerrilla reports later said that all Japanese-owned craft on Jolo were wiped out in this raid.

On 2 April one battalion of the 163rd Infantry was landed at Sanga Sanga Island, in the Tawi Tawi group only 30 miles from Borneo, by Captain John D. Murphy, VII 'Phib's representative at Zamboanga. About 30 Japanese were found on Bongao Island, in the same group, the same day. One week later, Captain Murphy landed the rest of the 163rd Infantry on Jolo Island, on beaches on the north shore about five miles from Jolo City, against no opposition. That afternoon a platoon was landed in the town. The 400 Japanese defenders elected to make their stand in the mountains near the center of the island on 2400-foot Mount Daho. It was only after several days of artillery preparation and air strikes that that position was taken out on 22 April. Remnants of the garrison held out on Mount Tuamtangas, in the western part of the island, until 30 June.

With the liberation of Tawi Tawi and Jolo, Eighth Army was

only a few miles from the great island of Borneo, which would be liberated by the Australian Army and U.S. Seventh Fleet.

After Jolo had been secured, General Eichelberger flew in to make a ceremonial call on the aged Sultan, Mohammed Janail Abirir II, spiritual leader of 300,000 Moslems in the Sulu Archipelago. He had once been an inveterate enemy to the Americans and in his youth led the Moro insurrection, which gave us great trouble in the early years of the century. After surrendering to Captain John J. Pershing, later General Pershing of World War I fame, Mohammed also attained a certain fame as hero of George Ade's popular musical comedy, *The Sultan of Sulu.* After his surrender the Sultan had remained steadfastly loyal to the United States. The Japanese, during their occupation, had stripped him of most of his possessions, including his prized gifts from Generals Pershing and Leonard Wood; but he had successfully defended himself with eight wives and numerous children and retainers at an armed camp in the mountains; and, although well over seventy years old, was now ready to take over the government and acquire a new wife.

CHAPTER X

The Southern Visayas

February–June 1945

1. *Panay* [1]

TWELVE days after the operation order for Palawan was issued, orders for clearing the Southern Visayas began to come
out of General MacArthur's headquarters. These envisaged the liberation of four major islands, Panay, Cebu, Negros and Bohol.
These "faraway places with strange-sounding names" — strange to
all but old hands of the Philippine Insurrection of 1898–1901 — had
been well developed during the first half of the twentieth century,
and were now the richest part of the Philippines except for the area
around Manila. Extensive sugar plantations and sugar centrals, business blocks, Hollywood-style houses and other signs of modern life
could be seen, as well as primitive conditions in the interior and
jungle-covered mountains. President Osmeña was a native of Cebu,
and Tomás Confesor, the prewar Governor of Panay, had maintained a loyal civil government in the mountains of that island. His
noble reply to the demand of the Japanese puppet president that he
surrender stamped him as a regular Old Roman, and the circulation
of it did much to keep up Filipino morale. [2]

Cebu City, second largest industrial center in the Philippines, and
Iloilo, third largest city and capital of Panay, were important objectives. They were wanted as staging points for troops redeployed
from Europe, for the intended assault on Japan itself; and in the

[1] CTG 78.3 (Rear Adm. Struble) Op Order and Action Report; Eighth Army
Report on Panay-Negros and Cebu Operations; R. R. Smith chap. xxx; Eichelberger *Jungle Road*.
[2] See quotation page in front matter of this volume.

islands of Cebu and Panay there were more than 30,000 Japanese whom General MacArthur had determined to eliminate. Guerrillas controlled most of the territory, but the Japanese Army held the cities and important industrial activities.

An operation order of 22 February 1945 set forth the instructions for VICTOR I. This included a landing on Panay, to be followed

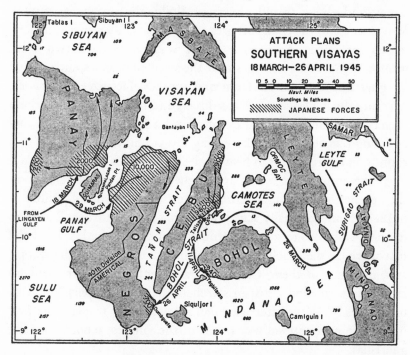

by the occupation of Negros Occidental (the northwest part of Negros), target date 18 March (G-day). The troops allocated were the 40th Division, reinforced, less one RCT, under Major General Rapp Brush, then in Luzon. Rear Admiral Arthur D. Struble, Commander Amphibious Group 9, was designated Attack Group commander, CTG 78.3, on 3 March. Plans were completed quickly, and embarkation and loading in beaching craft in Lingayen Gulf was completed on 14 March. No rehearsal was held because the assigned Army LCM detachment was at Mindoro, where it would join the overseas movement en route, and these landing craft had an important place in the assault waves. Rear Admiral Rigg's Crudiv 12 would cover and support the operation. Aërial bombardment by planes of V and XIII A.A.F. and Marine Air Group 14 began on 1 March.

Task Group 78.3 sortied from Lingayen 15 March and steamed straight to the objective, two sets of beaches on the south coast of Panay and about 12 miles west of Iloilo, the provincial capital. Movement into the transport area was preceded by a precautionary sweep for mines. At 0509 a report was received of two small groups of Japanese in villages near the selected beaches, surrounded by guerrillas and cut off from one another. Destroyer *Thatcher*, covering the minesweepers, was directed to fire on the first of these targets for about five minutes. She fired a few rounds before discovering that she was on the wrong target and then expended 119 rounds on the right one. This was the only bombardment that day.

As the amphibious forces approached, natives could be seen on the beaches, and Admiral Struble canceled all scheduled gunfire at 0748. H-hour, originally scheduled for 0830, was advanced to 0900 to enable all ships to get into proper position. As the LVTs of the first wave hit the beach, Filipinos rushed down to greet the troops, and, in honor of them, Colonel Peralta's guerrillas were lined up in parade formation, "stiff in starched khaki and resplendent with ornaments." [3] Wave after wave landed according to plan; the first opposition encountered was at one of the villages, reported by the guerrillas.

The reason was simple. At this time the Japanese garrison of Panay numbered 2000 to 2350 men, and several hundred Japanese civilians had moved in to exploit the sugar plantations and the natives. Lieutenant Colonel Totsuka, in command, planned to defend Iloilo only until it became untenable and then withdraw to what he called a "retrenchment position" on Inaman Hill, where he believed he could hold out indefinitely. This was a vivid indication of the change in Japanese thinking as the war went more and more against them.

[3] Eichelberger p. 208.

The 40th Division expanded the beachhead rapidly and ran into no serious resistance until it approached the outskirts of Iloilo. On 19 March a large explosion and fires were observed in the city and when troops entered next day not one Japanese was found. The citizens went "crazy with joy," laughing, cheering and throwing flowers at the troops, although a large part of their city had been destroyed by the Japanese when Colonel Totsuka ordered evacuation. Guerrillas harassed his column, but could not stop it, and, while 40th Division expanded the beachhead to a radius of 15 miles from the capital, it saw no reason to set out immediately in pursuit of the Japanese.

Destroyers *Thatcher* and *Claxton* fired star shell for the benefit of PT boats engaged in night searches in Iloilo Strait during the nights of 18–20 March, but received no calls for gunfire support. On the 20th, patrols sent out from Iloilo to nearby Guimaras Island found no signs of Japanese; guerrillas later wiped out a few stragglers. Two days later another patrol landed on Inampalagan Island, where a Japanese control station for electric mines in Guimaras Strait was located. The garrison got out in time to save its skin, but their control station was destroyed.

2. *Negros Occidental*

General Eichelberger entered Iloilo with General Brush on 20 March. He soon decided that it was timely to proceed with the second phase, the seizure of Negros Occidental, the northern and western part of that important sugar island, and set 29 March as target date. Admiral Struble remained at Iloilo to direct this movement and at once began planning for it. Reconnaissance showed that there was only one suitable point for the landing: near Pandan Point, opposite the center of Guimaras Island. That point, owing to an offshore bar, could be used by beaching craft no larger than

⁴ Jap. Mono. No. 7, *35th Army Operations, 1944–45* p. 126; Eighth Army Report of Panay-Negros and Cebu, Bohol, Negros Operation.

an LSM; LSTs would have to be unloaded outside. The assault was to be made by the 185th RCT, to be followed two days later by the 160th, less one battalion to remain on Panay. Upon call from Eighth Army, the 503rd Parachute RCT, then on Mindoro, would be dropped on the combat area. It was later flown to Panay and thence boated to Negros.

Guerrillas controlled about two thirds of Negros, but the Japanese had about 13,500 to 15,000 troops, under Lieutenant General Kono, in the northern half of the island, with headquarters at Bacolod. Another 800 to 1300 men under Lieutenant Colonel S. Oie were at Dumaguete in the southeastern corner. Both groups had prepared positions in the mountains to which they proposed to retire after destroying bridges and messing things up generally.

General Rapp Brush, who commanded the landing force, sent in a platoon under cover of darkness at about 0500 March 29 to seize an important bridge over the Bago River before the Japanese could blow it up. After a sharp fight with the Japanese guards the bridge was secured. The main force landed at 0900. As elsewhere, the enemy offered no opposition at the water's edge. If Kono had properly deployed his troops, according to General Eichelberger, he should have been able to wipe out the two battalions that landed on D-day; but beach defense was no longer Japanese doctrine, and Kono fought by the book. No naval support was needed for the landings. As the troops moved northward along the coast to seize the airfield near Bacolod, they met scattered opposition. Destroyers supported this movement during the night of 29–30 March, with star shell on call from the shore fire control party. *Thatcher* took up fire support on 2 April and illuminated through the night. She fired one close support mission on call of her shore fire control party at a target near Silay airfield, and continued to illuminate nightly until 5 April, when no more naval gunfire support was required.[5]

Hard fighting developed when the 40th Division pushed inland

[5] *Thatcher* Action Report 30 Apr. 1945.

against General Kono's inner fortress. There fighting continued until 4 June, when the Japanese withdrew deep into the unexplored mountains. This campaign for Negros cost the Army 370 killed and 1025 wounded.

3. Cebu [6]

Less than a week after issuing his order for the Panay operation, General MacArthur instructed Eighth Army and Seventh Fleet to execute VICTOR II — the recovery of Cebu, Bohol and Southern Negros. General Eichelberger assigned as ground troops the famous Americal Division (Major General William H. Arnold USA), which had won its spurs on Guadalcanal and in early 1945 was engaged in mopping up Leyte. Rear Admiral Fechteler, first to be named naval task group commander, was then detached for duty as Assistant Chief of Naval Personnel in Washington. Captain Albert T. Sprague, Admiral Barbey's chief of staff, relieved him as commander of this Task Group, 78.2. The target date, here called E-day, was set for 26 March, which gave time for a rehearsal at Leyte.

A beach near Talisay, about four miles west of Cebu City, was selected for the landing, to be made by two regiments abreast. It would be preceded by an hour and a half's bombardment by Admiral Berkey's cruiser division, which also covered the expedition from Leyte Gulf to Cebu.

Captain Sprague's task group, with troops embarked in APDs and beaching craft, sortied from Leyte Gulf and proceeded to the objective without incident. Minesweepers peeled off at 0200 March 26; prelanding bombardment began at 0700 and was lifted at 0822. Support craft and rocket LCI preceded the first wave of LVT to the beaches as usual. First wave touched down at 0828 and others followed at three-minute intervals.

[6] CTG 78.2 (Capt. A. T. Sprague) Action Report and Op Order, dated 4 Apr. 1945; Eighth Army Report cited in Note 4; Americal Division "After Action Report V-2 Operation"; Jap. Mono. No. 7.

These Cebu landings were exceptional, for Southern Philippines amphibious operations, in that the enemy here did offer serious opposition right on the beach. Of the Japanese troops on Cebu (about 14,500 in all) 85 per cent were concentrated in and around Cebu City. They were led by Major General Takeo Manjome and Rear Admiral Kaku Harada of the Naval Base Force. Lieutenant General Sosaku Suzuki, who had put up a stout defense at Leyte,[7] arrived 24 March and assumed over-all command, but did not interfere with Manjome's dispositions. These were designed to control and interdict rather than hold the city. He set up a first line of resistance in the rising ground above the coastal plain, about two and a half miles inland, a second line about one mile further inland, and numerous strong points in the rugged hills not far distant. This enterprising general had improved the five months since the Leyte landings to establish formidable defensive positions, pillboxes, caves, and the like, and had employed his men making beach and land mines out of 60-mm mortar shells. These were strewn liberally on the Talisay beaches and the roads leading thence towards the city. In addition to the mines he set up barriers and obstacles in the shape of sharpened bamboo stakes, antitank ditches and barriers built of logs and earth. General Manjome proposed, like Colonel Nakagawa at Peleliu, to offer better than token opposition on the beaches, but to exact a heavy price for our main objectives. Eighth Army as yet had encountered no mined beaches and, despite warnings from the guerrillas of what to expect, the Americal Division failed to provide enough engineers for mine clearance.

Seventh Fleet had learned from experience that every landing beach area must be bombarded, unless evidence of friendly natives being about was unmistakable. At Cebu, "Count" Berkey's cruiser division (*Phoenix, Boise,* H.M.A.S. *Hobart* and *Warramunga* and six U.S. destroyers) bombarded for an hour and a half. This had the happy effect of driving out elements of a Japanese sea transport regiment which had been detailed to defend the beaches, but it was

[7] *See* Vol. XII chap. xvi.

not enough to explode the land mines, which held up the Americal boys from 0830 to 1000.[8]

Ferdinand Magellan landed at the site of Cebu City on 7 April 1521 and promptly made an ally of the local Rajah. He lost his life on the nearby island of Mactan, on 28 April 1521 when personally leading an amphibious assault against one of the Rajah's enemies. The natives caught him in shoal water covering the retreat of his men, who were beyond the then very limited range of gunfire support, and with their spears did to death this greatest of navigators. Four hundred and twenty-four years later, Captain Sprague, walking almost in Magellan's footsteps, was also troubled by shoal water, but not hampered by any lack of gunfire support. Yet he had to surmount one hazard which Magellan never had to face — land mines. Ten of the first 15 LVT ashore were knocked out by mines when only a few yards inland. Subsequent boat waves of troops, eight of which had landed by 0910, piled up behind the first and the assault was stopped dead on the beaches. A submerged log boom held up beaching craft when they tried to land at 0920; and the LST and LST flotillas made wonderful targets for enemy artillery; but General Manjome had no artillery trained on the approach and missed this opportunity. By sailors off shore, exploding mines were taken to be enemy mortar fire, and at 0912 H.M.A.S. *Hobart* fired at a suspected mortar site; but there seems to have been no enemy gunfire of any kind at the water's edge. The beaching craft were allowed to come in without opposition, and by early afternoon had rigged pontoon causeways. The troops, once past the beach minefield, started at 1000 a cautious advance through abandoned Japanese defense positions.

[8] R. R. Smith chap. xxx compares the situation to that at Tarawa and gives the opinion that if Manjome had properly manned his beach defenses he might have had the unique distinction of repelling an amphibious assault, which had only once been done in the Pacific, by the Marines at Wake Island (see Vol. III chap. xii). To which it may be remarked that the new Japanese counter-amphibious tactics, whose objective was delay rather than victory, required him to save forces for defense of the interior, and that the pre-landing bombardment probably made his beach defenses untenable in any case.

Destroyer *Conyngham* at 1535 spotted something that looked like a periscope in the channel. Captain Sprague immediately got his group underway and formed cruising disposition, leaving two destroyers and two patrol craft to develop the contact. A small conning tower appeared, indicating a midget submarine. *Conyngham* and *Flusser* made several straddles on it from ranges of about 3000 yards, but observed no hits and the vessel submerged. *PC–1133*, closing in for a sonar search, grounded on a shoal in Cebu Harbor, and no further contact was made that day. But at 0038 next morning, *Newman* reported a surfaced midget submarine about seven miles south of the first sighting. She closed to within 100 yards of the boat, firing with automatic weapons, observed numerous hits around the little conning tower, and sank the midget.

The Japanese destroyed Cebu City almost as thoroughly as they did Manila, and the Americal Division marched in on 27 March. Next day they cleared Lahug airfield, two miles northeast of the city. Here the troops ran into resistance from Manjome's prepared positions, about a mile further inland. These, however, were within range of the American destroyers, which fired slow interdiction fire all night, and during the next few days and nights delivered call fire as requested by shore fire control parties, and continued to do so as long as enemy targets were within range. Evidence that this support was both welcome and effective is found in comments from the shore fire control parties, such as "Destroyer fire is excellent," and "Pillboxes destroyed on that ridge, the Japs were smoked out into the open where we mowed 'em down with automatic fire." [9]

On 18 April (third anniversary of the Halsey-Doolittle raid on Tokyo, and second anniversary of shooting down Admiral Yamamoto), General Manjome decided he had exhausted the possibilities of holding his prepared positions, and retired into the mountains. General Suzuki had already embarked with his staff in four small craft at Medellin, hoping to reach Davao and organize the de-

[9] Comdesron 5 (Capt. F. D. McCorkle) Action Report 5 Apr. 1945.

fense of Mindanao. Within a week this unit was bombed by American aircraft off Negros and Suzuki was killed.[10]

Except for destroyers, PCs and PTs covering minor shore-to-shore movements to outlying islands, Cebu offered no more work for the Navy.

The reserve regiment of the Americal Division, the 164th, arrived 9 April. Two battalions made an encircling maneuver, marching for three successive nights, concealed during the day, to get around Manjome's rear. An attack by them, concerted with a frontal attack by the other two RCTs (the 132nd and 182nd) forced the Japanese out of their last prepared positions into the mountains of northern Cebu, where they were no longer a menace.

The liberation of this island cost the U.S. Army 410 men killed, 1700 wounded and over 8000 nonbattle casualties, principally "victims of various jungle diseases." There were also a few naval casualties. Some 5500 Japanese were killed and 8500 surrendered at the end of the war; these included three generals and an admiral.

4. *Bohol and Southern Negros*

At the end of the first week of April, General Eichelberger urged General Arnold to get on with the clearing of Bohol and Southern Negros. On 11 April, LCMs and beaching craft lifted one battalion of the 164th Infantry to Tagbalaran, on the western coast of Bohol. The troops were met by guerrillas who had that part of the island under control. On 15 April patrols flushed the main body of about 330 Japanese in the hills about seven miles inland. They were not strongly emplaced and by 20 April were overrun.

On 26 April the rest of the 164th Infantry, having rested for a week after fighting on Cebu, landed unopposed on the southeastern coast of Negros, about five miles north of Dumaguete, the principal town in that part of the island. Presently they made contact with a patrol from the 40th Division which had made its way down

[10] Vol. XII 395.

the east coast without finding a single enemy. Dumaguete was occupied that afternoon. Two days later Lieutenant Colonel Oie and his 800 men were found in the hills about ten miles southwest of the town. Well dug in, they were not dislodged until 28 May; and not until 12 June did Oie give up organized resistance.

That is about the whole story of liberating the Southern Visayas, except for follow-up convoys and constant patrolling by PTs. By 20 June the Americal and the 40th Divisions had lost about 835 killed and 2300 wounded. About 500 Japanese had been captured and 10,250 killed. R. R. Smith assumes that another 4000 were killed or died from starvation between 20 June and 15 August. Nearly 17,500 surrendered on Panay, Negros, Cebu and Bohol at the end of the war. Several thousand more were killed by guerrillas or American patrols, or died of starvation, between 20 June and 15 August.[11] The liberation of the Southern Visayas was expensive for us, but still more for the enemy, and his futile defense of them gave him no corresponding advantage.

[11] R. R. Smith chap. xxx. These statistics include those quoted above for Cebu.

CHAPTER XI

Mindanao[1]

April–July 1945

1. The Malabang-Parang Landings

THE main part of Mindanao, which had been General Mac-
Arthur's initial target in his original plan for liberating the
Philippines, became the last, owing to the revision of plans in September 1944. The General, in his MONTCLAIR plan of February
1945, selected Illana Bay on Moro Gulf as the place for an amphibious landing with one army corps, setting target date (R-day) for
12 April. Shortage of shipping later caused this date to be shifted to
the 17th.

The terrain of Mindanao is very rugged and mountainous, covered with rain forest except for a certain amount of marsh and
grassland. Roads and other means of communication were very limited. The mountains yielded hardwood timber and the cultivated
part produced the abaca fiber from which manila line is made.
Most of the important abaca producers, even before the war, were
Japanese; Davao, the principal city, was the center of their activity.
Mindanao is peopled by Moros — Moslem Filipinos — who are stout
fighters. They never entirely gave up fighting the Spaniards, and
their resistance to American rule continued long after the Philippine Insurrection had subsided elsewhere in the Archipelago. An
old Malay custom that had plagued Americans for over forty years

[1] CTG 78.2 (Rear Adm. Noble) op order and Action Report 22 May 1945;
Eighth Army Report on the Mindanao Operation; R. R. Smith chap. xxxi; Eichelberger *Jungle Road* chaps. xvi–xvii (best account in print on the Mindanao campaign); Sherrod *Marine Corps Aviation;* Jap. Mono. No. 7 p. 115 and Map 15; Report of 24th Inf. Div. on V–5 Operation.

was "running amuck." A Moro who felt himself grieved would get hopped-up with drugs and rush about in a murderous frenzy, stabbing or killing everyone in his path. The Japanese stopped this by the simple expedient of executing all members of the offender's immediate family. And their treatment of such Moros as they controlled, leaving them without work, food or clothing, and flooding the island with worthless invasion money, made Mindanao ripe for liberation.

Imperial General Headquarters, assuming that MacArthur's original plan would be executed, had seen to it that part of the big island was well fortified and defended. Two regiments were transferred to Leyte in November 1944, but that left over 43,000 troops on Mindanao, under command of Lieutenant General G. Morozumi. His dispositions in mid-April were: the 100th Infantry Division and 32nd Naval Base Force north of Davao; 74th Infantry Regiment and 2nd Air Division at Malaybalay in the north center; about half the 30th Infantry Division (Lieutenant General Jiro Hirada) between that town and Cagayan on the north coast; and the 54th Independent Mixed Brigade at Zamboanga.

All these units of formidable paper strength were pinned down near the towns that they garrisoned by some 25,000 Filipino guerrillas under Colonel Wendel W. Fertig, who had been an American mining engineer before the war. Since the guerrillas controlled 95 per cent of the island, confining Japanese activity largely to the towns and principal roads, there seems, in retrospect, to have been no sound military reason for throwing American troops into this big island. Even the official Eighth Army Report admits that Mindanao had no strategic value after Luzon and the Visayas were secured; it even indicates that this operation was undertaken for reasons of prestige, and to please our Philippine allies.

Since General Morozumi's main strength was concentrated on Davao Gulf and along the main road (known as the Sayre Highway) which crossed the mountains thence to Cagayan, General Eichelberger made a sensible decision: to establish a beachhead on the lightly held western part of the island, then strike inland fast.

Zamboanga, on the tip end of the southwestern peninsula, had, as we have seen, been occupied by units of the 41st Infantry Division, Major General Jens Doe, on 10 March.[2] That was a good beginning, especially since the Japanese had made the bad guess that this was the only invasion of Mindanao contemplated by the Americans, and relaxed their efforts at defense.

General of the Army Douglas MacArthur's instructions for clearing the rest of Mindanao (Operation VICTOR V) were issued to Eighth Army on 11 March. Amphibious Group 8, of which Rear Admiral A. G. Noble assumed command 22 March, was designated to lift the X Corps. Detailed plans were issued on the 26th from Eighth Army headquarters on Leyte.

Task Group 78.2, as Admiral Noble's group was numbered, would lift the 24th Infantry Division (Major General R. B. Woodruff) and headquarters X Corps (Major General F. C. Sibert) from Mindoro to assault beaches near Malabang on R-day, 17 April, and then pick up the 31st Infantry Division (Major General C. A. Martin) at Morotai and land it at Parang, also on Illana Bay, on R-day plus 5. The mission of X Corps was to seize and develop a base whence further operations could be launched, in which Admiral Noble would coöperate. In this plan, General Eichelberger was making a calculated gamble. He believed that by striking quickly in unexpected places the enemy would be kept off balance and the island completely liberated earlier than could be accomplished by a slower and more careful advance.

On 11 April TG 78.2 departed Mindoro for Mindanao. On the same day word was received from Colonel Fertig that Malabang town and airstrip were already in the hands of his men. How that happened is an interesting story in itself.

The guerrillas had some 600 to 700 Japanese trapped in the outskirts of Malabang, but were unable to dislodge them. Since 3 April the Marine aviators, Colonel Jerome's "Magzam," had been land-

2 See Chap. IX sec. 2 above.

MINDANAO
17 April —— 12 July 1945

0   10   20   30
Naut. Miles
===Roads   ===Trails
Airstrip
Soundings in Fathoms

ing on the Malabang airstrip, conferring with the guerrillas on profitable targets and sending strikes against the Japanese positions. After ten days the enemy's numbers were cut to about 300. These broke through the guerrilla line on 14 April and fled southward, leaving the Filipinos in undisputed possession of both town and airstrip. Word of this reached Generals Sibert and Woodruff who embarked in *Wasatch* with Admiral Noble on the day of departure from Mindoro. On the assumption that the guerrillas could hold these gains until the arrival of the task group, the military and naval commanders worked out en route a completely new landing plan, a tribute to the training and flexibility of VII 'Phib. They decided to land one battalion at Malabang to ensure possession of that town and the airstrip, but to make the main effort at Parang, whence a road of sorts leads overland to Davao Gulf. This would gain at least two days. General Eichelberger, embarked in *Montpelier* with Admiral Riggs, approved the change by dispatch. The Parang landing also opened the possibility of using the Mindanao River for transportation and supply of troops inland. New orders were prepared and distributed while the task force was nearing the objective.

Approach and deployment were carried out on schedule and without incident. Admiral Riggs's cruisers bombarded the beach area as well as Cotabato, a key town near the mouth of the Mindanao River; the assault waves hit their assigned beaches less than a minute off schedule at 0900 April 17. There was no opposition and the landing proceeded in an orderly manner, hampered only by flat beach gradients and tidal conditions. A damaged pier in Parang was repaired and pontoon causeways were married to it promptly, permitting LSTs to land heavy equipment handily. An hour earlier a battalion of the 21st Infantry had landed at Malabang and quickly secured both town and airstrip. The troops moved rapidly inland and along Highway No. 1, connecting Illana Bay with Digos on Davao Gulf.

2. The Mindanao River Campaign

Although classed as a highway, No. 1 was little more than an improved trail incapable of supporting modern military vehicles, and the Japanese destroyed all bridges as they retired. As this had been anticipated it was planned to exploit the Mindanao River as a water route to the interior. The Army, since Philippine Insurrection days, had known the river to be navigable at least as far as Fort Pikit, thirty-five miles inland, where the highway crosses. And a short distance beyond Pikit is Kabakan, an important junction with the main road from Davao Gulf to Cagayan.

The Mindanao River forks about 15 miles from the coast and has two mouths. As R-day reconnaissance found no enemy about, a task unit was promptly set up to exploit the river route. It consisted of one battalion of infantry embarked in landing craft of the Army's 533rd Engineer Boat and Shore Regiment. Lieutenant Colonel Robert Amory USA commanded this flotilla of 5 LCM(G), 1 LCM(R),[3] 3 LCS(S), 24 LCM and 14 LCVP. With other craft belonging to the amphibian engineers, these had made the voyage from Lingayen to Moro Gulf on their own bottoms.[4]

At 0830 April 18, while Cleveland and Sigourney bombarded Tamontaka, the Army Engineers' fresh-water navy took off up both branches. Both units reached the forks at 1350, after clearing a few pockets of resistance. Before evening they seized Lomopog, where Moro guerrillas provided much valuable intelligence – as well as presenting a quantity of fresh duck eggs which gave all hands an ample breakfast next day.

Since Colonel Amory anticipated that Fort Pikit would be too tough for the automatic weapons in his LCM gunboats, he obtained

[3] These were LCMs converted by the Engineers as gunboats, with 40-mm, 25-mm and 20-mm guns, and LCMs equipped with rockets.
[4] Surf and Sand pp. 177–86; Guy Richards "Gunboat Blitz" Marine Corps Gazette Feb. 1946; information from Col. Amory, a New York lawyer and former head proctor at Harvard, who had joined the web-footed Engineers as a private in 1942.

for his task unit four PGM, 110-foot subchasers that had been converted to gunboats and whose armament included rocket launchers.[5] The PGM, together with two LCI(G), were sent upstream on 19 April to join the Engineers' navy. Lacking accurate charts and local pilots, they made slow progress, and the 110-footers had trouble negotiating some of the sharp river bends. Mechanical failure in one LCI halted them at Pagaluan, short of the objective, and not until the morning of 21 April did they catch up with Colonel Amory at Paidu Pulangi.

At 1100 that day the joint task unit made best speed upstream in two columns, each headed by a PGM. Guerrillas reported 800 Japanese with two cannon dug in near the ferry at the village of Balumis, just short of Fort Pikit. At 1521 the gunboats opened 3-inch fire against enemy positions below the ferry, and the Engineers landed a company of infantry a mile and a half downstream. The defenders could not have been more startled at the sight of battleships than they were at these 110-foot craft; they fled precipitately, leaving their supper half-eaten. A wrecked bridge held up the larger vessels, but Colonel Amory's 50-foot LCM(G)s worked past it, smothered enemy positions above the ferry with automatic weapons and rockets, and at 1600 landed troops to attack Fort Pikit. That, too, was abandoned by the enemy. The river was too shallow above this fort for the PGMs to continue upstream; but the LCMs, scraping bottom most of the way, made Kabakan, and occupied it 22 April in advance of the troops marching overland. The Japanese garrisons of Pikit and Kabakan retired to Basilan, where they were pinned down for the rest of the war.

This interesting revival of tactics used in the river and bayou operations of the American Civil War sped the advance of the 24th Division to the main battlefield above Davao Gulf. Admiral Noble, who at first took a dim view of a water-borne operation not con-

---

[5] These PGM were a part of a Close Support Unit, which included LCI(G), LCI(R) and LCS and was commanded by Capt. Rae E. Arison. Only three PGM, under Lt. Robert A. Pickering usnr, joined Col. Amory. The two LCI(G) were left behind, and *PGM-5* dropped out after fouling her propeller on a log.

ducted by sailors, commented "were it not for the successful completion of this river campaign, our forces would be at least a month behind their present schedule."

3. Davao Gulf Operations

On 22 April the 31st ("Dixie") Infantry Division began landing at Parang and Cotabato. General Sibert then split X Corps, as planned, ordering General Woodruff's 24th Division to push on along Highway No. 1 to Davao and General Martin's 31st to drive northward along the Sayre Highway from Kabakan. Marine Air Group 24 flew into Malabang from Luzon on 22 April to support both drives.

The 24th Division clashed only once with the enemy before reaching Digos on the Gulf of Davao on 27 April. It then continued north to Davao, encountering only lightly held road blocks, and on 3 May entered the city, which the enemy had pretty well wrecked. In this rapid advance, General Woodruff bypassed main Japanese defenses. These, which rendered his hold on Davao tenuous, were in the hills three thousand yards to four miles inland, and extended from a point about thirteen miles southwest of Davao to one about ten miles north of the city. To root the enemy out of this line proved to be a long process with hard fighting.

Admiral Noble now reënters the scene, wearing his flag in U.S.C.G.C. *Spencer*, in which General Eichelberger is embarked. TG 78.2 escorts an LSM group, carrying 1000 troops and 1500 tons of supplies from Parang to Digos, on 3–4 May. Cruiser *Denver* (Captain Thomas F. Darden) and three destroyers cover this movement. En route *Denver* shells and destroys a Japanese observation post on Balut Island, off the southern coast. When well inside Davao Gulf, she gets in touch with a shore fire control party and lobs 99 rounds of 6-inch shell into enemy positions in the hills behind the city.

This was the first of several "administrative movements," as these shore-to-shore operations were called by the Army. The next was to Taloma Bay, five miles southwest of Davao, which became the center of unloading activity on 6 May. Front lines there were only about 3000 yards from the beach. While unloading was in progress, destroyer *Flusser* fired 188 rounds of 5-inch on call from the shore fire control party.

The PGMs which had made the upriver excursion, under the command of Captain Rae E. Arison, together with three LCI(G), arrived in Taloma Bay south of Davao on 11 May. The previous night a tiny Japanese armed speedboat, at which nobody on our side had a good look, broke into the anchorage and sank a small Army freighter. Captain Arison, after agreeing upon targets with Army commanders ashore, began active patrolling on 12 May, shelling suspected enemy positions and bases on Samal Island. He also joined forces with PT boats in rooting out the enemy from the eastern shore of Davao Gulf.[6]

Motor Torpedo Boat Squadron 24, Lieutenant Edgar D. Hogland USNR, arrived 17 April but found no business on the west coast of Mindanao. Captain Bowling, the over-all PT commander, then tried his boats in what he called mobile support, using tender *Oyster Bay* anchored in Sarangani Bay as base. On the night of 26 April they patrolled Davao Gulf. A lone Japanese plane (the first and only one seen airborne by the liberating forces) attacked the boats, without effect. They returned to Sarangani 2 May, and thence moved into the Gulf on 6 May. The PTs performed useful services transporting Army scouts and Intelligence teams, but found few targets during their first week.

On 14 May *PT-335* and *PT-343*, with one of Captain Arison's LCI gunboats, patrolled the northeastern part of the Gulf, working with a Marine Corps Mitchell bomber which was based on Malabang. About noon, following up a report of a Japanese motor torpedo boat hideout near Piso Point opposite Davao, the two PTs steamed over there and found a concealed channel leading through mangroves into a cove, where six enemy PTs were so cleverly

6 CTU 78.2.58 (Capt. Arison) Action Report 19 May 1945.

camouflaged that at a hundred yards one could make them out only with the aid of binoculars. The two PTs opened fire with their 40-mm guns at point-blank range, blew the camouflage off one enemy boat, exploded its fuel tanks and fired some fuel drums ashore. The fire spread to an ammunition dump, which exploded with a tremendous blast, throwing debris 300 feet into the air and, incidentally, destroying another Japanese boat. The remaining four enemy craft were strafed and severely damaged before the raiders retired, well pleased with their day's work.

Next morning two other PTs, returning from night patrol, heard explosions near Piso Point and concluded that the Japanese were destroying their base. In the meantime Admiral Noble had detached destroyer escort *Key* to assist the PTs. She arrived off Piso Point in time to see them retiring under fire of heavy automatic weapons. After Lieutenant Hogland in *PT–106* had indicated profitable targets, *Key* fired 252 rounds of 5-inch, set for impact and air bursts, and 1072 rounds of 40-mm. Three large fires were ignited, and one explosion was heard. Two LCI gunboats then closed and used their 3-inch guns, setting more fires. Lieutenant Hogland now took two PTs into the cove, and at 75 yards shelled the four boats damaged the day before. Three of them caught fire and exploded, and the fourth, which was already partly burned out, was shelled again. A fifth, heavily camouflaged, was discovered and set afire.

When Hogland retired he found *Flusser* waiting to join the party, and selected targets for her. The destroyer laid on an area bombardment, expending 384 rounds of 5-inch to conclude this "Battle of Piso Point" on 15 May.

Since Japanese naval bases had a way of coming to life unexpectedly, the Piso Point hideout became a target for shoots and bombings almost daily for the next fortnight. Finally, on 29 May, 25 Liberators summoned from Morotai dropped 36 tons of bombs on this last refuge of the Japanese motor torpedo boats, and wiped it out completely.

4. *Macajalar and Minor Landings*

General Morozumi, expecting a landing at Macajalar Bay on the Mindanao Sea, neglected his defenses to the southward. This enabled the 31st Division temporarily to make rapid progress up the Sayre Highway, but by 5 May General Martin's boys were meeting stiff resistance and the fighting had settled into a slow, deliberate pattern. General of the Army Douglas MacArthur now decided to assist his own forces, and incidentally fulfill Morozumi's expectations, by a landing at Macajalar Bay. For this purpose Rear Admiral Struble lifted the 108th RCT of the 40th Division from Ormoc Bay, Leyte. Minesweepers, covered by destroyer *Meade*, entered Macajalar Bay ahead of the attack group, early on 10 May. Guerrillas controlled most of this region, but Japanese had been reported active and a destroyer bombardment was laid on as a precaution. The landing was made under assault conditions, but no opposition developed and it turned into another "administrative" affair. Patrols along the coast outside the beachhead perimeter were sent out in the next few days and beaching craft were used to ferry guerrillas into the beachhead.[7] The main body of troops worked their way inland over the Sayre Highway and made contact with elements of the 31st Division on 23 May.

By the end of the month Captain F. D. McCorkle (Comdesron 5), S.O.P.A. Davao Gulf, began organizing minor operations jointly with General Sibert's headquarters, to secure outlying Japanese radio stations and observation posts. Minesweepers had been at work for some time covering Davao Gulf and Sarangani Bay, largely controlled by guerrillas. Between 1 and 5 June, Japanese outposts were cleaned out at Luayon and Cape San Augustin, on the two entrances to Davao Gulf, Balut and Sarangani Islands. Captain McCorkle in *Flusser*, with destroyer escort *Leland E. Thomas*, LCI(R), LCI(G) and PTs, covered this movement of about 260 troops, who were embarked in the Army Engineers'

[7] CTG 78.3 (Rear Adm. Struble) Action Report 31 May.

LCMs. On 1 June, following an hour's bombardment by the two larger ships, and an air strike, the troops landed on Luayon and destroyed the Japanese radio station, whose garrison turned out to be one lone soldier. That afternoon the men reëmbarked, proceeded to the guerrilla-held village of Glan inside Sarangani Bay, and thence jumped off for Balut Island on 3 June. Here they encountered resistance and were unable to reach their hilltop objective until an auxiliary landing was made at another point, next morning. Having cleared the island and destroyed the radio station and other installations, the troops again took to their boats, to hit Cape San Augustin 5 June. PTs had reconnoitered the cape and brought off two plantation owners, who had accurate information on Japanese strength and dispositions. This landing was also preceded by a bombardment which chased the enemy into the jungle, and once more the troops met no opposition and destroyed Japanese installations at their leisure.

Returning to Sayre Highway, it was not until 10 June that the Japanese defense installations between Davao and Malaybalay were overrun by the 24th Division. Operations then entered the "mop-up and pursuit" phase. General Eichelberger declared organized resistance on Mindanao to be at an end on 30 June; but the enemy did not get the word, as usual in the Philippines, and mopping up continued. On 4 July PT boats lifted to Glan a reconnaissance platoon of the 24th Division, which, in conjunction with guerrillas working the other shore, secured that part of Mindanao by 11 July. The 1500 Japanese around Sarangani, cut off by the 24th Division's dash across the island, concentrated in the interior, about ten miles inland. Hence Sarangani Bay, first on General MacArthur's original target list for the Philippines, became the scene of the last amphibious landing in the Archipelago, on 12 July 1945. A BLT of the 21st Infantry Regiment was landed at the head of the Bay by Colonel Amory's craft. The troops pushed rapidly inland but were kept busy tracking down the enemy until mid-August.[8]

This Mindanao campaign was brief and brilliant, deserving more

[8] R. R. Smith chap. viii p. 67.

detailed study than we can afford, as an example of flexibility, improvisation and perfect coöperation between Army, Navy and Air Forces. It was costly to Eighth Army, but far more so to the enemy. By 7 September 1945, when General Tomochika (Suzuki's chief of staff who had escaped to Mindanao when his leader was bombed) signed the surrender document for Mindanao, the 30th Japanese Infantry Division had lost over 10,000 men, the 100th even more; and the 54th Independent Mixed Brigade, 4000 strong at the time of the American landing at Zamboanga in March, had been reduced to 800 men by sickness, starvation and guerrilla attacks.[9]

[9] Jap. Mono. No. 7 pp. 17, 118–23, 128; Eighth Army Report gives casualties as 761 killed, 3078 wounded. R. R. Smith chap. xxxi gives slightly different figures for both sides.

PART IV

Miscellaneous Operations

1942–1945

CHAPTER XII

Borneo

February–August 1945

1. *Borneo in Pacific Strategy* [1]

THE mountainous island of Borneo, whose area is more than twice as great as that of the entire Philippine Archipelago, is civilized (in the Western sense) only at a few points along the coast. Thinly inhabited by a variety of pagan tribes, such as the head-hunting Dyaks, the Dusuns and the Muruts, and by Moslem Malays, it was discovered for Europeans by Antonio d'Abreu in 1511. For over two centuries Europeans were content to trade along the Borneo coast, but when they withdrew toward the end of the eighteenth century, native pirates became such a nuisance in the South China Sea that the Dutch and the British moved in to control the island. Before World War II the greater part of it belonged to the Netherlands East Indies, but along the north coast were four areas under the British aegis — the sultanate of Sarawak, which Sir James ("Rajah") Brooke had made a British protectorate; Brunei, a tiny but very rich native sultanate, also under British protection; the crown colony of Labuan; and North Borneo, ruled by one of the last of those chartered companies which bore so large a part in the colonial history of North America. The interior was still left to the natives. Borneo was an economic backwater, exporting such things as rattan and edible birds' nests, until the twentieth

[1] See Vol. III Chaps, ix, xiv, xv, xvi; Vol. IX, under Burma; Maj. Gen. S. W. Kirby and others *The War Against Japan* (London 1957) I chap. xiii; John Ehrman *Grand Strategy* V (1956); Grace P. Hayes Ms. "History of the J.C.S." p. 67. Data furnished by Cdr. G. Hermon Gill RAN and Mr. Gavin Long O.B.E., general editor of the Australian war histories.

century, when oil was discovered in profitable quantities near the coast at Miri in Sarawak, Seria in Brunei, and at Tarakan, Balikpapan and other coastal points in the Dutch colony. Rubber plantations also were started. The Japanese wanted Borneo for its oil and its strategic position in the South China Sea. They captured it during the first few weeks of World War II, despite all efforts of the Royal Netherlands Navy, the United States Asiatic Fleet, and a small but valiant Punjabi garrison in the north.

Borneo under Japanese control became a major source of fuel oil for the Japanese Navy. As such, Allied strategists would have liked very much to recover the big island, but it lay too deep in enemy-held territory; either the Southern Philippines or Singapore would have to be liberated first. Thus, Borneo was left alone by the Allies for over two years, when it became the object of a curious strategic "After you!" business between the British and the American chiefs of staff.

The Joint Chiefs of Staff, in accordance with their hope and desire that the Royal Navy would return to the Pacific via the Indian Ocean and the Strait of Malacca, began early in 1944 urging their British opposite numbers to expel the Japanese from the oil-producing centers of Borneo, as an important contribution to the Pacific War. The British Chiefs of Staff lent a favorable ear, and in April and May 1944 were considering setting up a series of Anglo-Australian operations, to be mounted in Darwin, to recover both the Netherlands and the British coastal regions. It was also proposed and favored by the Australian government, that as soon as Germany was defeated, a formidable segment of the Royal Navy would support General MacArthur in this forward movement, reinforcing or relieving the Seventh Fleet. This plan was thrown into hotchpot in July, when the B.C.S. were informed of the yet inchoate American plan to assault Kyushu before the end of 1945. Mr. Churchill, Sir Alan Brooke, and others who determined British strategy, decided that the Royal Navy must get into the main show under, or beside, Admiral Nimitz. In that case, someone else would have to pick up the ball for Borneo; and as the Royal Netherlands

Navy had been almost completely destroyed in 1942, that meant your Uncle Sam.

Mr. Churchill, as usual, got what he wanted; although Admiral King almost upset the apple cart at the OCTAGON Conference at Quebec in September 1944 by letting it be known that he wanted no part of the British Navy in the Central Pacific. But President Roosevelt had already accepted Churchill's offer, and Admiral King grumbled in vain.[2] This decision – typical of political intervention in military strategy – was probably mistaken. The Royal Navy detachment, placed under Admiral Nimitz, was indeed a great help at Okinawa, but the United States Pacific Fleet could have got along without it; and had this detachment been allowed to operate in southern waters, in conjunction with the Australian Army, Singapore and a good part of the Netherlands East Indies might have been liberated before the war ended. That was what General MacArthur and Admiral King wanted and urged. Admiral Lord Mountbatten was eager to coöperate; but as we have seen in previous volumes, Mountbatten's forces in the Indian Ocean were starved in order to feed the Mediterranean.

Again, in March 1945, when General MacArthur was about to launch his attack on Borneo, he hoped to have the support of the British Pacific Fleet, now commanded by Admiral Sir Bruce Fraser RN. The J.C.S. objected, because Fraser's carrier force had been given an important rôle in the Okinawa operation coming up, and Admiral Nimitz was loath to release it. But, on the assumption that the British carriers would not be needed later than mid-April, the J.C.S. proposed that Admiral Fraser then be detached to cover an Australian invasion of Borneo, under MacArthur's supreme comman. This hook was baited with the tempting suggestion that Bru-

---

[2] Ehrman V 459–62, 472–85, 498–504, 517–24, goes into these discussions in great detail. Compare King & Whitehill *Fleet Admiral King* pp. 569–70. The reasons for Admiral King's opposition, which he failed to make clear at Quebec (at least the published minutes of the C.C.S. so indicate) were: (1) the inadequate Fleet Train of the R.N. (see Ehrman V 476–78), which caused him to fear that British ships in the Pacific far from their bases would have to depend on the already strained logistics of the U.S. Navy; and (2) belief that more profitable employment for the R.N. in the Pacific would be recovery of Singapore, Borneo and the N.E.I

nei Bay, North Borneo, would be an ideal base for the British Pacific Fleet, in lieu of Leyte Gulf, in the contemplated operations against Japan. But the British Chiefs of Staff refused to bite; they thought Brunei too remote to be useful, and it would have had to be built up; whilst eastern Leyte from Tacloban to Dulag was already a great logistics base. And, as Admiral Nimitz requested, the British carrier force remained in support of Fifth Fleet off Okinawa until that island was secured. The J.C.S., assuming that Mac-Arthur would soon be commanding an invasion of Japan's home islands, now came back with a proposal to create a new, all-British Southwest Pacific command in the late summer of 1945. That idea was still being batted about between London, Washington and Canberra when Japan surrendered.[3]

Allied indifference to Borneo was unfortunate for some two thousand prisoners, mostly Australian, whom the Japanese had kept since 1942 at Sandakan, North Borneo. In late 1944, when American warships began plowing the Sulu Sea, the Japanese commander in North Borneo guessed that his bailiwick would be the next Allied target and removed the prisoners to the interior. About three hundred sick were left at Sandakan, and all these died. The rest were sent to Ranau, close to Mt. Kina Balu, in a series of death marches, and put to work on the superhuman task of building an airfield in that rugged country. Conditions were even worse than on the River Thai; and by the time North Borneo was liberated, every one of these Australians, except six men who escaped to friendly natives, was dead.[4]

Borneo operations formed the tail end of General MacArthur's MONTCLAIR plan of 25 February 1945, and he issued instructions for the occupation of Tarakan (OBOE 1) on 21 March. At that time his, and Admiral King's, eyes were almost the only ones still focused on this neck of the Indies. Iwo Jima was practically secured and Oki-

[3] Ehrman VI 220–35.
[4] K. G. Tregonning *Under Chartered Company Rule — North Borneo 1881-1946* (Singapore, 1954) pp. 220–21.

nawa was coming up in a few days. The J.C.S. permitted MacArthur and Seventh Fleet to recover Borneo; but, as we shall see, they rejected his plans to follow this up by liberating Java and the other valuable islands which Japan had wrested from the Abda forces.

2. Tarakan [5]

Tarakan is a heart-shaped island, 15½ miles long by 11 miles at its widest point, lying in the swampy delta of the Sesajap River on the Dutch eastern coast of Borneo, bordering the Celebes Sea. The Japanese had captured it with slight difficulty on 11 January 1942.[6] The importance of this small island lay in its oilfields and airfield sites. Activity on the island was centered in the town of Tarakan, a mile and a half inland from the port of Lingkas, which had the only suitable landing place, a beach 2200 yards long, from which a pier for the oil tankers stretched out to deep water. This beach is mostly soft mud, and the part exposed at high water only 10 to 15 yards wide. Beaching of LSTs was out of the question, and dry-ramp beaching of LCTs and LCMs was doubtful. Not a very promising spot for an amphibious landing. And the problem of getting ashore there was complicated by offshore mines and beach obstacles. The mines were not only Dutch and Japanese, but influence mines that had been laid by Allied air forces over the past year, in the hope of forbidding access to the port by Japanese tankers. The Japanese garrison, about 2300 in number, had been occupied in protecting the beaches with four rows of beach obstacles, made of railway iron and hardwood posts joined by wire. But there were only six coast defense guns on Tarakan.

The over-all command of the Borneo landings was given by General MacArthur to I Australian Corps, Lieutenant General Sir Leslie Morshead, of which the 26th Brigade of the 9th Australian

[5] CTG 78.1 (Rear Adm. Royal) Action Report 5 May 1945; "Australian Military Forces Report on Operation Oboe I" 7 Aug. 1945; CTU 78.1.5 (Lt. Cdr. James R. Keefer USNR) Minesweeping Unit Action Report 8 May 1945.
[6] See Vol. III 281.

Infantry Division, Brigadier David A. Whitehead, obtained the assignment for Tarakan. And, owing to the Royal Navy's desire to join the big show at Okinawa, Seventh Fleet took care of the naval part of all Borneo operations. Rear Admiral Royal, after finishing his job at Zamboanga, was appointed Commander Tarakan Attack

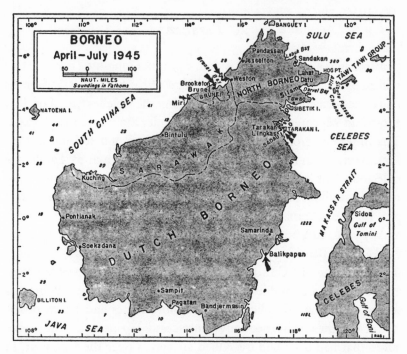

Group (TG 78.1) by Admiral Barbey, and on 7 April joined an advance planning team at the Corps headquarters at Morotai, where rehearsals were held between 19 and 24 April. "Peter Day," as D-day here was called, was set for 1 May 1945.

Minesweeping and clearing of beach obstacles would require several days of preparation, so there was no hope of achieving surprise. The minecraft and hydrographic units left Leyte on 22 April; Admiral Berkey's cruiser covering group and the close fire support unit left Subic Bay on 24 April, and these elements arrived off Tarakan on the 27th. H.M.A.S. *Lachlan* surveyed the passages and placed marker buoys. Sweeping was difficult, because of both the variety of mines and a three-knot tidal current. By Peter Day, 44 mines had been swept, at a cost of two motor minecraft damaged; but the approach channels were cleared.

A secondary assault echelon under Captain C. W. Gray left Morotai 26 April with a detachment of Australian troops and artillery to be landed on Sadau Island, a tiny islet in the channel between Borneo and Tarakan, on 30 April. The purpose was to emplace artillery to support the main landing next day and to cover combat demolition engineers while blowing breaches in the beach obstacles. After a short bombardment by *Philip*, the landing on Sadau Island was made without opposition around 0800 and promptly completed. *Philip* and *Jenkins* then took stations to bombard and cover the engineers at the main landing beaches on Tarakan. *Jenkins* in so doing struck a mine and suffered extensive hull damage.

Admiral Royal's task group arrived off Tarakan at 0530 May 1 and deployed for the landing. Admiral Berkey's covering force, cruisers *Phoenix, Boise*, H.M.A.S. *Hobart* and destroyers *Taylor, Nicholas, O'Bannon, Fletcher, Jenkins* and H.M.A.S. *Warramunga*, fired a pre-landing bombardment for about an hour. At 0811, when the first waves were 500 yards from the beach, all checked fire.[7]

The Allied assault force, predominantly Australian but including a United States Navy shore party, about 500 men of the United States Army and 400 Netherlanders (including officials to set up a civil administration), numbered about 18,000. They were lifted by two Australian LSIs, one U.S. Navy AKA, one LSD, and about 45 large U.S. beaching craft.

The first three waves for Beach Red 2 were landed in LCVPs, and the first four waves for the Beaches Green from amphtracs. One Australian battalion had a practically dry landing; the LVTs of the other battalions were stopped by an embankment at the high-water line and the troops disembarked into deep mud. Otherwise, landing operations unrolled as in a drill, the first LST beached at

[7] Comdesron 22 (Capt. C. W. Gray) Action Report 6 May 1945. Frigates H.M.A.S. *Burdekin, Barcoo* and *Hawkesbury* also participated.

0918, and twenty minutes later Admiral Royal ordered general unloading. At about 1020 the enemy opened light artillery and mortar fire on the beaches and support craft, but failed to interfere with the operation. Brigadier Whitehead assumed command ashore shortly after noon. By 1340 the docks were usable by hand labor, and a few minutes later the falling tide confined unloading to the piers.

Three destroyers, designated gunfire support ships for the three battalions ashore, by 1130 were getting calls for support. This support continued for nearly a month as the Japanese were driven back into the high ground in the center of Tarakan. Bombardment liaison officers, familiar with Australian techniques, were on board the ships to help with these fire support missions. The troops were highly pleased with the results and rewarded the destroyers with compliments.

On P plus 1 day (2 May) the Australians reached both Tarakan town and the airstrip. It took them three days more to clear the Japanese out of the town and from the high ground that dominates the field.

Captain Gray's destroyers remained off Tarakan until 8 May, when Lieutenant Commander Victor A. Dybdal, commanding officer of *Drayton*, took over the direction of fire support ships. That destroyer alone in 19 days fired 17 missions and expended 2574 rounds of 5-inch shell on enemy targets.

The most troublesome spot was a concealed enemy battery at Cape Djoeata, the high point on the northwestern side of Tarakan. On 2 May it suddenly opened up on the sweepers as they were working the narrow channel north and west of Tarakan. A hit caused *YMS-481* to explode and sink; two other YMS were hit but survived. Supporting gunboats and destroyer transport *Cofer* silenced the battery while the remaining four minesweepers retired. This battery defied all efforts to eliminate it until 23 May, when destroyer escort *Douglas A. Munro* gave it a thorough working over with 5-inch and automatic weapons, which knocked out the two 75-mm guns of which it consisted.

The Japanese garrison at Tarakan followed the new doctrine of doing most of its fighting inland, and it fought well. Not until 4 May was the high ground taken which commanded the beachhead. Next day, the Australians took Tarakan town and the airfield, but the enemy dug in north of the airfield and was not dislodged until 14 June. The invading troops had plenty of artillery, and needed little naval gunfire support after 8 May, by which time all warships but two had retired. H.M.A.S. *Barcoo* and destroyer escort *Formoe* stood by for call fire until the end of the month. In the final stage of shore operations, the Japanese were pressed into small units by the Australians, who lost only 225 men killed while inflicting a loss of 1775 (including 252 prisoners) on the enemy. The rest of the Japanese garrison surrendered at the war's end in August.

Altogether, this was a very well conducted amphibious operation, which attained its objectives with minimum loss.

3. *Brunei Bay* [8]

The next Borneo target on the MacArthur list was Brunei Bay, the spacious harbor of British North Borneo which Admiral King hoped to persuade the Royal Navy to use. Magellan's two surviving ships, *Vittoria* and *Trinidad*, spent about two weeks there, very pleasurably, in July 1521, being entertained by the Sultan with an elephant ride and sundry feasts. The Bay and its surrounding shores were still, in 1941, a sultanate under British protection; and the oil resources are such that the reigning potentate has been able to build the biggest mosque in the Far East.

Troops designated for Brunei Bay were a brigade of the 9th Australian Division, Major General G. F. Wootten; and for the last time Admiral Royal was designated Attack Group Commander. On 26 March the Admiral flew Captain Paul F. Dugan, his chief

[8] CTG 78.1 (Rear Adm. Royal) Action Report 19 June 1945; Amphibious Group 6 War Diary; daily reports received at Cincpac-Cincpoa headquarters in Guam, as noted by the writer.

of staff, and his plans and operations officers, to Morotai, to concert plans with the Australians. Royal himself left Tarakan for Morotai in his command ship *Rocky Mount* on 3 May.

Z-day, as General MacArthur designated D-day for Brunei, was originally set for 23 May, but troops and supplies were slow to arrive at Morotai and Z-day was postponed to 10 June. General Wootten's scheme of maneuver required two landings 20 miles apart, which caused Admiral Royal to divide his attack group into two units, one to land by LVT near the town of Victoria on the south side of Labuan Island, the other by LCVP on the spit marking the southwestern side of the bay east of Brunei Bluff. A subsidiary landing in LVT would be made later on a narrow beach on the eastern side of Muara Island, a small island inside the bight formed by the same spit. This complicated plan required several days of exercises and rehearsals, which were completed at Morotai on 1 June.

After our experience with assorted mines at Tarakan, several days of preliminary minesweeping were provided for Brunei Bay. Balabac Strait was swept by fleet minecraft between 22 and 29 April. Admiral Berkey's cruisers (*Boise, Phoenix, Nashville* and H.M.A.S. *Hobart*) with seven destroyers (including one Australian) covered the main sweep and provided pre-landing bombardment. The minecraft unit, consisting of 5 AM and 12 YMS, arrived off Brunei Bay early 7 June and began work promptly. All went well until 1515 June 8, when minesweeper *Salute* hit a contact mine. She lost four men killed and 12 seriously wounded, and sank eight hours later. Admiral Berkey's group, which arrived off Brunei simultaneously with the minecraft, covered the sweeps on 8 and 9 June. Underwater demolition teams reconnoitered the beaches without mishap. At 2115 June 9 the covering group made contact with Admiral Royal's attack group, which had sortied from Morotai 4 June. En route, Royal's group was joined by old "Noisy *Boise*" (Captain W. M. Downes), in which General MacArthur embarked to observe the landings.

Early on 10 June the attack group entered the roadstead and deployed. At 0650, after the Labuan unit (the 24th Brigade) had taken position off Labuan Island, it was attacked by a single twin-engined Nick, which dropped a bomb which missed, and escaped through a heavy volume of antiaircraft fire. Considering that the Japanese air forces had bases all around the N.E.I. and at Singapore, it is strange that so few air attacks developed.

Bombardment of the Labuan landing beaches began at 0805 and of the other sets of beaches at 0815. H-hour for all three was 0915. What Japanese there were in the vicinity fled from the bombardment, and the first waves landed exactly on time at all the beaches.[9] There was no opposition to the landing and little was encountered in the first few hours. By noon, troops were approaching the Labuan airstrip, and there real opposition began; although the field was captured 12 June a strong pocket of resistance in high ground westward held out until 21 June. An impressive group of high-ranking officers — Lieutenant General Morshead of the Australian Army, General Kenney of the A.A.F., Air Vice Marshal W. D. Bostock RAAF (who commanded air support for all Borneo operations), Rear Admiral Royal and General of the Army Douglas Mac-Arthur landed on Labuan Island for a look around. No enemy troops were found on Muara Island and by nightfall the Australians who landed in Brunei Bay had occupied Brooketon and moved some 3000 yards on towards Brunei town, which fell on the 15th.

General MacArthur, who also inspected progress at Brooketon, sent this parting message to the commanders at the objective: "The execution of the Brunei Bay operation has been flawless. Please accept for yourself and convey to your officers and men the pride and gratification I feel in such a splendid performance."

Motor torpedo boats of Squadrons 13 (Lieutenant Commander A. W. Fargo USNR) and 16 (Lieutenant R. H. Hallowell USNR), which arrived Brunei Bay on 9 June, ranged up and down the coast, destroyed a schooner and five barges, but soon ran out of targets. None were found in the Bay itself. The PTs were quickly reduced

9 The troops were lifted in 3 Australian LSI (*Westralia, Manoora* and *Kanimbla*) and U.S. Navy shipping: 1 LSD, 1 AKA, 17 LST, 8 LSM, and 5 LCI.

to making passes at targets in Jesselton, Miri and Kudat, and at enemy positions along the coast, as the Japanese retreated southward. Australian aircraft worked with them on these missions.

By 12 June the minecraft, having swept up 102 mines, could declare Brunei Bay clear, and next day began sweeping the Miri-Lutong-Baram area to the southward. On that day alone they cut 92 mines. They drew some inaccurate 75-mm fire, which ceased when covering destroyers closed in. At the objective a lone Nick was shot down by the dusk C.A.P. after it had dropped two bombs near *Charrette* with no damage. After dark on 14 June bombs were dropped on Labuan Island and at 2230 three planes were tracked in from the east. Ship antiaircraft fire splashed one of them.

Minesweeping continued in the Miri-Lutong area and by 16 June no fewer than 338 mines had been secured. Around Brunei Bay ground operations had reached the mop-up stage. Australian troop casualties to date were 40 killed and about 120 wounded. On 17 June a shore-to-shore movement of one battalion under Commander W. E. Verge occupied Weston on the shore of the Bay, while a second battalion and squadron of commandos landed at Mempakul on the northern headland two days later. The two forces drove toward a junction at Beaufort, which fell during 27–28 June.

Admiral Royal departed 17 June, leaving Captain H. B. Hudson as S.O.P.A. in charge of local operations. Anticipating his departure, General Morshead sent the Admiral a parting message: "On the eve of your departure I wish to express admiration and appreciation of the thorough, efficient and gallant and successful manner in which the naval force under your command carried out its vital rôle in both the Borneo operations."

This proved to be almost a funeral wreath for Admiral Royal. On 18 June, while en route to Leyte in *Rocky Mount*, he died suddenly of a heart attack. Overwork and strain had deprived the United States Navy, on the verge of victory, of a highly capable and greatly beloved flag officer.

The Australian 20th Brigade, having cleared the Japanese from the south side of Brunei Bay, moved along the coast towards the oil center of Seria, which fell on the 21st. The previous day another shore-to-shore movement had leapfrogged troops to Miri-Lutong in northern Sarawak, following a preliminary bombardment by destroyer *Metcalf*. Again there was no opposition, although *Metcalf* was called upon during the night of 20–21 June for harassing fire at an enemy troop concentration. By 1 July North Borneo was secured at a loss of only 114 men of the Australian Army, and 4 American sailors in *Salute*.

After the surrender of Japan, Australian troops occupied Jesselton (28 September) and Sandakan (19 October). Both towns had been wiped out by Allied bombers.

The Australian prisoners done to death by the Japanese were grimly revenged by the natives of Borneo. The Japanese troops, 21,000 of them in North Borneo alone, were ordered after their surrender to stack arms and march to Beaufort, where ships would embark them for home. This order opened a series of field days for the fierce Murut tribesmen. They harassed the unarmed Japanese columns day after day, and only a few hundred of those who surrendered ever reached Beaufort.[10]

4. Balikpapan [11]

The third Borneo target, OBOE II, was the oil center of Balikpapan, on the east coast across Makassar Strait from Celebes. This proved to be the final major amphibious operation for VII 'Phib, or for any Navy, in World War II. The pre-landing bombardment and target preparation, lasting 16 days, was the longest in any amphibious operation of this or probably of any other modern war.

A Japanese expeditionary force under Rear Admiral Nishimura, who subsequently lost his life in the Battle of Surigao Strait, occu-

10 K. G. Tregonning *North Borneo 1881–1946* p. 221.
11 CTG 78.2 (Rear Adm. Noble) Action Report 14 Aug., CTG 74.2 (Rear Adm. Riggs) Action Report 8 July, CTG 78.4 (Rear Adm. Sample) Action Report 24 July 1945.

pied Balikpapan on 23 January 1942, not without challenge from the sea; Commander Paul Talbot's valiant four-piper destroyers, *Ford, Pope, Parrott* and *Paul Jones*, stole into the transport area in the early hours of the 24th and sank four transports, then retired to rendezvous with Rear Admiral W. A. Glassford's flagship *Marblehead*.[12]

General MacArthur set 1 July 1945 as target date (F-day) for the seizure of Balikpapan. Admiral Barbey had already designated Rear Admiral Noble as Attack Group Commander. Troops assigned were the 7th Division, I Australian Corps, at Morotai, commanded by Major General E. J. Milford. Including units of the R.A.A.F., the invasion force was 35,000 strong. Rear Admiral Riggs commanded the cruiser and destroyer covering group. Noble flew to Manila on 17 May for a conference with Dan Barbey and returned on board his flagship *Wasatch*, on 20 May. Coast Guard Cutter *Spencer* then took a planning team from Davao to Morotai, and on 26 May Admiral Noble followed in *Wasatch*. If the reader cares to take the trouble to tabulate these operations, he will appreciate the planning problems of so close-coupled a series.

The assault on Balikpapan was complicated by a number of factors. As the principal oil center of Borneo it was known to be heavily defended, especially around Balikpapan City and the nearby Sepinggang and Manggar airfields. Many of the Japanese antiaircraft weapons could also be brought to bear on available landing beaches. Between 400 and 1000 yards inland from the high water mark, small wooded hills offered excellent defensive positions for coast defense guns, revetments, tunnels and pillboxes. On the narrow coastal plain the Japanese built tank traps 10 to 14 feet wide and partly filled some of them with water; it was feared that they might replace the water with oil which, when ignited, would present a fire barrier to assaulting troops. Burning oil drifting down the rivers and streams was another possibility. About 70 to 100 yards off shore there was a barrier constructed of logs driven like piles into the bottom, three or four logs deep and about 20 feet

[12] See Vol. III 285-91; S. Woodburn Kirby *The War Against Japan* I 297-98.

wide; and in some places there was a second log barrier, 60 to 80 yards seaward of the first.

Allied airmen had dropped more magnetic and acoustic mines off Balikpapan Harbor than anywhere in the Southwest Pacific. These, combined with prewar Netherlands minefields and suspected Japanese fields, made the minesweeping problem formidable. The approaches are so shallow (the 10-fathom curve lying 4 to 6 miles off shore) that the sweepers could expect no close-in gunfire support.

Intensive air strikes to soften up the target were begun a month before F-day. On 15 June, 16 motor minesweepers arrived off Balikpapan and began their operations, covered by light cruisers *Denver* and *Montpelier* and destroyers. This was but a small part of Admiral Riggs's group which, as F-day approached, built up to five U.S. light cruisers, including the much battered but now repaired *Columbia* ("The Gem"), Netherlands light cruiser *Tromp*, H.M.A.S. *Shropshire* and *Hobart*, with nine destroyers (one Australian) and two Australian frigates. Enemy aircraft from the Netherlands East Indies was expected to be active and fighter air cover was provided from Tawi Tawi, near the operating limit of fighters. Tarakan strip was not yet available owing to heavy rains.

For the first two days, as the sweepers worked well off shore, minesweeping was uneventful, but as they closed the harbor enemy reaction began. On 17 June the cruisers began their preliminary bombardment of targets at Balikpapan. These firings were coördinated with daily air strikes by Allied Air Forces. At 2000 three or four enemy planes dropped bombs near the cruisers and sweepers but caused no damage. Two more raids, with a total of seven planes, were equally harmless.

On 18 June occurred the first minecraft casualty. At 1255 *YMS-50* exploded a magnetic mine and at about the same time was fired on by a shore battery of two 75-mm guns. Covering ships, eagerly waiting for enemy batteries to expose themselves, took the offending battery under fire while landing craft attempted to move the sweeper to safety; but her back was broken, and at 1516, she had to be sunk by gunfire. The enemy reply to heavy counterbattery fire was to set off smudge fires to screen his installations. This became a daily occurrence. By 19 June harassing of the sweepers by shore gunfire increased and some were forced to jettison gear and clear out. The shore batteries ceased firing as soon as taken under counterbattery fire, in a deadly pattern of hide-and-seek that continued to F-day. Heavy air strikes, coördinated with bombardment and counterbattery whenever the minecraft were brought under fire, became daily routine.

The minesweepers bore the brunt of punishment, both from mines and enemy gunfire. Some 93 Allied magnetic mines were known to have been laid off Balikpapan with no gimmick installed to de-activate them after a definite period of time. In the two weeks of intensive sweeping before F-day only 27 mines, 18 of them magnetic, were swept by three fleet minesweepers and 38 YMS. They suffered extensive damage to their gear, especially the sensitive apparatus for dealing with magnetic mines, from bottom obstructions, electrical troubles and the understandable tendency of minecraft skippers to jettison gear in order to maneuver when under enemy fire. Yet the job was so well done that not one vessel, aside from the sweepers themselves, suffered mine damage at Balikpapan. Three motor minesweepers [13] were blown up, another was damaged by a mine and three were hit by enemy shellfire. Their casualties were 7 men killed and 43 wounded.

The underwater demolition teams also turned in a fine performance. Their work was simplified by a heavy blanket of gunfire support from cruisers and destroyers and close support of seven LCS(L) gunboats. Teams 11 and 18 arrived at Balikpapan in two APDs on 24 June. Next day, under the cover of heavy bombardment, both teams made a reconnaissance of beaches near Manggar, which they found poor for landing; but they blew gaps in the beach obstacles in order to deceive the enemy into thinking that this place would be used. On 27 June the teams made a reconnais-

[13] *YMS-50, -39, -365.*

sance of the preferred beaches at Klandasan, whose approaches had not yet been completely mineswept. Rendezvous with supporting gunboats was made at 0530 by LCPRs boating the UDTs, and the column was conned by destroyer *Stevens*, with radar and radio, to a point three thousand yards off the beaches. Heavy rain and smoke from the shore reduced visibility to near zero, but as the day advanced it improved and the boats had no difficulty dropping off swimmers on their designated beaches. The gunboats were continually under fire while the "frogmen" were doing their work, but the UDTs were able to retire without a single casualty and with complete information on the Klandasan beaches. No anti-boat or land mines were found, but the beaches were covered with heavy obstacles. In these, gaps had to be blown (as at Omaha Beach the previous year) to permit a reasonably safe landing.

To blow these gaps the boats approached in bright moonlight, beginning at 0500 June 25, and again conned by *Stevens*. The gunboats took station 1200 to 1500 yards off shore and were taken under enemy fire at once. They retaliated with heavy bombardment as the LCPRs made their way to the 500-yard line. The landing craft also received heavy fire at 800 to 1000 yards, but this slackened close to shore, thanks to a low ridge which protected them from inland fire. There were several 75-mm near-misses, and three boats received direct 37-mm hits but no casualties. The UDT swimmers fixed detonating charges on the obstacles and one set went off prematurely owing to a shell hit, injuring two swimmers — their only casualties. Withdrawal was made under heavy fire, while a white phosphorous screen was laid on the beaches by covering destroyers. *LCS(L)-28* was hit by three 75-mm shells but had only five wounded and soon returned to action.

No underwater work was done on 29 June, but on the 30th UDT-11 returned to the beach and demolished about three hundred more yards of obstacles. This job at Balikpapan was one of the bravest and best by the "frogmen" during the entire war.[14]

Combat air patrol from Tawi Tawi could not be maintained con-

[14] CTU 78.2.11 (Lt. L. A. States USNR) Action Report 2 July 1945.

tinuously owing to heavy rains and adverse weather. Enemy snoopers were about almost every day but made only one attack. In the evening of 25 June an estimated five to seven torpedo planes came in but caused no damage and lost three planes in the attempt. Admiral Noble requested CVEs to stand by during the critical first two days of the landings, and on 22 June Admiral Kinkaid passed the request to Admiral Nimitz, who lent him three of the five CVEs then at Leyte. These escort carriers had hit Kyushu on 16 June, the last day of two and one half months' continuous operation. Nevertheless, *Suwannee*, *Chenango* and *Gilbert Islands* (with Marine Air Group 2), under command of Rear Admiral William D. Sample, with six escorts, were immediately assigned to OBOE II as requested. They spent 1 to 3 July at Balikpapan, provided efficient C.A.P. and contributed to the landings by a strike on enemy positions on 3 July. Good old *Suwannee* and her companions set a record for mobility; Balikpapan is a good 2500 miles from the scene of their strikes two weeks earlier.

The Australian assault troops were lifted both in Australian and American transports, APDs and beaching craft.[15] A rehearsal was held on the east coast of Morotai, and on 26 June TG 78.2 sortied for the objective. Everyone seems to have felt that this would be one of the toughest shows yet, or one of the last; for it drew V.I.P.s like flies. On 25 June Vice Admiral Barbey arrived at Morotai and raised his flag in *Phoenix* as Commander Balikpapan Attack Force, but gave Admiral Noble tactical command of the operation. *Phoenix* shoved off ahead of the task force and on 29 June joined Admiral Sample's carrier group. Rear Admiral Berkey, in *Nashville*, also joined the CVEs; and at 1800 June 30 light cruiser *Cleveland*, with two destroyers escorting, arrived at Balikpapan with Commander in Chief Southwest Pacific Area, General of the Army Douglas MacArthur, embarked.

Task Group 78.2 arrived at the objective on the dot. H-hour was 0900. At daylight (0700) seven cruisers and as many destroyers

[15] In detail: 3 LSI of R.A.N. (*Westralia*, *Manoora* and *Kanimbla*), and the rest U.S.N.: 1 AKA, 1 LSD, 5 APD, 35 LST, 22 LSM, 16 LCI.

opened a two-hour intensive bombardment, which was suspended
only for an air strike and a rocket barrage from LCI(R)s around
0800. The enemy returned fire and several destroyers reported being straddled.

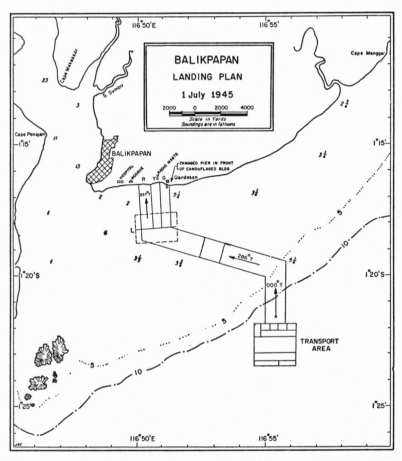

Conforming to the irregular bottom, a "double dog-leg" boat lane
was buoyed before F-day. The veteran web-feet took this in their
stride as they approached the beaches. Boat waves and close support
craft came under enemy fire but none were hit. Owing to a signal-
man's error the first wave was dispatched from the line of departure
slightly ahead of schedule, and, preceded by a second run of rock-

ets from the LCI(R)s, landed at 0855, five minutes early. Wave after wave followed at short intervals through sporadic artillery, mortar and small-arms fire; all, including the 17th which touched down at 1055, without a single casualty. This was a tribute to the heavy aërial and naval bombardment that preceded the landings, which added up to more than 3000 tons of bombs, 38,052 rounds of 3-inch to 8-inch shell, 114,000 rounds from automatic weapons and 7361 rockets. Another measure of its power lay in 460 enemy dead found near the beaches and in fortified positions northwest of them.

At first the Australians met only slight opposition as they fanned out to the north, west and east. Resistance stiffened as they moved into the higher ground where tunnels, revetted batteries, trenches and pillboxes were located. Cruisers and destroyers hit these strong points on call and the only enemy damage to naval shipping was to destroyer *Smith;* three 75-mm shells pierced her stack without exploding. By nightfall 1 July 10,500 troops (two brigades), 700 vehicles and 1950 tons of supplies had been landed, and 7th Division had reached its F-day phase line.

At 1130 that day General MacArthur, Admiral Barbey, Lieutenant General Morshead and Air Vice Marshal Bostock, the last two having arrived by air that morning, came ashore to observe progress. Pleased with what he had seen, General MacArthur departed in cruiser *Cleveland* at 1510.

On 2 July a third brigade landed. Unloading was slowed by surf and weather and the need to relocate a pontoon dock. Crudiv 12 (*Montpelier,* flag), present since 15 June, was released and proceeded to Leyte. The remaining cruisers and destroyers continued to deliver call-fire, and Allied aircraft were also on call for special strikes. In the early morning of 3 July two Japanese float planes approached; one was shot down by a CVE's night fighter and the other fled. Admiral Sample's escort carriers left for Leyte that afternoon, after launching a strike on enemy concentrations and supply dumps north of Sepinggang. At 0938 July 4, *Nashville, Phoenix* and five American destroyers commenced firing a 21-gun salute in honor of the day — which did double duty by being aimed at enemy positions — and an hour later a report was received to the effect that the salute had exploded a magazine. The Australian 21st Brigade, which had been advancing eastward along the coast, celebrated the Fourth by capturing Manggar airfield.

The Australians called freely for naval gunfire support; cruisers and destroyers were delighted to oblige, day or night. On 5 July, supported by a preliminary bombardment, troops landed at Point Penajam which the Japanese had abandoned the night before. Balikpapan town was completely cleared that day, and by 7 July conditions ashore were so stable that Admiral Noble departed for Leyte, leaving Captain C. W. Gray as VII 'Phib representative. Commodore Farncomb RAN, the Australian cruiser squadron commander in H.M.A.S. *Shropshire*, took over the direction of gunfire support. By 15 July one destroyer was enough to answer calls.

Eight PT boats, with their tender *Mobjack*, arrived off Balikpapan 27 June and commenced operating along the coast. Their early patrols, in the immediate vicinity, were to prevent the Japanese from restoring obstacles destroyed by the UDTs and from molesting navigational buoys laid by the minesweepers. This group was brought up to two-squadron strength on 6 July. Ranging up and down the coast of Borneo, around the Paternoster Islands in Makassar Strait and the west coast of Celebes, they destroyed a few luggers and an outlying radar station, but, as elsewhere in this region, quickly ran out of targets.[16] *Saufley* left Balikpapan on 19 July, after turning over bombardment liaison officer and fire support duties to *Conyngham*, which remained off the beachhead a few days longer. Her departure ended the U.S. Naval contribution to OBOE II.

While the 21st Brigade advanced from Manggar to Sambodja, the 25th pushed inland from Balikpapan towards Samarinda. The enemy resisted all along the line, but was overcome by 22 July, at the cost of 229 Australians.

[16] These were Squadrons 10 (Lt. Francis H. McAdoo USNR) and 27 (Lt. Henry S. Taylor USNR).

The outstanding features of this final amphibious operation of World War II were thorough minesweeping, excellent work by UDTs, and enormous expenditure of gunfire by the Australian and United States Navies. Before F-day, 23,767 rounds of 4.7-inch to 8-inch were fired; on F-day 11,884 rounds; and 11,158 more through 7 July. In addition, 114,000 rounds of 20-mm and 40-mm were fired from automatic weapons. For ammunition delivered in support of a one-division landing, this beats all records. The United States Army had been calling for more and more naval gunfire support as the Pacific War progressed; now the 7th Australian Division had cashed in on these accumulated demands — and how those Aussies loved it!

General MacArthur had always intended, after securing Balikpapan, to move the Australian troops into Java and restore the Netherlands government under Governor Van Mook. This proposal he presented to the J.C.S. on 26 February, with target date 27 June. The J.C.S. turned this over to the joint staff planners, who on 12 April were advised to cease consideration "in view of events." [17] The "events" they meant were not the death of President Roosevelt that day, but (1) the plan to concentrate all Allied effort on the expected invasion of Japan in the fall, and (2) the setting up for purposes of that invasion of a new command structure in the Pacific on 6 April, which gave MacArthur command of all Allied ground forces in the Pacific. With everyone looking and planning northward, the Netherlands East Indies were almost forgotten at Washington and London. After much debate, it was agreed on 7 June to augment Admiral Lord Mountbatten's Southeast Asia command by Borneo, Java and the Celebes. Mountbatten, who would have been only too glad to lead the liberation of Java, was unable to get at it as long as the Japanese held the straits leading thither from the Indian Ocean. Finally, on 2 August, when making the formal transfer of these islands to Mountbatten, the Combined Chiefs of Staff directed him to establish bridgeheads in

[17] Grace Hayes ms. "History of the J.C.S." II 366–7; Ehrman V 227–32, 254.

Java and Sumatra as soon as the Strait of Malacca was opened to Allied shipping. By that time, the war was over.

The result of this shilly-shallying was that the loyal population of Java had to wait a full month after the Japanese surrender for the Allies to exert any authority over their country. Not until 15 September 1945 did two cruisers, one British and one Dutch, put in at Batavia, and another two weeks elapsed before the first British troops landed. In the meantime the puppet government, supported by the Japanese garrison, was unable or unwilling to keep order, Netherlands authority was flouted, Dutch and other European nationals were left shut up in internment camps, and the economic life of the country suffered unnecessarily. But the Australians occupied the islands east of Lombok promptly, and in these there was little disorder.

CHAPTER XIII

Submarine Operations Southwest Pacific[1]

January–August 1945

1. *Japanese Prowlers in Philippine Waters*

AT the time of the Lingayen Gulf landings there were five Japanese submarines in Philippine waters and five more in Japan, preparing for active operations. The only ones which caused trouble were those west of the islands.

Attack transport *Cavalier*, in a convoy returning to Leyte from the Zambales landings, was torpedoed off the west coast of Luzon early on 30 January by an unidentified submarine, probably *RO-115*. She was not badly damaged, but a fleet tug towed her back to Leyte because her propeller was jammed. That afternoon a plane from one of Admiral Durgin's escort carriers sighted a submarine 60 miles northeast of Admiral Berkey's Covering Group. Three destroyers and a DE peeled off to hunt it but were unsuccessful.

Cruiser *Boise*, at 1955 on the last day of January, made a surface radar contact off Mindoro at 16,400 yards. A minute later this was picked up by destroyer *Bell* at 9250 yards, but at 5550 yards the target disappeared from the radarscope. *Bell* then picked it up, submerged, on her sound gear, approached and dropped a pattern of eleven depth charges. *O'Bannon* followed suit, and DE *Ulvert M.*

---

[1] See statement in Preface as to my sources for attacks on and sinkings of Japanese submarines and surface ships by the U.S. Navy. Further details on movements of Japanese submarines are in ATIS Document No. 16,268, the Japanese Naval HQ Tokyo War Diary.

Moore and destroyer *Jenkins* joined the hunt. At 2053 men on the fantail of *Bell* saw a dark object broaching, but it quickly disappeared. Contact was kept intermittently during the next three hours. At 0018 a heavy underwater explosion was heard and felt. This was *RO–115*, but she was not done for.

A week later, at 2222 February 7, destroyer escort *Thomason* had a radar contact at 14 miles when she and *Neuendorf* were acting as antisubmarine patrol for a convoy off Mindoro. This target was steering a course to intercept the convoy. When *Thomason*, about 4500 yards away, challenged with a flashing light, the target disappeared from the radar screens of both destroyer escorts. Some 1500 yards nearer, at 2307, sound contact was established. *Thomason's* skipper, Lieutenant Commander R. C. Barlow USNR, thought the object might be a stray small craft; but as he closed, sonar data proved it to be a submarine. When the range was down to 300 yards and the ship was about to fire a hedgehog pattern, the unmistakable outline of a submarine, down about 50 feet, appeared in the sonar pattern. Four to six explosions, so close together that they merged, were heard a few seconds after the hedgehogs were fired. But *Thomason's* target was the nine-lived *RO–55*, which had a few days' more grace.

Pacific Fleet submarine *Batfish* (Commander J. K. Fyfe), in Luzon Strait on her sixth war patrol, at 2250 February 9 picked up a radar contact at 11,000 yards. Forty minutes later, with the range down to 1850 yards, she fired four torpedoes – all of which missed. Commander Fyfe then closed to visual range and shortly after midnight his lookouts spotted a Japanese submarine at 1020 yards. Three torpedoes were fired and one hit the target and exploded. That was the last of *RO–55*.

At 1915 next evening, 10 February, Fyfe detected radar signals which sounded like those previously associated with Japanese submarines. Maneuvering carefully to determine the approximate bearing of this target, he sighted a submarine at 2037. Before torpedoes could be fired the target dived. Half an hour later *Batfish's* sound operator heard "blowing noises," indicating that the quarry was about to surface, and soon it appeared on the radar screen at 8650 yards. Fyfe made a surprise attack, closing by radar, and at 2202 fired four torpedoes. A heavy explosion and flash marked the last of *RO–112*.

Batfish's next victim was *RO–115*, which was trying to get home through Luzon Strait. This boat was picked up by radar at 0155 February 12. When the range closed to 7150 yards it dived. Fyfe put *Batfish* ahead of his target's track and about an hour later it surfaced. Duplicating his tactics against *RO–112*, he made an approach at radar depth. The submarine submerged, leaving the radar antenna on its mast above water. Fyfe then fired torpedoes and had the satisfaction of hearing a loud explosion which marked the end of *RO–115*. A box of navigational equipment and tables were recovered from the surface debris. Three enemy submarines in three days!

Following these losses, Japanese submarines did not again trouble the waters of the Philippines and South China Sea until *I–58* sank *Indianapolis* just as the war was ending. Their attention was mainly focused on the waters around Iwo Jima, and later Okinawa.

2. *American Submarine Operations* [2]

By January 1945 Japanese shipping in the South China Sea had thinned out to a mere trickle. To avoid Allied submarines the convoys steamed close to shore in shallow water along the coasts of China, Indochina and the Malay Peninsula.

Besugo (Commander T. L. Wogan) and *Hardhead* (Commander F. A. Greenup) were patrolling the Malayan coast not far from Singapore in scouting line on 6 January. At 1840 *Besugo* sighted a large tanker zigzagging on a northwesterly course. After closing

[2] War Diary Commander Submarines Seventh Fleet (Rear Adm. Fife); patrol reports of the individual submarines involved; Theodore Roscoe *Submarine* (1949); JANAC and *Imp. Jap. Navy in W. W. II.* Pacific Fleet SS operations will be related in Volume XIV.

and tracking this ship a destroyer and two smaller escorts appeared. At 2118 *Besugo* fired three torpedoes at the tanker. Two minutes later three hits were heard on 10,020-ton *Nichiei Maru*, and before diving the two commanders had the satisfaction of seeing her engulfed in flames. The escorts milled about but never came near the submarines, which calmly re-formed their scouting line and continued to search for shipping. *Sea Robin* (Commander P. C. Stimson) sank 5135-ton tanker *Tarakan Maru* off Hainan the same day.

Admiral Halsey's foray into the South China Sea in mid-January almost completely halted Japanese ship movements in those waters. But Rear Admiral James Fife,[3] who had relieved Admiral Christie as Commander Submarines Southwest Pacific on 30 December 1944, was taking no chances of missing anything and continued to maintain about 20 boats on station in that sea, and around Borneo. On 24 January one of them scored again. *Blackfin*, Commander W. L. Kitch, patrolling the same waters as *Besugo* and *Hardhead*, picked up a convoy, which included at least one tanker at 0502. Making a surface approach *Blackfin* began firing her bow tubes an hour later. One hit was observed on an escort vessel, which turned out to be destroyer *Shigure*, the miraculous survivor of Admiral Nishimura's force in the Battle of Surigao Strait, and she was sunk. The tanker, at which *Blackfin* discharged her stern tubes, was only damaged.

On the last day of January *Boarfish* (Commander R. C. Cross), which had been tracking a convoy off the Indochina coast since the 30th, sank a 7000-ton freighter, whose escorts succeeded in exploding a number of depth charges fairly close, but did no damage. Presumably *Boarfish* hit a second ship in this convoy and it was pol-

[3] James Fife, b. Nevada 1897. Annapolis '18. Served in World War I in *Tacoma* and *Chicago*, then became a submariner for almost his entire naval career. Comsubron 20 at time of Pearl Harbor; chief of staff to Admiral T. C. Hart to July 1942, Comsubron 2 to December; CTF 72 (submarines based on Brisbane) to March 1944; on Admiral King's staff for 8 months; Comsubsowespac and CTF 71, 30 Dec. 1944 to end of 1945; General Board, member strategic survey committee of J.C.S.; Comsubforlant April 1947 to June 1950; Assistant C.N.O. and Deputy C.N.O. to March 1953; Deputy Cincmed to August 1955, when retired. See also Vol. VI 67, 142.

ished off later in the day by Army bombers; for the sinking of 6890-ton *Daietsu Maru* at this time and place is jointly credited to her and to Army aircraft in postwar assessments.

Barbel (Lieutenant Commander C. L. Raguet), based at Fremantle, departed in January to patrol the South China Sea. Late that month she was ordered to form a wolf-pack with *Perch* (Commander B. C. Hills) and *Gabilan* (Commander W. B. Parham) to patrol off Balabac Strait and the southern entrance to Palawan Passage. On 3 February *Barbel* reported to *Tuna* (Commander E. F. Steffanides) and to *Blackfin* and *Gabilan* that these waters were being buzzed by Japanese aircraft and that she had been attacked three times with depth charges. This was the last message received from her. After the war Japanese aviators reported having attacked a submarine southwest of Palawan on 4 February and making a direct bomb hit near the conning tower. This was undoubtedly *Barbel*, lost with all hands.

Off the coast of Indochina on 23 February occurred one of the most bizarre accidents that can happen to a submarine — an underwater collision with a friendly boat. *Hoe* (Commander M. P. Refo) was patrolling submerged slightly to the north of *Flounder* (Commander J. E. Stevens). Since Commander Refo had observed a southerly drift of four miles during the day, he concluded that he was on the southern edge of his assigned area and came to course north at 1049, making only 1.8 knots. About six hours later, while running submerged at 60 feet, *Hoe* struck what her skipper at first thought to be a submerged rock. She angled and broached. Battle stations were manned at once, but from the bridge the only thing in sight was a vessel hull-down to the northeast, whose lights proved her to be a hospital ship. A quick check indicated that *Hoe* had taken in no water and that the pit log and sound head were working normally. Course was changed away from the hospital ship in order to make a more thorough inspection, but at 1711 a nearby Japanese float plane forced *Hoe* to dive. On surfacing again at 1932 she had SJ radar interference, which Commander Refo decided was caused by a nearby submarine. A few minutes later the interference suddenly ceased. At 2025 he intercepted a message from *Flounder,* reporting that her SJ radar was out of commission; and at 2355 a second message from the same boat sent word that she had been rammed by a submarine at the time and place where *Hoe's* skipper thought he had hit a rock.

When this freak collision occurred *Flounder* was on an easterly course while *Hoe* was steering due north. Fortunately Stevens was patrolling submerged at 65 feet, five feet deeper than Refo. At 1700 *Flounder* felt a peculiar shudder and dove deep. Water began to enter through a broken cable fitting, another shudder was felt, and the sound operator reported strong air swishes and fast propeller noises, which soon ceased. Eleven minutes later *Flounder* raised her periscope but sighted only the Japanese hospital ship in the distance. Commander Stevens then concluded that he had been in collision with another submarine, hopefully Japanese, and sunk. When darkness fell he surfaced and found that he had been hit just abaft the 4-inch gun. The deck structure was dented and the SJ radar antenna knocked out. He then sighted another surfaced submarine about 3000 yards away but identified her as American and did not attack. After making certain that his hull was secure, Stevens reported his damage to Admiral Fife and stated that *Flounder* was proceeding to Subic Bay. By this time he suspected that she had collided with *Hoe,* with which he had exchanged recognition signals early in the morning of 23 February. The fact that both boats were at or near neutral buoyancy when they collided accounts for *Hoe* being forced upward and broaching, while *Flounder* was forced down. They bounced off each other like a couple of slow-rolling billiard balls, and sustained but slight damage.

Hoe now extended her patrol to the coast of Indochina. There, during the afternoon of 24 February, she sighted a tanker and two escorts, which forced her to submerge while trying to reach an attack position. But she hung on to the contact and at 0244 February 25 fired four torpedoes at one of the escorts, DE *Shonan,* and sank her.

Southwest Pacific submarines continued to find victims in the

South China Sea and the approaches to Singapore. On 6 February, off the coast of Malaya, *Pampanito* (Commander P. E. Summers) sank a 7000-ton freighter and two days later bagged a 3520-ton passenger-cargo ship in the same vicinity. *Guavina* (Commander R. H. Lockwood) got another 7000-tonner off the Malayan coast next day, and on the 20th disposed of a 8700-ton tanker near Camranh Bay, giving her top score for February.

Four submarines had a desirable target in their periscopes on 12–13 February, but were not able to do much about it. First, at 1505 February 12, *Blackfin* sighted SE of Saigon the elusive *Ise* and *Hyuga*, together with one heavy cruiser and three destroyers, steering NNE at 15 knots. *Blackfin* maintained contact until 1730. *Charr* sighted the same group about the same time, but lost contact after trailing it for several hours. Next day, 13 February, the Japanese warships encountered two more submarines. At 1300 *Blower* (Commander J. H. Campbell), from ranges between 1800 and 2800 yards, fired six torpedoes at a heavy cruiser and a battleship which overlapped, and claimed two hits. Half an hour later *Bergall* (Commander J. M. Hyde) fired six torpedoes at the group from 4800 yards, and believed that one hit. Postwar assessments, however, indicate that no ship in this group was damaged; *Ise* and *Hyuga* had another reprieve.

Although fewer ships were now to be found in the South China Sea, they were being better escorted. Submarines knocked off a number of these escort vessels ranging in size from a destroyer to small subchasers. At 2342 February 19 *Pargo* (Commander D. B. Bell), patrolling off the coast of Indochina, picked up something promising on her radar at around 10,000 yards. While tracking and heading for an attack position, she identified the target as a large destroyer with a smaller vessel on a southerly course, zigzagging at 17 knots. By 0225 February 20 *Pargo* was in position and fired four torpedoes at 2500 yards. Two minutes later, as Commander Bell reported, the "first torpedo hit was immediately followed by a tremendous explosion which tore the destroyer stem from stern and blew the middle sky high. A column of fire and streaks of molten metal went up from under the bridge at least 3000 feet in the most spectacular sight any of us had ever seen. . . . The nearest thing that can describe it are the pictures of U.S.S. *Shaw* blowing up at Pearl Harbor on December 7th; so we have unofficially chalked this one up as, 'Revenge for the *Shaw!*' " This was the end of *Nokaze*, the 39th and last Japanese destroyer to be destroyed by American submarines.

At 1000 February 23, *Hammerhead* (Commander F. T. Smith) submerged off the Indochina coast north of Camranh Bay and sighted a small freighter close inshore, escorted by two vessels. While she was maneuvering for a good launching position, one of the escorts zigged to give her a perfect "down the throat" shot. Commander Smith promptly got his boat down to 150 feet, and in so doing heard two torpedo explosions which marked the end of 900-ton destroyer escort *Yaku*. The second escort vessel dropped a few depth charges close to *Hammerhead* but did her no damage.

Besugo, Bergall, Bowfin, Gato (Commander R. M. Farrell) and *Hawkbill* (Commander F. W. Scanland) bagged more small escorts during February. The largest ship sunk in the South China Sea during that month was the 10,000-ton tanker *Amato Maru*, torpedoed by *Blenny* (Commander W. H. Hazzard) off Saigon on the 26th.

The Japanese, desperately in need of oil, continued sending tankers to and from their southern fuel sources. Off the Indochina coast on 4 March *Baya* (Commander B. C. Jarvis) sank a 5200-ton tanker. Next day, between Hainan and Indochina, *Bashaw* (Commander H. S. Simpson) put down one twice as big. In the same region, near the end of the month, *Bluegill* (Commander Eric Barr) got a 5500-tonner. These were the last tankers sunk by submarines in the war. Aircraft would account for a few more.

Southwest Pacific submarines had now largely accomplished their mission of radically reducing the Japanese merchant fleet, and moved into other waters in search of different game. On 6 April *Besugo* reported a light cruiser in the Flores Sea between Soembawa and Flores Islands, zigzagging on a northwest course at 20 knots. She was escorted by three small vessels, of which *Besugo* sank one, the 630-ton minesweeper *No. 12*. The cruiser, *Isuzu*, which had been attacked by bombers of XIII A.A.F. earlier the same day, was sighted at 0400 next morning by submarine *Gabilan*, which got one torpedo into her. Submarine *Charr* (Commander F. D. Boyle), then in the vicinity, observed the explosion and got into the act. At 0820 *Charr* made three good torpedo hits on *Isuzu*. A British submarine, H.M.S. *Spark*, when closing to join the attack, saw the cruiser explode and go down; there was nothing left for *Spark* to do.

That 7th day of April was bad joss for the Japanese Navy. Up north, our fast carrier planes sank four destroyers, a light cruiser and mighty *Yamato;* in the Gulf of Siam U.S. submarine *Hardhead* sank 6900-ton freighter *Araosan Maru*.

During this month, owing to diminishing returns in the South China Sea, many Seventh Fleet submarines were transferred to Pacific Fleet upon completion of their patrols, and Admiral Fife moved his headquarters from Fremantle to Subic Bay.

A few good targets were encountered in waters off Indonesia. On 29 April *Bream* (Commander J. L. McCallum), patrolling south of Borneo, encountered a vessel of about 10,000 tons, steaming unescorted. Her first torpedo caused a tremendous explosion and fire, and the ship sank very promptly. *Besugo*, in the same vicinity, sighted the fire over the horizon and closed to investigate. She picked up a badly burned Japanese survivor. With no interpreter available, the most that could be learned from this man was the ship's route, from Balikpapan to Batavia, and the fact that she flew the German flag. Her identity remains a mystery to this day. *Besugo* continued into the Java Sea and on 23 April sank German submarine *U-183*.[4]

By the end of April only 33 Seventh Fleet submarines were operating, and during May they bagged only four ships, the biggest being a 6000-ton passenger-cargo vessel sunk by *Hammerhead* in the Gulf of Siam on 15 May. This ship had been sighted the previous afternoon and tracked all night. An alert escort lobbed a few

[4] See Vol. X 303.

4.7-inch shells close to *Hammerhead* as she was making a surface approach. *Cobia* (Commander A. L. Becker) joined the chase and observed the ship sinking after *Hammerhead* had fired her last three torpedoes.

On 29 May *Bluegill* launched a foray of her own. With two Australian Army officers embarked, she performed a one-ship amphibious operation on Pratas Reef, or Island, about 150 miles SE of Hong Kong. "Captured Bluegill, formerly Pratas, Island," reported Commander Barr. "Softened up island with bombardment by *Bluegill*, sent ten-man landing force ashore, encountered slight opposition, raised American flag 29 May with appropriate ceremonies, installed plaque commemorating ourselves, destroyed Japanese meteorological station and a 2000-gallon fuel dump. Now, on to Tokyo! Please have invasion medals struck immediately!" [5] Unfortunately China has renamed the island Tungsha Tao instead of Bluegill.

Early that month *Lagarto*, Commander F. D. Latta, became a casualty. When patrolling the Gulf of Siam she made contact with *Baya*, engaged at that time in tracking a heavily escorted tanker. *Baya* reported that the escorts had 10-cm radar and had attacked her with gunfire. The two skippers agreed to submerge ahead of the convoy's track, about 12 miles apart, and parted. Messages were exchanged during 2 and 3 May, but when *Baya* tried to raise *Lagarto* by radio on the 4th she got no reply. After the war was over it was found that Japanese minelayer *Hatsutaka* reported attacking a submarine at the time and place where *Lagarto* should have been. But on 16 May *Hawkbill* revenged *Lagarto* by sinking *Hatsutaka* as she was moving along the Malayan coast.

This almost ends the story of American submarines in the South China Sea. In June the total score was 2 small freighters and 5 escort vessels, most of the latter being sunk by gunfire. One notable achievement took place in July, last full month of the war. Late on

---

[5] Cdr. Barr's dispatch, received at Cincpac-Cincpoa HQ, Guam, when the writer was there. It seems that the Japanese had evacuated Pratas, leaving only a few caretakers.

the 14th *Bluefish*, Lieutenant Commander G. W. Forbes, patrolling northeast of Great Natoena Island, received a contact report from nearby *Blower* and closed to investigate. At 0223 July 15 she heard torpedo explosions and an hour later received a report from *Blower* that she had attacked something, she did not know what, with doubtful results. About an hour later *Bluefish* encountered the "something," which was zigzagging, and identified it as a surfaced Japanese submarine. She fired a torpedo spread at 0411 and observed two hits. The submarine, which proved to be *I-351*, caught fire, broke in two and sank almost immediately. A gasoline fire on the surface prevented immediate search, but after daylight *Bluefish* recovered three Japanese sailors from the water, one of the few instances during the Pacific War when any survivors from a Japanese submarine were rescued. This high mortality of enemy submariners was caused not by unwillingness to rescue survivors on the part of the United States Navy, but by the enemy's doctrine that compelled sailors to go down with their boats. The three men from *I-351* were topside when she broke up, and floated off.

On 6 August *Bullhead* (Lieutenant Commander E. R. Holt) reported that she was passing through Lombok Strait en route to the Java Sea. This was the last heard from her, or any of her crew. A Japanese Army pilot reported depth-charging a submarine off the Bali coast on the same day, claiming two direct hits and starting a gush of oil. Presumably that was the end of *Bullhead*, lost with all hands.

A new, profitable hunting ground for small game was found in late July in the Gulf of Siam. From 23 July to 11 August, *Bugara*, (Commander A. F. Schade), and *Blenny* between them sank 115 small trading and fishing vessels. *Ray* (Commander W. T. Kinsella) disposed of 24 in one day, 7 August, off the Kra Isthmus. In all, 220 vessels, mostly of less than 100 tons' burthen, were sunk by Sowespac submarines in these waters before the end of the war.

CHAPTER XIV

The U.S. Naval Group, China[1]

1. The "Rice Paddy Navy"

OF ALL the far-flung operations of the United States Navy in World War II, the most bizarre was that of the United States Naval Group, China, popularly known as the "Rice Paddy Navy." Starting with one commander USN, and one Chinese general, it expanded by the end of the war to 2500 American volunteers drawn from the Navy, Army, Marine Corps and Coast Guard, in close collaboration with some fifty thousand Chinese sailors, fishermen and pirates, and many times that number of guerrillas. This group engaged in a variety of cloak-and-dagger activities in the interior of China, and the only members who even saw the ocean were the coast watchers.

Even before Pearl Harbor, planners in Washington counted on more than military assistance from China in the event of a war with Japan. Weather reports were the first desideratum for the Pacific Fleet, since Western Pacific weather is formed over Asia. Reports on Japanese naval and shipping activities along the China coast would be of great value, as well as detailed intelligence on possible landing beaches along the China coast. The Navy (as we have seen), until out-argued by General MacArthur, looked forward to establishing a big beachhead in China as springboard for the final assault on Japan.

Rear Admiral Willis A. Lee, one of the Navy's top planners in

---

[1] Roy O. Stratton *SACO — The Rice Paddy Navy* (Pleasantville, N.Y., 1950); Rear Admiral Milton E. Miles "The U.S. Naval Group, China," *U.S. Naval Institute Proceedings* LXXII (July, 1946) 921; Lectures in 1949 and 1958 at the Naval War College by Admiral Miles.

Washington, chose for this unusual assignment Commander Milton E. Miles, universally known by his World War I nickname of "Mary." [2] On the day after Pearl Harbor, Miles was routed out of bed by Admiral Lee and told to get ready to go to China and lay the Navy's problems before Chiang Kai-shek. As it took time to clear this mission with the Chinese government, it was May 1942 before Commander Miles managed to reach Chungking.

Admiral Lee knew his man. As a young officer fresh out of the Naval Academy, Miles had spent five years in the Asiatic Fleet. On his shore leaves and liberties it was his habit to travel inland, off the beaten paths, and observe native customs. At the close of this tour of duty, with his wife and three small sons, he crossed Asia by what was later known as the Burma Road, and continued across India to Afghanistan and across Persia. He picked up a working knowledge of a few Chinese dialects and, even more important, acquired respect for and understanding of the Chinese people.

Upon his arrival in Chungking, Miles was taken in charge by Lieutenant General Tai Li, Chief of the Bureau of Investigation and Statistics of the National Military Council, which was compared with the American F.B.I. by his friends and with Hitler's Gestapo by his enemies. Miles and Tai formed a warm friendship, and Miles came to regard Chiang Kai-shek as one of the world's greatest men. He loved to quote one of the Generalissimo's sayings, "The more you sweat in peace, the less you will bleed in war." Tai Li, whose organization had infiltrated everywhere in Japanese-held China, undertook to collect weather and other information that the United States Navy wanted. But the Japanese tracked down every new weather radio station and destroyed it.

By the end of 1942 Miles realized that the weather-reporting net-

---

[2] Said to have been derived from the name of Mary Miles Minter, a popular movie actress of the era. Born Arizona 1900. Annapolis '22. Served in six different ships of the Asiatic Fleet to 1927. M.S. Columbia in electrical engineering, 1929. Served in *Saratoga* to 1932; in BuEng to 1934; exec. *Wickes*, staff of Comdesron 5 on Asiatic station, 1934. C.O. *John D. Edwards* 1939; ordered to Washington Mar. 1942, when recruited by Rear Adm. Lee for U.S. Navy Group, China. After the service here described, became C.O. *Columbus*, and successively Comcrudiv 10, 6 and 4. Director Pan-American affairs and U.S. Naval missions 1950; Com Fifteen 1954; Com Three 1956; retired 1958.

work would have to be turned into a secret army to be really useful. Tai Li needed more guerrillas to protect the weather man, and more Americans to train the Chinese. On Commander Miles's recommendation an agreement was signed 15 April 1943, establishing the Sino-American Coöperative Organization (SACO), commanded by Tai Li, with Miles as his deputy. Volunteers were carefully screened by the SACO office in Washington and put through a special training course before being sent out to China. No "old China hands" with preconceived ideas were wanted. The young Americans recruited were completely integrated into Chinese formations; their orders were drafted in Chinese and English and signed jointly by Tai Li and Miles. At a headquarters called "Happy Valley," about ten miles from Chungking, the men received their final training before going into the field.

Unit One, first to take the field, consisted of Major John H. Masters USMC and five men, later increased to twenty. They went overland by truck to a small mountain village in Anwhei Province, deep behind Japanese lines, but less than two hundred miles from Shanghai and Nanking, arriving 1 April 1943. Their duty was to train Tai Li's guerrillas in the use of small arms and submachine guns, and in sabotage and intelligence work. Scouting, patrolling, and aircraft and ship identification were later added to the curriculum. Seven more guerrilla training units were established within the next year and placed in the field in key spots, ranging from Shensi Province in the north to Kweichow Province, on the Chinese mainland opposite Formosa.

A medical department of SACO was next set up; doctors and Navy corpsmen were recruited and given special training. SACO eventually had twenty-four medical dispensaries and three mobile field hospitals in China, operating mostly behind the Japanese lines. The first, set up in western Hunan in November 1943, trained Chinese doctors and hospital attendants. Few Chinese with the necessary background could be found, but a small class of doctors and medical assistants were graduated before the summer of 1944, when the school had to be evacuated because of the Japanese advance along the Hankow–Canton railway. The unit then moved by truck overland to a site about forty miles west of Hangchow. Truck travel in China, a high adventure at any time, was doubly so in wartime. The usual fuel was charcoal, alcohol and tung oil. Baling wire and Chinese paper money served for bolts and gaskets. One of Tai Li's groups specialized in stealing tires from the Japanese and smuggling them through the lines.

This hospital unit was pursued and attacked by the Japanese as it moved eastward, but the guerrillas successfully covered and protected it to the destination in a pocket of the mountains. There an old Buddhist temple served as hospital, and training courses were resumed. On a clear night the lights of Shanghai were visible from a nearby hilltop. It was not uncommon for an American or British prisoner, who had escaped from the prisons and concentration camps near Shanghai, to be brought into "Pact Doc," as this unit was called, by guerrillas. Here they were kept until strong enough to push on to freedom.

Systematic weather information and weather reports were one of the principal purposes of the Naval Group in China. The Navy Department authorized an aërological complement of thirty-six officers and one hundred and twenty men, and equipment, to establish three hundred weather stations; a weather central was set up near Chungking, and in August 1943 Commander Irwin F. Beyerly arrived to take charge. He and an assistant moved inland to train Chinese students — over seven hundred of them — at a local radio school in weather reporting and ship and aircraft identification. By November, when it became evident that many reports from Chinese agencies were sent in irregularly and received to late to be useful, it was decided to create a weather service within SACO. Aërological units were attached to each of the guerrilla training teams in the field and at other SACO installation behind the lines, and Commander Beyerly's unit was absorbed. By October 1944, comprehensive weather maps were being broadcast daily to the Pacific Fleet.

The Intelligence group, formed early in 1943, was headed by

Commander David D. Wight. This became the most widespread activity of the U.S. Naval Group, China. It had liaison officers and photo interpretation units with General Chennault's XIV A.A.F. and acted as that force's Intelligence agency. It planted watchers along the China coast from Shanghai to Hong Kong and worked hand in glove with Tai Li's far-flung network.

The biggest trouble for SACO was not the enemy but the problem of supply. It had a unit in Washington to look after procurement and shipment of supplies to Bombay, where Captain Miles maintained an office to receive and forward all that came in, and to procure what he could locally. The Joint Chiefs of Staff allocated 150 tons a month to SACO in the airlift over the "Hump." That allowance was so pitifully small that it had to be used for highest priority equipment and supplies. General Joseph W. Stilwell USA, who took a dim view of an independent command in his bailiwick,[3] once held up all SACO's air shipments for six months.

No sooner had the supply problem been partially solved than another rose to harass Naval Group, China. Major General William Donovan's Office of Strategic Services attempted to do much the same thing that SACO was already accomplishing. After a preliminary wrangle, "Wild Bill" Donovan named "Mary" Miles director of O.S.S. in China; but some of Donovan's orders were so displeasing to Tai Li, the real boss of SACO, that this arrangement had to be given up.

By June of 1944, SACO was a going concern with good communications and active units feeding a wealth of information to Chungking. This, in turn was being relayed regularly to the Pacific and Seventh Fleets, to the Army Air Forces, and to other interested commands. So important did Pacific Fleet submarines consider SACO reports of Japanese ship movements along the China coast that they kept a liaison officer in Chungking to make certain of getting the word promptly.

[3] C. F. Romanus & Riley Sunderland *Stilwell's Command Problems* (Washington, 1955), 470.

2. The Pony-back Navy

Captain Miles wished to set up a weather station in Suiyuan Province, near the border of Inner Mongolia. Major Victor R. Bisceglia USMC commanded the unit of twelve men, most of them sailors. They left Happy Valley on 18 November 1943 in twelve charcoal-burning trucks driven by Chinese drivers, guarded by a detachment of eighty guerrillas. The convoy was held up at a crossing of the Yellow River in Kansu Province, about seventy-five miles west of Lanchow, until 8 January 1944, when the ice was strong enough to cross. There followed a ninety-mile trek across desert country and two more crossings of the Yellow River in sub-zero weather. The party would have been in serious want of food, fuel and clothing had not General Ma Hung Kwei, Governor of Ningshia Province, given the men all they needed, including an outfit of padded clothing and goatskin coats and caps, so that they were difficult to distinguish from nomadic Mongols.

Major Bisceglia's unit reached its destination in Suiyuan 18 January and the trucks returned to Chungking. Now the men were isolated; their only means of escape in the event of imminent capture was by horseback. So each man was given a Mongolian pony by the Governor of Suiyuan. The unit set up headquarters in a former Catholic mission about forty miles north of the Yellow River. In addition to collecting weather information, Bisceglia's men trained nearly six hundred Chinese soldiers in a course similar to that given United States Marines. Columns of these guerrillas operated against Japanese outposts in the direction of Peiping. They destroyed railroad equipment, attacked small towns occupied by Japanese troops, and persuaded several thousand Chinese puppet troops to change sides.

The high point of these operations occurred in March 1945 when Lieutenant Donald M. Wilcox, with an aërographer and a hospital corpsman, mounted on ponies, set out with two hundred Chinese guerrillas toward Peiping. On 15 May they were attacked by a Japanese armored column of six tanks, five armored Bren gun carriers and about four hundred cavalry. After a spirited two-hour battle the surviving Japanese retreated.

3. The Yangtze Raiders

Hankow, the metropolis of central China, lies at the head of deep-water navigation six hundred miles up the Yangtze River, and is also the terminus of the Peiping–Hankow–Canton railway. The Japanese used Hankow as their principal base and distributing point in support of military operations in southwest China.

In the spring of 1944 it was decided to establish a SACO unit here to train guerrillas and saboteurs to work against the railroads and shipping. Designated Unit 13, it was generally known as the Yangtze Raiders. Originally consisting of Lieutenant Joseph E. Champe USNR and five men, this team set up headquarters at a town in the mountains about 50 miles south of the Yangtze in July 1944. First a group of Chinese were trained in sabotage; next a school was opened to teach American methods to 500 guerrilla soldiers. Supplies and equipment had to be brought over 130 miles of mountain trails on the backs of 450 coolies. Headquarters were established in a former temple, which Yankee ingenuity and sense of humor managed to provide with something resembling modern secretarial and sanitary facilities.

The first combat unit of 250 guerrillas, with two Americans, moved out in bitter winter weather in early December 1944. Most of their traveling was done at night. In mid-February, when the group had reached a lake near the Yangtze, it was almost surrounded by about 2000 Japanese and 8000 puppet troops who had moved across the river especially to get them. The Chinese guerrilla commander, using Stonewall Jackson strategy, sent a squad to create a disturbance north of his main body. This drew off enough Japanese to create a gap out of which the guerrillas slipped. The unit then resumed its foray, blew up bridges, cut telephone and telegraph lines and generally raised the devil almost under the eyes of the Japanese.

In March 1945 a second Yangtze Raider unit succeeded in overcoming the Japanese guards in a town near Wuning and destroyed their supply warehouses. Presently three raider units were in the field harassing the Japanese in central China. The Chinese saboteurs, as distinguished from the guerrillas, operated in small groups of three men each and took tremendous risks. The Canton–Hankow railway was heavily protected, some of it by an electric fence, as well as by guards and big dogs. Yet on 20 April 1945 a short distance from Wuchang (across the river from Hankow) a sabotage team blew up an ammunition train by placing a 50-pound TNT charge on the tracks between the time the reconnaissance train passed and the ammunition train arrived. A locomotive and seven cars were blown over a cliff. Another team, operating around Kiukiang, sank two steamers with a device invented by Lieutenant Champe. Charges were suspended from bamboo floats about two feet under water. These floats were joined by a long line and pulled out in the river by sampans. One float was released inshore of the anchored target ship and the other on the offshore side. The current carried the line across the vessel's bows, when the charges trailed down stream, and were exploded when they hit the ship. Two members of the team worked as stevedores on a Japanese ammunition ship at Kiukiang to learn about her cargo before sinking it by this method.

These patterns of guerrilla and sabotage activity were followed until the end of hostilities. Two or three Americans accompanied each of the guerrilla field units but no one was even wounded in the many brushes that occurred.

4. *The Coast Watchers*

Obtaining information on Japanese shipping along the China coast was also one of the main objectives of the U.S. Naval Group,

China. In the early stages of SACO this was entrusted to Chinese coast watchers, who were willing and eager but had difficulty in identifying ships accurately.

When the Japanese split China by their drive southward from Hankow in the summer of 1944 and drove XIV Army Air Force from their advanced bases, it became obvious that the only way to get at Japanese coastal shipping was from the air or by submarine. The one method was unusually risky because of the long distance of the China coast from air bases in the Philippines or western China, and submarines were troubled by the shoal water off the coast. Thus, accurate intelligence of ship movements was doubly necessary, and this could be had only from well trained coast watchers. After a reconnaissance in July 1944, Commodore Miles selected Changchow, a town twenty-five miles inland from Japanese occupied Amoy, as headquarters for an Intelligence unit concerned primarily with keeping track of Japanese shipping. Americans were trained for this duty and manned the coast watching stations in the fall.

In January 1945 a United States submarine wolf pack consisting of *Queenfish*, *Picuda* and *Barb*, commanded by Commander C. E. Loughlin and known as "Loughlin's Loopers," was operating in Formosa Strait. On 8 January it broke up a convoy off Takao, but no more targets could be found. Naval Group China informed the submarines on 20 January that Japanese traffic was holing up at night and running by day close inshore, in less than ten fathoms of water. *Barb*, Commander E. B. ("Gene") Fluckey, had penetrated a junk flotilla inside the ten-fathom curve a few days earlier in search of targets and found none, but observed that no navigational lights were burning along the coast. He reasoned that since most of the ships reported by SACO were using Lam Yit Bay, about 80 miles northeast of Amoy, yet not rounding Turnabout Light, they must be using some inner passage. The only one he could find on his chart was a very shallow one called Hai Tan Strait. SACO, asked to investigate next day, reported that Hai Tan was being used by large ships. This convinced Fluckey that shipping was moving only in daylight in water too shallow for him to attack. But a northbound convoy, which Naval Group, China was reporting regularly, should anchor in Foochow that night. He planned to tag along with the junk fleet north of Hai Tan to try to locate it.

Shortly after dark 22 January *Barb* passed through the junks and took a position north of Hai Tan Strait in nine fathoms of water. In the meantime Sergeant William M. Stewart usmc, a coast watcher at Nam Kwan Bay, reported to Changchow "Eleven Jap transports anchored two miles south of me. Am sending pirates aboard to get the dope." This was relayed promptly from Changchow to Chungking and to the submarines off the coast. *Barb* is reported to have intercepted Stewart's message and sent him a message, "Save prize for me." *Barb* then moved toward Nam Kwan Bay, working into a position through suspected minefields to a point only 6000 yards from the anchored convoy and six miles inside the ten-fathom line. At 0404 January 23 she fired a spread of ten torpedoes at what the skipper reported to be "the most beautiful target of the war." [4] The ships were anchored in three columns which from *Barb's* viewpoint overlapped, providing a continuous target over two miles long. At least eight hits were heard and observed, with two ships exploding and fires observed on others; but according to the generally accurate postwar Japanese compilations, all that *Barb* sank was the 5244-ton freighter *Taikyo Maru.*[5]

After firing her spread *Barb* highballed out to sea to get more depth for diving. As he headed out, Commander Fluckey radioed to Sergeant Stewart, "Next time I'll put wheels on my keel!"

By 1 March 1945 the coast watcher network was in full operation. Each post was manned by two American sailors, a Chinese interpreter, a Chinese weather man and six or more guerrillas. On 20 March, twelve B–25s, from newly acquired fields on Luzon, raided Amoy. This raid was observed by a coast watcher team cov-

---

[4] *Barb* Report of 11th War Patrol 15 Feb. 1945.
[5] It is possible that other ships of the convoy were beached and so not listed as lost.

ering the harbor of Amoy. The watchers were instrumental in saving the entire crew of one B-25, forced down in Japanese-held territory. Two days later the Amoy coast watchers reported that the tail of a PB4Y-2 had been shot off by antiaircraft fire from Amoy and been splashed. Boatswain's Mate H. W. Tucker, walking along a road on the north shore of Amoy Harbor, saw it happen. He changed route to investigate, and at sundown saw seven white men and several Chinese approaching. Tucker greeted them with "Hi ya fellows, who are you?" The astonished aviators replied, "We're from the U.S. Navy. Who are you?" "I'm Navy too," said Tucker. "Come on!" — and led the party safely back to Changchow. Don Bell, a radio-news correspondent who was one of the rescued party, reported: "Imagine our gasps of amazed delight when told that there was a U.S. Naval Station just 80 li (about 27 miles) away. Here we had been shot down less than a mile from a Jap garrison, we had been chased by motor boats and searched for by Jap planes less than two hours before, and here was a man telling us we were within a few hours of safety. . . . When we saw Tucker swinging along with a Tommy gun over one shoulder and a bag of iron rations over the other — well, you can talk about a sailor's welcome but you haven't seen anything!"

This rescue paid off two months later when a Privateer buzzed the Changchow SACO unit and dropped a note saying there would be a package drop on the next pass. Down came a box loaded with ship's service items that had only been a dream until then. A note explained that the contents were a gift of the Squadron to which the PB4Y-2 belonged, and of the Red Cross.

By July 1945 guerrilla operations were reaching to the coast and the Japanese began to stir around to break them up. Preparations were made to evacuate Changchow if necessary but the enemy never came near it. SACO forces received support from the air and helped the fliers locate targets by means of long, white panel arrows on the ground. They continued to coöperate with aviators and to receive supplies after the Japanese surrendered and until the bases were closed down for return to the United States.

5. The Final Naval Battle of World War II [6]

Immediately after the armistice on 15 August 1945, all SACO units in the field received orders to close down and make their way to Hankow, Shanghai or Chungking, whichever was the nearest. But even the folding up of activities provided some strange doings in this most irregular naval organization.

Unit 8, with headquarters at Tsingtien in Chekiang Province, had the unusual experience of fighting the last naval battle of the war, in a manner reminiscent of the War of 1812. Following President Truman's announcement of Japan's surrender, Unit 8 was ordered to break camp and proceed to Shanghai. Lieutenant Livingston ("Swede") Swentzel with a party of eight then left for Wenchow on the coast. There he commandeered two sailing junks and shoved off for Shanghai, with Chinese fishermen crews and a battery consisting of one bazooka rocket-launcher. On the morning of 20 August they sighted a large black junk armed with a 75-mm howitzer standing out from a nearby island, and it acted so suspiciously that Swentzel gave chase. As he approached, the black junk presented her broadside, opened fire with her 75-mm gun and scored a direct hit on Swentzel's "flagship," killing two Chinese, wounding two others and damaging her rudder so that she drifted off to leeward. The second SACO junk, commanded by Lieutenant Stuart L. Pittman USMCR, then opened fire on the enemy with machine and Tommy guns. The Japanese replied in kind, but Pittman managed to maneuver his junk by sail within 100 yards of them, a good bazooka range. A young seaman manned the bazooka and managed to shoot three rockets into the black junk. The third exploded in her hold, knocking out her 3-inch gun and taking all the fight out of the Japanese, who begged for quarter by displaying a dirty white undershirt on a bayonet. As some of them continued to fire with rifles, Pittman decided to board, and commanded the

[6] Vice Adm. Miles's Lecture at Naval War College, 9 May 1958; Lt. Pittman's story, as told to Lt. Cdr. H. Brooks Beck USNR in 1948.

boarding party himself. The Japanese skipper, who, though badly wounded, was still able to handle a revolver, attempted to take a pot shot at Pittman when he entered the hold, but was thwarted by the quick action of an American sailor who pumped several rifle shots into him. Before the skipper died, Pittman was able to hear his version of the affair — he had mistaken the Americans for Chinese pirates. The carnage wrought in this wooden ship by the bazooka rocket was terrific — 48 of the crew killed, and all but four of the surviving 39 wounded; but the junk was still able to sail, so Swentzel placed a prize crew on board and returned to Haimen to dispose of his prisoners. All three junks arrived at Shanghai on 24 August.

It is ironic that this fight of 20 August 1945, the final naval battle of a war in which aircraft, carriers, and a galaxy of new weapons were employed, should have been fought by sailing ships, and concluded by the classic tactics of boarding. Perhaps there is a subtle lesson in this incident to a world of ever-expanding wonders. After a war of annihilation, the sailing frigate, the cutlass and the boarding pike may stage a comeback. Sailors, never forget how to sail!

At the time of Japan's surrender, SACO held three seaports and about two hundred miles of the China coast. Elements of the Rice Paddy Navy had some trying and delicate moments in moving into Japanese-occupied cities before the formal surrender document was signed on 2 September and communicated to the Japanese troops in China. "Swede" Swentzel's unit was the first to arrive in Shanghai. The Lieutenant himself entered the city in search of further orders, and the remainder of the unit were quartered with Chinese troops in Pootung. On 2 September the group tried to enter the city but were prevented by surly Japanese. An English-speaking Japanese officer, declaring that the Emperor's surrender did not apply to Shanghai, placed Swentzel's party under arrest and bundled it off to a compound, but the prisoners were soon released. SACO's disbursing officer flew with Tai Li and several other Chinese officers from Chungking to Shanghai on

9 September, carrying half a billion Chinese dollars and $1,000,000 U.S. currency to set up a pay office for SACO and Seventh Fleet. By the time Admiral Kinkaid arrived on 19 September he found the nucleus of a naval organization functioning in Shanghai.

Unit 7 broke camp on 25 August with orders to proceed to Hangchow, where its C.O., Lieutenant Lloyd M. Felmly USNR, had some difficulty in convincing the Japanese commander that the war was over. The Yangtze Raiders assembled at Hankow and had no trouble. Others of Naval Group China made their way to major cities, on foot or by sampan, whence they were moved to evacuation centers by more modern means of transportation. Some of the officers and men remained in China until 1946, but most of the men shipped home, and the Rice Paddy Navy gradually disintegrated. They had helped the common cause far more than their slender numbers would indicate. They carried away a feeling of great friendliness for the Chinese, and gratitude for the efforts of poor farmers and fishermen to help them. This sound basis for future friendship between two great countries was shattered within a few years, alas, by the Communist propaganda of Mao's government.

Task Organization for the Invasion of Luzon[1]

January 1945

COMMANDER IN CHIEF
General of the Army Douglas MacArthur USA in BOISE

TF 77 LUZON ATTACK FORCE
Vice Admiral T. C. Kinkaid in WASATCH

Deputy Commander, Vice Admiral T. S. Wilkinson
in MOUNT OLYMPUS

Commanding General, Lieutenant General Walter Krueger in WASATCH

TG 77.1 FLEET FLAGSHIP GROUP, Vice Admiral Kinkaid

Fleet Flagship Unit, Captain A. M. Granum

Commander Air Support Control Units, Captain F. N. Taylor

WASATCH Capt. Granum; destroyers SMITH Lt. Cdr. E. H. Huff, FRAZIER Cdr.
F. O'C. Fletcher.

Cruiser Unit, Captain W. M. Downes

Light cruiser BOISE Capt. Downes; destroyers COGHLAN (with Comdesron 14,
Capt. G. L. Sims, embarked) Cdr. B. B. Cheatham, EDWARDS Lt. Cdr. S. E. Ramey.

TG 77.2 BOMBARDMENT AND FIRE SUPPORT GROUP
Vice Admiral J. B. Oldendorf in CALIFORNIA

San Fabian Fire Support Unit, Rear Admiral G. L. Weyler in NEW MEXICO

Unit "M," Commo. H. B. Farncomb RAN: Heavy cruiser H.M.A.S. AUSTRALIA
Capt. J. M. Armstrong RN; battleship MISSISSIPPI Capt. H. J. Redfield; destroyers
ALLEN M. SUMNER (with Comdesdiv 120, Cdr. J. C. Zahn, embarked) Cdr. N. J.
Sampson, LOWRY Cdr. E. S. Miller.

Unit "N," Rear Admiral I. C. Sowell (Combatdiv 4): Battleship WEST VIRGINIA

---

[1] Compiled from the op plan and war diaries of participating groups; those in command on S-day verified from ships' war diaries and Action Reports. Air groups squadrons from their war diaries and histories, and number and types of planes are from "Weekly Location of U.S. Naval Aircraft." First ship mentioned in a group is flagship unless otherwise stated.

Capt. H. V. Wiley; heavy cruiser H.M.A.S. SHROPSHIRE Capt. G. A. G. Nicholas RN; destroyers LAFFEY Cdr. F. J. Becton, O'BRIEN Cdr. W. W. Outerbridge.
Unit "O," Rear Admiral Weyler: Battleship NEW MEXICO Capt. R. W. Fleming; [2] heavy cruiser MINNEAPOLIS Capt. H. B. Slocum; destroyers BARTON (with Comdesron 60, Capt. W. L. Freseman, embarked) Cdr. E. B. Dexter, MOALE Cdr. W. M. Foster, INGRAHAM Cdr. J. F. Harper, WALKE Cdr. G. F. Davis.[3]

LINGAYEN FIRE SUPPORT UNIT, Vice Admiral Oldendorf

Battleships CALIFORNIA Capt. S. B. Brewer, PENNSYLVANIA Capt. C. F. Martin, COLORADO Capt W. S. Macaulay; heavy cruisers LOUISVILLE Capt. R. L. Hicks,[4] PORTLAND Capt. T. G. W. Settle; light cruiser COLUMBIA Capt. M. E. Curts; destroyers LEUTZE Cdr. B. A. Robbins, HEYWOOD L. EDWARDS Cdr. A. L. Shepherd, KIMBERLY Cdr. J. D. Whitfield, NEWCOMB (with Comdesron 56, Capt. R. N. Smoot, embarked) Cdr. I. E. McMillian, RICHARD P. LEARY Cdr. D. P. Dixon, WILLIAM D. PORTER Cdr. C. M. Keyes, BENNION Cdr R. H. Holmes, BRYANT Cdr. P. L. High, IZARD (with Comdesdiv 112, Capt. T. F. Conley, embarked) Cdr. M. T. Dayton, H.M.A.S. ARUNTA Cdr. A. E. Buchanan RAN, H.M.A.S. WARRAMUNGA Lt. Cdr. J. M. Alliston RN.

BEACH DEMOLITION GROUP, Lieutenant Commander O. B. Murphy USNR

Embarking Underwater Demolition Teams, Capt. B. H. Hanlon: UDT 8 Lt. Cdr. D. E. Young USNR, UDT 10 Lt. A. O. Choate USNR, UDT 14 Lt. A. B. Onderdonk USNR, UDT 5 Lt. J. K. DeBold USNR, UDT 9 Lt. H. F. Stevenson USNR, UDT 15 Lt. H. F. Brooks.
High speed transports GEORGE E. BADGER Lt. Cdr. E. M. Higgins USNR, DICKERSON Lt. Cdr. R. E. Lounsbury, RATHBURNE Lt. Cdr. R. L. Welch USNR, CLEMSON Lt. W. F. Moran USNR, BULL Lt. J. B. McLaughlin USNR, HUMPHREYS Lt. Cdr. O. B. Murphy USNR, SANDS Lt. J. M. Samuels USNR, OVERTON Lt. Cdr. D. K. O'Connor USNR, BELKNAP Lt. R. Childs USNR, BLESSMAN Lt. P. LeBoutiller USNR.

TG 77.3 CLOSE COVERING GROUP, Rear Admiral R. S. Berkey

Light cruisers PHOENIX Capt. J. H. Duncan, MONTPELIER Capt. H. D. Hoffman, DENVER (with Comcrudiv 12, Rear Admiral R. S. Riggs, embarked) Capt. A. M. Bledsoe; destroyers NICHOLAS (with Comdesron 21, Capt. J. K. B. Ginder, embarked) Cdr. R. T. S. Keith, FLETCHER Cdr. J. L. Foster, RADFORD Lt. Cdr. J. E. Mansfield, O'BANNON Lt. Cdr. J. A. Pridmore, TAYLOR Lt. Cdr. H. H. de Laureal, HOPEWELL Cdr. W. S. Rodimon.

TG 77.4 ESCORT CARRIER GROUP
Rear Admiral C. T. Durgin

LINGAYEN CARRIER GROUP, Rear Admiral Durgin

MAKIN ISLAND, Capt. W. B. Whaley, with Composite Squadron 84, Cdr. W. H. Rogers USNR: 16 FM-2 (Wildcat), 12 TBM-3 (Avenger).
LUNGA POINT, Capt. G. A. T. Washburn, with Compron 85, Lt. Cdr. F. C. Herriman: 14-FM-2, 12 TBM-3.
BISMARCK SEA, Capt. J. L. Pratt, with Compron 86, Lt. B. M. Lakin USNR: 16 FM-2, 12 TBM-3.

[2] Killed 6 Jan.; Cdr. J. T. Warren became C.O. until relieved by Capt. J. M. Haines 9 Feb.
[3] Killed 6 Jan.; Lt. J. S. Burns USNR became C.O.
[4] Wounded 5 Jan., when command passed to the exec. Commander W. P. McCarty.

SALAMAUA, Capt. J. I. Taylor, with Compron 87, Lt. H. N. Heisel: 14 FM-2, 10 TBM-3.
HOGGATT BAY, Capt. J. A. Briggs, with Compron 88, *Lt. Cdr. E. N. Webb: 16 FM-2, 12 TBM-1C.

LINGAYEN PROTECTIVE GROUP, Rear Admiral R. A. Ofstie

KITKUN BAY, Capt. Albert Handly, with Compron 91, *Lt. Cdr. B. D. Mack: 5 16 FM-2, 1 FM-2P, 11 TBM-3.
SHAMROCK BAY, Capt. F. T. Ward, with Compron 94, Lt. Cdr. J. F. Patterson USNR: 20 FM-2, 11 TBM-3, 1 TBM-3P.
Destroyer escorts JOHN C. BUTLER Lt. Cdr. J. E. Pace, O'FLAHERTY Lt. Cdr. D. W. Farnham USNR.

HUNTER-KILLER GROUP, Captain J. C. Cronin

TULAGI, Capt. Cronin, with Compron 92, Lt. J. B. Wallace: 11 FM-2, 12 TBM-3.
Destroyer escorts STAFFORD Lt. Cdr. V. H. Craig USNR, WILLIAM SIEVERLING Lt. Cdr. C. F. Adams USNR, ULVERT M. MOORE Lt. Cdr. F. D. Roosevelt Jr. USNR, KENDALL C. CAMPBELL Lt. Cdr. R. W. Johnson USNR, GOSS Lt. Cdr. C. S. Kirkpatrick USNR.

Screen, Captain V. D. Long (Comdesron 6)

Destroyers MAURY Lt. Cdr. D. L. Harris, GRIDLEY Lt. Cdr. G. F. Dalton, BAGLEY Cdr. W. H. Shea, HELM Cdr. S. K. Santmyers, RALPH TALBOT Lt. Cdr. W. S. Brown USNR, PATTERSON Lt. Cdr. W. A. Hering, McCALL Lt. Cdr. J. B. Carroll, EDMONDS Lt. Cdr. J. S. Burrows USNR, HOWARD D. CLARK Lt. Cdr. D. C. Miller USNR.

SAN FABIAN CARRIER GROUP, Rear Admiral F. B. Stump

NATOMA BAY, Capt. A. K. Morehouse, with Compron 81, Lt. Cdr. R. C. Barnes: 18 FM-2, 12 TBM-1C.
MANILA BAY, Capt. Fitzhugh Lee, with Compron 80, Lt. Cdr. H. K. Stubbs USNR: 20 FM-2, 12 TBM-1C.
WAKE ISLAND, Capt. A. V. Magly, with Comspotron 6 1, Lt. Cdr. W. F. Bringle: 23 FM-2, 12 TBM-3.
STEAMER BAY, Capt. Steadman Teller, with Compron 90, Lt. Cdr. R. A. O'Neill: 16 FM-2, 12 TBM-3.
SAVO ISLAND, Capt. C. E. Ekstrom, with Compron 27, Lt. Cdr. P. W. Jackson: 19 FM-2, 11 TBM-1C, 1 TBM-1CP.
† OMMANEY BAY, Capt. H. L. Young, with Compron 75, Lt. Cdr. A. W. Smith USNR: 19 FM-2, 10 TBM-1C, 1 TBM-1CP, 1 TBM-3.

Screen, Captain H. J. Martin (Comdesron 51)

Destroyers HALL Cdr. L. C. Baldauf, HALLIGAN Cdr. C. E. Cortner, BELL Cdr. J. S. C. Gabbert, BURNS Cdr. J. T. Bullen, PAUL HAMILTON Cdr. Dan Carlson, TWIGGS Cdr. George Philip, ABBOT Cdr. F. W. Ingling.

CLOSE COVERING GROUP, Rear Admiral G. R. Henderson

SAGINAW BAY, Capt. F. C. Sutton, with Compron 78, Lt. F. G. Lewis USNR: 20 FM-2, 12 TBM-3.

* Lost or killed in this operation.
† Sunk 4 Jan.

5 Lt. F. M. Blanchard USNR became Com Compron 91 Jan. 5.
6 Composite Spotting Squadron.

KADASHAN BAY, Capt. R. N. Hunter, with Compron 20, Lt. Cdr. J. F. McRoberts: 24 FM-2, 10 TBM-1C, 1 TBM-1CP.
MARCUS ISLAND, Capt. C. F. Greber, with Compron 21, Lt. Cdr. T. O. Murray USNR: 24 FM-2, 9 TBM-1C.
PETROF BAY, Capt. R. S. Clarke, with Compron 76, Cdr. J. W. McCauley: 20 FM-2, 12 TBM-1C.

Screen, Captain J. W. Callahan (Comdesdiv 104)

Destroyers CHARRETTE Lt. Cdr. G. P. Joyce, CONNER Cdr. W. E. Kaitner, RICHARD S. BULL Lt. Cdr. F. S. Moseley USNR, RICHARD M. ROWELL Cdr. H. A. Barnard.

TG 77.6 MINESWEEPING AND HYDROGRAPHIC GROUP
Commander W. R. Loud

Sweep Unit 1, Cdr. Loud (Cominron 2): Minesweepers HOPKINS Lt. D. P. Payne USNR, CHANDLER Lt. F. M. Murphy USNR, SOUTHARD Lt. Cdr. J. E. Brennan USNR, * HOVEY Lt. B. N. Cole USNR, * LONG Lt. Stanley Caplan USNR; minelayer PREBLE Lt. Cdr. E. F. Baldridge; high speed transport BROOKS Lt. S. C. Rassmussen USNR; 4 LCPR.

Sweep Unit 2, Lt. Cdr. John Clague USNR: Minesweepers HAMILTON Lt. Cdr. Clague, DORSEY, Lt. J. M. Hayes USNR, * PALMER Lt. W. E. McGuirk USNR, HOGAN Lt. Cdr. J. P. Conway USNR, HOWARD Lt. Cdr. O. F. Salvia; minelayer BREESE Lt. Cdr. G. W. McKnight USNR.

Sweep Unit 3, Lt. Cdr. H. R. Peirce USNR: Minesweepers REQUISITE Lt. Cdr. Peirce, PURSUIT Lt. Cdr. R. F. Good USNR, SAGE Lt. Cdr. F. K. Zinn USNR, SCUFFLE Lt. Cdr. E. A. Johnson USNR, TRIUMPH Lt. Cdr. C. R. Cunningham USNR.

Sweep Unit 4, Lt. Cdr. J. R. Keefer: Minesweepers SAUNTER Lt. Cdr. Keefer, SALUTE Lt. J. R. Hodges USNR, SCOUT Lt. E. G. Anderson USNR, SCRIMMAGE Lt. Robert Van Winkle USNR, SENTRY Lt. Cdr. T. R. Fonick USNR.

Other Sweep Units: 5, Lt. J. S. Dement, 8 YMS; 6, Lt. W. A. Latta USNR, 8 YMS; 7, Lt. Paul Schminke USNR, 8 YMS; 8, Lt. E. O. Saltmarsh USNR, 8 YMS; 9, Lt. G. L. O'Neil USNR, 5 YMS; 10, Lt. W. H. Boutell USNR, 5 YMS; 11, 4 LCPR (equipped as sweepers).

Hydrographic Unit, Cdr. R. B. A. Hunt RAN: Frigates H.M.A.S. GASCOYNE, WARREGO; surveying ship H.M.A.S. BENALLA; *HDML-1074; YMS-316.*

Service Unit, Lt. Cdr. J. E. Cole USNR: Minelayer MONADNOCK Lt. Cdr. Cole.

TG 77.7 SCREENING GROUP, Captain J. B. McLean (Comdesdiv 48)

Destroyers BUSH Cdr. R. E. Westholm, STANLY Cdr. J. B. Morland, HALFORD Cdr. R. J. Hardy, STEMBEL Cdr. W. L. Tagg.

TG 77.8 SALVAGE AND RESCUE GROUP, Commander B. S. Huie USNR

Salvage Vessels GRASP Lt. Cdr. J. F. Lawson, GRAPPLE Lt. R. K. Thurman USNR, CABLE Lt. Cdr. Hartwell Pond USNR; Repair ships AMYCUS Lt. Cdr. E. W. Wunch (Ret.), EGERIA Lt. A. H. Wilson USNR; Fleet tugs APACHE Lt. C. S. Horner, CHICKASAW Lt. Cdr. L. C. Olson USNR, CHOWANOC Lt. R. F. Snipes, POTAWATOMI Lt. C. H. Stedman; Ocean tugs HIDATSA Lt. C. F. Johnson USNR, QUAPAW Lt. Cdr. R. H. Donnell USNR, RAIL Lt. (jg) T. P. Pierce USNR; *ATR-61;* 8 LCI(L).

TG 77.9 REINFORCEMENT GROUP, Rear Admiral R. L. Conolly

Embarking U.S. 25th Infantry Division, Maj. Gen. C. L. Mullins; 158th Reg. Combat Team, Brig. Gen. H. MacNider; 13th Armored Group, Col. M. E. Jones.

* Sunk in this operation.

Force flagship APPALACHIAN Capt. C. R. Jeffs; Destroyer REMEY Cdr. R. P. Fiala. Nouméa Transport Unit, Commo. H. W. Graf in *Zeilin:* Attack transports PRESIDENT JACKSON (with Comtransdiv 23, Capt. W. S. Popham, embarked) Cdr. C. B. Hamblett USNR, PRESIDENT ADAMS Capt. M. C. Erwin, LA PORTE Cdr. M. C. Thompson, LATIMER Capt. J. P. Dix, OXFORD Capt. P. S. Crandell, ZEILIN Capt. T. B. Fitzpatrick, OCONTO Cdr. P. Jackson USNR, LAURENS Capt. D. McGregor, AUDRAIN Lt. Cdr. G. O. Forrest USNR; transports PRESIDENT MONROE Cdr. J. M. Payne USNR, COMET Lt. Cdr. J. B. Blee USNR; attack cargo ALGOL Lt. Cdr. A. T. Jones USNR; S.S. NAVAJO VICTORY, MANDERSON V., LAS VEGAS V., BEDFORD V., H. T. DODGE, SOLON TURMAN, WRANGELL, FOMALHAUT.

Screen, Cdr. M. L. McCullough: Destroyers MCNAIR Cdr. McCullough, NORMAN SCOTT Cdr. W. B. Porter, MELVIN Cdr. B. K. Atkins.

Bougainville Unit, Cdr. C. J. Ballreich: Transport PRESIDENT POLK Cdr. Ballreich; attack transport LIBRA Cdr. G. W. McCormick USNR; DE HARMON Lt. Cdr. T. U. Weekes USNR.

Milne Bay Unit: Attack transport WARREN Cdr. E. S. Stoker; DE DARBY Lt. Cdr. M. W. Martin USNR.

Oro Bay Unit: Attack cargo UVALDE Lt. Cdr. W. M. McCloy; DE J. DOUGLAS BLACKWOOD Lt. Cdr. J. L. Johnston USNR.

Lae Unit: Attack transport OLMSTED (with Comtransdiv 5, Capt. R. W. Abbott, embarked) Capt. C. L. C. Atkeson.

Finschhafen Unit: Hospital ship TRYON Cdr. W. G. Jones; attack cargo WARRICK Lt. Cdr. E. J. Grey.

Hollandia Unit: Transport WINGED ARROW Cdr. J. E. Shomier; attack transport APPLING Lt. Cdr. A. L. Stuart USNR; high speed transport COOLBAUGH Lt. Cdr. S. T. Hotchkiss USNR.

Noemfoor Unit, Capt. J. K. Davis: Attack transports LEON Capt. H. B. Southworth, ADAIR Capt. S. P. Comly, HASKELL Cdr. A. L. Mare; attack cargo DIPHDA Lt. Cdr. R. C. Willson USNR; high speed transports KILTY (with Comtransdiv 100, Cdr. R. A. Wilhelm, embarked) Lt. L. G. Benson USNR, SCHLEY Lt. Cdr. E. T. Farley USNR, CROSBY Lt. G. G. Moffatt USNR, HERBERT Lt. G. S. Hewitt USNR, LLOYD (with Comtransdiv 103, Cdr. W. S. Parsons, embarked) Lt. Cdr. P. N. Gammelgard USNR, NEWMAN Lt. Cdr. R. I. Thieme USNR, KEPHART Lt. Cdr. I. H. Cammarn USNR, COFER Lt. H. C. McClees USNR, TALBOT (with Comtransdiv 107-T, Lt. Cdr. C. C. Morgan USNR, embarked), TALBOT Lt. Cdr. Morgan, MANLEY Lt. Cdr. R. C. Foster USNR, GOLDSBOROUGH Lt. C. E. Caton USNR.

Leyte Transport Unit, Cdr. H. B. Olsen USNR: Attack transport GILLIAM Cdr. Olsen; *PC-1128;* tankers BENNINGTON, BIRCH COULIE.

LST Unit, Commander A. A. Ageton (ComLSTflot 3)[7]

Bougainville LST Unit, Cdr. R. D. DeKay USNR: Destroyer escort GREENWOOD Lt. Cdr. D. G. Bryce USNR, 3 LST; Oro Bay LST Unit, Cdr. G. R. Berner: Destroyer escort LOESER Lt. Cdr. J. Proctor USNR, 5 LST; Hollandia LST Unit, Cdr. Ageton: Destroyer MONSSEN Lt. Cdr. E. G. Sanderson, 7 LST, *SC-735;* 7 merchant ships; Noemfoor LST Unit, Cdr. N. W. Nelson USCG: 6 LST, *PC-462, -563;* Sansapor LST Unit, Lt. Roy Collier USNR: *LST-219, PC-464;* Morotai LST Unit, Cdr. L. A. Drexler: Destroyers MCDERMUT Cdr. C. B. Jennings, MCGOWAN Cdr. W. R. Cox, MERTZ Cdr. W. S. Estabrook; 13 LST. Leyte LST Unit, Cdr. E. C. Parsons USNR: 15 LST.

TG 77.10 SERVICE GROUP, Rear Admiral R. O. Glover

Leyte Service Unit, Captain E. P. Hylant

Tankers CARIBOU Lt. J. B. Humphrey USNR, CARONDELET Lt. R. H. Grasmere USNR, SILVER CLOUD Lt. Cdr. H. R. Will USNR, SHIKELLAMY Lt. E. J. Blewitt USNR, SUSQUEHANNA Lt. J. C. Brown USNR; Royal Fleet Auxiliary BISHOPDALE Cdr. N. W. Westlake RNR; Royal Australian Fleet Auxiliary KURUMBA Lt. J. T. Maurey RANR; water ship STAG Lt. E. A. Winkler USNR; ammunition ships PYRO Lt. Cdr. S. J. Reiffel USNR, H.M.A.S. YUNNAN Lt. D. Morrison RANR; cargo ships MURZIM Lt. Cdr. D. S. Walton USCGR, BOOTES Lt. N. W. Anderson USNR; general stores ACUBENS Cdr. E. B. Ellis USNR; net tenders TEABERRY, SATINLEAF, TEAK, SILVERBELL; repair ship MIDAS; Drydock No. 19; merchant ships IRAN VICTORY, MERIDIAN V.

Lingayen Service Unit, Captain T. J. Kelly

Tankers TALLULAH Lt. Cdr. W. F. Huckaby USNR, SCHUYLKILL Cdr. J. B. McVey, CHEPACHET Lt. Cdr. H. K. Wallace, MINK Lt. W. J. Meagher USNR, ANDREW DORIA Lt. Howard Buehler USNR, KENWOOD Lt. Cdr. R. L. West USNR; water ship SEVERN Lt. Cdr. O. Rees; ammunition ships ELMIRA VICTORY, PROVO V.; 2 LST; net tender INDUS.

Mindoro Service Unit, Captain J. D. Beard

Tankers SUAMICO Cdr. A. S. Johnson, SALAMONIE Cdr. L. J. Johns, WINOOSKI Lt. Cdr. T. B. Christenson USNR, PECOS Lt. Cdr. G. W. Renegar USNR, COWANESQUE Cdr. L. S. McKenzie USNR, PANDA Lt. J. A. Arnold USNR; ammunition ships DURHAM VICTORY, BLUEFIELD V., CYRENE.

Screen, Commander W. H. Putnam USNR

Destroyer escorts THOMASON Lt. Cdr. C. B. Henriques USNR, LOVELACE Lt. Cdr. E. L. de Kieffer USNR, MANNING Lt. Cdr. J. I. Mingay USNR, NEUENDORF Lt. Cdr. R. C. Barlow USNR, JAMES E. CRAIG Lt. Cdr. E. F. Andrews USNR, EICHENBERGER Lt. Cdr. N. Harrell.

TF 78 SAN FABIAN ATTACK FORCE
Vice Admiral D. E. Barbey

Embarking United States I Army Corps, Maj. Gen. I. P. Swift; 43rd Infantry Division, Maj. Gen. L. F. Wing.

Force Flagship BLUE RIDGE, Captain H. B. Brumbaugh

TG 78.1 WHITE BEACH ATTACK GROUP, Vice Admiral Barbey

White Beach Transport Group, Commodore C. G. Richardson

Transport Group A, Capt. P. P. Welch: Attack transports DU PAGE Capt. G. M. Wauchope USNR, FULLER Capt. N. M. Pigman, WAYNE Capt. T. V. Cooper; transport JOHN LAND Cdr. F. A. Graf; cargo AQUARIUS Cdr. I. E. Eskridge USCG.

Transport Group B, Commodore Richardson: Attack transports CAVALIER Capt. A. G. Hall USCG, FELAND Cdr. G. F. Prestwich; transport GOLDEN CITY Cdr. C. M. Furlow USNR; cargo THUBAN Capt. J. C. Campbell USNR; LSD SHADWELL Lt. Cdr. W. K. Brooks USNR.

Transport Group C, Capt. D. L. Ryan: Attack transports FAYETTE Capt. J. C. Lester, HEYWOOD Cdr. G. M. Jones USNR, LEEDSTOWN Capt. H. A. Carlisle; cargo HERCULES Cdr. W. H. Turnquist USNR; LSDs EPPING FOREST Cdr. L. Martin USNR, WHITE MARSH Capt. G. H. Eppelman USNR.

LST GROUP, Captain R. M. Scruggs in *LST-466*
LST Unit "A," Cdr. J. E. Van Zandt USNR: 10 LST.
Unit "B," Cdr. D. M. Baker: 10 LST.
LSM Group, Lt. Cdr. W. A. Burgett: 10 LSM.
LCI Smoke Group, Capt. H. F. McGee: 13 LCI.
LCT Group, Lt. K. L. Black USNR: 6 LCT.
Control Unit, Capt. S. G. Barchet: 4 SC, 3 PC.
LCI Support Unit, Lt. F. C. Nevius USNR: 3 LCI(M), 11 LCI(G), 5 LCI(R).
Beach Parties, Lt. Cdr. J. B. Avery USNR: Party No. 6, Lt. Cdr. Avery; Party
No. 4, Lt. E. J. Zinser USNR.

White Beach Attack Group Screen, Captain T. B. Dugan (Comdesron 23)
Destroyers CHARLES AUSBURNE Lt. Cdr. H. W. Baker, DRAYTON Lt. Cdr. V. A.
Dybdal, SHAW Lt. Cdr. V. B. Graff, RUSSELL Lt. Cdr. J. E. Wicks, JENKINS Cdr.
P. D. Gallery, LAVALLETTE Cdr. Wells Thompson, CONVERSE (with Comdesdiv 46,
Capt. R. W. Cavenagh, embarked) Lt. Cdr. E. H. McDowell, FOOTE Cdr. Alston
Ramsay, BRAINE Cdr. W. W. Fitts; destroyer escorts CHARLES J. KIMMEL (with
Comcortdiv 71, Cdr. W. C. F. Robards, embarked) Lt. Cdr. F. G. Storey,
THOMAS F. NICKEL Lt. Cdr. C. S. Farmer; 2 PC.

TG 78.5 BLUE BEACH ATTACK GROUP
Rear Admiral W. M. Fechteler

Embarking 6th U.S. Infantry Division, Maj. Gen. E. D. Patrick USA.
Group Flagship FREMONT, Captain C. V. Conlan

Blue Beach Transport Group, Commodore D. W. Loomis
Transdiv 20, Commo. Loomis: Attack transports LEONARD WOOD Capt. H. C.
Perkins USCG, PIERCE Capt. F. M. Adams, JAMES O'HARA Capt. E. W. Irish; transport
LA SALLE Cdr. F. C. Fluegel USNR; attack cargo ELECTRA Lt. Cdr. D. S. Holler USNR;
cargo AURIGA Cdr. J. G. Hart USNR; LSD BELLE GROVE Cdr. Morris Seavey USNR.
Transdiv 26, Capt. H. J. Wright: Attack transports CALLAWAY Capt. D. C.
McNeil USCG, SUMTER Cdr. J. T. O'Pry USNR; transport STORM KING Cdr. H. J. Han-
sen; cargo JUPITER Cdr. J. M. Bristol; LSV MONITOR Cdr. K. J. Olsen; LSD
GUNSTON HALL Cdr. D. E. Collins USNR.
Transdiv 32-T, Capt. J. L. Allen: Attack transports BARNSTABLE Capt. H. T.
Walsh, ELMORE Capt. D. Harrison, BANNER Lt. Cdr. J. R. Pace USNR; transport
HERALD OF THE MORNING Cdr. H. A. Dunn; cargo MERCURY Lt. Cdr. N. D. Salmon
USNR: hospital ship RIXEY Capt. P. H. Jenkins.
Tractor Unit, Capt. O. R. Swigart: 30 LST. LSM Unit, Lt. Cdr. E. G. Smith:
10 LSM. Control Unit, Capt. J. J. Wright: 3 PC, 4 SC Support Unit, Lt. Cdr.
A. M. Holmes: 2 LCI(G). Rocket & LCI Unit, Lt. C. M. Goodman: 5 LCI,
7 LCI(R). LCT Unit, Lt. (jg) K. C. Jackson USNR: 6 LCT. Beach Parties, Lt.
J. L. Williams: Party No. 5, Lt. Williams; Party No. 2, Lt. (jg) C. E. Lundin
USNR. Salvage Unit, Lt. Cdr. P. W. Porter USNR: 2 LCI; *ATR-61;* Fleet tug POTA-
WATOMI Lt. C. H. Stedman; Repair ship EGERIA Lt. A. H. Wilson USNR.

Blue Beach Attack Group Screen, Captain J. H. Wellings (Comdesron 2)
Destroyers MORRIS Lt. Cdr. R. V. Wheeler, LANG (with Comdesdiv 4, Cdr.
W. T. McCarry, embarked) Lt. Cdr. J. T. Bland, STACK Cdr. R. E. Wheeler,
STERETT Cdr. F. J. Blouin, MUSTIN Lt. Cdr. J. G. Hughes, DASHIELL Cdr. D. L.
Cordiner, WILSON Cdr. C. J. MacKenzie; destroyer escorts DAY Lt. Cdr. K. E. Read
USNR, HODGES Lt. Cdr. J. A. Gorham USNR, PEIFFER Lt. Cdr. W. F. Jones USNR,
TINSMAN Lt. W. G. Grote USNR.

TF 79 LINGAYEN ATTACK FORCE
Vice Admiral T. S. Wilkinson

Embarking XIV Corps, Maj. Gen. O. W. Griswold USA.
Group Flagship MOUNT OLYMPUS, Captain J. H. Shultz

TG 79.1 ATTACK GROUP "ABLE," Rear Admiral I. N. Kiland
Embarking 37th Infantry Division, Maj. Gen. R. S. Beightler USA.
Flagship MOUNT MCKINLEY, Captain W. N. Gamet

TG 79.3, Transport Group "ABLE," Commodore M. O. Carlson
Transdiv 28–T, Commo. Carlson: Attack transports HARRIS Capt. M. E. Murphy, DOYEN Cdr. J. G. McClaughry, BOLIVAR Capt. W. L. Field, SHERIDAN Capt. P. H. Weidorn; cargo ALMAACK Lt. Cdr. C. O. Hicks USNR; LSV OZARK Capt. F. P. Williams; LSD OAK HILL Cdr. C. A. Peterson USNR.
Transdiv 8–T, Capt. S. P. Jenkins: Attack transport SARASOTA Cdr. J. I. MacPherson USNR; attack cargo TITANIA Cdr. M. W. Callahan (Ret.); LSIs H.M.A.S. MANOORA Cdr. A. P. Cousins RANR; H.M.A.S. KANIMBLA Cdr. A. V. Bunyan RANR, WESTRALIA Lt. Cdr. E. W. Livinstone RANR.
Transdiv 38–T, Capt. G. W. Johnson: Attack transports LAMAR Capt. B. K. Culver, HARRY LEE Capt. J. C. Pomeroy, ALPINE Cdr. G. K. G. Reilly; transport STARLIGHT Capt. E. C. Holden USNR; hospital ship PINKNEY Cdr. A. A. Downing USNR; ALSHAIN Capt. Roland E. Krause.

TG 79.5 Tractor Group "ABLE," Captain J. S. Laidlaw
LST Assault Unit, Capt. J. R. Clark: 8 LST. LST Reserve Unit, Lt. Cdr. E. L. Jungerheld USNR: 11 LST. LST Assault Unit, Cdr. W. J. Morrison: 7 LSM. LSM Reserve Unit, Cdr. W. E. Verge: 11 LSM. LCT Unit: 6 LCT.

TG 79.7 LCI Group, Commander A. R. Montgomery
Salvage & Fire Fighting Unit, Cdr. Montgomery: 3 LCI(L). Rocket Gunboat Unit, Lt. Cdr. R. S. Rickabaugh USNR: 13 LCI(G). Mortar Unit, Lt. Cdr. C. F. Robinson USNR: 6 LCI(M).

TG 79.9 Control Group "ABLE," Lieutenant Commander B. H. Katschinski USNR
Destroyer Escort ABERCROMBIE Lt. Cdr. Katschinski; 3 PC; 3 PCS; 3 YMS; 1 SC.

TG 79.11 Screen, Captain R. H. Smith (Comdesron 22)
Transport Group "A" Screen, Capt. Smith: Destroyers WALLER Cdr. H. L. Thompson, SAUFLEY Cdr. D. E. Cochran, PHILIP Cdr. J. B. Rutter, RENSHAW Cdr. G. H. Cairnes, CONY Cdr. A. W. Moore, ROBINSON Cdr. E. B. Grantham; Destroyer Escorts LE RAY WILSON Lt. Cdr. M. V. Carson USNR, GILLIGAN Lt. Cdr. C. E. Bull USNR.

TG 79.2 ATTACK GROUP "BAKER," Rear Admiral F. B. Royal
Embarking 40th Infantry Division, Maj. Gen. Rapp Brush USA.

Flagship ROCKY MOUNT Captain F. A. Hardesty

TG 79.4 Transport Group "BAKER," Commodore H. B. Knowles in CAMBRIA
Transdiv 10–T, Capt. S. M. Haight: Attack transports CLAY Capt. N. B. Van Bergen, WILLIAM P. BIDDLE Capt. R. W. Berry, ARTHUR MIDDLETON Capt. S. A. Olsen

uscg, BAXTER Capt. V. R. Sinclair; transport GEORGE F. ELLIOT Cdr. *N*. F. Weidner; LSV CATSKILL Capt. R. W. Chambers USNR; attack cargo CAPRICORNUS Lt. Cdr. B. F. McGuckin USNR.
Transdiv 18-T, Commo. Knowles: Attack transports CAMBRIA Capt. C. W. Dean uscg, MONROVIA Capt. J. D. Kelsey, FREDERICK FUNSTON Capt. C. C. Anderson; transport WAR HAWK Capt. S. H. Thompson USNR; attack cargo ALCYONE Cdr. H. P. Knockerbocker.
Transdiv 30-T, Capt. E. T. Short: Attack transports KNOX Capt. J. H. Brady, CALVERT Cdr. J. F. Warris, CUSTER Capt. W. E. Terry; attack cargo CHARA Cdr. J. P. Clark USNR; LSDs LINDENWALD Capt. R. W. Cutler USNR, ASHLAND Lt. Cdr. W. A. Caughey USNR, CASA GRANDE Lt. Cdr. F. E. Strumm USNR.
Landing Craft Control Unit, Lt. Cdr. J. W. Stedman USNR: Destroyer Escort WALTER C. WANN Lt. Cdr. Stedman; 3 PC; 4 SC; 2 PCE(R).

TG 79.6 Tractor Group "BAKER," Captain E. A. Seay
Assault Unit Green, Cdr. George Reith USNR: 5 LST.
Assault Unit Orange, Lt. Cdr. J. F. Dore USNR: 4 LST.
LST Reserve Unit, Capt. Ethelbert Watts: 10 LST.
LSM Reserve Unit, Capt. J. P. B. Barrett: 31 LSM.
LCT Unit, Lt. J. P. McKeon USNR: 6 LCT.

TG 79.8 LCI SUPPORT GROUP, Captain T. W. Rimer
Mortar Unit, Lt. Cdr. G. W. Hannett USNR: 6 LCI(M).
Rocket & Gunboat Unit, Lt. F. R. Giliberty USNR: 13 LCI(G).
Salvage Unit, Capt. Rimer: 2 LCI(L).

Transport Group "B" Screen, Captain J. B. McLean (Comdesdiv 48)
Destroyers BUSH Cdr. R. E. Westholm, HALFORD Cdr. R. J. Hardy, CONWAY (with Comdesdiv 44, Capt. W. L. Dyer, embarked) Cdr. J. H. Besson, EATON Cdr. Chesford Brown, SIGOURNEY Lt. Cdr. Fletcher Hale, STEMBEL Cdr. W. L. Tagg; destroyer escorts RICHARD W. SUESENS (with Comcortdiv 69, Cdr. T. C. Phifer, embarked), Lt. Cdr. R. W. Graham USNR, OBERRENDER Lt. Cdr. Samuel Spencer USNR.

Landing Craft Screen, Captain E. R. McLean (Comdesron 49)
Destroyers PICKING Cdr. B. J. Semmes, ISHERWOOD (with Comdesdiv 98, Cdr. M. H. Hubbard, embarked) Cdr. L. E. Schmidt, LUCE Cdr. H. A. Owens, SPROSTON Cdr. M. J. Luosey, WICKES Lt. Cdr. J. B. Cresap, YOUNG Cdr. D. G. Dockum, CHARLES J. BADGER Cdr. J. H. Cotten.

TF 73 COMMANDER AIR SEVENTH FLEET
Rear Admiral F. D. Wagner

TG 73.1, FLAGSHIP GROUP, Captain W. A. Evans

TG 73.2, LINGAYEN GROUP, Rear Admiral Wagner

Search & A/S W Unit, Rear Admiral Wagner
Seaplane tenders CURRITUCK Capt. Evans, BARATARIA Cdr. G. S. Coleman; 3 crash boats (AVR).
VPB-20, Lt. Cdr. R. M. Harper: 11 PBM-3D (Mariner).
VPB-71, Cdr. N. C. Gillette: 12 PBY-5A (Catalina).
Spotting & Rescue Unit, Cdr. E. O. Rigsbee: Seaplane tender ORCA Cdr. Rigsbee.
VPB-54 (half), Cdr. K. J. Sanger: 6 PBY-5A.

TG 73.3 MANUS GROUP, Captain J. O. Lambrecht

VS-61, Lt. Cdr. W. J. Camp: 12 VSB (Helldiver).
VPB-146, Lt. Cdr. J. P. Robinson: 12 PV-1 (Ventura).
Carrier Replacement Pool, Groups and Squadrons.

TG 73.4 MOROTAI GROUP, Captain C. B. Jones

Seaplane Tender HERON Lt. J. M. Norcott USNR; 2 crash boats
VPB-101, Cdr. J. A. Miller: 9 PB4Y (Liberator).
VPB-130, Lt. Cdr. C. R. Dodds: 12 PV-1.

TG 73.5 LEYTE RESCUE GROUP, Commander M. K. Fleming

Seaplane Tender TANGIER, Cdr. Fleming; 1 crash boat
VPB-54 (Half), Cdr. Sanger: 6 PBY-5A.

TG 73.6 LEYTE SEARCH GROUP, Commander J. C. Renard

VPB-104, Lt. Cdr. Whitney Wright: 12 PB4Y.
VPB-117, Lt. Cdr. T. P. Mulvihill USNR: 15 PB4Y.
VPB-137, Lt. Cdr. J. A. Porter USNR: 12 PV-1.

TG 73.7 MINDORO GROUP, Commander J. I. Bandy

Seaplane Tenders HALF MOON Cdr. Bandy, SAN PABLO Cdr. C. S. Willard
VPB-25, Lt. Cdr. J. C. Skorcz USNR: 12 PBM.

TG 78.4 FIRST LINGAYEN REINFORCEMENT GROUP,[8]
Commodore H. B. Knowles

Transdiv 34, Commo. Knowles: CAMBRIA, ADAIR, GILLIAM, PRESIDENT MONROE.
Transdiv 35, Capt. S. P. Jenkins: CLAY, LEON, ARTHUR MIDDLETON, CATSKILL.
Transdiv 36, Capt. G. W. Johnson: MONROVIA, FULLER, SUMTER, WAYNE.

Screen, Captain W. L. Freseman

BARTON, WALKE, O'BRIEN, MUSTIN, LAFFEY.

TG 78.5 SECOND LINGAYEN REINFORCEMENT GROUP,[9]
Commodore H. W. Graf

Maffin Bay Unit

Transdiv 41, Capt. H. J. Wright: OLMSTEAD, LA PORTE, BANNER, LAURENS, GEORGE F.
ELLIOT, DIPHDA.
Transdiv 42, Capt. E. T. Short: ZEILIN, LATIMER, BARNSTABLE, OXFORD, COMET.

Morotai Unit

Transdiv 21: TITANIA; H.M.A.S. KANIMBLA, WESTRALIA, MANOORA.

Screen, Captain R. H. Smith

WALLER, PHILIP, SIGOURNEY, SAUFLEY, RENSHAW.

[8] C.O.s not repeated, as most ships were in the assault landing. This group returned to
Leyte, picked up 1st Cav. Div., 32nd Inf. and 112th RCT, for transport to Lingayen, arriving 27 Jan.
[9] Returned again to Lingayen with 33rd Inf. Div. 8 Feb.

Appendix I

TG 78.6 THIRD LINGAYEN REINFORCEMENT GROUP,[10]
Captain R. W. Abbott

Transdiv 11, Capt. J. L. Allen: LEONARD WOOD, OCONTO, WARREN, HERALD OF THE MORNING, WAR HAWK, JOHN LAND, UVALDE.
Transdiv 12, Capt. Abbott: AUDRAIN, WILLIAM P. BIDDLE, STORM KING, HEYWOOD, CALVERT, STARLIGHT, ELECTRA, THUBAN.

Screen, Captain W. L. Dyer (Comdesdiv 44)
CONWAY, EATON, LOWRY, CONY, ROBINSON.

TG 78.9 LINGAYEN LST REINFORCEMENT GROUP,[11]
Captain L. J. Manees

Group 26, Cdr. A. E. Fitzwilliam: 6 LST. Group 27, Cdr. H. Ridout: 1 LST. Group 28, Lt. R. R. Shake: 3 LST. Group 29, Lt. H. J. Thompson: 3 LST. Group 30, Cdr. P. J. Nelson: 8 LST. Group 31, Lt. R. L. Conkling: 1 LST. Group 32, Capt. R. C. Webb: 9 LST. Group 33, Lt. H. G. Coit: 5 LST. Group 34, Capt. D. W. Hardin: 4 LST. Group 35, Capt. Manees: 3 LST. Group 36, Lt. Cdr. E. H. Pope: 4 LST. Group 37, Capt. K. A. Thieme: 5 LST. Group 38, Lt. A. Lozica USNR: 1 LST, 6 LCI, 1 APC, Merchant ships BEN GRIERSON, DAVID D. FIELD, E. A. BURNETT, C. FRANCIS JENKINS, JAMES ROLPH, STEVEN BENET, JOE HARRIS, JUSTO AROSO-MENO, HENRY BARNARD, JOHN PAGE, SIDNEY EDGARTON, SIMON BOLIVAR, JOSEPH TOOLE, O. L. BODENHAMMER, EDWARD WESTCOTT, PANAMA VICTORY, JOHN HART, OTIS SKINNER, CHARLES M. RUSSELL, JOE FELLOWS, HARRIET MONROE, GEORGE TAYLOR, OWEN SUMMERS, HENRY MEIGGS, ROBERT F. BROUSSARD, CHARLES GOODNIGHT, KYLE V. JOHNSON, RALPH T. O'NEILL.

Screen, Captain W. M. Cole (Comdesron 5)

Destroyers FLUSSER Lt. Cdr. K. G. Robinson, CONYNGHAM Lt. Cdr. B. Taylor, STEVENS Cdr. W. M. Rakow, CLAXTON Cdr. M. W. Firth, HOWORTH Cdr. E. S. Burns; Destroyer Escorts RILEY (Comcortdiv 67, Cdr. F. G. Gould) Lt. Cdr. D. H. Johnson USNR, LESLIE B. KNOX Lt. Cdr. J. A. Moffett USNR, MCNULTY Lt. Cdr. D. A. Crafts USNR, METIVIER Lt. Cdr. E. H. Maher USNR, GEORGE A. JOHNSON Lt. Cdr. A. T. Horn USNR, EUGENE E. ELMORE Lt. Cdr. R. F. Creath USNR.

LINGAYEN MOTOR TORPEDO BOATS,
Lieutenant Commander F. D. Tappaan USNR

MTB Tender WACHAPREAGUE Lt. Cdr. H. A. Stewart USNR
MTBRon 28, Lt. Cdr. G. A. Matteson USNR: PT-378, -379, -380, -381, -383, -546, -547, -548, -549, -550, -551.
MTBRon 36, Lt. J. W. Morrison USNR: PT-522, -523, -524, -525, -526, -527, -528, -529, -530, -531, -532.

TG 78.7 LST REINFORCEMENT AND RESUPPLY GROUP,
Captain F. J. Mee
Leyte LST Unit, Captain J. S. Laidlaw

LST Flot 3, Cdr. A. A. Ageton: 21 LST; Flot 6, Capt. Laidlaw: 16 LST. Group 38, Capt. J. R. Clark: 23 LST.

[10] Loaded 41st Inf. Div. at Biak, returned to Lingayen 10 Feb.
[11] Arrived Lingayen 13 Jan.

Screen, Captain J. G. Coward (Comdesdiv 107)

Destroyers REMEY, NORMAN SCOTT, MONSSEN, STACK, MERTZ; destroyer escorts RILEY (Comcortdiv 67, Cdr. F. G. Gould), LESLIE B. KNOX, METIVIER, GEORGE A. MCNULTY, EUGENE E. ELMORE.

First LST Resupply Unit,[12] Captain O. R. Swigart
LST Flot 8, Capt. Swigart: 18 LST.
LSM Group 5, Lt. Cdr. E. G. Smith: 5 LSM.
Screened by Captain Coward's group.

TG 78.8 LSD REINFORCEMENT GROUP, Captain R. W. Cutler USNR

Landing ship docks LINDENWALD, OAK HILL, CASA GRANDE, EPPING FOREST, WHITE MARSH, SHADWELL.
Screen: Cdr. F. J. Blouin: Destroyers STERETT, WILSON.

[12] Transported Sixth Army elements and Air Force units to Lingayen, 27 Jan.

Task Organization for the Third Fleet[1]

1 December 1944–23 January 1945

THIRD FLEET
Admiral William F. Halsey in NEW JERSEY

TF 38 FAST CARRIER FORCE
Vice Admiral J. S. McCain in HANCOCK

TG 38.1 TASK GROUP ONE, Rear Admiral A. E. Montgomery[2]

Carrier		YORKTOWN	Captain T. S. Combs
		Air Group 3: Commander Mac. B. Williams	
VF-3	2 F6F-3, 46 F6F-5, 6 F6F-5P (all Hellcats)		Lt. Cdr. W. L. Lamberson
VB-3	3 SB2C-3, 21 SB2C-4 (all Helldivers)		Cdr. J. T. Lowe
VT-3	18 TBM-1C (Avenger)		Cdr. C. H. Turner

Carrier		WASP	Captain O. A. Weller
		Air Group 81: Commander F. J. Brush	
VF-81	13 F6F-3, 1 F6F-3P, 1 F6F-3N, 36 F6F-5, 3 F6F-5N,		Cdr. F. K. Upham
VB-81	9 SB2C-3, 12 SBW-3 (Helldiver)		Lt. Cdr. H. P. Lanham
VT-81	18 TBM-1C		Lt. Cdr. G. D. M. Cunha

Light carrier		COWPENS	Captain G. H. Debaun
		Air Group 22: Lieutenant Commander T. H. Jenkins USNR	
VF-22	24 F6F-5, 1 F6F-5P		Lt. L. L. Johnson USNR
VT-22	9 TBM-1C		Lt. Cdr. Jenkins

Light carrier		MONTEREY	Captain S. H. Ingersoll
		Air Group 28: Lieutenant Commander R. W. Mehle	
VF-28	3 F6F-3, 21 F6F-5, 1 F6F-5P		Lt. Cdr. Mehle
VT-28	9 TBM-1C		Lt. R. P. Gift USNR

[1] Admiral Halsey's Action Reports and sources given in Appendix I, note 1. Ships were constantly being shifted from one carrier group to another, as well as additional ships joining.

[2] Relieved by Rear Adm. Arthur W. Radford 29 Dec.

SUPPORT UNIT, Vice Admiral W. A. Lee in SOUTH DAKOTA
Batdiv 8, Rear Admiral G. B. Davis: ⁸ MASSACHUSETTS Capt. W. W. Warlick
ALABAMA Capt. V. R. Murphy.
Crudiv 6, Rear Admiral C. Turner Joy: Heavy cruisers SAN FRANCISCO Capt.
H. E. Overesch, BALTIMORE Capt. C. K. Fink.
Crudiv 10, Rear Admiral L. J. Wiltse: Heavy cruiser BOSTON Capt. E. E. Herr-
mann; Light cruisers ASTORIA Capt. G. C. Dyer, SAN DIEGO Capt. W. E. A. Mullan,
OAKLAND Capt. K. S. Reed.
Destroyers DEHAVEN (with Comdesron 61, Capt J. H. Carter, embarked) Cdr.
J. B. Dimmick, MANSFIELD Cdr. R. E. Braddy, LYMAN K. SWENSON Cdr. F. T. Wil-
liamson, COLLETT Cdr. J. D. Collett, MADDOX Cdr. J. S. Willis, BLUE (with Comdes-
div 122, Cdr. C. K. Bergin, embarked) Cdr. Lot Ensey, BRUSH Cdr. J. E. Edwards,
TAUSSIG Cdr. J. A. Robbins, SAMUEL N. MOORE Cdr. H. A. Lincoln, CUSHING (with
Comdesron 53, Capt. H. B. Jarrett, embarked) Cdr. L. F. Volk, BUCHANAN Cdr.
R. W. Curtis, HOBBY Cdr. G. W. Pressey, WELLES Lt. Cdr. J. S. Slaughter, DYSON
Cdr. L. E. Ruff, * SPENCE * Lt. Cdr. J. P. Andrea THATCHER Cdr. W. A. Cockell,
COLAHAN Cdr. D. T. Wilber, HALSEY POWELL Cdr. S. D. B. Merrill, BENHAM Cdr.
F. S. Keeler, YARNALL (with Comdesdiv 106, Cdr. J. H. Hogg, embarked) Cdr.
J. B. Denny, STOCKHAM Cdrs. E. P. Holmes, M. G. Johnson, WEDDERBURN Cdr.
C. H. Kendall, HAILEY Cdr. P. H. Brady, FRANKS Cdr. D. R. Stephan, UHLMANN
Cdr. S. G. Hooper.

TG 38.2, TASK GROUP TWO, Rear Admiral Gerald F. Bogan

Carrier   LEXINGTON   Captain E. W. Litch

Air Group 20: Commander D. F. Smith

VF-20	1 F6F-3, 68 F6F-5, 3 F6F-5N	Cdrs. F. E. Bakutis, J. S. Gray
VB-20	15 SB2C-3	Lt. Cdr. R. E. Moore
VT-20	15 TBM-1C	Lt Cdr. S. L. Prickett

Carrier   HANCOCK   Captain R. F. Hickey

Air Group 7: Commander J. D. Lamade

VF-7	50 F6F-5, 2 F6F-5P, 2 F6F-5N	Lt. Cdr. * L. J. Check
VB-7	8 SB2C-3, 7 SB2C-3E, 10 SBW-3	Lt. Cdrs. * J. L. Erickson, D. C. Caldwell
VT-7	18 TBM-1C	Lt. Cdr. L. E. Ewoldt

Carrier   HORNET (Cardiv 5, Rear Adm. J. J. Clark)   Captain A. K. Doyle

Air Group 11: Commander R. E. Riera

VF-11	15 F6F-3, 33 F6F-5, 3 F6F-5N	Lt. Cdr. E. G. Fairfax
VB-11	18 SB2C-3, 5 SBW-3	Lt. Cdr. E. J. Kroeger USNR
VT-11	18 TBM-1C	Lt. W. J. Engman USNR, Lt. Cdr. J. A. Fidel

Light carrier   CABOT   Captain S. J. Michael

Air Group 29: Lieutenant Commander W. E. Eder

| VF-29 | 4 F6F-3, 21 F6F-5 | Lt. Cdr. Eder |
| VT-29 | 9 TBM-1C | Lt. I. H. McPherson USNR |

* Lost in these operations.

⁸ Relieved by Rear Adm. John F. Shafroth 26 Dec.

Appendix II

317

SUPPORT UNIT, Rear Admiral E. W. Hanson

Batdiv 4, Rear Admiral Hanson: NEW JERSEY Capt. C. F. Holden, WISCONSIN Capt. E. E. Stone.
Batdiv 7, Rear Admiral O. C. Badger: IOWA Capt. J. L. Holloway.
Crudiv 17, Rear Admiral J. C. Jones: Light cruisers PASADENA Capt. R. B. Tuggle, ASTORIA Capt. G. C. Dyer, SAN JUAN Capt. J. F. Donovan, MIAMI Capt. J. G. Crawford, WILKES-BARRE Capt. R. L. Porter.
Destroyers CAPPS (with Comdesdiv 102, Cdr. J. W. Callaghan, embarked) Cdr. J. M. Wood, DAVID W. TAYLOR Cdr. W. H. Johnsen, EVANS Cdr. B. N. Wev, JOHN D. HENLEY Cdr. C. H. Smith, BOYD Cdr. A. E. Teall, BROWN Cdr. T. H. Copeman, COWELL Cdr. C. W. Parker, TRATHEN Cdr. J. R. Millet, HAZELWOOD Cdr. V. P. Douw, OWEN (with Comdesdiv 103, Capt. J. P. Womble, embarked) Cdr. C. B. Jones, MILLER Lt. Cdr. D. L. Johnson, THE SULLIVANS Lt. Cdr. J. R. Baum, STEPHEN POTTER Cdr. L. W. Pancoast, Lt. Cdr. G. R. Muse, TINGEY Cdrs. J. O. Minor, K. S. Shook, HICKOX (with Comdesdiv 104, Capt. W. T. Kenny, embarked) Lt. Cdr. J. H. Wesson, HUNT Cdr. H. A. Knoertzer, LEWIS HANCOCK Cdr. W. M. Searles, MARSHALL Cdr. J. D. McKinney, AULT (with Comdesdiv 123, Capt. J. M. Higgins, embarked) Cdr. J. C. Wylie, ENGLISH Cdr. J. T. Smith, CHARLES S. SPERRY Cdr. H. H. McIlhenny, WALDRON Cdr. G. E. Peckham, HAYNSWORTH Cdr. S. N. Tackney, JOHN W. WEEKS (with Comdesdiv 124, Cdr. R. W. Smith, embarked) Cdr. R. A. Theobald, HANK Cdr. G. M. Chambers.

TG 38.3, TASK GROUP THREE, Rear Admiral F. C. Sherman

| Carrier | | ESSEX | Captain C. W. Wieber |

Air Group 4: * Commander G. O. Klinsmann, Captain F. K. Upham

VF-4	27 F6F-3, 17 F6F-5	* Lt. Cdr. K. G. Hammond, Lt. L. M. Boykin
VB-4	24 SB2C-3	Lt. Cdr. C. V. Johnson
VT-4	18 TBM-1C	Lt. P. J. Davis USNR
VMF-124	18 F4U-1D (Corsair)	Lt. Col. W. A. Millington USMC
VMF-213	18 F4U-1	Maj. D. E. Marshall USMC

| Carrier | | TICONDEROGA | Captain Dixie Kiefer |

Air Group 80: Commander A. O. Vorse

VF-80	68 F6F-5, 2 F6F-5P, 3 F6F-5N	Lt. Cdr. L. W. J. Keith USNR
VB-80	22 SB2C-3	Lt. Cdr. E. L. Anderson
VT-80	14 TBM-3, 1 TBM-1C, 1 TBM-3P	Lt. Cdr. C. W. Shattuck USNR

| Light carrier | | LANGLEY | Captain J. F. Wegforth |

Air Group 44: Commander M. T. Wordell

| VF-44 | 20 F6F-5, 4 F6F-3, 1 F6F-5P | Cdr. Wordell |
| VT-44 | 9 TBM-1C | Lt. Cdr. H. H. Klare |

| Light carrier | | SAN JACINTO | Captain M. H. Kernodle |

Air Group 45: Commander G. E. Schechter

| VF-45 | 10 F6F-3, 13 F6F-5, 1 F6F-5P | Cdr. Schechter |
| VT-45 | 7 TBM-1C, 2 TBM-3 | Lt. J. G. Piegari USNR |

* Lost in these operations.

HEAVY SUPPORT, Rear Admiral T. R. Cooley

Batdiv 6, Rear Admiral Cooley: WASHINGTON Capt. R. F. Good, NORTH CARO-
LINA Capt. O. S. Colclough, SOUTH DAKOTA Capts. R. S. Riggs, C. B. Momsen.

LIGHT SUPPORT, Rear Admiral M. L. Deyo

Crudiv 13, Rear Admiral Deyo: Light cruisers SANTA FE Capt. H. C. Fitz, MO-
BILE Capt. C. C. Miller, BILOXI Capt. P. R. Heineman.
Crudiv 14, Rear Admiral F. E. M. Whiting: Light cruisers VINCENNES Capt.
A. D. Brown, FLINT Capt. C. R. Will.
Destroyers CLARENCE K. BRONSON (with Capt. E. R. Wilkinson, Comdesron 50,
embarked) Cdr. Gifford Scull, COTTEN Cdr. P. W. Winston, DORTCH Cdr. R. E.
Myers, GATLING Cdrs. A. F. Richardson, V. J. Meola, HEALY Cdr. J. C. Atkeson,
COGSWELL (with Comdesdiv 100, Capt. W. J. Miller, embarked) Cdr. R. E. Lock-
wood, CAPERTON Cdr. G. K. Carmichael, INGERSOLL Cdr. A. C. Veasey, KNAPP Cdr.
W. B. Brown, PORTERFIELD (with Comdesron 55, Capt. A. E. Jarrell, embarked)
Cdr. D. W. Wulzen, CALLAGHAN Cdr. C. M. Bertholf, CASSIN YOUNG Cdr. J. W.
Ailes, PRESTON Cdr. G. S. Patrick, LAWS (with Comdesdiv 110, Cdr. W. R. Edsall,
embarked) Cdr. L. O. Wood, LONGSHAW Cdr. R. N. Speck, PRICHETT Cdr. C. M.
Bowley, HALSEY POWELL Cdr. S. D. B. Merrill.

TG 38.5, TASK GROUP FIVE,[4] Rear Admiral M. B. Gardner

Carrier   ENTERPRISE   Captain G. B. H. Hall

Night Air Group 90: Commander W. I. Martin

VFN-90   16 F6F-5E, 16 F6F-5N, 2 F6F-5P   Lt. Cdr. R. J. McCullough USNR
VTN-90   27 TBM-3D   Lt. R. F. Kippen USNR

Light Carrier   INDEPENDENCE   Captain E. C. Ewen

Night Air Group 41: Commander T. F. Caldwell

VFN-41   9 F6F-5N   Cdr. Caldwell
VTN-41   4 TBM-1D, 4 TBM-3D   Lt. W. R. Taylor USNR

Screen, Captain I. H. Nunn (Comdesron 47)

Desdiv 93, Capt. Nunn: MCCORD Cdr. F. D. Michael, TRATHEN Cdr. J. R. Millet,
HAZELWOOD Cdr. V. P. Douw.
Desdiv 94, Capt. L. K. Reynolds: HAGGARD Cdr. D. A. Harris, Lt. Cdr. V. J.
Soballe, BUCHANAN Cdr. R. W. Curtis, FRANKS Cdr. D. R. Stephan.

TG 30.8 AT SEA LOGISTICS GROUP THIRD FLEET
Captain J. T. Acuff [5]

Oilers: ATASCOSA Cdr. H. L. DeRivera, AUCILLA Lt. Cdr. C. L. Cover USNR,
CACAPON Lt. Cdr. George Eyth USNR, CACHE Lt. Cdr. C. R. Cosgrove USNR, CALI-
ENTE Lt. Cdrs. A. E. Stiff and F. N. Lang USNR, CHICOPEE Cdr. C. O. Peak USNR,
CHIKASKIA Lt. Cdr. George Zimmerman USNR, CIMARRON Lt. Cdr. H. G. Schnaars
USNR, ENOREE Lt. Cdr. E. L. Jurewicz USNR, GUADALUPE Cdr. H. A. Anderson,
Lt. Cdr. C. A. Boddy USNR, HOUSATONIC Lt. Cdr. J. R. Ducat USNR, KANKAKEE
Lt. Cdr. W. G. Frundt USNR, KENNEBAGO Lt. Cdr. C. W. Brockway USNR, LACKA-
WANNA Cdr. A. J. Homann, MANATEE Lt. Cdr. J. B. Smyth USNR, MARIAS Cdr. J. G.
Olsen USNR, MASCOMA Lt. Cdr. H. P. Timmers USNR, MERRIMACK Capt. Vaughn
Bailey, MILLICOMA Cdr. G. E. Ely USNR, MONONGAHELA Cdr. F. J. Ilsemann, NAN-

[4] The night-flying group, formed 5 Jan. and dissolved 12th.
[5] Capt. Acuff's successive flagships were destroyers *John D. Henley, Aylwin* and
Welles. No division commanders accompanied CVEs on this duty.

TAHALA Capt. P. M. Gunnell, NECHES Cdr. H. G. Hansen USNR, NEOSHO Lt. Cdr. F. P. Parkinson USNR, NIOBRARA Cdr. R. C. Spaulding USNR, PAMANSET Cdr. D. J. Houle, Lt. Cdr. C. B. Gjedsted USNR, PATUXENT Lt. Cdr. F. P. Ferrell USNR, SAUGA-TUCK Lt. Cdr. J. F. Ardagh USNR, TALUGA Cdr. H. M. Mikkelsen USNR, TOMAHAWK Lt. Cdr. W. L. Eagleton USNR.

Escort Carriers with replacement planes: ALTAMAHA Capt. A. C. Olney, ANZIO Capt. G. C. Montgomery, CAPE ESPERANCE Capt. R. W. Bockius, KWAJALEIN Capt. R. C. Warrack, SHIPLEY BAY Capt. E. T. Neale, NEHENTA BAY Capt H. B. Butterfield, SARGENT BAY Capt. W. T. Rassieur, RUDYERD BAY Capt. C. S. Smiley.

Screen: [6] Destroyers DEWEY (with Comdesron 1, Capt. P. V. Mercer, embarked) Lt. Cdr. C. R. Calhoun, AYLWIN Lt. Cdr. W. K. Rogers, DALE Lt. Cdr. S. M. Zimmy, DYSON Cdr. L. E. Ruff, FARRAGUT (with Comdesdiv 2, Capt. J. F. Walsh, embarked) Lt. Cdr. C. C. Hartigan, HAILEY Cdr. P. H. Brady, HICKOX Lt. Cdr. J. H. Wesson, HOBBY (with Comdesdiv 38, Capt. J. B. Cochran, embarked) Cdr. G. W. Pressey, * HULL Lt. Cdr. J. A. Marks, MCDONOUGH Lt. Cdr. B. H. Shupper, * MONAGHAN * Lt. Cdr. F. Bruce Garrett, THATCHER Cdr. W. A. Cockell, THORN Lt. Cdr. F. H. Schneider, WELLES Lt. Cdr. J. S. Slaughter.

Destroyer Escorts BANGUST Lt. Cdr. C. F. MacNish USNR, CROWLEY Lt. Cdr. T. J. Skewes USNR, DONALDSON Lt. Cdr. H. G. Hartmann USNR, GEORGE Lt. Cdr. F. W. Just USNR, GRADY Lt. Cdr. F. R. King USNR, HILBERT Lt. Cdr. J. W. Darroch USNR, KYNE Lt. Cdr. C. F. Sweet USNR, LAKE Lt. Cdr. A. D. Weekes USNR, LAMONS Lt. Cdr. H. C. M. Lamkin USNR, LAWRENCE C. TAYLOR Cdr. Ralph Cullinan, LEWIS Lt. Cdr. F. A. Reece USNR, LYMAN Lt. Cdr. J. W. Wilson USNR, MELVIN R. NAWMAN Lt. Cdr. F. W. Kinsley, MITCHELL Lt. Cdr. J. H. Carpenter USNR, OLIVER MITCHELL Lt. Cdr. K. J. Barclay USNR, O'NEILL Lt. Cdr. D. S. Bill, OSMUS Lt. Cdr. B. W. Pattishall USNR, REYNOLDS Lt. Cdr. H. Marvin-Smith USNR, RIDDLE Lt. Cdr. F. P. Steel USNR, ROBERT F. KELLER Lt. Cdr. J. R. Hinton USNR, SWEARER Lt. J. M. Trent USNR, TABBERER Lt. Cdr. H. L. Plage USNR, WATERMAN Lt. Cdr. J. H. Stahle USNR, WEAVER Lt. Cdr. W. A. Taylor USNR, WESSON Lt. Henry Sears USNR.

Ammunition Ships SANGAY, MAUNA LOA, S.S. AUSTRALIA VICTORY, PROVO V., RAINIER, MOUNT BAKER, NITRO; Fleet Tugs HITCHITI, JICARILLA, MATACO, MOLALA, SIOUX, TEKESTA, ZUNI.

TF 17 SUPPORTING SUBMARINES PACIFIC FLEET
Vice Admiral Charles A. Lockwood

"Loughlin's Loopers": QUEENFISH Cdr. C. E. Loughlin, PICUDA Cdr. E. T. Shepard, BARB Cdr. E. B. Fluckey.

"Clementson's Clippers": BLUEBACK Cdr. M. K. Clementson, SEA FOX Cdr. R. C. Klinker, PUFFER Lt. Cdr. Carl Dwyer.

"Bennett's Blazers": SEA OWL Cdr. C. L. Bennett, SEA POACHER Cdr. F. M. Gambacorta, PIRANHA Cdr. H. E. Ruble.

"Post's Panzers": SPOT Cdr. W. S. Post, BALAO Cdr. M. F. Ramirez de Arellano, ICEFISH Cdr. R. W. Peterson.

"Rebel's Rippers": SEA DOG Cdr. V. L. Lowrance, SEA ROBIN Cdr. P. C. Stimson, GUARDFISH Cdr. D. T. Hammond.

SILVERSIDES Cdr. J. C. Nichols, TAUTOG Cdr. T. S. Basket, KINGFISH Lt. Cdr. T. E. Harper, SPEARFISH Lt. Cdr. C. Cole.

* Lost in these operations.

[6] Because screens were frequently reformed to accompany oiler and CVE groups going to and fro, there was no over-all screen commander.

TG 71.1 SUPPORTING SUBMARINES SEVENTH FLEET
Rear Admiral Ralph W. Christie [7]

ANGLER Lt. Cdr. Howard Bissell USNR, BARBEL Cdr. R. A. Keating, BESUGO Cdr. T. L. Wogan, BLACKFIN Cdr. W. L. Kitch, BLUEGILL Cdr. E. P. Barr, BOARFISH Cdr. R. L. Gross, BREAM Cdr. J. L. P. McCallum, CAIMAN Cdr. F. C. Lucas, COBIA Cdr. A. L. Becker, GABILAN Cdr. W. B. Parham, GUITARRO Cdr. T. B. Dabney, GURNARD Cdr. N. D. Gage, HARDHEAD Cdr. F. A. Greenup, KRAKEN Cdr. T. H. Henry, PERCH Cdr. B. C. Hill, ROCK Cdr. J. J. Flachsenhar, SEALION Lt. Cdr. C. F. Putman.

The names of Seventh Fleet Submarines which patrolled South China Sea in 1945, together with those of their commanding officers, will be found in Chapter XIII.

[7] Relieved by Rear Adm. James Fife 30 Dec. 1944.

Task Organizations in Operations to Liberate the Southern Philippines

February–April 1945

(*The Chain of Command for all was as follows*)

SUPREME COMMANDER, ALLIED FORCES, SOUTHWEST PACIFIC AREA
General of the Army Douglas MacArthur USA

COMMANDING GENERAL EIGHTH ARMY
Lieutenant General Robert C. Eichelberger USA

COMMANDER SEVENTH FLEET
Vice Admiral Thomas C. Kinkaid [1]

COMMANDER VII AMPHIBIOUS FORCE
Vice Admiral Daniel E. Barbey in AGC BLUE RIDGE,
Captain H. B. Brumbaugh

(*Abbreviated Task Organizations for each operation follow. The commanding officers will mostly be found in Appendix I.*)

1. *Palawan* (*Victor III*), *28 February 1945*

TG 78.2 AMPHIBIOUS GROUP 8, Rear Admiral W. M. Fechteler
in U.S.C.G.C. SPENCER, Commander J. R. Hinnant USCG
Embarking 186th RCT, Brigadier General Harold H. Haney USA.

TG 74.2 COVERING AND SUPPORT GROUP, Rear Admiral R. S. Riggs
CLs DENVER, MONTPELIER, CLEVELAND; DDs FLETCHER, O'BANNON, JENKINS, ABBOT
Transport Unit, Commander W. V. Deutermann
APD Unit, Cdr. W. S. Parsons: LLOYD, KEPHART, NEWMAN, COFER; LSD RUSHMORE

1 Promoted Admiral 3 Apr. 1945.

LCI Unit, Cdr. Deutermann: 10 LCI(L)
LSM Unit, Cdr. W. E. Verge: 20 LSM
LST Unit, Cdr. D. P. Stickley: 6 LST
Support Unit, Cdr. D. H. Day: 7 LCI(R), 3 LCI(M), 4 LCS(L)
Control Unit, Cdr. J. H. Petersen USNR: 1 PC, 3 SC

Screen, Capt. W. M. Cole: DDs FLUSSER, CONYNGHAM, SMITH, DRAYTON, SHAW
Minesweeping Unit, Lt. E. O. Saltmarsh USNR: 4 YMS
Beach Party, Lt. E. J. Zinser USNR
Naval Combat Demolition Unit in 1 LCI(D)
Reinforcement Echelon, Capt. R. H. Smith: DDs WALLER, SIGOURNEY, MCCALLA;
19 LST
Salvage Unit, Lt. Cdr. R. H. Donnell USNR: ATF QUAPAW
MTB Unit, Lt. J. H. Van Sicklen USNR: AGP WILLOUGHBY; 2 MTBrons
Slow Tow, Cdr. H. M. Jones USNR: DE JOBB; AOG SAKATONCHEE; ATR 86
(towing PT dock)

2. Zamboanga (Victor IV), 10–18 March 1945

TG 78.1 AMPHIBIOUS GROUP 6, Rear Admiral Forrest B. Royal
       in ROCKY MOUNT, Commander F. A. Hardesty

Embarking 41st Infantry Division, Major General Jens A. Doe USA.

TG 74.3 CRUISER COVERING GROUP, Rear Admiral R. S. Berkey

CLs PHOENIX, BOISE; DDs FLETCHER, NICHOLAS, TAYLOR, JENKINS, ABBOT

Transports, Captain L. J. Manees

APD Unit: Same as for Palawan
LST Unit, Capt. Manees: 23 LST
LSM Unit, Cdr. D. J. Weintraub: 21 LSM
LCI Unit, Cdr. A. V. Jannotta USNR: 32 LCI

Screen, Captain R. H. Smith

DDs WALLER, SAUFLEY, PHILIP, SIGOURNEY, ROBINSON, MCCALLA, BANCROFT, BAILEY;
DEs RUDDEROW, CHAFFEE

Support Craft Unit: Captain R. E. Arison

7 LCS(L); 5 LCI(R); 2 LCI(M); 2 LCI(D); 1 LCI; 2 Naval Combat Demolition Teams

Landing Craft Control and Beachmaster Unit

Lieutenant Commander W. W. Sullivan USNR

2 PC; 2 SC; 2 Beachmaster Teams

Minesweeping Unit: Lieutenant E. O. Saltmarsh USNR

11 YMS

ATF QUAPAW; *ATR-61;* PF H.M.A.S. WARREGO; AN CINNAMON

MTB Unit: Lieutenant R. A. Williamson USNR

Service Unit:
AGP OYSTER BAY; 2 MTBrons

3. *Panay* (*Victor I*), *18 March and W. Negros, 29 March 1945*

TG 74.3 AMPHIBIOUS GROUP 9, Rear Admiral Arthur D. Struble
in u.s.c.g.c. ingham, Cdr. K. O. A. Zittel uscg
Embarking 40th Infantry Division, Major General Rapp Brush usa

TG 74.2 COVERING GROUP, Rear Admiral R. S. Riggs
CL cleveland; DDs conway, stevens, eaton
LST Unit, Cdr. G. C. Berner: 16 LST
LSM Unit, Cdr. W. E. Verge: 10 LSM
LCI Unit, Cdr. F. B. C. Martin: 13 LCI
Escort Unit, Captain T. B. Dugan
DDs charles ausburne, thatcher, claxton, converse, dyson
Minesweeping Unit, Lt. W. H. Nicholls usnr: 5 YMS
Salvage and Rescue Unit: *ATR–61*
Control and Inshore Support Unit: 2 SC, 4 LCI(R), 1 LCI(M), 1 LCI(D)
LCM Unit, Capt. J. J. Huetter usa
Beach Party No. 9, Lt. D. T. Radajkowski usnr
Hydrographic Unit, Cdr. K. E. Oom ran: PF h.m.a.s. warrego

4. *Cebu* (*Victor II*), *26 March 1945*

TG 78.2 AMPHIBIOUS GROUP 8, Captain A. T. Sprague
in U.S.C.G.C. spencer, Commander Hinnant
Embarking Americal Division, Major General William H. Arnold.

COVERING AND SUPPORT GROUP, Rear Admiral Berkey
Same as in 2 (*Zamboanga*), *H.M.A.S.* hobart *relieving* boise
APD Unit, Cdr. W. S. Parsons: APDs lloyd, newman, kephart, cofer
LCI Unit, Cdr. W. V. Deutermann: 15 LCI(L)
LSM Unit, Lt. Cdr. G. F. Baker: 11 LSM
LST Unit, Capt. H. B. Hudson: 13 LST; 3 LCT
LST Tractor Unit, Cdr. D. P. Stickley: 4 LST
Support Unit, Cdr. D. H. Day: 5 LCI(R), 4 LCS(L)
Control Unit, Cdr. J. H. Petersen usnr: 2 PC
Screen Unit, Capt. F. D. McCorkle: DDs flusser, shaw, conyngham, smith, drayton
Minesweeping Unit, Lt. G. L. O'Neil usnr: 8 YMS
Beach Party No. 5, Lt. M. Williams usnr: *LCI(D)–228* lifting one UDT; *ATA–179*

5. *Mindanao* (*Victor V*), *17–18 April 1945*

TG 78.2 AMPHIBIOUS GROUP 8, Rear Admiral Albert G. Noble
in WASATCH, Captain K. D. Ringle
Embarking X Corps, Major General Franklin C. Sibert USA, comprising 24th
Infantry Div., Major General Ross B. Woodruff USA, and 31st Infantry Div.,
Major General Clarence A. Martin USA.

TG 74.2 SUPPORT AND COVERING GROUP, Rear Admiral R. S. Riggs

CLs MONTPELIER, DENVER, CLEVELAND; DDs CONWAY, EATON, STEVENS, YOUNG,
CONY, SIGOURNEY

"GREEN" Beach Attack Unit, Rear Admiral Noble

Screen, Capt. T. B. Dugan: DDs CHARLES AUSBURNE, BRAINE, ROBINSON, CLAXTON

APD Unit, Cdr. W. S. Parsons: APDs LLOYD, ALEX DIACHENKO, KEPHART

LST Unit, Capt. O. R. Swigart: AGP PORTUNUS; 14 LST; 7 LCT

LCI Unit, Cdr. M. M. Byrd: 11 LCI

LSM Unit, Cdr. D. J. Weintraub: 13 LSM

Morotai Staged Unit, Captain F. J. Mee

23 LST; S. S. SOTER ORTYNSKY, JOHN DOCKWEILER, HEBER CREEL, JIM BRIDGER,
A. S. DUNNIWAY, JEFFERSON DAVIS; 11 LCI; DDs FLUSSER, AULICK, CONYNGHAM; DEs
JOBB, ALBERT T. HARRIS

Zamboanga Layover Unit, Commander Horatio Ridout

14 LST; S.S. CHARLES WOLCOTT, T. A. JOHNSON

Control Unit, Cdr. J. H. Petersen USNR: 2 PC
Beach Party No. 11, Cdr. J. P. Graff
Minesweeping Unit, Lt. W. H. Boutell: 5 YMS
Close Support Unit, Capt. R. E. Arison: 1 LCI, 8 LCI(R), 4 LCI(G), 3 LCS(L);
ATF QUAPAW; *LCI* (*D*)–*228* carrying UDT

"RED" Beach Attack Unit, Captain G. D. Zurmuehlen
in U.S.C.G.C. SPENCER

DDs DYSON, MCCALLA; 13 LST; 2 LSM; 5 LST; 2 SC; 2 YMS; 1 LCI(R);
2 LCI(G); 4 PGM; *ATR–61; LCI*(*D*)–*227* lifting UDT
Floating Reserve Unit: APDs NEWMAN, LIDDLE; 2 LST; 5 LCI; 1 LSM
MTB Unit. Capt. S. S. Bowling: 1 AGP, 8 MTBs
Hydrographic Unit, Lt. Cdr. G. C. Tancred RAN: H.M.S. LACHLAN

Ships Hit or Near-missed, and Casualties Inflicted, by Kamikaze Attacks in Lingayen Operation[1]

January 1945

Day	Time	Type	Ship	Extent of Damage	Casualties Killed	Casualties Wounded
3	0728	AO	COWANESQUE	Minor	2	1
4	1712	CVE	* OMMANEY BAY	Sunk	93	65
5	1651	DD	HELM	Minor	0	6
5	1706	CA	LOUISVILLE (1)	Moderate	1	59
5	1735	CA	H.M.A.S. AUSTRALIA (1)	Minor	30	46
5	1735	DD	H.M.A.S. ARUNTA	Minor	2	4
5	1739	ATF	APACHE	Minor	0	3
5	1740		LCI(G)-70	Moderate	6	9
5	1745	DE	STAFFORD	Extensive	2	12
5	1745	CVE	MANILA BAY	Moderate	22	56
5	1750	CVE	SAVO ISLAND	Negligible	0	0
6	1145	DD	ALLEN M. SUMNER	Extensive	14	29
6	1145	DD	RICHARD P. LEARY	Minor	0	1
6	1159	BB	NEW MEXICO	Minor	30	87
6	1201	DD	WALKE	Extensive	13	34
6	1215	DMS	* LONG	Sunk	1	35
6	1252	APD	BROOKS	Extensive	3	11
6	1424	CL	COLUMBIA (1)	Minor	0	1
6	1427	DD	O'BRIEN	Moderate	0	0
6	1437	CA	MINNEAPOLIS	Minor	0	2
6	1545	AVP	ORCA	Minor	0	4
6	1720	BB	CALIFORNIA	Minor	45	151
6	1720	DD	NEWCOMB	Minor	2	15
6	1729	CL	COLUMBIA (2)	Extensive	13	44
6	1730	CA	LOUISVILLE (2)	Extensive	32	56
6	1732	DMS	SOUTHARD	Moderate	0	6
6	1734	CA	H.M.A.S. AUSTRALIA (2)	Serious	14	26
7	0430	DMS	HOVEY [2]	Sunk	46	3

* Sunk in this operation.

[1] For stories of most of these attacks, see Chaps. IV, V and VI.

[2] *Hovey* and *Palmer* have been included although the one was sunk by an aerial torpedo and the other by two bombs.

Day	Time	Type	Ship	Extent of Damage	Casualties Killed	Wounded
7	1835	DMS	PALMER	Sunk	28	38
8	0545		LST-912	Minor	4	3
8	0720	CA	H.M.A.S. AUSTRALIA (3)	Minor	0	0
8	0739	CA	H.M.A.S. AUSTRALIA (4)	Extensive	0	0
8	0751	CVE	KADASHAN BAY	Serious	0	3
8	0755	APA	CALLAWAY	Minor	29	22
8	1857	CVE	KITKUN BAY	Extensive	17	36
8	1903	LSI	H.M.A.S. WESTRALIA	Minor	0	0
9	0700	DE	HODGES	Minor	0	0
9	0745	CL	COLUMBIA (3)	Serious	24	68
9	1302	BB	MISSISSIPPI	Minor	23	63
9	1311	CA	H.M.A.S. AUSTRALIA (5)	Minor	0	0
10	0710	DE	LE RAY WILSON	Extensive	6	7
10	1915	APA	DU PAGE	Minor	32	157
12	0658	DE	GILLIGAN	Extensive	12	13
12	0729	DE	RICHARD W. SUESENS	Slight	0	11
12	0753	APD	BELKNAP	Extensive	38	49
12	0815		LST-700 (1)	Extensive	0	6
12	1250	S.S.	OTIS SKINNER	Extensive	0	0
12	1830	S.S.	KYLE V. JOHNSON	Extensive	129	0
12	1830		LST-778	None	0	0
12	1830	S.S.	DAVID DUDLEY FIELD	Minor	0	0
12	1830	S.S.	EDWARD N. WESTCOTT	Substantial	0	13
13	0810		LST-700 (2)	Extensive	2	2
13	0821	APA	ZEILIN	Extensive	8	32
13	0858	CVE	SALAMAUA	Extensive	15	88

Index

Names of Combatant Ships in SMALL CAPITALS
Names of Lettered Combatant Ships such as LSTs, and of
Merchant Ships, in *Italics*

Only main headings of Organizations are indexed.

Index

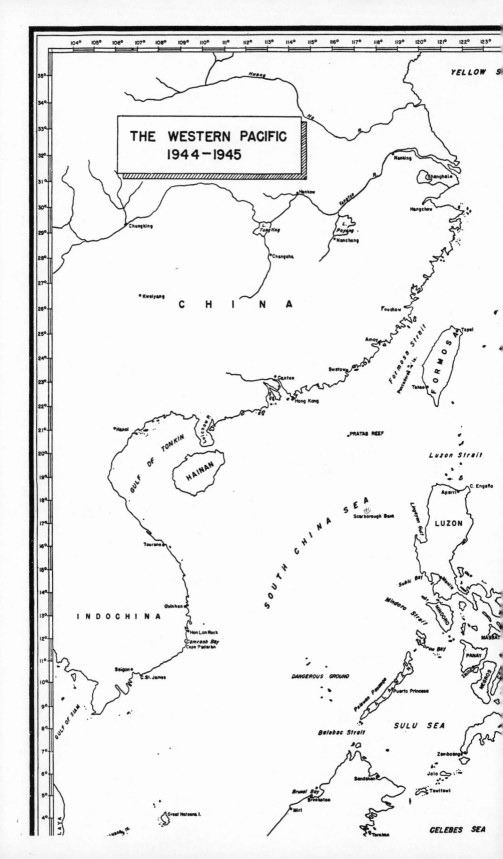

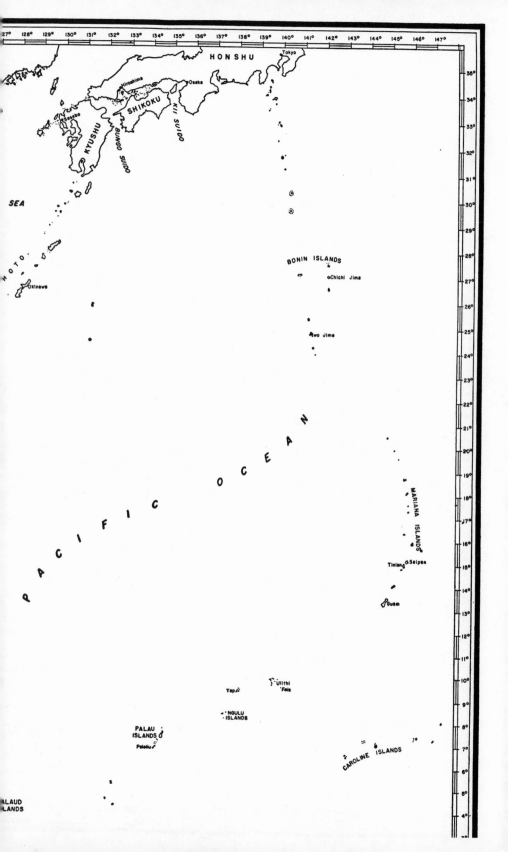

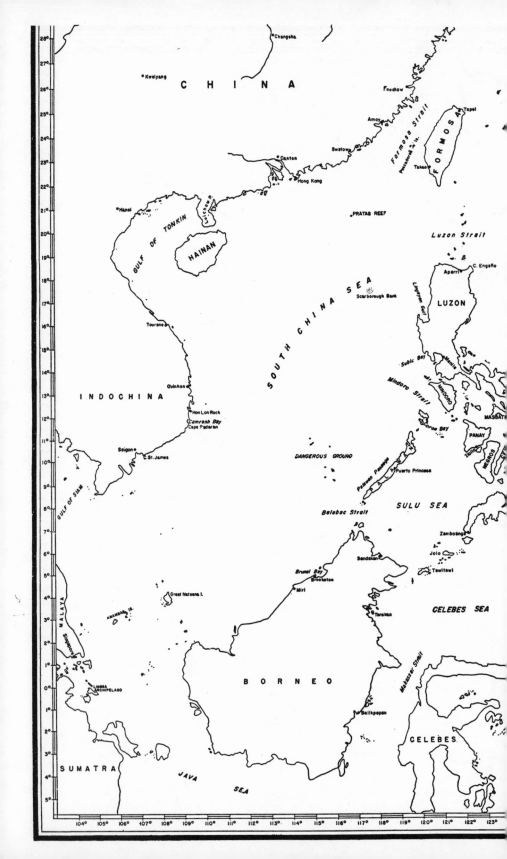

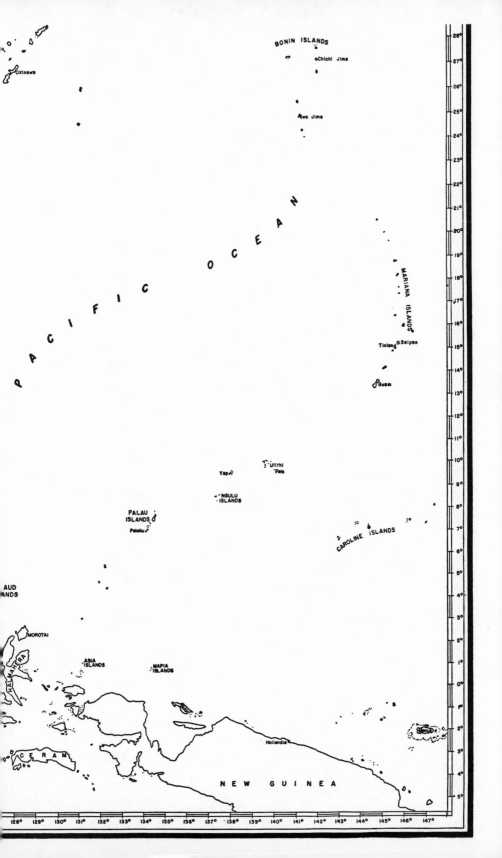